Understanding School Management

Understanding School Management

Edited by

**Ron Glatter, Margaret Preedy,
Colin Riches and Mary Masterton
at the Open University**

Open University Press
Milton Keynes · Philadelphia

Open University Press
12 Cofferidge Close
Stony Stratford
Milton Keynes MK11 1BY

and

1900 Frost Road, Suite 101
Bristol, PA 19007, USA

First published 1988
Reprinted 1989

British Library Cataloguing in Publication Data
Understanding school management.——(E325).
1. School management and organization——Great Britain
I. Glatter, Ron
371.2'00941   LB2901

ISBN 0-335-15559-6
ISBN 0-335-15552-9 Pbk

Library of Congress Cataloging-in-Publication Data
Understanding school management.
"E325 course reader."
Includes indexes.
1. School management and organization——Great Britain.   I. Glatter, Ron.
LB2901.U53   1987   371.2'00941   87-22114

ISBN 0-335-15559-6
ISBN 0-335-15552-9 (pbk.)

Typeset by Colset (Pte) Ltd, Singapore
Printed and bound in Great Britain by
Biddles Ltd, Guildford and King's Lynn

Contents

Tables and figures

Acknowledgements

Essays in this collection come from the following sources, to whose publishers grateful acknowledgement is made:

1.1 'Leadership in professionally staffed organizations', by Hughes, M., in Hughes, M., Ribbins, P. and Thomas, H. (eds), *Managing Education: The System and the Institution*, London, Holt, Rinehart and Winston, (1985).

1.2 'Leadership and mission', by Hoyle, E., in Hoyle, E., *The Politics of School Management*, London, Hodder and Stoughton, (1986).

1.3 'Primary headship and collegiality', by Southworth, G., in Southworth, G. (ed.), *Readings in Primary School Management*, Lewes, Falmer Press, (1987).

1.4 'The role of the middle manager in the secondary school', by Ribbins, P., in Hughes, M., Ribbins, P., and Thomas, H. (eds), *Managing Education: The System and the Institution*, London, Holt, Rinehart and Winston, (1985).

1.5 'Headteachers at work: practice and policy', by Hall, V., Mackay, H. and Morgan, C., in Hall, V., Mackay, H. and Morgan, C., *Headteachers at Work*, Milton Keynes, Open University Press, (1986).

1.6 'How heads manage change', by Weindling, D. and Earley, P., *School Organization*, vol. 6, no. 3, pp. 327–338, (1986).

2.1 'Cultural forces in schools', by Handy, C., in Handy, C., *Taken for Granted? Looking at Schools as Organizations*, Harlow, Longman, (1984).

2.2 'Key factors for effective junior schooling', by Mortimore, P., Sammons, P., Stoll, L., Lewis, D. and Ecob, R., in Inner London Education Authority Research and Statistics Branch, *The Junior School Project: a Summary of the Main Report*, (1986).

2.3 'The management of school improvement', by Glatter, R., in Hoyle, E. and McMahon, A. (eds), *World Yearbook of Education 1986: the Management of Schools*, London, Kogan Page.

3.1 'Normative models of accountability', by Kogan, M., in Kogan, M., *Educational Accountability*, London, Hutchinson, (1986).

3.2 'Models of governing bodies', by Packwood, T., in Kogan. M., Johnson, D.,
Packwood, T. and Whitaker, T., *School Governing Bodies*, London,
Heinemann, (1984).

4.1 'The school and curriculum decisions', by Skilbeck, M., in Skilbeck, M.,
School-based Curriculum Development, London, Harper and Row. Paul
Chapman Publishing (1984).

4.2 'Research into educational innovation', by Fullan, M., in Gray, H. L. (ed),
The Management of Educational Institutions: Theory, Research and Consultancy,
Lewes, Falmer Press, (1982).

4.3 The conduct of the curriculum: the roles and deployment of teachers; in The
Education, Science and Arts Committee of the House of Commons, *Third
Report: Achievement in Primary Schools*, London, HMSO, (1986). Reproduced
with the permission of the Controller of Her Majesty's Stationary Office.

4.4 'Conflict and strain in the postholder's role', from Campbell, R. J. (Jim)
Developing the Primary School Curriculum, London, Holt, Rinehart and
Winston, (1985).

4.5 'Pastoral needs in schools', by Marland, M., in Lang, P. and Marland, M.
(eds), *New Directions in Pastoral Care*, Oxford, Basil Blackwell in association
with the National Association for Pastoral Care in Education and the Economic and Social Research Council, (1985).

4.6 'Primary school resource management: a case study', by Gray, L., © The
Open University 1984, by permission of the Open University.

4.7 'Information technology in schools: responses and effects', by Lancaster, D.,
in *Educational Management and Administration*, 13(2), pp. 140–145, (1985).

5.1 'Reference groups in primary teaching: talking, listening and identity',
by Nias, J., in Ball, S. J. and Goodson, I. F. (eds), *Issues in Education and
Training Series 3: Teachers' Lives and Careers*, Lewes, Falmer Press, (1985).

5.2 'Some legal aspects of employment in schools', Lyons, G. and Stenning, R.,
in Lyons, G. and Stenning R., *Managing Staff in Schools: a Handbook*, London,
Hutchinson, (1986).

5.3 'The selection and appointment of heads', by Morgan, C., in Hoyle, E. and
McMahon, A. (eds), *World Yearbook of Education 1986: the Management of
Schools*, London, Kogan Page.

5.4 'INSET and professional development for teachers', Advisory Committee
on the Supply and Education of Teachers, Department of Education and
Science, (1984).

5.5 'Towards a staff development review', Samuel, G., *School Organization*, vol. 4,
no. 3, pp. 205–210, (1984).

5.6 'The management of school-based staff development: an example',
Oldroyd, D., *British Journal of In-service Education*, vol. 11, no. 2, pp. 82–90,
spring, (1985).

Preface

This reader comprises a collection of papers published in connection with the Open University course E325, entitled 'Managing Schools', which examines the concepts of education management in the light of actual management situations and decision-making processes in schools.

This reader is one part of an Open University integrated teaching system and the selection is therefore related to other material available to students. The editors have attempted nevertheless to make it of value to all those concerned with school management. Opinions expressed in it are not necessarily those of the course team or of the University.

It is not necessary to become an undergraduate of the Open University in order to take the course of which this reader is part. Further information about the course and about the Advanced Diploma in Educational Management, of which it can form a component, may be obtained by writing to: The Associate Student Central Office, The Open University, PO Box 76, Milton Keynes, MK7 6AN.

Introduction

This reader, which supports the Open University course E325 'Managing Schools', is the successor to Bush, *et al* (1980) *Approaches to School Management* which was linked with E323 'Management and the School'. The intervening years have seen an increasing emphasis on understanding management issues within our schools – and in education generally – and the importance of good management in school effectiveness. There has been a major growth in support for school management training and development by central government and local authorities. These trends have been accompanied by several major research studies in this field and the arrival of much new literature. Since the publication of the E323 reader, the Centre for Education Policy and Management at the Open University has reflected some of this work through its other courses in this field (which now all form part of an Advanced Diploma in Educational Management) and the readers which are attached to them (Boyd-Barrett *et al* 1984; Bell *et al* 1984; Goulding *et al* 1984).

No single volume of readings could adequately represent the breadth and variety of recent writing on school management. Some of what is missing may be found in the other readers referred to above, in the published correspondence texts for E325, or in other courses. However, we believe that all the studies included here contribute to an understanding of school management and are worthy of attention by busy staff in schools who have a concern or responsibility for management within them, and by those in local authorities, higher education or elsewhere, whose task is to facilitate and support school development.

Any collection such as this invites the question 'Why should we examine and seek to understand school management?' Only the briefest discussion of such a large issue is possible here. The growth of interest in school management in the 1980s has inevitably been greatly stimulated by contextual factors: severe reductions in resources, heightened pressures for accountability and answerability to external publics, a pupil population which was sharply declining in most areas, expectations of increased effectiveness, efficiency, productivity, and 'value for money', and a strong promotion in some quarters of the processes and practices of private sector industry and commerce as models for the operation of public services. This has led some to regard this increasing emphasis on school management as undesirably mechanistic, and to claim that values implicit in the management of schools tend to go unquestioned (see, for example, Maw *et al* 1984).

John Sayer, a distinguished former headteacher, has effectively countered such a view:

> Instead of registering that management, like the motor car, is itself valueless, we should be agreeing that if we have goals we have to equip ourselves to head towards them; if we have values it is no good just proclaiming them, we have to find ways to put them into practice. Too often education has proclaimed values and outcomes which are not reflected in what has actually been happening.
>
> (Sayer 1986, p. 3)

In line with this approach, the stance taken in this reader is that school management is a highly practical activity concerned with creating effective organizational means to ensure that educational values, goals and intentions are put into practice. To understand school management in practice we must analyse *both* the ways goals and intentions are determined *and* the methods used to implement them as well as the results which are obtained. This understanding requires much more than finding and teaching suitable and specific techniques and skills for more effective performance; it calls for *reflection* on how theoretical concepts and models, and the findings of empirical studies, can illuminate and guide the ways in which managers act. Thus the readings deal with many themes covering concepts and models of management, role analysis, research reports, national reviews of educational management, curriculum management, and various case studies touching on one or more of these themes.

Clearly there are many ways in which we might have arranged the sequencing of the selected contributions. Section 1 deals with the major theme of 'Leadership in schools'. Hughes (1.1.) provides a review of the literature on leadership and professionalism, particularly in the context of educational organizations, drawing upon his own research in this field, and emphasizing the political dimension involved in leadership. In 1.2 Hoyle takes up the theme of school leadership in a micro-political arena, and moves forward to analyse the notion of school mission, which he considers to be 'a neglected aspect of the role of the head'. In 'Primary headship and collegiality' (1.3) Southworth turns our attention to the tensions and problems created when collegiality coexists with leadership and examines some possible incompatibilities. Ribbins's examination (1.4) of the roles of middle managers in secondary schools gives centrality to their importance in pupil achievement. He is, however, 'sceptical' about traditional definitions of middle-management roles, which are often 'decontextualized' in the sense that they are either considered in isolation from other role holders with whom they interact or without regard to the nature of the particular institution within which they are enacted. The Weindling and Earley extract (1.6) is based on their research into the first years of secondary headship, and focuses on the way heads manage change.

Section 2 on 'School cultures and effectiveness' begins with a chapter by Handy (2.1) which was a part product of an investigation, sponsored by the Schools Council, into what light someone with experience of *industrial* management could shed on *school* management following a series of 'conversations' with heads and staffs of primary and secondary schools. Handy sought to apply to schools a classification of cultures from organizational theory. Establishing the most appropriate cultural mix is an important recipe for success. The significance of school culture or climate in school effectiveness is one of the findings of the ILEA investigation into factors involved in the progress and development of children in junior schools, summarized in 2.2. In 2.3 Glatter reflects on school improvement and its interrelationship with school maintenance, examines various models for explaining how change occurs in schools and supports a multiperspective view of school improvement and the way that effectiveness might be achieved.

Section 3 is entitled 'The school and its context' and explores some key issues of accountability. The first of its two chapters is a theoretical analysis by Kogan (3.1) of some models of accountability, in which the author critically examines the empirical work carried out by the Sussex and Cambridge projects on accountability. Packwood (3.2) looks at various models of governing bodies within the local education system and concludes that they have a number of possibilities in the way they perform their roles; these need to be clarified and the resource implications worked out.

Section 4 on 'Curriculum and resource management' contains papers of wide diversity and interest. Skilbeck (4.1) argues the case for the school as the centre for curriculum development in a partnership between all the stake-holders. In 4.2 Fullan analyses the implementation of curriculum change and what has to be done to help people in educational institutions to deal effectively with innovation by bringing about changes in three key areas: materials for teaching, methods of teaching and educational beliefs. The extract from the House of Commons Select Committee Report (4.3) is a discussion of evidence received by the committee on the conduct of the curriculum in the primary schools of England and Wales and the roles of teachers in this process, especially stressing the importance of coordinators in primary schools to carry out specialist functions. Campbell (4.4) deals in greater depth with the ambiguities and resulting stresses which face such coordinators in seeking to do their daily work. In chapter 4.5, Marland examines the limited research which has been carried out into the needs of students and tutors, the structures for pastoral care and key aspects of the pastoral curriculum, and he suggests ways in which research might move forward.

The last two chapters of Section 4 probe two neglected aspects of school management, namely resource management and the use of information technology in schools. Gray (4.6) produces a case study of resource allocation in the primary school and looks in turn at the internal allocation procedures, the ways needs are identified and met throughout the year and how LEA and non-LEA funds are deployed. Lancaster's paper (4.7) deals with the implications of the rapid introduction of microcomputers into the curriculum and administration of schools and demonstrates the varied pattern of use between schools, resulting in distinctive adaptations of job roles and the modification of organizational structures.

In 'Issues in staff management' (Section 5) three of the six chapters are the products of recent research and two are case studies of current practice. Nias (5.1) explores the way primary teachers in her research established their own identities and sought social and cognitive support for their educational views and commitments, and how these related to their career expectations. Lyons and Stenning (5.2) describe the legal framework which governs the employment of staff in schools and examine some problems which can result from ignoring or misinterpreting employment legislation. In 5.3 Morgan discusses the findings of the 'POST' project on the selection and appointment of headteachers in secondary schools. He is critical of present procedures and criteria for selection and examines some alternative practices in selection. For the rest of the papers in this section attention turns from the selection of staff to their development. The document from the Advisory Committee on the Supply and Education of Teachers (ACSET) (5.4) discusses the case for INSET, the types of provision, the conditions for its effectiveness and the role of the school in the process. Samuel (5.5) writes about a staff development review and appraisal in one school and Oldroyd (5.6) describes and analyses the management of staff development in another.

As we have said, it is impossible to achieve comprehensiveness given the amount and range of work which is now available. Some of the topics omitted here are covered in the associated E325 course texts. Many of the items included here do, however, challenge conventional thinking about school management. We are particularly glad to have represented several of the major empirical research studies which have been conducted in this field in recent years, including some which place emphasis on how those who are involved in or affected by management themselves perceive the process. Such systematic studies undertaken within schools are the best corrective to an excessively abstract and theoretical approach, of which academic work in education, and in management, is often justly accused by those who practise these arts. Empirical studies, allied with individuals' experience and reflection, are the most valuable means towards achieving an understanding of management in schools at a time when the difficulty and centrality of the management task have never been more evident.

Finally we wish to recognize the major part played by our secretaries in assembling this reader and we thank Caroline Fawcus, Helen Knowles and Betty Russell both for their technical contribution and for their sustaining cheerfulness.

References

BELL, J., BUSH, T., FOX, A., GOODEY, J. and GOULDING, S. (1984). *Conducting*

Small-Scale Investigations in Educational Management, Harper and Row for the Open University.

BOYD-BARRETT, O., BUSH, T., GOODEY, J., McNAY, I. and PREEDY, M. (1983). *Approaches to Post-School Management*, London, Harper and Row for the Open University.

BUSH, T., GLATTER, R., GOODEY, J. and RICHES, C. (1980). *Approaches to School Management*, London, Harper and Row for the Open University.

GOULDING, S., BELL, J., BUSH, T., FOX, A. and GOODEY, J. (1984). *Case studies in Educational Management*, London, Harper and Row for the Open University.

MAW, J. *et al* (1986). *Education PLC? Headteachers and the New Training Initiative*, Bedford Way Papers 20, Institute of Education, University of London (distributed by Heinemann).

SAYER, J. (1986) 'Management as a technology for values: philosophy in practice', unpublished draft of a paper presented to the 1986 Annual Conference of the British Educational Management and Administration Society (BEMAS), Westfield College, London, September 1986.

Section 1

Leadership in schools

Leadership in professionally staffed organisations

Meredydd Hughes

Introduction

Leadership and profession are terms of wide application which conjure up a variety of interpretations. At different times they have both given rise to controversy in public discussion, each having many overtones, both positive and negative. Both concepts have generated a formidable social science literature.

The first [. . .] section of the chapter will provide [. . .] an inevitably brief survey of the concept of professionalism, giving attention in particular to studies in an organisational context. The leadership of professionals in organisational settings which will be considered in the [second] section, has been comparatively neglected in the general literature. It will be considered mainly in the specific context of the leadership of educational institutions, but will draw as appropriate on relevant ideas and research of a more general kind which is described in the earlier section.

The issues involved are somewhat complex, but are of importance in the management of education and more widely. Many of the approaches discussed are firmly grounded within the system/functionalist paradigm [. . .] but attention is also given to contemporary challenges to traditional concepts of leadership and profession. A micro-political viewpoint is finally advocated [. . .]

Professionalism and the Management of Organisations

In this section consideration will first be given to the different views which have been expressed concerning the nature of professionalism, earlier assumptions concerning essential characteristics of professions being more recently questioned. The implications for organisational management of employing a professional work force will then be considered, including the potential for conflict and how such conflict can be resolved or avoided.

The concept of professionalism

Profession, like leadership, is an elusive concept and is a word with variations of meaning in the social science literature and even more so in general usage. Millerson (1964, p. 5) noted 23 distinct traits which have been included in various definitions of the term profession. According to Goode (1960), many of the characteristics that have been proposed are derivative, the two core characteristics in his view being a lengthy period of training in a body of abstract knowledge and a strong service orientation. Elsewhere he described the characteristics of a professional community as a sense of identity associated with shared values, an agreed role definition, a common technical language, and a recognition that the professional group has power over its members (Goode 1957, pp. 194–209). His work may be cited as an example of sociological studies which tended to accept, somewhat uncritically, the rhetoric of prominent professional groups and their unduly idealistic self-definitions of their special characteristics. As Johnson (1972, p. 25) has aptly observed, 'while the service ethic may be an important part of the ideology of many professional groups, it is not so clear that practitioners are necessarily so motivated'.

In contrast to the 'trait' approach adopted, though in a compressed form, by Goode, Barber (1963) looked for characteristics of professionalism which might be regarded as having functional relevance for the relationship of professional to client or for society generally. He identified four such characteristics: a high degree of systematic knowledge, orientation to community interest, control through a code of ethics emanating from a voluntary association, and a system of rewards which is 'primarily a set of symbols of work achievement' (p. 672). The underlying assumption that there is a universally recognised community interest, which is distinctively served by highly qualified occupational groups whose members are expected to place symbolic rewards above monetary gain, and generally do so, is one which may understandably give rise to scepticism, as Jackson (1970, p. 8) has noted. In a later definition of professional behaviour Barber (1978, p. 601) essentially retained the first three characteristics but made no reference to symbolic rewards.

A consistent advocate of a more critical approach to professionalism has been Everett Hughes, who cogently argued that the available evidence indicated that 'the concept "professional" in all societies is not so much a descriptive term as one of value and prestige' (Hughes 1958, p. 44). He later proposed that attention should be given to the empirical question of how professionalised certain occupations are at a particular time, rather than seeking to determine whether they are professions in some absolute sense (Hughes 1963). He was followed by Ben-David (1963–4), who analysed professions in relation to the class system of different societies, and Prandy (1965), who examined professional associations as status bodies which bestow a qualification and seek to maintain and enhance its prestige. Oleson and Whitaker (1970), p. 184), in a review of studies of professional socialisation, conclude that there is a tendency 'to overlook major discrepancies between the symbol of profession and the everyday human realities on which it rests'. In a similar realistic vein, Larson (1977, p. xvi) saw professionalisation as 'the process by which producers of special services sought to constitute and control a market for their expertise'.

Hall (1969) followed up his previous study of the elements of bureaucracy [. . .] by a similar dimensional approach to professionalism. He examined the structural aspects of 27 professions and the attitudes expressed by their members, and found significant discrepancies between structural and attitudinal scores (pp. 87–8, Table 4.2). Professionalised occupations structurally did not rank as highly as some others in terms of belief in service to the public or of sense of calling to the field. They invariably had the highest ranks, however, in terms of belief in self-regulation and the use of the professional organisation as a reference group.

The structures and procedures within professions which ensure a substantial measure of professional autonomy and control are increasingly being vigorously challenged by those who use professional services, as Barber (1978) and Wirt (1981) have clearly shown. Wirt has provided an instructive developmental model of political conflict between professionals and non-professionals, i.e. 'the laity'. He distinguishes five phases as follows: *quiescence*, which entails professional dominance; *issue emergence*, involving a growing number of random individual complaints by clients; *turbulence*, characterised by strong challenges and militant pressure groups, and in some cases by the emergence of inside agitators' within the professional ranks; *resolution*, the phases in which both the professional and lay representatives are engaged in vigorous debate and action, and which may also involve government as mediator or adjudicator; and finally *closure*, signifying the reduction of conflict as the professionals typically accept some redefinition of professional services, whether voluntarily or as a result of legally imposed constraints. Wirt's illustrative examples relate mainly to medical and legal services in the USA, but he also includes apposite references to parental concern and governmental intervention in education in both the USA and UK. The resulting involvement of professionals in external political activity, both at a micro level and at group level, albeit in a non-party sense in most cases, is well documented in Wirt's paper.

This brief review may be summed up with the observation that the early phases of Wirt's developmental model appear to be relevant to the concept of professionalism itself. The period up to about 1960 was largely one of quiescence, when the self perceptions of the professionals themselves, reinforced by their professional associations, were largely accepted not only by the relevant client groups but also by most social scientists. The 1960s and early 1970s may be regarded as a period of issue emergence, when the rhetoric of the professions began to be questioned, first by social science academics and then, in more robust terms, by individual clients and client groups. Since the mid-1970s there has clearly been a period of turbulence when the challenges are stronger and more co-ordinated and some of the professional groups are themselves more active and vociferous in defending their interests, younger professionals themselves sometimes schizophrenically challenging established practice. Politicking flourishes, and there is little sign as yet of an abatement of conflict between the seemingly elitist aspirations of professionals and a widespread populist revolt which receives encouragement from radicals of both the political left and the political right. At the general level under consideration it appears that Wirt's final categories, resolution and closure, are difficult to envisage, being quite remote from the practical politics of life today.

Factors conducive to conflict within organisations

Professionals employed in organisations are liable to have difficulties from time to time in their relationships, not only with their clients or the public at large, but also with those in authority in their employing organisation. Professionals, it has been claimed, are unreasonably resistant to administrative control (Abrahamson 1967). Studies of scientists in research establishments (Hall and Lawler 1970), studies of doctors and nurses in hospitals and clinics (Engel 1970; Corwin 1961), studies of social workers in local authority departments (Jordan 1979; Glastonbury and Cooper 1982), studies of accountants in large commercial firms (Sorenson and Sorenson 1974), studies of teachers and lecturers in schools and colleges (Corwin 1965; Noble and Pym 1970) all share a common characteristic. They display similar patterns of latent or actual conflict between the occupational group and organisational requirements which cannot be simply explained away in terms of the recalcitrance of awkward individuals. The real issue, it appears, in the ubiquitous strain between professions and organisations is the relationship between two institutions, not merely between organisations and individuals' (Kornhauser 1963, p. 8).

Areas of conflict have been comprehensively reviewed on a number of occasions (Scott 1966; Etzioni 1969; Harries-Jenkins 1970; Rotondi 1975; Larson 1977). Many aspects have been discussed, Etzioni for instance suggesting that teachers, social workers and nurses might appropriately be regarded as semi-professionals on the two assumptions that they are more amenable than other professionals to bureaucratisation and that a higher proportion of them are women. The suggestion that these two assumptions are interconnected has been vigorously challenged (Neuse 1978, p. 440), and the concept of semi-professionalism has largely been discarded, having proved to be even more elusive than that of professionalism itself.

Returning to the main theme, one can broadly distinguish in the literature between problems related to the professional's claim to autonomy within the organisation, and problems arising as a result of his or her external orientation and affiliations.

The professional's claim to autonomy
Because of their specialised training, professionals expect to be accorded a large measure of discretion in dealing with matters considered to be within their area of expertise. It is argued that it is by using their trained judgement in professional matters that they can best contribute to the objectives of their employing

organisation. If they are employed in a highly structured, tight bureaucracy, a certain level of endemic conflict, erupting from time to time in major incidents, appears to be an almost inevitable consequence, as evidenced by research in different contexts.

A comprehensive study by Hall (1968) provides support for the proposition that the professional's quest for autonomy is the professional value which causes most difficulty in organisations. The research included doctors, nurses, lawyers, accountants, social workers and teachers. Bureaucratisation scales were developed for the organisational units within which the various professionals worked, and measures were obtained on attitudes towards professional values such as service to the public and sense of autonomy. Whereas other relationships proved to be relatively weak, Hall found a strong negative relationship between 'feeling of autonomy' and each of his five bureaucratic dimensions, namely, hierarchy of authority, division of labour, rules, procedures, and impersonality. He concluded that increased bureaucratisation threatens professional autonomy. The strong professional drive for autonomy, he noted, 'may come into direct conflict with organisationally based job requirements. At the same time the organisation may be threatened by strong professional desires on the part of at least some of its members' (Hall 1968, pp. 102–3).

A related issue is the professional's reluctance to accept without qualification the legitimacy of a hierarchy of authority. Professionals are well aware that technical expertise does not necessarily increase with position in the formal hierarchy. The extent of resistance to hierarchical control varies according to circumstances, as will be noted later, the availability of appeal and consultative procedures being a significant factor. The quality of the professional commitment at the different organisational levels seems also to make a difference. Thus Scott (1965) found that social workers who regarded their supervisors as professionally oriented were less hostile to routine supervision than those who designated their supervisors as less professional, the supervision being acceptable when seen as an opportunity for helpful guidance by a senior colleague. On the other hand it was the more professionally oriented workers who were generally more critical of the control system than their less professionally motivated colleagues. A similar polarisation of attitude has been found among teachers and lecturers, identified by Corwin (1965) as a difference between *professional* and *employee* orientations, which is of relevance to the discussion of leadership in education later in the chapter.

The professional's external orientation
The second basic factor which tends to create problems is that the ideal stereotype of a professional establishes him or her as an incorrigible cosmopolitan. In a study of professionals in public agencies, Reissman (1949, p. 309) found that, in contrast to other employees, the professionals had a strong tendency 'to face outwards and away from the bureaucratic structure of their organisation'. With the accelerating increase of knowledge in all specialisms, the external aspect of professionalism has steadily increased in importance, familiarity with current

professional literature and contact with colleagues across organisational boundaries being essential for the maintenance of standards and the further development of expertise. By such means professional credibility is retained and renewed, but this may sometimes be at the expense of the immediate organisational task. It is not surprising that frustrated, locally based administrators, who have to be concerned with the mundane task of organisation maintenance, become sceptical about the priorities and organisational loyalty of professional staff. Such differences of perspective are commonplace, for instance, in universities and polytechnics.

A notable pioneering study in this area was carried out by Gouldner (1957), who studied three aspects of the role orientation of the staff of a liberal arts college. He found that a high commitment to professional skills was positively related to an outside reference group orientation, and that both were negatively related to loyalty to the employing organisation as indicated by a wish to remain indefinitely in the organisation. Adopting a distinction drawn by Merton (1957) between *cosmopolitan* and *local* community leaders, Gouldner defined as 'cosmopolitan' the members of an organisation high in commitment to specialist skills and strongly oriented to outside reference groups, but low in organisational loyalty. The 'locals' were opposite in each respect. There is tension, Gouldner concluded, between an organisation's instrumental need for expertise which is provided by the cosmopolitans and its social need for loyalty which is provided by the locals.

Whereas the idea of a single cosmopolitan–local continuum of role orientations has had a powerful influence on later writers, Gouldner's assumption that his three variables, professional commitment, reference group orientation and organisational commitment, were so highly associated that they formed a single continuum was only partially supported by his research findings. Subsequent research has clearly demonstrated that the cosmopolitan–local typology is an over-simplification (Grimes and Berger 1970) and that at the very least one must consider two independent dimensions, related respectively to professional commitment (or cosmopolitan orientation) and to organisational commitment (or local orientation). In addition to Gouldner's 'cosmopolitans' and 'locals', a two-dimensional model thus envisages two further categories, the 'cosmopolitan-locals' (i.e. those high on both dimensions), and the 'indifferents' (i.e. those low on both dimensions). That many persons do in fact manage to combine loyalty to their profession and to their organisation has been repeatedly shown in empirical research (Blau and Scott 1963; Corwin 1965; Thornton 1970; Goldberg 1976; Jauch, et al 1978). Goldberg showed, additionally, that commitment to organisational goals could be an incentive to professionals to increase their professional expertise.

While recent research has thus shown that it is misleading and unhelpful to automatically equate professionalism with disloyalty to the organisation, it is equally important not to lose sight of the fact that the insight of Reissman and Gouldner retains at least partial validity. It has to be accepted that, if professional expertise is to be credible and relevant in the modern world, a cosmopolitan, outward-looking stance is an essential element in the role orientation of professionals in organisations. Like the claim to autonomy, however, it is liable to give rise to tensions and problems in organisations which employ professionals.

Modes of organisational accommodation

In spite of the rhetoric which flies around when conflict erupts, it may be noted that although strains and tension do arise between professional and organisational loyalties they seldom lead to major confrontation, accommodation being nearly always somehow achieved. A major reason for this, according to Blau and Scott (1963 pp. 60–3), is that bureaucracies and professions have many things in common.

In their classic contribution on this topic Blau and Scott suggest that, in spite of differences between bureaucratic and professional perspectives, there are important common elements. Both are concerned to establish and uphold general standards of performance, which can be rationally defended. They are similar in studiously avoiding exaggerated claims: professional expertise is specific and limited, bureaucratic authority is explicitly defined and circumscribed. For both the professional and the bureaucrat, relationships with clients are expected to be psychologically detached, avoiding emotional involvement. Professional recognition and advancement is the result of specific achievement as assessed by the colleague group; similarly bureaucratic advancement is expected to be determined by objective criteria rather than by personal considerations. In view of these common characteristics it is not surprising that at least some professionals find little difficulty in adapting to organisational life.

Research by Blau and others tends to support this kind of interpretation. Blau (1968) found that the presence of a clear hierarchy is welcomed by the professionals if it is perceived to facilitate effective two-way communication with senior management. La Porte (1965, p. 37) found that a hierarchical structure is acceptable if it 'acts as a filter of organisational uncertainty', making it possible for the work of the professionals to proceed without extensive bureaucratic interference. Hall (1982, p. 109), in a later comment on his own research, previously mentioned, observed that a strong negative relationship between professional attitudes and hierarchy of authority was only established in the case of attitude to autonomy (Hall 1968, p. 102). 'The presence of a relatively rigid hierarchy', he concluded, 'may not adversely affect the work of professionals if the hierarchy is recognised as legitimate.'

Focusing on another bureaucratic characteristic, Organ and Greene (1981) examined the extent to which formalisation, defined as 'the control of job activities by administrative rules and procedures' (p. 238), results in conflict between administrative imperatives and professional norms. They found that conflict 'is neither omnipresent nor inevitable' (p. 251). To some extent formalisation did increase role conflict for professionals, but this was more than offset by its effect in reducing role ambiguity and in enhancing identification with the organisation. The organisation might become more meaningful to the professional, they suggested, 'by providing a Gestalt within which he can define more reassuringly the nature of his own contribution to the larger enterprise' (p. 250).

An entirely different perspective on factors to be considered in achieving harmonious working relationships has been provided by Tuma and Grimes (1981). Though their research interest was focused on role conceptions, they concluded from their study of academic and administrative staff at a large research-oriented university that 'the organisational and professional settings are as important as a person's role orientations in determining how the person performs professional and organisational roles' (p. 187). Their study considered separately the three dimensions originally proposed in Gouldner's (1957) study, namely *professional commitment, external or reference group orientation* and *local orientation* as indicated by intended organisational immobility. They added another measure of organisational commitment, *commitment to organisational goals*, on the grounds that it cannot be assumed, when employment opportunities are diminishing, that a wish to continue in an organisation necessarily implies such a commitment. A further refinement was their recognition of the importance of another role dimension, *concern with advancement*, which relates to the basic human desire to get on, whether this was achieved through the profession or the organisation.

Tuma and Grimes found that there was some association between the five conceptually distinct aspects of role orientation which they had identified. In explaining such relationships, they conceded that cognitive congruence, as proposed by Gouldner operated to some extent, but suggested that two organisationally related mechanisms were also likely to be influential. These are:

(a) The recruiting policies which determine the criteria whereby organisational members are appointed.
(b) The behavioural feedback by means of which role aspirations within the organisation may adapt to the career opportunities available.

The latter mechanism, and the related recognition of 'concern for advancement' as a significant variable that over-rides the idealised professional–organisational dichotomy, brings a note of realism into the literature, which is in accord with the critical political analysis provided by commentators such as Johnson (1972) and Wirt (1981).

From the accounts which have been given of recent research in different contexts and from different standpoints, it may be concluded that some oversimplification was inevitably involved in our separate discussion of factors conducive to conflict and accommodation in the management of professionally staffed organisations. Neither internally, in relation to formalisation and control structures, nor externally, in relation to the recognised cosmopolitan orientation of professionals, is the situation as clear-cut as some of the earlier literature might suggest. Hierarchy, for instance, can be seen either as an impediment to professionals or as facilitating professional input into organisational decision-making. Conflict and accommodation are intertwined, and it is evident that, as

Tuma and Grimes observed, the organisational and professional settings are of crucial importance in achieving co-operation rather than disharmony.

A considerable challenge is thus presented to those in leadership positions in professional organisations, i.e. in organisations which are largely staffed by professionals and have a recognised professional function such as healing the sick or providing education. As the cited research suggests, the challenge is partly that posed by the subtle and fascinating internal complexity of professionally staffed organisations which may be recognised as revealing a hitherto largely neglected arena of micro-political activity. There is also the challenge to professional authority and control posed by powerful external forces, which is of increasing importance and again has a political dimension in the non-party sense, at both micro and macro levels.

The implications of this double challenge for the leadership of professionally staffed organisations will now be considered. Without neglecting issues applicable to professional organisations generally, the discussion will be focused specifically on the role of leadership in the management of educational institutions.

Leadership roles in educational institutions

In general, those who have managerial and leadership responsibilities in educational institutions would claim to be educational professionals. This gives rise to ambiguities as well as to opportunities. The strains and tensions which have to be accommodated will include those which are personal to the individual concerned, who may conveniently be referred to in this context as the professional-as-administrator. The scope of the discussion is widened as it is recognised that *all* teachers have managerial, as well as academic, responsibilities.

A dual role model is proposed which seeks to take account of the situation that arises when the *chief executive* of a professionally staffed organisation may also be considered to be its *leading professional*. An essential element in the model is the close interdependency of the two aspects. This is demonstrated in relation to school headship, but is equally applicable at other levels and in different types of educational organisation.

The chapter ends by considering some of the challenging tasks which face the educational professional-as-administrator in three domains of professional leadership. The first two domains are concerned respectively with instrumental and expressive aspects of the internal activities of the organisation, the third being concerned with external aspects and the extent to which the professional-as-administrator may be able to develop a positive, pro-active, representative role.

The professional-as-administrator

In professionally staffed organisations it is usual for institutional heads to be appointed who have a strong professional background in the relevant area of expertise. Such appointments may be regarded as co-opting devices designed to defuse tensions between practising professionals and their managers. As noted by Moore (1970, p. 211). '. . . the manager who has some basis for understanding the problems intrinsic to the professional role and its organisational setting is likely to elicit somewhat greater confidence than would be accorded a mere layman'. Moore also observed that there is a representative as well as an internal co-ordinating function to be performed and that a similar point applies: representation by 'one of their own kind' is more acceptable to professionals than by 'anyone viewed as an outsider'. The role of the *professional-as-administrator* may thus be presented, in structural-functional terms, as the ultimate accommodating technique: it legitimises hierarchy, helps to ensure that bureaucratic formalisation does not restrict professional autonomy, and provides external representation which expresses a professional standpoint. Whether it works like that in practice is another matter. The implication that, in terminology first introduced in relation to secondary school headship, the leading professional of the organisation is simultaneously its chief executive (Hughes 1972) is an attractive concept, but ultimately depends for its justification on the extent to which a leadership style is adopted which elicits the co-operation of the professional group.

That the appointment to high office of committed and inspired professionals does not necessarily ensure a collegial style of leadership is easily demonstrated by considering some of the familiar names that might grace a pantheon of educational leaders. Moodie and Eustace (1974), in their well-known chapter on university vice-chancellors, singled out Hetherington of Liverpool, and then of Glasgow, and Irvine of St. Andrews for special mention as outstanding leaders. A later principal of St. Andrews wrote about Irvine twenty years after his death, 'I have been told that professors trembled when called before him. I have also been told that they felt that this was only right and proper' (Moodie and Eustace 1974, p. 149). There was a similar tradition of directive autocratic leadership in further education [. . .].

Arnold of Rugby and Thring of Uppingham, doyens of what has been called the 'headmaster tradition' of the English public schools (Baron 1975), would also, it may be assumed, have an honoured place in the pantheon. On the one hand they were certainly leading professionals, and on the other they fitted Norwood's description, quoted by Baron, of the headmaster as 'an autocrat of autocrats', so that 'the very mention of the title conjures up in the minds of most people a figure before whom they trembled in their youth, and with which they have never felt quite comfortable even in mature life' (Norwood and Hope 1909, p. 213).

It would be unwise to draw general conclusions, particularly as it has been noted that little reliance can be placed on a trait or 'great man' theory of leadership. There is, however, at least one significant characteristic which is common to Hetherington, Irvine, Arnold and Thring: each had a strong commitment to the education of those in their charge, and not simply to carrying out the managerial duties of their office. They each illustrate Hall's dictum, quoted earlier, that one of the conditions necessary for the leader's behaviour to have a large impact is that 'the leadership is expected to have a great deal to do with

what goes on in the organisation' (Hall 1982, p. 173). Because of their acknowledged wisdom as educational experts in their particular field, they were able to
exert influence also externally on behalf of their institutions. It is on record that
much of the funding of St. Andrews University and of Rugby School depended
during their periods of office, on the personal initiative and effort of Irvine and
Arnold respectively.

The strong professional commitment of such archetypal father figures is a
quality shared to varying extents by the heads and other senior staff in schools,
colleges, and universities. Those with leadership responsibilities at different
levels in educational institutions, ranging from the small primary school to the
large university or polytechnic, aspire to professional authority as educators as
much as to positional authority as managers of organisations. A similar reliance
on professional, as well as on organisational, authority may be attributed to
inspectors and advisers, [. . .] and applies to considerable extent also to local
education officers (Bush and Kogan 1982, pp. 9–12).

Though it is at the school level that the co-existence of professional and
organisational authority systems has been given most attention (e.g. Thomason
1974), it has also been recognised in higher and further education. In discussing
leadership in higher education, Becher and Kogan (1980, p. 64) refer to 'the
dual system of hierarchy and collegium running through the system', which is
epitomised in the Janus-like role of university vice-chancellors, polytechnic
directors and college principals. For vice-chancellors this view is confirmed in
studies by Szreter (1968; 1979) and by Moodie and Eustace (1974, p. 127) who
observe of vice-chancellors that 'although their day to day activities within the
university may conveniently be described as "administrative", they are
expected to be, and in fact often are, academic in purpose and outlook.'[1] The
description of 'chief academic and administrative officer', used of vice-
chancellors in university charters since 1948, was significantly adopted in
describing college principals in DES Circular 7/70. The duality is recognised in a
NATFHE college administration handbook in a chapter (Edwards and Easton
1980) which recognised both that 'in administrative matters the principal may
be regarded as a manager acting on behalf of the LEA' (p. 148) and that 'clearly,
within the college, the principal has responsibility for being an educational
initiator, either by introducing new ideas or encouraging others to bring forward
ideas' (p. 146)[. . .]

It may be concluded that, with some difference of emphasis, the professional-
as-administrator is an ever present phenomenon in the educational system, in
each sector and at every level. The strain involved in the occupancy of such
positions is not always fully recognised, external accommodation being often
achieved at the expense of internal conflict. The potential clash of loyalties is
similar to that experienced by the scientist involved in both research and
research administration. 'As an administrator, he must make decisions that are
in the organisation's interest. As a scientist he has scientific values and peers in
the scientific community whose approval and support he desires. What happens
when organisational and research interests diverge . . .?' (Lambright and Teich

1978, p. 135). A related discussion by Feldman (1978) of the administration of the mental health service is of particular interest because of the similar professional ideology of mental health and education. An initial reluctance to be involved in the exercise of power and control was noted, but Feldman concluded that 'the mental health professional in government who is able to blend the use of power with an understanding of human needs is likely to be an extremely effective administrator' (p. 142).

The dual (leading professional–chief executive) role model

In order to examine more closely the professional-as-administrator phenomenon at the headship level, it has been conceptualised (Hughes 1972) as the simultaneous activation of two sub-roles which deeply inter-penetrate each other: the role of *leading professional* (LP) and the role of *chief executive* (CE). As a tentative first approximation one can then visualise the two sub-roles as distinct entities. This involves differentiating between activities which are *prima facie* professional and those which are *prima facie* executive (managerial), while also explicitly recognising that there are internal and external aspects to both role conceptions. The resulting dual (LP—CE) role model of headship is shown in Figure 1.1.1 below as applied to secondary school headship (Hughes 1976), but could easily be formulated for use in other contexts.

The inter-relationships of elements of the model will be explained by briefly describing aspects of the empirical research in which it was used, which involved interviews with the heads of 72 schools and with a stratified sample of teaching staff and school governors.

The research first revealed significant inter-relationships between internal and external aspects of each of the two sub-roles. Within the LP sub-role, heads who were strong in their external professional orientation (i.e. cosmopolitans, in Gouldner's classification) tended to – and were expected by staff to – take an innovatory stance in their internal professional role, i.e. they were pre-eminently the heads who encouraged colleagues to try out new ideas and media. Within the CE sub-role, heads granted recognition and autonomy by external authority were more like than those not so recognised to take initiative themselves internally in executive matters and to delegate effectively to members of staff. Within both sub-roles internal and external aspects were inter-related.

More significantly it was found that elements of the two sub-roles were related to each other so that, as suspected, the notional separation into distinct sub-roles proves to be no more than a convenient heuristic device. Matters related to teaching by the head, for instance, (e.g. whether the head should teach, how much, which classes and at what level) were mainly considered by heads and by others not in terms of their professional implication for the head as teacher and for the pupils taught, but in terms of the implications of the head's teaching for the school as an organisation. Conversely the head's supervision of staff in the interest of the school as an organisation (an aspect of the CE sub-role) was more acceptable when it could be regarded by both heads and staff as an opportunity

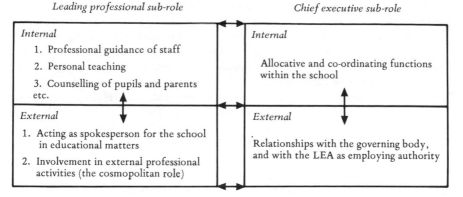

Figure 1.1.1 *The dual (leading professional-chief executive) role model*

for providing professional guidance to inexperienced staff (an aspect of the LP sub-role).

The research identified areas in which the LP and CE sub-roles were supportive, those in which they appeared not to relate, and those in which there was potential conflict. There were two aspects of the CE sub-role, one internal and one external, for which the head's claims to be a leading professional appeared particularly relevant:

(a) Allocating resources.
(b) Presenting and interpreting to the governing body and the LEA information concerning the school's academic achievement.

In general the research confirmed a substantial inter-penetration of the two sub-roles. It seems that the professional-as-administrator does not act in some matters as a leading professional and in others as a chief executive. Professional knowledge, skills and attitudes are likely to have a profound effect on the whole range of tasks undertaken by the head of a professional organisation.

It may be noted that Morgan, Hall and Mackay (1983, p. 13) have recently referred to the LP–CE conceptualisation as helpful in their categorisation of the managerial tasks of the secondary school head. They also drew on Robert Katz's (1974) analysis of administrative skills as *technical, human* and *conceptual*, the latter referring to the ability to see the enterprise as a whole. Designating task categories to match the three types of skill, they added a fourth category of *external management* tasks [. . .].

It must be added, however, as the issue is of some importance, that Morgan, Hall and Mackay appear not to have recognised the integrative significance of the professional-as-administrator concept. They assume a close relationship between the LP sub-role and their technical (i.e. educational) task category, but only apparently at the expense of regarding the human, conceptual and external management task categories as exclusively with the CE sub-role (p. 13). Subsequently, when those with whom the head interacts are identified, the dichotomy

is formulated differently, internal school management generally being designated as 'the professional domain' and the school's external management as 'the
public domain' (p. 15, Table 2). Either way the implied separation, though
useful in generating a job description, does not appear to take account of the
complexity of the linkages between professional and executive elements. The
sharp professional/executive differentiation of heads' tasks, proposed by Morgan
and colleagues might appear to be taken a step further by Handy (1984) who
argues that schools should have both leaders (senior professionals) and
administrators (lay bursars). 'To combine the two roles in one person', he
observes, 'is an invitation to stress' (p. 23). Handy is, however, using the term
'administration' to refer solely to subordinate, regulatory activities, as is common usage in commercial management, whereas 'leadership' for him 'includes
the "direction" of the institution, the setting of its vision and its standards, and
the oversight of its working' (Handy 1984, p. 35), i.e. it effectively includes both
the LP and the CE sub-roles, as conceptualised in the dual role model.

   An implicit assumption in regarding these two sub-roles as separate and
mutually exclusive, as Ouston (1984) has observed, is that 'the head-as-
professional can be left to the educational theorists, whereas the head-as-
executive is a management issue' (p. 54). This is a view which has, in fact, been
put forward in relation to headteacher training and development (Everard 1984,
p. 52). Such a division, Ouston considers, would be 'artificial and possibly
dangerous', a comment with which I fully agree. It may therefore be permissible
in concluding this section to recall the unequivocal standpoint adopted under the
sub-heading 'Towards a unified role model of headship', in the original formulation of the construct:

> Though they are useful as analytical and heuristic devices, it has to be recognised that
> our (LP-CE) role models are but abstractions, which only partially reflect the reality.
> In seeking to develop a more unified role model it is therefore salutory to recall that
> many heads to some extent, and some heads to a great extent, succeed in simulta-
> neously activating and integrating the contrasting and potentially conflicting aspects
> of their total role.
>
>   (Hughes 1976, p. 59)

In applying the dual role model at other levels in educational organisations, a
similarly integrative approach would be appropriate.

The domains of professional leadership

Drawing on the earlier discussion of approaches to leadership in organisations, it
is appropriate finally to consider three broad areas in each of which the professional-as-administrator has a significant part to play. Professional leadership, as
has been shown, is concerned with task achievement, with group maintenance
and development, and with the external, representative aspects of the role.
These are considered in turn.

Task achievement

Only in the small school is the direct contribution to task achievement of the professional leader, such as through personal teaching, likely to be unavoidable. Many secondary as well as primary school heads would, however, regard being involved in some personal teaching as having substantial symbolic significance. This would not be so likely in further education, even at head of department level. Heads of department in universities, more perhaps than in polytechnics, would attach importance to their teaching role as a form of leadership by example. This would not normally apply, however, to university vice-chancellors or to polytechnic directors.

The most significant professional contribution of the positional leader to task achievement will be indirect. The opportunities for leader participation may conveniently be expressed in terms of a classical management cycle, as applied to education in a number of management by objectives formulations (e.g. Davies 1975). The leader is likely to be involved in:

(a) Any attempt that is made to identify aims and objectives for the organisation.
(b) The broad formulation of means by which the resulting decisions are to be implemented.
(c) The measures adopted, whether formally or informally, to judge the extent to which agreed objectives are being achieved.
(d) Any further action which is taken as a result of the assessments made.

It will be noted that though the above are unmistakably elements of the management process, the crucial decisions which have to be made at each stage are essentially professional, involving value judgements which would often benefit from explicit philosophical analysis.

The kind of leader participation will vary. It may involve contributing personally some of the new ideas relating to goal identification, policies for implementation, and outcome appraisal. This would be more likely to occur on a substantial scale in a school than in the more complex situation of a university or polytechnic. Even at the school level, however, it may be argued that the head should primarily be a facilitator or convener of organisational problem-solving rather than attempting to solve all problems personally (Schmuck and Nelson 1977; John 1980).

Additionally or alternatively, therefore, the leader inevitably will be involved in a critical appraisal of the contributions of others and in the use of professional and political judgement in co-ordinating, reconciling and integrating those contributions. Such processes can be formalised, as happened in 1984 at the University of Birmingham, where the vice-chancellor took the initiative, against a background of diminishing resources, in establishing an Advisory Planning Committee, under his chairmanship, to develop new academic initiatives, which will then be more widely considered through the normal channels of academic decision-making.

It is, of course, not only at the summit of the organisational hierarchy that the professional-as-administrator concept is relevant to task achievement. The initiation of structure within universities, polytechnics and colleges by deans of faculties, heads of department and individual lecturers, gives rise to issues of both professional and organisational significance, the consideration of which typically takes place within a well developed committee structure. Similarly in schools, though the formal structures may be less elaborate, there is room for a concept which differentiates between curricular and interpersonal management skills in considering task achievement at every level and not simply in relation to the role of the head (Campbell 1984).

Group maintenance and development

The appointment of professional persons as heads of professionally staffed organisations has mainly been advocated, not in terms of their contribution to task achievement but on the grounds that such persons are well placed to have the confidence, and to elicit the co-operation, of professional staff. Etzioni (1964, p. 82), for instance, observed that having a professional at the head of the authority structure will mean that 'the needs of professionals will be more likely to receive sympathetic attention'. Similar views have been expressed by Abrahamson (1967, p. 83), by Moore (1970, p. 211) and by Cyert (1978, p. 345). It is not simply that, because of a shared commitment to professional values, the professional staff will expect to find the organisational head sympathetic to their viewpoint and welfare, but that for the same reason professional influence will also flow in reverse, the views and wishes of the professional head being more likely to be heeded, other things being equal, than those of a lay manager.

Human relations theorists have shown that a rigid hierarchial emphasis can make the achievement of a genuine colleague relationship very difficult. Thus Bennis (1959) discussed the hierarchical superior as 'an instrument and arm of reality, a man with power over the subordinate', who is also potentially an agent of growth, 'a helper, trainer, consultant and co-ordinator'. The two aspects, he concluded, are liable to be in conflict, and 'a commitment to maturity' is required on both sides to activate the two roles simultaneously.

In practice the situation is likely to be even more complicated, for the extent to which there is a significant commitment to professional values will vary within the subordinate group, as it will among the positional leaders themselves (Corwin 1965). Hoyle (1975, p. 37) has usefully differentiated within the teacher group between restricted professionality, confined to work in the classroom, and extended professionality which additionally includes an awareness of wider dimensions. Sensitivity to such differences of attitude is clearly advisable for heads of department who wish to obtain the co-operation of their colleagues in planning for change and in working together to achieve it (Watts 1977).

Innovative school heads, it has been reported (Hughes 1975), are particularly aware that informal contacts with staff colleagues, such as over a cup of coffee in the common room, are highly political occasions, providing opportunities for collegial influence to be exerted in both directions, through 'dropping hints', 'sowing the seed', 'deliberate kite flying', and the most subtle manipulative activity of all, 'making it appear that the new idea has come from someone else'. There is clearly scope for more detailed study of such informal occasions, using the methods of symbolic interactionists and ethnomethodologists.

A parallel case study of teacher-principal interaction in American schools (Hanson 1976) reported examples of manipulative behavioural management by both teachers and principals, both parties relying on a common commitment to professional values. Democratic procedures and informal bargaining served as conflict reduction mechanisms, and principals, through their control of the reward structures of teachers, had an additional powerful organisational resource at their disposal.

Both studies thus provide examples in the domain of group maintenance and development of the inter penetration of the LP and CE sub-roles, as previously described:

> The innovating head, it appears, relies partly on exerting influence on staff colleagues as a fellow professional; equally, however, he accepts his position as chief executive, and uses the organisational controls which are available to him to get things moving. Professional and executive considerations reinforce each other as complementary aspects of a coherent and unified strategy
>
> (Hughes 1976, p. 58)

[. . .] Formal staff participation, which has long been a familiar feature of university government and is now a recognised part of the management of further education and, to a lesser extent, of schools, may be seen as the institutionalisation of the informal collegial interaction of positional leader and professional group which was described in the Hughes and Hanson studies. Whether it occurs formally or informally, staff participation is liable to come into conflict with interpretations of organisational accountability which are currently strongly supported [. . .]. The professional-as-administrator then has a particularly difficult role in achieving a balance, if not a reconciliation, between the conflicting demands, which is accentuated as a national assessment scheme to monitor teacher performance becomes a matter of public debate.

Implicit in the above is the idea of a close connection between the task achievement and the group maintenance and development domains. In a useful discussion of the management of higher education institutions in a period of contraction and uncertainty, Davies and Morgan (1983) discuss policy formation in terms of four successive phases: an *ambiguous* stage, a *political* stage, a *collegial* stage and an *executive* stage. Davies and Morgan suggest that 'to miss any phase, or to allow insufficient time for it, is to invite problems subsequently . . .' (p. 172). They refer to the significant role of the university head in creating communication links and dialogues between parties who may have the capability to develop new perspectives. 'At its most sophisticated, the vice-chancellor's or administrator's role involves coalition building between potentially like-minded groups' (Davies and Morgan 1983, p. 173).

The encouragement of systematic, institution-wide staff development [. . .] may thus be seen as one of the leadership tasks of the senior professional-as-administrator, who, in virtue of his or her formal position, has some control over organisational resources. Tom Bone (1982, p. 277) has suggested that the best forms of staff development are side-effects of participative management, and institutional heads are thus especially well placed to contribute to the develop-ment of members of their senior management team, encouraging them in turn to assist in the professional development of their colleagues generally.

A fruitful concept at each level is 'action-centred leadership' (Adair 1973), which seeks to achieve a balance among the overlapping requirements of the *task*, the *individual* and the *team*, the term 'team' significantly replacing the impersonal 'setting' of the familiar 'tri-dimensional concept' of job, person and setting (Ostrander and Dethy 1968, p. 384). Action-centred leadership can be further accommodated within the comprehensive framework of organisation (or human resources) development (OD/HRD), the essential principle of which is to involve organisational members themselves 'in the diagnosis, transformation and evaluation of their own social system' (Schmuck 1982).

Experiential learning in a group setting is an important ingredient in OD-type collaborative problem-solving, task-related information being fully and frankly shared. The approach has been shown to work well when the participants per-ceive themselves as the 'owners' of the programme and its outcome (Milstein 1982), but the exercise quickly becomes sterile when the members consider themselves manipulated (Wolcott 1977) or to be under threat in a situation of contracting resources (Cyert 1978). The challenging, but sometimes unenviable, nature of the professional-as-administrator's leadership respon-sibility for maintaining and developing the group becomes very apparent (Taylor 1980; Bone 1982).

The external domain
In discussing the problems facing professions in the public service, Mosher (1978) mentioned a number of major social changes which significantly add to the complexity of the role of professional leadership. He drew attention particu-larly to the erosion of the line conventionally drawn between the roles of the professional expert and the politician acting as the people's representative, which he coupled with a growing demand for public involvement in making and executing domestic policy. Other significant factors, he suggested, were the greater concern within society for equal rights and opportunities, wherever disadvantage could be perceived, and the growing strength and militancy of unions in the public service, including those of the professionals themselves.

Mosher was writing of public service professions in the USA, but his words have a familiar ring in a UK context, and particularly in relation to education. Marten Shipman (1984, p. 5), in a book on education as a public service, sees the education service as a net, which depends for its shape on the various pressure groups pulling away at the corners. On the one hand there are administrative influences through national and local government and the voluntary bodies; on the other hand there are varied professional and academic pressures. Development, he suggests, is the result of interaction between these two groups of factors *within* the education service, but taking account also of pressures from a disparate set of other influences, the *external* forces. Among these he includes not only other government departments, the Manpower Services Commission, the Racial Equality and Equal Opportunities Commissions, etc., but also parents, employers, trade unions and others 'acting through interest groups both to affect the legal and financial basis of the service and to influence professional practices' (p. 6). It was these latter group; which Lord Morris (1975) had in mind when he referred to a new kind of politics, which would mean that 'the new Machiavelli can no longer make up his mind what he wants to do, and then bring the people round to putting up with it' (p. 14). 'All sections of the community', he added, 'divided up and organising themselves in very crisscross ways, are going to speak up for themselves without apology and if necessary with vigour' (p. 18)[. . .]

Given the turbulent environmental uncertainties with which educational institutions are faced, it is evident that there is an important external aspect to the professional leadership expected of the professional-as-administrator, which accords with Handy's insistence, noted earlier, on the representative or ambassadorial role of the leader. It is also noteworthy that authority as a leading professional and not simply as a chief executive is frequently required in relationships with clients and their parents, with the community and with governmental and other agencies. The professional leader also has the complementary task of making visible and interpreting to the professional group the concerns and interests of increasingly influential external groups and authorities.

In recently expressing a personal view on the changing nature of headship skills and public confidence, Ken Lambert (1984) quotes Yukl's view that school heads will need to spend more time in external activities such as shaping community expectations, soliciting co-operation and support and conducting public relations activities. Declining enrolments and economic stringency are factors which tend to strengthen the pressure for such involvement. Similar issues also arise in relation to further and higher education, as Tom Bone (1982) has shown.

The need for professional leaders to cultivate a sensitive political awareness, already mentioned in the internal institutional context, becomes even more evident in relation to the external domain. This had been foreseen by Lord Morris (1975, p. 18) in his forecast that administration in education, as in the other public services, would move towards the activities of politics, not in the party sense but in fundamental approach. Its practitioners would have to show more of the arts and skills of politics. Essentially the same message was expressed in a more radical guise in a volume, *Professions for the People: The Politics of Skill* (Gerstl and Jacobs 1976), which includes a sustained critique of education as a professional activity (Wenger 1976).

Earlier in the chapter Wirt's (1981) developmental model of dynamic political interaction between professions and their environment was described. The model has become particularly applicable to education. The phases of *issue emergence* and *turbulence* have become very familiar, and the idea of government involvement, whether as mediator or adjudicator, in a subsequent *resolution* phase can be recognised as more than a possibility. Though Wirt does not refer specifically to the part played by the professional leader in the achievement of *resolution* and *closure*, his analysis provides convincing confirmation of the importance for the external aspect of the professional-as-administrator role of political skill combined with a recognised integrity of purpose, recognised both by external groups and by the leader's professional colleagues.

Conclusion

In seeking to understand the nature of leadership in educational institutions, regarded as professionally staffed organisations, much ground has been covered, and an attempt has been made to uncover similarities and inter-relationships at various levels. [. . .]

In the [first part of this chapter] the considerable literature on professionalism and on professionals in organisations was drawn on to discuss aspects of the professional's internal and external orientation which are liable to result in conflict between professionals and the ever increasing constraints of their employing organisation. Ways in which accommodation is achieved were considered, bearing in mind particularly recent research findings which have relevance to educational organisations.

In the [second] section of the chapter the challenging but equivocal leadership role of the professional-as-administrator at different organisational levels has been considered, a dual role model being outlined which incorporates both a *leading professional* and a *chief executive* sub-role. The inter-penetration of these two aspects was emphasised as a necessary step towards achieving a more unified concept of the professional leadership role in the final part of the section. This was considered in action-centred leadership terms in relation to task achievement, group maintenance and development, and the external domain. The need for professional commitment to be balanced by political awareness and skill has been a dominant theme in the latter part of the discussion, as account has been taken of internal and external pressures. It is appropriate to end by quoting yet again from Lord Morris (1975, p. 19), who, referring to the educational administrator, wrote as follows:

> . . . it is his task to present an *acceptable* scheme; for today only acceptable schemes are operable. In all parts of the world this is a task which is likely to prove a formidable and exciting challenge to the educational administrator in the years ahead.

Notes

1 The same duality is recognised, but with a significant difference of emphasis, in the Jarratt Report (Jarratt 1985):

No one can doubt the need for the Vice-Chancellor to be recognised as the academic leader of his institution and in no way should other responsibilities be seen as diminishing this. But to enable the institution at least to survive and to seize the opportunities open to it in the future, the Vice-Chancellor will have to adopt a clear role as the executive leader as well – and have the necessary authority to carry it out (p. 26).

References

ABRAHAMSON, M. (1967). *The Professional in the Organisation*. Chicago, Rand McNally.

ADAIR, J. (1973). *Action Centred Leadership*. New York, McGraw-Hill.

BARBER, B. (1963). 'Some problems in the sociology of the professions', *Daedalus,* **92**, 669–88.

BARBER, B. (1978). 'Control and responsibility in the powerful professions', *Political Science Quarterly,* **93**, 599–615.

BARON, G. (1975). 'Some aspects of the "Headmaster Tradition" ', in HOUGHTON, V., McHUGH, R. and MORGAN, C (ed.), *Management in Education, Reader 1: The Management of Organisations and Individuals*, London, Ward Lock Educational.

BECHER, T. and KOGAN, M. (1980). *Process and Structure in Higher Education*, London, Heinemann.

BEN-DAVID, J. (1963–4). 'Professions in the class system of present-day societies: a trend report and bibliography; *Current Sociology,* **12**, 247–330.

BENNIS. W. G. (1959). 'Leadership theory and administrative behaviour: the problem of authority', *Administrative Science Quarterly,* **4**, 259–301.

BENNIS, W. G. (1973). *The Leaning Ivory Tower*, New York, Jossey-Bass.

BLAU, P. M. (1968). 'The hierarchy of authority in organisations', *American Journal of Sociology,* **73**(14), 453–67.

BLAU, P. M. and SCOTT, W. R. (1963). *Formal Organisations: A Comparative Approach*, London, Routledge and Kegan Paul.

BONE, T. (1982). 'Problems of institutional management in a period of contraction', in GRAY, H. L. (ed.), *The Management of Educational Institutions*. Barcombe, Lewes, Falmer Press.

BUSH, T. and KOGAN, M. (1982). *Directors of Education*, London, Allen and Unwin.

CAMPBELL, R. J. (1984). 'In-school development: the role of the curriculum postholder', *School Organisation,* **4**(4), 345–57.

CORWIN, R. G. (1961). 'The professional employee: a study of conflict in nursing roles', *American Journal of Sociology,* **66**, 604–15.

CORWIN, R. G. (1965). 'Militant professionalism, initiative and compliance in public education', *Sociology of Education,* **38**, 310–31.

CYERT, R. M. (1978). 'The management of universities of constant or decreasing size', *Public Administration Review,* **38**(4), 344–9.

DAVIES, J. (1975). 'A discussion of the use of PPBS and MBO in educational planning and administration', in DOBSON, L., GEAR, T. and WESTOBY, A. (ed.), *Management in Education, Reader 2: Some Techniques and Systems*, London, Ward Lock Educational.

DAVIES, J. L. and MORGAN, A. W. (1983). 'Management of higher education institutions, in a period of contraction and uncertainty', in BOYD-BARRETT, O. et al (ed.), *Approaches to Post-School Management*, London, Harper and Row.

EDWARDS, D. B. and EASTON, W. A. G. (1980). 'The role of the principal', in WAITT, I. (ed.), *College Administration: A Handbook*. London, National Association of Teachers in Further and Higher Education.

ENGEL, G. V. (1970). 'Professional autonomy and bureaucratic organisation', *Administrative Science Quarterly, 51,* 50–60.

ETZIONI, A. (1964). *Modern Organisations*. Englewood Cliffs, New Jersey, Prentice-Hall.

ETZIONI, A. (ed.) (1969). *The Semi-Professions and their Organisation*. New York, The Free Press.

EVERARD, K. B. (1984). *Management in Comprehensive Schools – What can be Learned from Industry?*, 2nd edition University of York, Centre for the Study of Comprehensive Schools.

FELDMAN, S. (1978). 'Conflict and convergence: the mental health professional in government', *Public Administration Review, 38*(2) 139–44.

GERSTL, J. and JACOBS, G. (ed.) (1976). *Professions for the People: The Politics of Skill*, Cambridge, Massachusetts, Schenkman Publishing.

GLASTONBURY, B. and COOPER, D. M. (1982). 'Case studies of bureau-cratisation', in GLASTONBURY, B. et al. *Social Work in Conflict*, London, British Association of Social Workers.

GOLDBERG, A. I. (1976). 'The relevance of cosmopolitan/local orientations to professional values and behaviour', *Sociology of Work and Occupations, 3,* 331–56.

GOODE, W. J. (1957). 'Community within a community: the profession', *American Sociological Review, 22,* 194–200.

GOODE, W. J. (1960). 'Encroachment, charlatanism and the emerging professions: psychology, sociology and medicine', *American Sociological Review, 25,* 902–13.

GOULDNER, A. W. (1957). 'Cosmopolitans and locals: towards an analysis of latent social roles: I and II, *Administrative Science Quarterly, 2,* 281–306 and 444–80.

GRIMES, A. J. and BERGER, P. K. (1970). 'Cosmopolitan-local: evaluation of the construct', *Administrative Science Quarterly, 15,* 407–16.

HALL, D. T. and LAWLER, E. E. (1970). 'Job characteristics and pressures and the organisational integration of professionals', *Administrative Science Quarterly, 12,* 461–78.

HALL, R. H. (1968). 'Professionalisation and bureaucratisation', *American Sociological Review, 33*(1) 92–104.

HALL, R. H. (1969). *Occupations and the Social Structure*, Englewood Cliffs, New Jersey, Prentice-Hall.

HALL, R. H. (1982). *Organisations: Structure and Process, 3rd edition*, Englewood Cliffs. New Jersey: Prentice-Hall.

HANDY, C. B. (1984). *Taken for Granted? Understanding Schools as Organisations*, London, Longman.

HANSON, E. M. (1976). 'The professional/bureaucratic interface: a case study', *Urban Education, 11*(3) 313–32.

HARRIES-JENKINS, G. (1970). 'Professionals in organisations', in JACKSON, J. A. (ed.), *Professions and Professionalisation*. London, Cambridge University Press.

HOYLE, E. (1975). 'Leadership and decision-making in education', in HUGHES, M. G. (ed.) *Administering Education: International Challenge*, London, Athlone.

HUGHES, E. C. (1958). *Men and their Work*. Glencoe, Illinois, The Free Press.

HUGHES, E. C. (1963). 'Professions', *Daedalus, 92,* 655–68.

HUGHES, M. G. (1972). *The Role of the Secondary School Head*, Ph.D thesis, University of

Wales (University College, Cardiff).

HUGHES, M. G. (1975). 'The innovating school head: autocratic initiator or catalyst of co-operation?', *Educational Administration* 4(1) 29–47.

HUGHES, M. G. (ed.) (1975). *Administering Education: International Challenge*. London, Athlone.

HUGHES, M. G. (1976). 'The professional-as-administrator: the case of the secondary school head', in PETERS, R. S. (ed.), *The Role of the Head*, London, Routledge and Kegan Paul.

JACKSON, J. A. (ed.) (1970). *Professions and Professionalization*, London, Cambridge University Press.

JARRATT, Sir A. (Chairman) (1985). *Report on the Steering Committee for Efficiency Studies in Universities*, London, Committee of Vice-Chancellors and Principals.

JAUCH, L. R., GLUECK, W. F. and OSBORN, R. N. (1978). 'Organisational loyalty, professional commitment and academic research productivity', *Academy of Management Journal,* **21**, 84–92.

JOHN, D. (1980). *Leadership in Schools*, London, Heinemann.

JOHNSON, T. J. (1972). *Professions and Power*, London, Macmillan.

JORDAN, B. (1979). *Helping in Social Work*. London, Routledge and Kegan Paul.

KATZ, R. L. (1974). 'Skills of an effective administrator,' *Harvard Business Review*, **52**, 90–102.

KORNHAUSER, W. (1963), *Scientists in Industry: Conflict and Accommodation*, Berkeley, University of California Press.

LA PORTE, T. A. (1965), 'Conditions of strain and accommodation in industrial research organisations', *Administrative Science Quarterly,* **10**, 21–38.

LAMBERT, K. (1984). 'The changing nature of headship skills and public confidence: a personal view', *Educational Management and Administration,* **12**(2) 123–126.

LAMBRIGHT, W. H. and TEICH, A. H. (1978). 'Scientists and government: a case of professional ambivalence', *Public Administration Review,* **38(2)**, 133–9.

LARSON, M. S. (1977). *The Rise of Professionalism*, Berkeley, University of California Press.

LORD MORRIS OF GRASMERE (1975). 'Acceptability: the new emphasis in educational administration', in HUGHES, M .G. (ed.), *Administering Education: International Challenge*, London, Athlone.

MERTON, R. K. (1957). *Social Theory and Social Structure*, revised edition, Glencoe, Illinois, The Free Press.

MILLERSON, G. (1964). *The Qualifying Associations: a Study in Professionalisation*. London, Routledge and Kegan Paul.

MILSTEIN, M. M. (1982). 'Training internal change agents for schools', in GRAY, H. L. (ed.), *The Management of Educational Institutions*, Barcombe, Lewes, Falmer Press.

MOODIE, G. C. and EUSTACE, R. (1974). *Power and Authority in British Universities*, London, Allen and Unwin.

MOORE, W. E. (1970). *The Professions: Roles and Rules*, New York, Russell Sage Foundation.

MORGAN, C., HALL, V. and MACKAY, H. (1983). *The Selection of Secondary School Headteachers*, Milton Keynes, Open University Press.

MOSHER, F. C. (1978). 'Professions in public service', *Public Administration Review,* **38**(2), 144–50.

NEUSE, S. M. (1978). 'Professionalism and authority: women in public service', *Public Administration Review,* **38**(5), 436–41.

NOBLE, T. and PYM, B. (1970). 'Collegial authority and the receding locus of power', *British Journal of Sociology,* **21**, 431–45.

NORWOOD, C. and HOPE, A. H. (1909). *The Higher Education of Boys in England.*

OLESON, V. and WHITAKER, E. W. (1970). 'Critical notes on sociological studies of professional socialisation', in JACKSON, J. A. (ed.), *Professions and Professionalisation*, London, Cambridge University Press.

ORGAŃ, D. W. and GREENE, C. N. (1981). 'The effects of formalisation on professional involvement: a compensatory process approach', *Administrative Science Quarterly,* **26**(2) 237–252.

OSTRANDER, R. H. and DETHY, R. C. (1968). *A Values Approach to Educational Administration*, New York, American Book Company.

OUSTON, J. (1984). 'The role of the secondary school head', in WHITE, J. (ed.), *Education plc?* Bedford Way Papers 20, London, University of London Institute of Education.

PRANDY, K. (1965). *Professional Employees: a Study of Scientists and Engineers*, London, Faber.

REISSMAN, L. (1949). 'A Study of role conceptions in bureaucracy', *Social Forces,* **27**, 305–10.

ROTONDI, T. (1975). 'Organisational identification: issues and implications', *Organisational Behaviour and Human Performance,* **13**, 95–109.

SCHMUCK, R. A. (1982). 'Organisation development for the 1980s' in GRAY, H. L. (ed.), *The Management of Educational Institutions*, Barcombe, Lewes, Falmer Press.

SCHMUCK, R. and NELSON, J. (1977). 'The principal as convener of organisational problem solving', in SCHMUCK, R. A. et al, *The Second Handbook of Organisation Development in Schools*, Palo Alto, California, Mayfield.

SCOTT, W. R. (1965). 'Reactions to supervision in a heterogeneous professional organisation', *Administrative Science Quarterly,* **10**, 65–81.

SCOTT, W. R. (1966). 'Professionals in bureaucracies – areas of conflict', in VOLLMER, H. M. and MILLS, D. L. (ed.), *Professionalisation*, Englewood Cliffs, New Jersey, Prentice-Hall.

SHIPMAN, M. (1984). *Education as a Public Service*, London, Harper and Row.

SORENSEN, J. E. and SORENSEN, T. L. (1974). 'The conflict of professionals in bureaucratic organisations', *Administrative Science Quarterly,* **19**, 98–106.

SZRETER, R. (1968). 'An academic patriciate – vice-chancellors 1966–7', *Universities Quarterly,* **23**(1) 17–45.

SZRETER, R. (1979). 'The committee of vice-chancellors revisited: the pattern ten years later', *Educational Studies,* **5**(1) 1–6.

TAYLOR, W. (1980). 'Managing contraction', in FARQUHAR, R. H. and HOUSEGO, I. E. (ed.), *Canadian and Comparative Educational Administration*, Vancouver, University of British Columbia.

THOMASON, G. F. (1974). 'Organisation and Management', in HUGHES, M. G. (ed.), *Secondary School Administration: A Management Approach, 2nd edition*, Oxford, Pergamon.

THORNTON, R. (1970). 'Organisational involvement and commitment to organisation and profession', *Administrative Science Quarterly,* **15**, 417–26.

TUMA, N. B. and GRIMES, A. J. (1981). 'A comparison of models of role orientations of professionals in a research-oriented university', *Administrative Science Quarterly,* **26(2)** 187–206.

WATTS, J. (ed.) (1977). *The Countesthorpe Experience: The First Five Years*, London, Allen and Unwin.

WENGER, M. G. (1976). 'The case of academia: demythologisation in a non-profession', in GERSTL, J. and JACOBS, G. (ed.), *Professions for the People: The Politics of Skill*. Cambridge, Massachusetts, Schenkman Publishing.

WIRT, F. (1981). 'Professionalism and political conflict: a developmental model', *Journal of Public Policy,* **1**(1) 61–93.

WOLCOTT, H. F. (1977). *Teachers Versus Technocrats*, Eugene, University of Oregon Centre for Educational Policy and Management.

YUKL. G. (1971). 'Toward a Behavioural Theory of Leadership', *Organisational Behaviour and Human Performance,* **6**, 414–40. Also in HOUGHTON, V., McHUGH, R. and MORGAN, C. (1975) *Management in Education Reader I*, London, Ward Lock.

1.2

Leadership and mission

Eric Hoyle

This chapter explores a neglected aspect of the role of the head, that of identifying a 'mission' for the school. [. . .] One reason for this neglect is that identifying 'mission' is a somewhat diffuse activity which is rooted in a person's stance towards educational issues and conveyed via language and actions of a symbolic kind rather than through clearly identifiable tasks. It is not amenable therefore to research in the conventional mode. The other reason [. . .] is that the notion of 'mission' smacks of a discredited approach to leadership, the heroic 'man on horse-back' image which is certainly at odds with the ideas of educational leadership which emerged in the 1960s whereby a head is seen as *primus inter pares* in a collegial system and perhaps more a servant of the teachers, facilitating their professional activities, than inducing a commitment to a particular vision.

The role of the head has certainly changed in recent years. It has become overloaded with expectations to the point at which, were heads to seek to meet them all, they would risk the burn-out which is affecting so many. One of the dilemmas of the head is to select from the range and diversity of expectations those to which they should give most time and attention. We have a good idea of what school leaders actually *do* from the growing number of studies which have sampled their activities (e.g. Wolcott, 1973; O'Dempsey, 1976; Peterson, 1976; Willis, 1980; Martin and Willower, 1981; Sproull, 1981). These studies not only illuminate the diversity of the tasks of heads but how, typically, these change with great rapidity if not from minute to minute then from quarter hour to quarter hour. No doubt many of the actions of these heads are concerned with building a mission for their schools, but the diffuse nature of this task means that it is implicit in the welter of specific tasks which heads constantly undertake in response to the immediate and contingent [. . .]

By and large, management theory and research do not engage with this aspect of the role of head because their focus is largely on the management of personnel and resources rather than the more elusive idiographic and inspirational aspects of the role. Some recent developments in the theory and practice of school management such as school-based curriculum development, school-focused in-service training and the self evaluation of schools (Bolam, 1982; Dalin and Rust, 1983; McMahon, 1986) are putting a premium, perhaps for the first time, on the public clarification of a mission for each school. Conventional research offers little guide as to how heads have in the past sought to construct and convey a mission nor how they might do so.

[. . .]

School leaders: managers, politicians, philosophers

The study of educational leadership is embedded in management theory which, in turn, has its intellectual roots in social psychology. In spite of much excellent work in this field, [. . .] there is something missing. One element in this 'something' is [. . .] that management theories of leadership are apolitical or, at least, leave the political element implicit. Organisations are characterised by micro-political activity and leadership is to a considerable degree a political task. There is an increasing consciousness of this aspect of educational leadership. [. . .]

However, having added the political dimension, there is still something else missing. [. . .] It would seem that the 'something' is the leader's capacity to grasp the configuration of forces at work in the environment, to construct an achievable mission – the art of the possible – to convey this mission to others often through the skilful use of language and symbol, and to attain a commitment to the mission.

To suggest that theories of school leadership should incorporate these charismatic, even heroic, aspects of leadership may be seen as pure bathos. It would certainly fuel staffroom humour about school leadership. To imagine that the thousands of school leaders might be touched by the heroic is rather absurd. Certainly the present writer has deep reservations about 'the man-on-horseback' approach to leadership. And yet effective school leadership depends, even in situations in which school policies are centralised, on the capacity of the head to articulate a mission for the school.

Consideration of leadership has recently been enhanced by the philosophical approach of Hodgkinson (1983). [. . .] His basic taxonomy is reproduced in Figure 1.2.1 overleaf. He writes:

> Within this scheme the ideal typical sequence is as follows. Organisational values are articulated by top level administration through philosophical processes (argument, dialectic, logic, rhetoric and value clarification). This is the level of *idea*. The idea emergent from this first phase must be translated into some sort of plan and reduced to a written, persisting and communicable form. This form must then be entered into a political process of persuasion. This is the domain of power, resource, control and politics, and we have moved from the level of ideas to the level of *people*. Coalitions must be formed, levers pulled, persons persuaded as power and support are marshalled around the project or plan. Each of these three process phases of administration can be subsumed under the rubric of policy-making.
>
> When power is aligned and resources are committed, the next stage (still a *people* stage) requires the mobilisation and organising of what economists call the factors of

Eric Hoyle

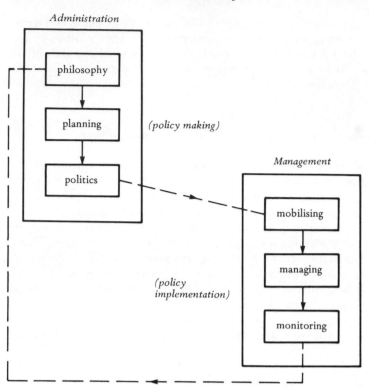

Figure 1.2.1 *(From Hodgkinson, C. (1983)* The Philosophy of Leadership, *Blackwell)*

production – land, labour and capital – around the organisational purposes. This phase is critical and involves, metaphorically speaking, a shift of gears from the administrative into the managerial phase. This phase is an intermediate one of art between the philosophy of policy making on the one hand and the science of management on the other; it is here where, if at all, the pieces are put together and philosophy is moved to the realm of facts, action and *things*.

The taxonomy is valuable in many ways. Firstly, it reaffirms the importance of the *idea* of leadership. Secondly, it recognises and locates the political dimension of leadership. And thirdly, in his extension of the model, Hodgkinson distinguishes between three levels of reality: philosophy and planning which are concerned with *ideas*, politics and mobilising which are tasks involved in achieving a transition from ideas to action and are concerned with *people*, and *managing* and *monitoring* which are concerned with *things*. Current theories of leadership are mainly concerned with people, and to a lesser degree with things.[. . .]

Theories of leadership

The initial assumption about leadership was that it was a function of personal characteristics – the *trait* approach. However, this approach proved to have little power in predicating effective leadership since it excluded consideration of leadership *style* and the context of leadership. No 'timeless leadership qualities' were satisfactorily identified and effective leadership was seen to be relevant to context. Some *clusters* of effective leadership have been identified (Stogdill, 1948) but it is the exercise of these clusters through a *leadership style* in relation to a particular *context* which is important.

Early work on *leadership style* centred on *democratic, authoritarian* and *laissez faire* styles with the evidence purporting to demonstrate the greater effectiveness of the democratic style. [. . .] These particular concepts were influenced by a prevailing ideology which, in the 1930s and 1940s when many of these studies were carried out, ensured a predeliction for the democratic style of leadership. However, this particular set of concepts was challenged by developments in leadership studies from the 1950s onwards. It was not that authoritarian leadership turned out to be more effective than democratic leadership, but to conceptualise leadership in this way was to miss the point that although *successful* democratic leadership was more effective than successful *authoritarian* leadership, even the latter led to a higher level of effectiveness and satisfaction than *unsuccessful* leadership. Effective leadership in terms of achievement and group satisfaction was the outcome not only of interpersonal relationships, but also of the sense of achievement arising from a task completed.

From the 1950s onwards almost all those undertaking research into leadership identified two key dimensions of leadership: *personal relationships* and *task achievement*. [. . .] The effective leader ensures that tasks are accomplished and at the same time colleagues feel that their social needs are being met.

Of [various] pairs of concepts [emphasising these two aspects of leadership] *initiating structure* and *consideration* have perhaps been [. . .] used most frequently in the study of the management of schools. Halpin (1966) defined them as follows:

> *Initiating structure* refers to the leader's behaviour in delineating the relationship between himself and members of his work group; and in endeavouring to establish well-defined patterns of organisation, channels of communication, and methods of procedure.
> *Consideration* refers to behaviour indicative of friendship, mutual trust, respect, and warmth in the relationship between the leader and members of his staff.

The two factors emerged from a tradition of research into leadership based on the Leader Behaviour Discipline Questionnaire (LBDQ). Although many leadership styles have been identified, indicating that there are many roads to effectiveness, the two concepts remain basic to most patterns. Halpin took this research tradition forward to develop a questionnaire for determining the organisational climates of schools, i.e. teachers' perceptions of the behaviour of their principals and of the effects of this behaviour on their own job satisfaction.

A first step was to identify four characteristics of principals' behaviour and four characteristics of teachers' behaviour.

1 *Disengagement* refers to the teachers' tendency to be 'not with it'. This dimension describes a group which is 'going through the motions', a group that is 'not in gear' with respect to the task at hand. [. . .] This subtest focuses upon the teachers' behaviour in a task-orientated situation.
2 *Hindrance* refers to the teachers' feeling that the principal burdens them with routine duties, committee demands, and other requirements which the teachers construe as unnecessary 'busywork' [. . .] [which] hinders rather than facilitates their work.
3 *Esprit* refers to morale. The teachers feel that their social needs are being satisfied, and that they are, at the same time, enjoying a sense of accomplishment in their job.
4 *Intimacy* refers to the teachers' enjoyment of friendly social relations with each other. This dimension describes a social-needs satisfaction which is not necessarily associated with task-accomplishment.

Principal's behaviour:

5 *Aloofness* refers to behaviour by the principal which is characterised as formal and impersonal. He 'goes by the book' and prefers to be guided by rules and policies rather than to deal with the teachers in an informal, face-to-face situation. [. . .] To maintain this style, he keeps himself at least, 'emotionally' – at a distance from his staff.
6 *Production emphasis* refers to behaviour by the principal which is characterised by close supervision of the staff. He is highly directive and plays the role of a 'straw boss'. His communication goes in only one direction, and he is not sensitive to feedback from the staff.
7 *Thrust* refers to behaviour by the principal which is characterised by his evident effort in trying to 'move the organisation'. Thrust behaviour is marked not by close supervision, but by the principal's attempt to motivate the teachers through the example which he personally sets. [. . .] This behaviour, though starkly task-orientated, is nonetheless viewed favourably by the teachers.
8 *Consideration* refers to behaviour by the principal which is characterised by an inclination to treat the teachers 'humanly', to try to do a little something extra for them in human terms.

The next stage was to combine the responses for each school to yield a school profile and then to establish by factor analysis whether these school scores combined to yield distinctive figurations. He identified six distinctive configurations which he termed *organisational climates* which he labelled: *open, autonomous, controlled, familar, paternal, closed.* [. . .]

Current theories of leadership are still dominated by powerful evidence for the existence of these two key factors. However, two additional elements in prevailing leadership theory are relevant. [. . .] The first is [. . .] that effective leadership is context based. Tannenbaum, Weischler and Massarik (1961) noted that the effective leader takes into account four sets of forces when deciding what actions to take. These are: forces in the leader, forces in subordinates, forces in the situation (e.g. type of organisation, the nature of the task and the availability of time) and forces in the environment (this latter aspect was added after reflection on earlier work, see Tannenbaum and Schmidt, 1958). The inclusion of the context in which leadership is exercised is referred to as the *contingency theory of leadership*.[. . .] Perhaps the best known on such theory is that developed and tested by Fiedler (1965). However, although Fiedler's work takes account of context, it is the immediate work-group context which is dominant and the emphasis remains on forces in the leader and forces in subordinates. The *path-goal theory of leadership* (House, 1971; House and Dessler, 1974) emphasises the importance of leadership behaviour which encourages realistic and positive expectations amongst subordinates and provides structures for their attainment. It also emphasises the point that effective leadership styles will vary with context and that the leader must match style to context, what Getzels and Guba (1957) earlier termed a *transactional style*. However, the path-goal theory remains largely concerned with the immediate work-group, the authority system and the task as the contextual factors, with the task being largely conceptualised in limited and immediate terms. As Hanson (1979b) points out, contingency theories of leadership have received little application to educational contexts [. . .] and have paid relatively little attention to the socio-political context outside the organisation. [He] suggests the need for an open-systems perspective on leadership, a point to which we will return later in this chapter.

A second development in leadership theory which is relevant to the present discussion is the identification of a third dimension in relation to the basic *task* and *person* dimensions. It is hardly surprising that additional factors have been 'discovered'. [. . .] Yukl (1975) adds to Halpin's *initiating structure* and *consideration* a third factor: *decision-centralisation*, i.e. the degree of leader influence over group decisions, the participative dimension. The potential significance of this dimension can be seen in the work of Nias (1980) which showed that the *de*-centralisation of decisions did not necessarily increase the job satisfaction of teachers. In fact, the teachers in her sample generally responded well to what Nias calls *positive leadership* but negatively both to passive and Bourbon (i.e. authoritarian) leadership. Teachers' responses similarly indicated a desire for 'common goals', 'continuity', 'consistency', 'direction', 'coherent philosophy' and 'priorities'. She writes:

> [. . .] Typical comments about 'positive' heads were : 'The headteacher set the direction of the school. He was an old-fashioned patriarch in many ways, but the staff were an open group, and the fact that the place was full of certainties made it a good place to start in.' 'It's much better at this school. We're given a lead. We're under quite strong pressure from the head to conform in certain ways, but that's better I think than at (his previous school) where you were left entirely to do your own thing.'

Nias's work is based on a relatively small sample and would need much more support before the findings could be regarded as a contribution to leadership theory for schools. Moreover, there needs to be further support for the separate factor of *decision-centralisation* as identified by Yukl since it could be argued that its components are, in effect, a sub-set of the components of Halpin's *initiating structure* factor. Nevertheless, the possibility of a separate factor raises some interesting issues, in particular, the importance to a school of a distinctive and positive 'mission' and for the head to initiate and sustain this 'mission'.

A third development in leadership theory is education-specific and is concerned with the influence of heads on school improvement. Hall and colleagues at the University of Texas have worked on the leadership styles of school principals and Leithwood and colleagues at the Ontario Institute for the Study of Education have worked on principal profiles, detailed descriptions of their behaviour. It would be a misrepresentation of their work to argue that they demonstrate the effective principal as the one who can create a staff commitment to a mission. The data in both cases is far too sophisticated to have imposed on them this global and simplistic notion. However, their findings are not wholly unrelated to the present discussion.

Leithwood and Montgomery (1984) identified four stages of profile 'growth' involving a move from the *administrator* (low) through the *humanitarian* and the *programme manager* to the *problem-solver* (high). The latter, the effective principal, selects goals from a number of public sources, transforms them into short term planning goals and uses them to increase conviction and consistency amongst staff members. This suggests vision, a capacity to analyse and a capacity to motivate. The research suggests that this vision may be pursued in conflict with the views of district administrators. Leithwood and Montgomery (1984) further suggest that a comparison can be made between these 'profiles' and Hall's 'styles' (Hall *et al.*, 1982). [. . .] This tradition of research suggests that effective principals fulfil the task and social relations dimensions but transcend their immediate organisational environment in their quest for goals.

> Highly effective principals systematically selected their goals from those espoused for students by agencies of the state, the local school board, perceived needs of the community and students served by the school. Because the least effective principals, described by the profile, valued running a smooth ship (administratively) these goals were derived from a sense of the administrative tasks requiring attention for this to be achieved. Goals did not often spring from curricular, instructional or interpersonal considerations.
>
> (Leithwood and Montgomery 1984)

The concept of 'mission'

'Mission' is somewhat vague and is defined in different ways, but, given a particular connotation, it is a useful term to use in relation to the functions of the school. At one end of a possible range of connotations is the military concept of mission. This conveys a highly rational activity. Here mission suggests a clear objective to be achieved within a finite time scale and to which can be attached relatively clear criteria of success. [. . .] At the other end of the hypothesised continuum is the connotation of mission as a process of establishing and maintaining religious faith which may embrace the specific task of conversion duly marked by an appropriate ritual, but is more broadly concerned with the transcendental character of a religion.

The connotation of mission adopted in this chapter lies between the two. It is more than the achievement of a set of specific educational objectives, although these may be encompassed by it. On the other hand it lacks [. . .] the ineffable character of a religious mission. [. . .] Mission is viewed here as a cluster of goals which the school meets from the [. . .] diffuse and diverse range covered by the broad aims of education. [. . .] Schools will make their own selection from the range of possible goals. There are two reasons why such a selection is made. One, of course, is the fact that schools cannot do all that is expected of them and even though a constraint on their possible range of goals is imposed from without, there will remain the need to impose further limitations. The other reason is [. . .] that schools will seek to forge a distinctive identity. Their members like to have a sense of distinctiveness, to feel that their enterprise is somewhat different from that of others. This is noticeable at conferences where teachers tend to speak of their own schools as somehow different from the norm. The 'mission' of the school, then, is the distinctive, or presumed-to-be-distinctive, cluster of goals with associated beliefs, attitudes and activities. This cluster is more than the curriculum of this school where curriculum is narrowly defined in terms of content, but obviously the curriculum in this sense is central and the 'mission' may be generated out of decisions about content. Otherwise, curriculum content will certainly flow from the concept of mission. In practice, concept and content are likely to be the outcome of an interactive process.

There are few organisational theorists whose work contributes to this sort of thinking about organisations, but an important exception is Selznick. In *Leadership and Administration* (1957) he advances the need for organisations to have a mission which he defines broadly as the general aims of the organisation. He points out that an organisational mission cannot be specified in detail nor is it unchanging. He sees it as one of the indispensable tasks of leadership to formulate and present the organisational mission. [. . .] Selznick distinguishes between *organisation* which is 'an expendable tool, a rational instrument engineered to do a job' and an *institution* which is more nearly 'a natural product of social needs and pressures – a responsible and adaptive organism'. Thus organisation is the limited structural and administrative component of the social unit, and institution the global entity including its values. Hence mission relates to the institution and for Selznick has to represent a balance between 'the internal state of the system, the strivings, inhibitions and competences that exist within the organisation' and 'the external expectations that determine what must be sought or achieved if the institution is to survive'. The distinctive 'character' of the school and the prevailing mission, will be outcomes of the balance struck between these two functions.[. . .]

Although the terms 'mission' and 'character' are very slippery indeed the ideas behind them are worth exploring. It is perhaps easiest to do so in terms of the related functions of leadership. This entails, of course, making the assumption that the head will retain the capacity to exert a strong influence on the direction of the school.

The articulation of a mission

Theories of leadership, even contingency theories of leadership, tend to be mainly concerned with the twin functions of task achievement and social needs satisfaction. [. . .] To be sure, leadership theory is ostensibly concerned with policy formulation but in fact has little to say about the leadership skill needs or the practices to be followed in constructing a mission. Moreover, there is some ambivalence in the literature which on the one hand portrays the heroic charac-ter of certain leaders and on the other portrays the good organisational leader as someone who appears to take the mission as given and focuses on derived tasks. There is the additional factor that the 1950s and 1960s was a time which saw a burgeoning of management theory but it was also a time when there was a social and political climate which emphasised participation and democratisation and when in consequence the heroic aspect of leadership was relatively low-key. [. . .] Social theories are products of their time and we are perhaps seeing a re-emergence of an older concept of leadership which entails the identification and articulation of a mission. Leadership in this sense is perhaps treated with less suspicion. Hodgkinson (1983) makes the following distinction:

> Administration refers then to the more thinking, qualitative, humane and strategic aspects of the comprehensive executive function, while 'management' refers to the more doing, quantitative, material and tutorial aspects.

When he argues that administration is philosophy in action, in this context, philosophy may be 'in the mode of articulated policy utterances or of inchoate and unaltered values daily translated into action through the devices of the organisation'. As far as the argument of this chapter is concerned, mission can be conveyed either as a clear articulation with the head as the person on the white charger, or can be conveyed much more subtly through a succession of lead-ership actions which would need careful observation to be distinguished from management as Hodgkinson defines it.

Hodgkinson points four maxims for leadership:

> The leader has four responsibilities. He should:
> 1 Know the task.
> 2 Know the situation.
> 3 Know his followership.
> 4 Know himself.

These obviously have some affinity with Tannenbaum's four 'forces'. Hodgkinson's second maxim can be taken to include the organisational situation, and, of course, Maxim 3 on followership would also imply a knowledge of both the organisation and its environment. Although the contingency theorists, following Tannenbaum and Schmidt, invariably include a knowledge of the environment in lists of management tasks, there is, in fact, relatively little discussion in the literature of the skills required and strategies entailed in the leader transforming the forces in the environment into a mission for the organisation. Hodgkinson gets much closer to this in his conception of administration-as-philosophy. We can explore some of the implications of the construction and presentation of a mission for the head.

An expectation of heads is that they will be alert to the forces in the environment of the school which have potential relevance for its internal activities. These forces can be divided into two clusters. One cluster will contain relevant knowledge of what is happening in the broader educational world. This would largely entail a knowledge of existing and emerging educational policies at national and local levels. This knowledge would be acquired through a reading of policy statements, reports (or, at least, reports of reports), the educational press, and through interaction with other heads, advisers, lecturers, etc. through courses, conferences, in-service days, etc. Underpinning these policies will be a body of educational and curricular theory and associated research on which the well-prepared head could call, to put them in a wider philosophical and empirical context. The second cluster relates to the clientele of the school and would include a knowledge of social background, parental aspirations, community resources, job opportunities, etc.

The head who would create a mission for the school would have the continuous task of selecting from these clusters of knowledge which, as modified by an awareness of forces within the head and within the teachers currently teaching in the school and such other organisational forces as structures and resources, would fashion a set of goals for the school which could be construed as a mission. Different leadership styles entail differences in the degree to which heads construct missions alone or in collaboration with members of staff who would have been encouraged to contribute to the negotiation of a mission on the basis of *their* knowledge of environmental forces and forces within themselves. To the head would fall the task of articulating and presenting the mission. This would be achieved through verbalisation, through the deliberate deployment of symbols, or through a series of less obtrusive symbolic acts. At this point the task merges into the middle elements of Hodgkinson's model: *politics* and *mobilising*. This involves the securing of staff commitment to the mission. The task then moves to the operationalisation stage and merges with the *managerial* components of the Hodgkinson model. This involves the fulfilment of the two basic dimensions of leadership: task achievement and social needs satisfaction.

Mission and style

The literature on leadership signposts a plethora of styles. [. . .] One of the best-known typologies is Weber's distinction between *charismatic, traditional* and *bureaucratic* leadership. A more psychological typology is Zaleznik's (1966) tripartite typology of *proactive, reactive* and *mediative* styles. Reddin (1970) offers a more extended typology including *compromisers, developers, missionaries, autocrats,* etc. However, we can refer again to Hodgkinson's work which offers the following typology of leadership 'archetypes': *careerist, politician, technician* and *poet.*

Any of Hodgkinson's archetypes could conceivably generate a mission. The *careerist* could do so because the self-regarding nature of this type of leader will, in the cause of self-advancement, create a distinctive mission for their organisations. For Hodgkinson this is 'the lowest archetype from the point of view of moral or ethical approbation'. The *politician* could do so through mobilising teachers on the basis of their professional interests in achieving certain educational goals. The politican-leader differs from the careerist because of an interest in the work-group. The probability of the *technician* generating a mission seems unlikely since this style suggests a preoccupation with means rather than ends. But Hodgkinson notes that it is a mistake to treat the technician-leader as value-neutral or value-neutered since the rationality which such a leader expresses can become an end in itself so that once there is a given aim, though it will not be the technician-leader who prescribes this aim, the technician-as-mandarin will endow the rational means to the achievement of this aim with the status of mission. But, for Hodgkinson, it is the *poet* who is the leader with a mission. Of this archetype he writes:

> According to the theory of archetypes, the true poet would subsume the lower categories. He would therefore be acting on the highest ethical plane and thereby seeking higher states of welfare for his organisation, states not necessarily perceptible to all subordinates since their clear perception would be a function of the leader's greater value consciousness. The poet would transcend the value forms of life associated with the lower archetypes. He has a sense of the unconditioned and the unconditional; an authority intensified by moral force. He may appear as the 'man of principle' or the 'man of conscience' or the 'man of intuition' whose value commitments are such that they cannot be compromised, even if they fly in the face of the sweetest arguments of prudence and calculation.

Hodgkinson is naturally aware of the dangers in this form of leadership, the close line between the guardian and the megalomaniac. He writes:

> Generally, then, for this archetype there can be but one maxim of praxis: beware charisma! The charismatic leader may wish to lead where others cannot or ought not to follow. To beware does not necessarily mean or entail 'Avoid'!: there can be greatness and glory here as well as danger – superlative rewards for superlative risks – but it does enjoin consciousness. Be *aware!* Then choose.

These archetypes are heuristic. They are not rooted in statistical analysis. They are the outcome of a considerable amount of reflection on the nature of leadership. We will not flog them to death here by applying them systematically to case material of educational leaders, though the reader may like to undertake this exercise. However, they are useful points of reference in the subsequent discussion.

The poet articulates and embodies a mission and colleagues respond in an effective way. To be wholly successful this type of leader must have strong elements of the politician in mobilising teachers, and of the technician in ensuring that aims are effectively pursued. The careerist component is less clear. It may be that the poet can be a careerist or that careerism precludes poetry. Of course, this is at the highest level of abstraction and the apotheosis of the headteacher-as-poet will strike many, if not most, readers as a somewhat bizarre notion. Since there are thousands of heads in this country it would be to fly in the face of reason to assume that many even approximate to the ideal-type of poet. Most are probably making the best of their own qualities and the situations in which they find themselves.

We have our examples of heads as poet-leaders in the independent sector from, say, Arnold to Neill, but in the state schools we have fewer examples for two reasons. One is that it can be assumed that it is harder in a state school for the head to establish a distinctive 'mission', because, despite the relatively high degree of autonomy in the British system, there *are* external constraints and because, although independent schools are, to a degree, 'wild' and must meet the expectations of parents if they are to stay in business, the parents know what they are buying and there is likely to be a greater congruence between the 'mission' of the independent school and the expectations of parents than is the case in the state sector. The other point is that there are fewer accounts of headteachers-as-leaders for state-school heads simply because the schools produce fewer biographies and because it is much more difficult and politically-sensitive to write about a state-school head except in atypical cases. We can only, therefore, hypothesise some patterns for state schools.

Perhaps the basic distinction is between those heads who lead from the front and, if successful, inspire teachers to follow, and those who whilst not lacking a degree of muted charisma, succeed in building a mission through democratic means involving much negotiation. The former kind is more likely to be careerist, to articulate the mission via language and symbol, and to be committed to greater and more radical change. The latter type of head is more likely to convey a mission in a much more subtle way through everyday actions. Within each broad category there will be many variations. [. . .] Elizabeth Richardson's study of Nailsea School (Richardson, 1973) [. . .] illustrates the way in which Denys John, the head, sought to create a mission:

> At times – particularly when he had been under pressure from parents or governors about standards of work, of behaviour, of dress – he would almost lecture the staff on the ways in which he felt they were falling down, though he would be careful to use the pronoun 'we' rather than 'you', thus acknowledging his own share of responsibility for the school's image in the neighbourhood. Sometimes he would offer intellectual leads, in the manner of a seminar leader, through duplicated papers on fundamental topics such as staff participation in policy making, the nature of authority, the theoretical bases of curricular development. Sometimes he would set out proposals, almost in the style of a government report or memorandum, on such problems as the re-organisation of courses, the setting and supervision of homework and the stand-ardisation of assessment procedures. On some occasions he would protect people from their own feelings by avoiding staff discussion of an important event; on others, he

would devote a whole meeting to the exploration of attitudes and feelings about such an event. He might introduce a discussion with a careful, detailed explanation of the theme to be considered, or he might wait for others to take the initiative after only the barest of introductions, if necessary holding an uncomfortable silence. In all these situations it seemed that the staff experienced discomfort, either because they felt lumbered with his prepared thoughts and therefore inadequate by comparison, or because they felt helpless, leaderless and so at the mercy of their own uncertainty about what kind of thoughts it would be appropriate to bring forward.

This extract neatly illuminates the way in which a mission can be constructed by the head-as-leader in collaboration with his colleagues. Although typologies such as Hodgkinson's are valuable, there is a need for case studies of the ways in which heads exercise leadership, undertaken by skilful social scientists who also have a high level of literary ability. The process is complex, subtle and heavily reliant on symbolic modes of communication.

A suggestive piece of research is that of Hughes (1973) in which, on the basis of empirical evidence, a distinction is made between the head-as-administrator and the head-as-professional. It is through the latter component of the role that leadership is exercised. Hughes' work indicates that the professional head encourages a professional response from colleagues and although the published data does not explicitly demonstrate that professional heads are those who conceptualise a mission in collaboration with colleagues, it is perhaps reasonable to speculate that this is likely to be the case.

The ambivalence of teachers

Teachers are inevitably critical of their headteachers. The range and diversity of the tasks expected of the head are such that they inevitably fall short of teachers' ideals, which themselves may be in conflict. Teacher talk about heads often focuses on the [. . .] inevitable shortfall between the ideal and the real. These criticisms will be differently expressed, sometimes vitriolically and sometimes more gently in a humorous context. The functions served by this criticism are themselves diverse and beyond the scope of the present discussion. Of particular interest here is the ambivalence of teachers' attitudes towards the mission-building activities of the head and the susceptibility of this activity to criticism and humour.

This ambivalence probably has its roots in the loosely-coupled nature of schools. Teachers value their autonomy and will yield this only with reluctance. This structural autonomy may well be associated with what might be termed a conceptual autonomy, an individualistic commitment to a set of beliefs about teaching which may be largely intuitive (Jackson, 1968) and to a restricted form of professionality (Hoyle, 1974). At the same time, teachers may experience a desire to participate in and identify with a larger enterprise than classroom teaching, the school and its mission. Thus the 'balance between autonomy and control' and equilibrium point in a loosely-coupled system may have its counterpart in the relationship between a personal classroom mission and a collective school mission.

A school mission identified and constructed by the head may appear as threatening to the individual teacher. A defence against this will be criticism and often ridicule. The head who attempts to articulate a grandiose mission for the school, unless he or she has the charisma to carry along an enthusiastic group of teachers, will inevitably run the danger of being the object of staffroom humour. We have few studies of this staffroom humour but one of the best (Woods, 1979), whilst not dealing specifically with the issue of mission, illustrates well the vulnerability of the head to teacher humour. [. . .]

Yet, although there would seem to be teacher resistance to the articulation of a school mission, as studies by Nias and others have shown, teachers nevertheless respond positively to heads who are providing positive leadership and even a 'coherent philosophy'. This suggests that the head's task of articulating a mission is particularly difficult and sensitive. Teachers will respond to positive leadership, but the pull of autonomy ensures that their response will be guarded and balanced by a self-protecting humour. However, this is an area very much in need of further study.

Missions that fade and missions that fail

In this section we are concerned with two modes in which there can be a decline of a mission which had previously been successfully established. The first mode is the result of managerial entropy. Heads get older and there is the ever-present possibility of a slow winding down. This is not, of course, universal. A. S. Neill sustained his sense of mission until his death at the age of ninety. [. . .] There is no hard evidence of the incidence, or indeed the existence, of this phenomenon. There is the evidence of an increase in the rate of early retirement amongst headteachers, but no assumptions can be made about the relationship between this and managerial entropy. Opportunities for early retirement have increased in recent years encouraged by LEAs who wish to create promotion opportunities in a stable state. It is generally held that the greater incidence of early retirement is due to increased stress experienced by heads. But again, it is difficult to relate stress to managerial entropy.

In Britain at least, there is no policy for offsetting the potential run-down of a school mission. There is currently a move on the part of government to subject heads to systematic external evaluation for the first time, but it is not clear so far just how effectiveness will be assessed or whether there will be any attempt to assess the degree to which they have created a mission for the school. Some heads cope with this potential problem by choosing to move to the headship of a different school, not necessarily for promotion or increased salary, but simply to present themselves with a new challenge.

The failure of a mission is quite a different phenomenon and can arise when a head fails to interpret the environment correctly and therefore establishes an inappropriate mission which is doomed to failure, or fails to involve his staff with a sense of mission, or fails to convert the mission into policy or practice. There have been one or two spectacular failures of this kind in education which have received much publicity. However, the educational enterprise is such that spectacular failures are unusual and the shortfall between intention and action does not have the grandeur of disaster. [. . .] A failure of mission is usually a matter of degree.

The reasons for acute or relative failure are usually the result of a misjudgment of one or more sets of forces which impinge on the leadership role. It will be recalled that Hodgkinson's four maxims were that the leader should know the task, the situation, the followers and himself or herself. 'Failure' can result from being unable to fulfil more and more of these maxims. There are examples in the literature of failures of mission due to a head's misjudgment about outside forces. These have sometimes been failures to carry parents along with the mission. Parents are likely to be more conservative than educationists and any mission which involves innovation beyond the experience of most parents should ensure that they become committed to that mission and in those circumstances it is a key task of the leadership of the school to achieve this. In other instances, heads have misjudged the expectations of the local education authority and the mission has foundered through lack of external support or even hostility.

In some other instances, heads have pressed a mission beyond the level of acceptance of the staff and have alternatively found themselves isolated. Michael Duane at Risinghill (Berg, 1968) and Robert Mackenzie at Braehead (Mackenzie, 1970) each had a personal mission which was not accepted by the majority of staff. Terry Ellis at William Tyndale (Auld, 1976) shared a strong commitment to a distinctive mission with some of his colleagues but it was a mission which was violently opposed by others.

A third problem occurs where the head has a mission, succeeds in getting staff committed to it, but it is then found that the task is beyond the professional and organisational means to accomplish. This frequently entails an attempt to undertake a radical restructuring of the organisation, curriculum and pedagogy of the school but the grand design turns to ashes as the practicalities get out of hand and disruption and disillusion follow. This is a case of a head not fully understanding the task which has been set for the school and misjudging the personal capacities required to bring it about.

Two final points can be made about mission and leadership. One is that what appears as a failure of leadership in one school at a particular time may have positive long term consequences for the educational system as a whole. The injunction to know the task, situation, followers and self probably leads to the majority of schools having modest missions and the educational process changing very slowly through disjointed incrementalism. On the other hand, the spectacular failure may be a pathbreaker which others will follow. The second points is that given the turbulence of the environment, the limits to rationality, and the scope for the operation of sheer chance, the failure of a mission may be more due to sheer bad luck than to an inappropriate leadership style.

Conclusion

There is an extensive body of research on organisational leadership including the leadership of schools. This research emphasises the importance of two basic leadership functions – task achievement and the fulfilment of the social needs of colleagues – as essential to effectiveness. The theory also emphasises the contingent nature of leadership and the need to take account of forces outside the organisation. However, two elements are missing from this body of research. One is the recognition of the micropolitical dimension of leadership – the models presented are a little too rational and altruistic. [. . .] The other omission is the somewhat nebulous function of leadership which is the function of identifying, conceptualising, transmitting and gaining acceptance of a mission for the school, an idea or image of where it is heading.

It has been the purpose of this chapter to put this nebulous but nevertheless important aspect of leadership on the agenda. There is a danger that the idea of mission conjures up a discredited view of leadership as a sword-waving man on a charger. Or, because the conceptualisation of a mission is an educational process, there is the opposite danger of seeing such a leader as an ineffective dreamer. Hodgkinson's model of leadership tasks usefully draws attention to the importance of the continuity of the relationship between the policy formulation and implementation aspects of leadership. We need to know much more about how heads formulate policy, and about the direct and subtly indirect and symbolic means whereby it is transmitted.

References

AULD, R. (1976). *Report of the Public Inquiry into the William Tyndale junior and infant schools*, London, ILEA.

BERG, L. (1968). *Risinghill*, Harmondsworth, Penguin.

BOLAM, R. (ed.) (1982). *School-focused In-service Training*, London, Heinemann.

DALIN, P. and RUST, V. D. (1983). *Can Schools Learn?* London, NFER/Nelson.

FIEDLER, F. (1965). 'Engineer the job to fit the manager', *Harvard Business Review*, Sept–Oct.

GETZELS, J. W. and GUBA, E. G. (1957). 'Social behaviour and the administrative process', *School Review*, 65 winter.

HALL, G. E. *et al* (1982). 'Three change-facilitator styles', paper presented at the annual meeting of AERA, New York, 1982.

HALPIN, A. (1966). *Theory and Research in Administration*, New York, Macmillan.

HANSON, E. M. (1979). 'School management and contingency theory: an emerging perspective', *Educational Administration Quarterly*, 15(2).

HODGKINSON, C. (1953). *The Philosophy of Leadership*. Oxford, Blackwell.

HOUSE, R. (1971). 'A path—goal theory of leader effectiveness', *Administrative Science Quarterly*, 16.

HOUSE, R. and DESSLER, G. (1974). 'The path—goal theory of leadership: some post hoc and a priori tests', in HUNT, J. and LARSON, L. (eds), *Contingency Approaches to Leadership*, Carbondale, Illinois, Southern Illinois University Press.

HOYLE, E. (1974). 'Professionality, professionalism and control in teaching', *London Educational Review* 3(2).

HUGHES, M. (1973). 'The professional as administrator: the case of the secondary school head', *Educational Administration Bulletin*, 2(1).

JACKSON, P. W. (1968). *Life in Classrooms*, New York, Holt, Rinehart and Winston.

LEITHWOOD, K. and MONTGOMERY, D. J. (1984). 'Patterns of growth in principal effectiveness', paper presented at the Annual Meeting of AERA, New Orleans, April, 1984.

MACKENZIE, R. (1970). *State School*, Harmondsworth, Penguin.

McMAHON, A. (1986). 'The self-evaluation of schools' in HOYLE, E. and McMAHON, A. (eds), *World Yearbook of Education, 1986: The Management of Schools*, London, Kogan Page.

MARTIN, W. J. and WILLOWER, D. (1981). 'The managerial behaviour of high school principals', *Education Administration Quarterly*, 17.

NIAS, J. (1980). 'Leadership styles and job satisfaction in primary schools' in BUSH, T. *et al* (ed), *Approaches to School Management*, London, Harper and Row/Oxford University Press.

O'DEMPSEY, K. (1976). 'The analysis of work-patterns and roles of high school principals', *Administrator's Bulletin*, 7(8).

PETERSON, K. (1976). 'The principal's tasks', *Administrator's Notebook*, 26(8).

REDDIN, W. J. (1970). *Managerial Effectiveness*, New York, McGraw-Hill.

RICHARDSON, E. (1973). *The Teacher, the School and the task of Management*, London, Heinemann.

SELZNICK, P. (1957). *Leadership in Administration*, New York, Harper and Row.

SPROULL, L. (1981). 'Managing educational programs: a micro-behavioural analysis', *Human Organization*, 40.

STOGDILL, R. (1948). 'Personal factors associated with leadership', *Journal of Psychology*, 25.

TANNENBAUM, R. and SCHMIDT, W. H. (1958). 'How to choose a leadership pattern', *Harvard Business Review*, 51(3).

TANNENBAUM, R., WEISCHLER, I. and MASSARIK, F. (1961). *Leadership and Organization: a Behavioural Science Approach*, Urbana, Illinois, University of Illinois Press.

WEBER, M. (1947). *The Theory of Social and Economic Organization*, (trans. Henderson, A. and Parsons, T.), New York, Free Press.

WILLIS, Q. (1980). 'The work activity of school principals: an observational study', *Journal of Educational Administration*, 18.

WOLCOTT, H. (1973). *The Man in the Principal's Office*, New York, Holt, Rinehart and Winston.

WOODS, P. (1979). *The Divided School*, London, Routledge and Kegan Paul.

YUKL, G. (1975). 'Towards a behavioural theory of leadership' in HOUGHTON, V. *et al* (ed), *The Management of Organizations and Individuals*, London, Ward Lock.

ZALEZNIK, A. (1966). *Human Dilemmas of Leadership*, New York, Harper and Row.

Primary headship and collegiality

Geoff Southworth

Introduction

Those who work in primary schools are currently receiving many messages about how they should operate. This article will look at two of these messages: those to do with leadership and those to do with collegiality. On the one hand there is a persistent acceptance of schools as being hierarchical organisation requiring top-down management and leadership (DES 1977). On the other hand the value of involving teachers in the decision-making process is being promoted (DES Welsh Office 1985). It is also common to see both being advertised at the same time:

> The head is always, in law as well as in fact, responsible for the situations in his or her school. Successful heads have interpreted these considerable powers and duties wisely. They have not been authoritarian, consultative, or participative as a matter of principle; they have been all three at different times as the conditions seemed to warrant, though most often participative. Their success has often come from choosing well, from knowing when to take the lead and when to confirm the leadership offered by their colleagues.
>
> (ILEA 1985 para. 3.25)

This quote suggests that the two can be synthesized, that there is little conflict between leadership and collegiality, and that they are compatible. I think this assumes rather too much. Leadership and collegiality warrant examination, in their own right and because of the tensions which are created by their coexistence. This article will review such research data as exists, look at some of the perspectives in the literature, and embody observations based on work with headteachers on management courses and my personal experience of primary headship.

Perceptions of headteachers in primary schools

Headteachers cannot be understood separately from their contexts, the most important aspect of which is the school. Yet even this apparently simple term has different meanings in different countries. King (1983) shows that in England we regard the school as a *community*, unlike the USA where schools are seen as *part* of the community. In England the school is a unique collection of people (Oldroyd 1984), a fact which has two implications for headship. First, the head is not just head of a school but the leader of a community. Headteachers often act as leaders of their particular school community. For example, at school ceremonies the head who welcomes parents to a special assembly, or concert, or event, and who thanks the staff and children and parents for their participation is signalling a leadership role since the fact that s/he is making these remarks to everyone present is part of the message (King 1983). Second, because each school is unique the head has a degree of autonomy. For the head the context of the school creates a leadership role in relation to his/her colleagues and some freedom from others outside the school so that s/he can lead the community of the school in his/her own way, since only s/he as head will know what the conditions warrant. Small's (1984) investigation into five headteachers illustrates how the role of each is affected by the circumstances of the school s/he is in and how these differences also make them independent. The title of the study is significant: 'A Scandal of Particularity? Headship in the mid-1980s'.

One effect of this sense of separateness is that the head's boundary and fil- tering roles are emphasized. Richardson (1975) identified a boundary role for the headteacher. Those 'outside' the school customarily approach those in the school via the headteacher (e.g. parents, LEA advisers, welfare and support agencies). Frequently those communications coming out of the school require the headteacher's acknowledgement, if not approval (e.g. pupil reports, INSET course attendance requiring day release, letters to parents). Although his/her consent may be given in an informal, non-bureaucratic manner, the fact that it is deemed necessary emphasizes the head's boundary role. Coulson (1980) sug- gests that the head also acts as a 'filter', for example in relation to school governors. The 1980 Education Act makes schools accountable to their gover- nors. Yet if materials intended for school governor training (NAGM 1981; Sallis 1982) and personal experience are valid indicators, a headteacher's ability to 'filter' information by means of their reports to governors is not significantly diminished.

Another effect of this idea of heads leading a community is that heads develop a sense of attachment to the school. Coulson (1980) provides evidence that heads and the schools they lead become so closely identified that he calls it 'ego- identification'. Heads talk about 'their' school and refer also to 'my' staff, and 'my' deputy. However, this identification is more than a sense of placement, it is frequently a feeling state. The majority of heads I have worked with genuinely *feel* a strong sense of responsibility for much, if not all, that happens in 'their' school.

This feeling of personal attachment and involvement suggests that we should be trying to understand not just the sociological and organizational aspects of headship but also its 'psychology'. We need to examine the roles of headteachers in terms of their feelings, motives, perceptions and judgements. At present we can say only that primary heads *are* closely attached to 'their' schools, and that by a sense of boundary they are identified with that particular school. There is, however, a great deal more we need to know about what this means for the individual head.

However, there is also a need to highlight some other features which affect the headteacher. The first of these can be labelled school ethos. Heads appear to feel that they have the responsibility for determining 'their' school's 'ethos'. The underlying philosophy of the school should be the head's (see Coulson 1980). This seems to arise from their sense of example. Primary heads are typically promoted straight from the classroom. It is their practical abilities as a class-teacher which has kudos with the selectors (King 1983). They are therefore expected by the selectors to exert an influence. The very title is significant – *head*teacher. The process of promotion effectively approves the individual's professional values. Moreover on becoming a head the person may feel that his/her teaching is of such an order that it is worthy of emulation by others. Whitaker (1983) speaks of a 'sense of mission' accompanying a person's entry into a new headship. An issue then is that the head, as an individual, arrives at a level of influence feeling a sense of professional self belief and example and accepting a responsibility to project these values onto the school. The head is not just the leader of the school, s/he is now the leading exemplar for the school.

As leading exemplar the head's values become the significant benchmarks for the school. Dearden (1968) has argued that there are no aims of primary educa-tion, only aims of education. This implies that there are no terminal points for primary education; there is no time or stage at which teachers can say they have achieved the aims. Primary teachers often feel that there is always more they could be doing. Alternatively, many argue that primary education should be viewed in terms of its processes and evaluated by reference to the kinds of expe-riences and activities that constitute it rather than to the anticipated outcomes (Blenkin and Kelly 1981). In the face of a lack of consensus as to what primary education should be achieving and how to evaluate this it may mean that, on a day-to-day basis, the headteacher's values become the adopted ones, since they are more tangible than any other indicators.

Given this set of features the challenge for heads is to generate commitment to 'their' values. Whatever the exact nature of a headteacher's roles and respon-sibilities in a particular school most heads attempt to exercise a unifying influ-ence on the school. Coulson (1980) describes how heads 'generate commitment' and foster loyalty not so much to the abstract idea of the school but to themselves as individuals. Certainly this personal relationship exists between heads and 'their' deputies. The role relations of head and deputy frequently operate on the basis of a code of conduct whereby heads and deputies do not disagree on matters of school policy in 'public', that is in front of other staff. Disagreements are only allowed to surface in 'private'. Given other features of the deputy head's role, which will be mentioned later, this pact tends to work often to the benefit of the head. Deputies seldom question the head's ruling or decision in formal situations such as staff meetings, and are expected to actively support decisions at such times. It is my experience that at times of deputy head selection acceptance of this code of conduct by candidates is examined by the headteacher. Certainly, many heads and deputy heads subscribe to this view of 'loyalty' believing it to be an acceptable arrangement.

However, 'loyalty' is only one way of creating unity in the school. The recruitment and selection of staff to vacant posts is a tactic of considerable significance. The strong feelings expressed by groups of heads when discussing how much, or how little opportunity they have had to recruit staff is an indicator of how central this aspect of management is to them. When a head talks about 'his/her' school to another and describes the situation, responsibilities of staff, curriculum developments, rates of change, staff relations and so on, the listening head will very quickly seek to discover how many of the staff the head has appointed. And often heads will say 'I appointed' this teacher when in fact it was the appointment of the school governors. Indeed, amongst heads there is a belief that the ideal state of school leadership is when the head has selected all of his or her 'own' staff. If that cannot be achieved then the next best thing is to have appointed 'one's own' deputy.

Staffing may also be used less directly to unify a school through job descriptions. Such descriptions do a number of things. First they frequently make it quite clear to teachers that they are directly responsible to the headteacher (Lancashire LEA 1980). Second, teachers often have job descriptions but the headteacher does not, which suggests that whilst teachers each have a framed and clearly delineated set of tasks or functions the head has an over-arching, omnipotent role. Third, job descriptions also seek to direct teachers into areas of activity which, broadly, are congruent with the head's philosophy and long-term aspirations for the school.

Teacher appraisal systems may also be used to unify a school. Although the specific proposals are only now emerging (Suffolk 1985) appraisal looks to be taking place within the existing hierarchies and conventions. What is likely is that headteachers will articulate a set of views on the teachers' competences according to some agreed schedule. However, whilst a schedule of teacher appraisal may structure much of the context and some of the content, it is obvious that a headteacher's adoption and interpretation of these schedules will also incorporate their senses of example and loyalty. In other words, quite properly, their professional values will pervade the whole enterprise. Given the points already made about the head's role one can clearly see appraisal as a device whereby the head consciously and unconsciously can apply pressure to unify the school.

What is not being suggested, of course, is a mirror-like correspondence between the teachers and the head. Heads cannot clone. Yet this idea of unity is intended to bring out the opportunities that a headteacher has to affect the parameters of divergence. It looks as if the head becomes the norm to whom the staff refer.

Another way to determine the headteacher's influence on the school is to consider not his/her role but that of the deputy head. In a primary school the deputy head is typically in an ambiguous position. The scant literature on the deputy head's role shows that there is no common agreement as to the nature of the role. Bush (1981) is unequivocal in saying that the position of deputy has little substance or meaning because the leadership of the primary school is over-whelmingly the function of the head. In addition, primary deputies are seldom released from their class teaching duties and as Coulson (1976) noted it is rare that the deputy's job, on a day-to-day basis, differs from that of other teachers. The ILEA report 'Improving Primary Schools' (ILEA 1985) says that the deputy should be regarded as a trainee head. This implies that there is no intrinsic need for deputies in the school. The meaning of the role is cast into the future, not the present.

In reality what deputies do rests almost entirely upon what the head allows them to do. Some small-scale research into the headteacher's conceptions of the deputy head's role (Southworth 1985a) revealed that high priority is given to the deputy being a 'good' teacher. Discussions with groups of primary headteachers suggests that heads ideally see deputies as 'disciples'. The deputy should be appointed by the head-in-post, selected on the basis of a close match to the head's image of a 'successful' teacher. The deputy would then spend most of his/her time working in the classroom providing a good example for other teachers to follow. Deputies, therefore, are classroom surrogates of the headteacher. This is also useful because heads in large and medium-sized primary schools will have been 'promoted out' of the classroom which has been the basis of their exemplary activity. Heads thus need to find a substitute. Deputies, therefore, are not there to help the head unload some of his/her duties. Ideally, deputies are regarded as putting into operation, in the classroom, a set of values on behalf of their sponsor, the head. If this is achieved then the head will have doubled the forces of influence (Whitaker 1983). The head will have influence over the whole school *and* a classroom disciple providing a direct example for teachers to follow.

The influence of heads upon 'their' school is also revealed during periods of headteacher succession. When heads talk about 'taking over' from another head it is unusual, in my experience, that the succeeding head is full of conviction for their predecessor's regime. Often there are doubts expressed about certain ways of doing things, or of procedures strangely absent. It is common that the incoming head is critical of aspects of the school.

There are two things to focus on here. First, it suggests that there is some discontinuity at the time of headteacher succession. This is consistent with the picture drawn here. If heads are autonomous, able to set the ethos for the school and 'unify' the staff within a framework of values compatible with the head's beliefs, then one would expect that there would be discontinuity. Second, when these differences relate to the curriculum, teaching and learning issues, then such discontinuity is potentially disruptive and even damaging. When a change of head occurs what could be happening is a change in the school's value system.

At this point it is useful to look at some of the implications of the perspective which has been outlined. It is widely accepted that primary heads have a formidable concentration of power (Alexander 1984). However, that is not to say that all heads are autocratic or paternalistic. Heads can choose to exercise their power in different ways. A great deal of what is described here is *latent*. How an individual activates these patterns of control, if at all, will be a matter of individual practice. Nevertheless, the analysis offered does support the idea of heads having considerable scope for influence. The analysis, moreover, does not rely solely on an organizational perspective to do with role, position or function. The viewpoint presented here also substantially relies upon subjective states such as personal beliefs, values and felt perceptions. This raises some important issues concerning the current views on leadership.

First, primary heads now have greater opportunities to acquire management skills (DES 3/83; 3/85). These skills may help them with many aspects of their job but how useful will these skills be unless primary management courses also analyse the headteacher's role? If so much power resides with the head then management courses should focus on this. Heads need to understand the nuances of their position and power since heads are as likely to be the obstacles to development as the creators of change. Unfortunately the programmes of many primary management courses tend to mean that primary heads consider many other roles and managerial functions but seldom focus on *their* role in 'their' school.

Second, how helpful is it for heads to be told that the single most important factor in a successful school is a good head (DES 1977; DES Welsh Office 1985). The notion that a good head equates with a good school is far too simplistic (see Winkley 1984). For one thing it only adds to the headteacher's heavy sense of responsibility – if the school's success is also the head's success, its failure is also the head's failure (King 1983). Such a crude equation is likely to be stressful to many headteachers. It is also a negation of the role of many, many teachers. It certainly does not help to develop a sense of collegiality.

Third, this analysis has important implications for heads as individuals. Elsewhere (Southworth 1985) I have advocated the need for support mechanisms for headteachers because they find their responsibilities a heavy burden. They also find the role often isolates them from others in the school. Work with cohorts of headteachers who have attended management courses suggest that whilst these heads hold views which support this analysis they also demonstrate associated pressures and strains. They need to talk about 'their' schools, about the challenges, changes and developments which face or confront them: headteachers are people too (Coulson 1985). A problem with role theory, and some of those who use it to describe headship, is that role theory does not throw light on the individuality of actors. If the primary head's leadership role is to continue or change then greater support will be needed for them as individuals.

Fourth, it follows from much of this that it is the *person* of the head, his/her perceptions and values, which are of fundamental concern (Coulson 1985). If leadership is to alter in the primary school then some serious attempts will have to be made to meet the personal needs of the individual head.

Lastly, primary heads evidently have influence and power and feel the strains of these responsibilities, but this accumulation of power is at odds with the model of primary school development which is currently being promoted and which I label as collegiality.

Collegiality

Collegiality has become a popular notion and is advocated by a number of sources. One can be identified as 'professional accountability' (Elliott *et al* 1981; Campbell 1985), where all members of the school, regardless of role or status, see themselves as mutually accountable. Another source is that of certain organizational theorists (McGregor 1960; Herzberg 1966) who have encouraged participation. Thirdly, there are those who offer collegiality as an alternative to the headteacher's concentration of power (Hargreaves 1973; Coulson 1980), since as Handy (1984) says, in a democratic society schools can look strangely feudal to the outsider.

The idealized 'collegial school' has small working groups of teachers feeding back suggestions for school-wide change to the collectivity of the whole staff meeting for decision-making. These working groups are usually led by curriculum 'leaders' or 'consultants' who might also work alongside teacher-colleagues. This collaboration is supported by heads who have committed themselves to devolving responsibilities to the staff group and to servicing such activity (Campbell 1985). Campbell's distillation of collegiality is supported by official policies from several sources, some of which are given verbatim below:

> Where teachers with responsibilities for a particular area of the curriculum were effective in influencing the work of the school this was apparent in a number of ways: in the case of English language and mathematics there was evidence of teachers planning programmes of work in consultation with the head, advising other teachers and helping to encourage a consistent approach to the work in these subjects.
> (DES 1978, *Primary Education in England: A Survey by HM Inspectors of Schools*, para 4.5)

> Few teachers are expert in all parts of the curriculum. It becomes increasingly difficult for an individual teacher to provide the width and depth of all the work required to be taught. . . The necessary help, support and advice may in part be given by heads and local advisers. It may also be provided by other teachers on the staff who have a special interest, enthusiasm and responsibility for a part of the curriculum and who act as consultants. Such teachers may give support in a variety of ways: by producing guidelines and schemes of work; by leading discussions and organizing study groups; by disseminating work done on in-service courses; by working alongside classteachers; by assembling and organizing resources; and occasionally by teaching classes other than their own.'
> (DES 1982, *Education 5 to 9: an Illustrative Survey of 80 First Schools in England*, para 3.19)

> Usually the whole staff were involved in the process throughout and were all members of the specific review and development teams. This was possible because of their

comparatively small staff size and it did facilitate a good, if informal, exchange of information about the review and development process.

(McMahon *et al* 1984, *Guidelines for Review and Internal Development in Schools: Primary School Handbook* (GRIDS), Schools Council Programme 1, p. 56)

The professionalism of the teacher also involves playing a part in the corporate development of the school. HMI reports frequently refer to the importance of professional team work, where the teachers within a school agree together on the overall goals of the school, on the policies for the curriculum in the widest sense, including policies for the standard of behaviour expected of pupils and for the relationship expected between teacher and pupils. The pupils' own ability to co-operate and work well with each other is enhanced by the experience of members of staff working productively together in a professional relationship. HMI reports also draw attention to the value of agreed policies for marking and assessment within a school

(DES 1985, *Better Schools*, Cmnd 9469, para 143)

We believe that many primary schools would benefit from increased delegation of responsibilities to members of staff. . . . It is a matter of high priority that each school should have a sense of wholeness. That can be achieved only through clear and sensitive leadership. . . . It is important to be sure that the various aspects of the curriculum cohere for the school as a whole.

(ILEA 1985, *Improving Primary Schools*, paras 3.27, 3.28 and 3.43)

A key issue in extending the influence of teachers with posts of special responsibility is the willingness of heads to delegate and to give scale post teachers the necessary support and authority. This has been achieved in one junior school where all posts of responsibility are for curriculum development. Each scale post teacher was asked to produce detailed schemes of work and all have done so. These have commendable depth in terms of aims, objectives, approaches and content, although to date only the language scheme has a built-in assessment schedule. Considerable whole school discussion accompanied the production of the schemes, and all teachers have a clear understanding of the aims and all share a common purpose in implementing them. Curriculum leaders call at least one meeting a term to discuss their specialism, to evaluate the schemes in practice and to invite ideas for future development. A recent initiative has been the involvement of curriculum leaders in teaching alongside colleagues and subsequently discussing the work. The discussion occurs when a peripatetic teacher takes the class. A rota of team teaching has been drawn up and according to staff all are enjoying the experience and feel they are gaining from it. A sense of corporate team work has been established within which scale post teachers have made a substantial mark upon the work of the school as a whole. This is a model worthy of wider emulation.

(DES Welsh Office 1985, *Leadership in Primary Schools: Primary Education in Wales*)

Two things emerge from these statements. First, one can see the key components of collegiality: consultation, communication, continuity, coordination and coherence. All have been part of the vocabulary of curriculum planning and organization for some time (see Blyth and Derricott 1977), but have now been adopted as school management strategies. In one sense this is encouraging since it maintains the connection between school and curriculum management structures, between curriculum development and school development. However, school management involves rather more than curriculum management. External communications and internal relations will only partially be accommodated by such curriculum strategies. Moreover, each of these key components deserves detailed scrutiny. For example, continuity is now being given careful attention (Derricott 1985) and can be seen to have two distinguishable meanings – communicational and structural (Southworth 1985c). Continuity as communication describes teachers reporting what they have covered in curriculum content. Continuity as structure is to do with how teachers conceive 'development', and 'knowledge'. Nor is the meaning of consultation clear. Some DES documents (DES 1984) use the term consultation within a top-down framework. What is not being offered is a partnership of equals (Southworth 1985c). Schools are probably more consultative now but it does not follow that they are more democratic. Much of the language of curriculum management is couched in terms of staff meetings, working parties and in-service course dissemination. A lot of this may simply be the exchange of information and have little bearing on decision-making. Indeed, it can be argued that the model of curriculum management seemingly offered by HMI provides heads with greater opportunities to unify 'their' schools since whole-school coordination and coherence lend themselves as much to that interpretation as to colleagues working collaboratively and democratically. The key words of collegiality require careful study. At the moment they are used far too loosely, are ambiguous and may be misleading.

The second thing to emerge is that collegiality will change the existing role relations in school. Collegiality is likely to reduce the predominance of the headteacher and the autonomy of the classteacher. The former will occur through increased delegation and participation. The latter because classteachers are now being encouraged to take on a dual role: the responsibility within general school policies for the coherence of the programme of work of their class; and an advisory/consultancy role in some aspect of the curriculum throughout the school (ILEA 1985 para 3.37). Both of these role changes will be major changes.

I can find no acknowledgement in the writings of those who advocate collegiality that it will involve major change. Indeed, the documents which promote collegiality seem to ignore how collegiality will be implemented and developed. The absence of any discussion as to the challenges this change will create tends to leave one with the impression that collegiality is easy to adopt. The foregoing discussion of the head's role obviously presents many barriers. Packwood's case study (1984) reveals that introducing a collegial approach will be far from easy. Packwood describes how a Junior school changed its responsibility structure so that subject responsibilities could be delegated to teachers. There are three things which should be highlighted from this study. First, the idea of 'subject specialists' needs considerable clarification. Secondly, Packwood shows how even within this particular school's staff there were differences as to how a specialist should proceed, and what the job involved. Thirdly, the case study points towards the fact that collegiality will not just affect formal role relations, but the nature of all relationships.

Focusing on the third point one can anticipate that collegiality would alter adult interactions both individually and in groups. Collegiality would affect the whole nature of school discourse, decision-making and evaluation. It would test the whole professional culture of primary education and the power structure of individual schools (Alexander 1984). Moreover, collegiality would intrude into areas often seen as 'private'. Handy (1984) notes that because schools are faced with blurred aims, conflicting functions and no simple way of measuring success, every judgement is subjective and personal. To encourage teachers to come together to discuss plans, practice and evaluation is to ask teachers to examine their different approaches, methods, values and beliefs. This will undoubtedly create tensions, competition and sometimes conflicts. It turns the practical into the political and the interpersonal.

Change usually brings with it uncertainties, but a switch to collegiality would bring uncertainty *and* some risks. Differences in practice and philosophy have in many schools been avoided because the individuals are convinced that they cannot (or would not) cope with the turbulence created by facing them and talking about them. To ask that teachers now do this is to underestimate the nature and structures of feeling which any individual and all organisations embody. Collegiality *will* affect the adults in the school because collegiality will disturb both formal and informal group processes. In addition there is a lack of published work to help guide schools towards a collegial approach. Those who try will be working in the dark.

There are other problems too. First the rate of change is problematical. The time taken to switch to a collegial approach, and the time collegial processes take in school are both likely to be slower than autocratically announced changes. Oldroyd (1984) in his account of how a Canadian school moved towards group cohesion and collegiality, says that sufficient trust emerged only after a two-year process of incremental development. Is this a pace which is in harmony with the rates of change implied in the current rash of curriculum policy documents? Reports emanating from the DES and HMI (see Southworth 1985d) who are designating and redesignating the areas of the curriculum, stimulating interest in CDT and technology, science education, and home economics, imply a faster rate of change than Oldroyd's case study depicts. A second problem is that the call for collegial ways has occurred during a time when primary schools have been adversely affected by falling pupil rolls. The problems this has created have not been conducive to headteachers attempting to re-model their leadership patterns. Issues of redeployment, early retirement, or whether a school will be amalgamated or closed are too fraught to provide the stability needed for a change to collegiality. In any case the idea of heads delegating more tasks has come when the head may well have fewer staff to delegate to. These turbulent conditions have probably inhibited interest in collegiality whilst the barrage of curriculum documentation has further hindered the adoption of a collegial approach.

Conclusion

It would appear from this examination that leadership and collegiality are not necessarily compatible. Collegiality is aimed at reducing the heads' load through increasing their scale of delegation. In this way it is hoped that the excesses of monopolistic headship will be avoided and that staff will be more participative. In the first instance this fails to take sufficient account of the headteachers' perceptions of their role and their strong feelings of responsibility for the school.

A second issue is that collegiality has enormous implications for staff development. If collegiality is to be encouraged then we need to look very carefully at how headteachers are to be developed and might need to change. The kinds of management courses which primary heads need are not so much ones of systems theory, instrumental rationality and industrial production as of curriculum awareness, social understanding and interpersonal skills. The head will probably need to act more as a facilitator (Southworth 1984). As a facilitator the head needs a particular order of insights and skills. To quote Shaw (1983) s/he must be able to make complex, synthetic judgements of the type needed in ethics, politics or diplomacy, not like those needed in engineering or economics.

It was noted that this is a major role change for headteachers. Therefore, before collegiality can become a viable option heads need to be able to examine and understand the dynamics and consequences of their present leadership role. It needs to be recognized that in offering heads a collegial approach they are being asked to do something which is both complex and uncertain. Few of us will go out of our way to do that. Heads are being asked to change their role and become more active in curricular leadership in the school. This role change is a far more important innovation to the head than any other specific curriculum innovation. Role changes for heads and teachers will create ambivalence even among those willing to try (Fullan 1982). As there is already a need for support for headteachers (Southworth 1985b) further support facilities are likely to be needed.

Then there is the matter of management training for heads. It has been suggested that a feature of these courses should be that heads devote attention to their role in 'their' school. However, one needs to ask more fundamental questions of the way management training is being conceived. How helpful is it at a time when collegiality is being promoted for only heads to be given management training? Surely, if collegiality is to be taken seriously we need to be looking at courses for the whole staff group.

Another aspect of the staff development implications is the consideration which teachers will also need. They too will need considerable help. Some of this could take place as part of school-based staff development, but there are also reasons why some of this should take place away from the school site and the staff group. Initial work on leadership and communication in the staff group is possibly best done with teachers from other schools and under the tutelage of those proficient in group processes, communication and counselling. Teachers who accept a curricular responsibility will also need to enhance their knowledge both of the chosen area and of change processes and evaluation.

All of these staff development programmes will require rather more than a short course taken after school. The existing low levels of funding for in-service training, the lack of day release in many LEAs and the frequent absence of these kinds of course in some areas, suggest that collegiality will suffer because of impoverished resourcing.

The third issue to raise is that if collegiality is to be more widely accepted and adopted then it needs to be more thoroughly discussed. Before we rush into collegial ways a more sophisticated understanding needs to be developed. At present we only have the advocates' word that it works well. Surely we need further research data and case studies, since only then can we examine in detail the tensions between headship, leadership and collegiality. At present we need to regard both leadership and collegiality as invitations to enquiry, not as a rhetoric of conclusion (Eisner 1985).

References

ALEXANDER, R. J. (1984). *Primary Teaching*, Holt, Rinehart & Winston, London.

BLENKIN, G. M. and KELLY, A. V. (1981). *The Primary Curriculum*, Harper & Row, London.

BLYTH, W. A. L. and DERRICOTT, R. (1977). *The Social Significance of Middle Schools*, Batsford, London.

BUSH, T. (1981). 'Key roles in school management', in Open University (1981), *Policy-making organisation and leadership in school*, E323, Block, 4, Part 3, Open University Press, Milton Keynes, p. 84.

CAMPBELL, R. (1985). *Developing the Primary School Curriculum*, Holt, Rinehart and Winston, London.

COULSON, A. A. (1976). 'Leadership function in primary schools', in *Educational Administration*, 5(1) pp. 37–48.

COULSON, A. A. (1980). 'The role of the primary head', in BUSH, T. *et al* (eds), (1980), *Approaches to School Management*, Harper & Row, London.

COULSON, A. A. (1985). 'Recruitment and management development for primary headship', *School Organization*, vol. 5, no. 2, pp. 111–123.

DEARDEN, R. (1968). *Philosophy of Primary Education: An Introduction*, Routledge & Kegan Paul, London.

DES (1977). *Ten Good Schools*, HMSO, London.

DES (1978). *Primary Education in England: A Survey by HM Inspectors of Schools*, HMSO, London.

DES (1982). *Education 5 to 9: an Illustrative Survey of 80 First Schools in England*, HMSO, London.

DES (1983). Circular 3/83.

DES (1984). *Parental Influence at School*, Cmnd 9242, HMSO, London.

DES (1985). *Better Schools*, Cmnd 9469, HMSO, London.

DES Welsh Office (1985). *Leadership in Primary Schools: HMI (Wales) Occasional Paper*, HMSO, Cardiff.

DES (1985). Circular 3/85.

DERRICOTT, R. (1985). *Curriculum Continuity: primary to secondary*, NFER-Nelson, Windsor.

EISNER, E. W. (1985). 'Emerging models for educational evaluation', in EISNER, E. W., *The Art of Educational Evaluation: A Personal View*, Falmer, London, p. 71.

FULLAN, M. (1982). *The Meaning of Educational Change*, Teachers College Press, Columbia Univ., New York.

HANDY, C. B. (1984). *Taken for Granted? Looking at Schools as Organisations*, Schools Council Programme 1, Longmans/Schools Council, York.

HARGREAVES, D. (1973). 'Do we need headteachers?' in *Education 3–13*.

HERZBERG, F. (1966). *Work and the Nature of Man*, World Publishing Co., New York.

ILEA (1985). *Improving Primary Schools*, Report of the Committee on Primary Education, ILEA, London.

KING, R. (1983). *The Sociology of School Organisation*, Methuen, London.

LANCASHIRE EDUCATION AUTHORITY (1980). Job Description for Scale Post Holder, Lancashire Mimeo.

McGREGOR, D. (1960). *The Human Side of Enterprise*, McGraw-Hill, New York.

McMAHON, A. *et al* (1984). *Guidelines for Review and Internal Development in Schools: Primary School Handbook (GRIDS)*, Schools Council Programme 1, Longmans/Schools Council, York.

NAGM (National Association of Governors and Managers) (1981). 'The role of the chairman', Paper No. 17, NAGM Secretary, Sheffield.

OLDROYD, D. (1984). 'School-based staff development: lessons from Canada', in *School Organisation*, vol. 4, no. 1, pp. 35–40.

PACKWOOD, T. (1984). 'The introduction of staff responsibility for subject development in a junior school', in GOULDING S., *et al* (1984), *Case Studies in Educational Management*, Harper & Row, London, pp. 85–98.

RICHARDSON, T. E. (1975). *The Teacher, the School and the Task of Management*, Heinemann, London, p. 96.

SALLIS, J. (1982). *The Effective School Governor: a Guide to the Practice of School Government*, Advisory Centre for Education, London. 2nd ed.

SHAW, K. E. (1983). 'Rationality, experience and theory', in *Educational Management and Administration*, 11(3), pp. 167–172.

SMALL, N. (1984). 'A scandal of particularity? Headship in the 1980s', conference paper BEMAS conference, Cambridge 1984.

SOUTHWORTH, G. W. (1984). 'Development of staff in primary schools: some ideas and implications', in *British Journal of In-Service Education*, vol. 10, no. 3, pp. 6–15.

SOUTHWORTH, G. W. (1985a). The role of the primary deputy head – unpublished data collection of 50 headteachers' views: 1983–5.

SOUTHWORTH, G. W. (1985b). 'Primary Heads' Reflection on Training', in *Education*, vol. 165, no. 25, p. 560.

SOUTHWORTH, G. W. (1985c). 'Perspectives on the primary curriculum', in *Cambridge Journal of Education*, vol. 15, no. 1, pp. 41–49.

SOUTHWORTH, G. W. (1985d). 'Further perspectives on the primary curriculum', in Cambridge Journal of Education, vol. 15, no. 3.

SUFFOLK EDUCATION AUTHORITY (1985). 'Those having torches: teacher appraisal: a study'.

WHITAKER, P. (1983). *The Primary Head*, Heinemann, London.

WINKLEY, D. (1984). 'Educational management and school leadership: an evolutionary perspective', in HARLING, P., (ed.), *New Directions in Educational Leadership*, Falmer Press, London, pp. 205–22.

1.4

The role of the middle manager in the secondary school

Peter Ribbins

Introduction

Do secondary schools need middle managers? If so, how many and of what kind? Since the fifties successive salary settlements have enabled more and more teachers to receive extra payments for carrying 'additional responsibilities'. But what these are and how they ought to be discharged has rarely been given precise definition and the need for *heads of subject* and *pastoral leaders* has been assumed rather than justified (see Ribbins 1985, 1986).

This chapter will examine ideas about the role of the middle manager within the secondary school. This is a topic which has attracted increasing attention in public and academic debate, far too much of which has treated the concept of 'role' itself as unproblematic.

The concepts of 'role' and 'role structure'

As Morgan and Turner (1976) have put it, 'the way in which people should and do behave in organisations, is frequently explained by role theory . . . the concept of role has been a pervasive one in administrative theory. There is a plethora of papers and also some severe critics' (p. 8). A major problem lies in the fact that the meaning given to 'role' and 'role structure' varies according to the sociological paradigm within which they are located.

In commonsense usage, the term 'role' is often taken to mean a designated *position* (e.g. 'head of house') within a *structure* of positions (e.g. 'house'). For the organisational theorist a role is more than just a position in a structure; it is the behaviours associated with it which those in other positions expect the role incumbent to engage in. Roles are therefore defined in the relationships between positions in a structure expressed in the behaviours considered appropriate rather than merely in the designated positions themselves.

Adherents of the functionalist perspective tend to emphasise the needs of the organisation as determining its role structure and therefore the behaviour of its members. From such a perspective, the organised, consensual character of the school is stressed, with particular teacher or pupil roles being reduced to a network of inter-related, articulated and coherent set of behaviours maintained by shared norms and by publicly agreed expectations involving high levels of prescription.

All this would seem to leave little room for conflict. Yet some degree of role strain and conflict appears to be a pervasive part of everyday life within all kinds of social groups. How is this to be explained? First, what is 'role strain' and 'role conflict'? Briefly, role strain may be thought of as the tensions which an individual role incumbent experiences as a result of some form of role conflict. Both concepts are closely tied to the notion of 'expectation' and, it must be said, are often used as if they were interchangeable. Thus Peeke (1983) suggests that: 'Role strain occurs when expectations are contradicted or actors do not hold expectations in common' (p. 226) and Morgan and Turner (1976) argue that: 'Role conflict refers to the incompatibility in the demands and expectations a role incumbent faces' (p. 8).

Hargreaves (1972) identifies eight sources of role conflict which Peeke (1983) lists as follows:

1 Where an actor simultaneously occupies two positions whose roles are incompatible.
2 Where there is a lack of consensus amongst the occupants of a position about the content of a role.
3 Where there is a lack of consensus amongst the occupants of one of the complementary role positions.
4 Where an actor's conception of his role conflicts with the expectations of a role partner.
5 Where various role partners have conflicting expectations.
6 Where a single role partner has incompatible expectations.
7 Where role expectations are unclear.
8 Where an actor lacks basic qualities required for adequate role performance.
  (p. 226)

Since Hargreaves was writing from an essentially interactionist perspective we might well expect the notion of role conflict to play a significant part in any account of interpersonal relations which he offers. However, some level of role conflict, may also be explained within a functionalist approach. It must be remembered that the model of social life upon which it is based is essentially an 'ideal type'. In practice some degree of variation always exists in the ways in which people play the roles they are allotted. Possible reasons for such variation include: imperfections within the culture, structure and methods of socialisation which exist within organisations; the fact that individuals within organisations perceive the expectations as to the particular roles they are filling with a greater or lesser degree of accuracy; because, as Morgan and Turner (1976) argue, 'Freedom of individual action is partly preserved by the large degree of latitude to many roles, where the powerful expectations are of prohibition rather than prescription' (p. 7). The idea of 'continuums' of 'compulsion' are further developed by Silverman (1970), who distinguishes between 'must', 'should' and 'could' prescriptions, and by Schein (1965) who differentiates between the 'pivotal', 'relevant' and 'peripheral' norms or attributes relevant to a particular role.

Morgan and Turner (1976) identify three main forms of role conflict: conflict between roles; conflict within a role; and conflict within a *role set*. Woodland (1979) distinguishes two levels at which an individual may experience role conflict 'first, within his own body of roles, and second between his own roles and those of other actors' (p. 161). Two examples of the former are identified. First, if there is a discrepancy between ego's perception of his role and his perception of his actual behaviour, this could have harmful effects on his self image (p. 161). Best *et al* (1983) discuss just such a case in their account of the conflicts experienced by Mrs Chalmers during her probationary year at Rivendell (pp. 142–147). Second, conflict can also occur when an individual 'perceives some incompatibility between performing certain prescriptions of one of his roles and carrying out those of another of his roles' (Woodland 1979, p. 161). Once again, Mrs Chalmers offers a case in point as she struggled to meet what she saw as the conflicting demands of her role as a tutor with those of her role as a teacher.

Conflict, as Woodland (1979) argues, 'may arise at a second level when the way ego perceives his role differs from the definition of his role by the occupants in counter positions' (p. 161). This form of conflict was the subject of research by Gross *et al* (1958) whose work 'represents a major attempt to measure how the actor actually defines his role and the extent of consensus in such role definitions between different role occupants' (Woodland 1979, p. 162). This study of the role of the school superintendent is concerned with both *intrapositional* consensus (agreement on role definition between holders of similar roles) and *interpositional* consensus (agreement on role definition between different positions within the role set). Gross also offers an analysis of the means of resolving role conflict in which the player of a particular role 'chooses, avoids or compromises between conflicting expectations of other actors in terms of how legitimate he perceives these expectations to be, how strong he perceives the sanctions against his nonconformity to these expectations to be, and whether he gives priority to the sanctions or the legitimacy of the expectations, or compromises between the two'.

Morgan and Turner (1976) take 'an essentially *structural* conception of role, which asserts that individuals occupy organisational offices and social positions, to which are attached constraining expectations and demands' (however) 'in spite of the pervasive influence of other people's expectations, the role player retains substantial opportunity for choice in his role performance . . . Role theory in our view does not of necessity provide a deterministic and conforming view of behaviour . . .' (p. 13). As regards the usefulness of 'role theory', they suggest that:

1 Role theory offers a useful tool of analysis through which to identify the set of expectations associated with a particular status position;
2 it also conceptualises the elements, systematic and personal, which constitute a status position;
3 in its deployment of role conflict, it incorporates the 'problem' of lack of consensus among varying expectations of the holder of a particular status position.

The relevance of these ideas to the study and practice of educational management is the specific concern of a paper by Burnham (1969). Although a brief reference is made to the interactionist ideas of Turner (1969), in his analysis Burnham also adopts a functionalist approach. In this analysis 'the concepts of role and role expectation provide one way of thinking about administrative behaviour. In this sense, administration can be seen as the process of defining, allocating and integrating roles and personnel to maximise the probability of achieving the goals of the organisations' (p. 202). As applied to the head of a contemporary comprehensive school:

> The genius of administration, according to Nolte (1966) lies in this endless process of diagnosing, defining, classifying and interpreting roles, in the context of an intimate knowledge of the personalities of a large and varied staff. It is a competency which requires to be based in a clear understanding of the social and educational goals of the institution, a thorough analysis of the jobs to be done, and a perceptive awareness of the interests, skills and idiosyncrasies of the staff. (p. 204).

Much the same may be said of the middle manager.

Best *et al* (1983) discuss the attractions of an alternative conception of role which is based on an *interactionist* perspective. They stress that the formal structure of roles that exist in schools such as Rivendell may be viewed both as a 'social fact', with an objective reality over and above any individual teacher's perception of it, and, in an important sense, as existing only in the conceptions which teachers hold of it and in the recognition they give to it. To fail to take account of this is 'to ignore the dynamic aspect of role-play as teachers negotiate the complexities of their professional and personal lives on a day-to-day basis' (p. 53). Role incumbents do not just 'step into' a role. Rather:

> as Symbolic Interactionists have been at pains to point out, roles are also . . . the product of interaction between social actors. Each 'role incumbent' is active in construing the roles he 'plays', and in the interpersonal negotiation which characterises interaction between roles. To some extent this is a question of the *interpretation* of formal role expectations such that it is possible to talk of the *style* with which the individual meets them, but it may also be a matter of intentional variation and redefinition of the formal role by the actor himself.
>
> (Best *et al* 1983)

As Turner (1969) points out, social actors do not merely 'take' roles as they are presented to them, but actively 'make' them what they are. Furthermore, even if an actor does appear to 'take on' a role, this does not explain why he does so.

Functionalists would point to the 'fact' that such behaviours are 'functional' to the needs of the organisation but other explanations may be equally plausible. For example, Goffman (1977) argues that adequate role-play often requires an actor to 'present a front' and for his fellow actors collectively to 'sustain a front'. But such an actor may meet the formal requirements of the role he is playing in two ways. Thus, Goffman distinguishes between *role commitment* (a situation in which he accepts the formal requirements of the role as ones he must meet but in which he does not much value his role performace as a person) and *role-attachment* (a situation in which he identifies his role performance with his own values and his own needs as a person). Goffman uses the term 'role distance' to describe the situation in which an actor plays the role adequately but in a more-or-less offhand manner.

For all these reasons there will be differences between the formal designation of roles within an organisation and the way in which those roles are actually perceived and 'played'. Moreover, as Hargreaves (1972) has shown, the officially designated roles are by no means the only roles to be found in schools. On the contrary, there are a host of ascribed, achieved or confirmed *informal roles* which are an important part of the social structure of the school. As Best *et al* (1983) conclude, 'the structure of officially designated roles is one thing, but the reality in practice may be something else altogether' (p. 54).

But Best *et al* (1983) also recognise that:

> it is tempting to exaggerate the degree of freedom which the individual can exercise over the shape of his role. This is especially true where roles are institutionalised in formal organisations like the school . . . The reality is of a dynamic, complex and often tense relationship between the free and rational actor on the one hand and the formal structure of role expectations on the other. (p. 54).

From this perspective a satisfactory explanation of the academic, the pastoral, etc. provision of a school must approach its caring or curricular systems as both social facts external to, and constraining the role incumbent's behaviour, and as the subjective interpretation and negotiation of role which individual actors make. It must also be seen as the product of an ongoing interaction between *both* these sets of 'realities'. Best *et al* (1983) illustrate this point with reference to an account of three successive regimes of heads at Rivendell (Chapter 8) and also by examining the ways in which different pairs of teachers played what were ostensibly the same role. In doing so they explore,

> how different teachers responded in very different ways to the relationship between personal fulfilment and formal role expectation and the varying degrees of 'attachment' and 'commitment' which characterized their role play . . . how role-performance is to some extent dependent upon the 'perspectives' which teachers adopt on their sub-roles and the ideologies which seem to underlie them or which they are in the process of constructing as they work out the more or less tense encounters which make up their daily life. (p. 142)

With these theoretical frameworks in mind, what can we learn from the literature of the role of the academic and pastoral middle manager?

The role of the pastoral and academic middle manager

No attempt will be made to offer a comprehensive review of the growing literature dealing with the role of the middle manager within the secondary school.
Rather, a number of topics will be identified and discussed which might serve to
illustrate the scope and character of 'what we know' on this topic.

Marland (1981), who has done as much as any writer to shape our thinking
about the role of the middle manager within the comprehensive school, argues
that 'their function is unique to this country, and is a clear practical demonstration of the philosophy of the devolved system of educational responsibility in
Britain' (p. 1). The way this devolution has effected the nature of the school can
be summed up as follows:

1 The UK school is largely autonomous, and therefore its structure, procedure, curriculum and counselling can be devised within the school . . .
2 The professional career structure and additional payments see promotion clearly as
related to further *responsibility* . . .
3 Administration and pedagogy are fused . . .
4 The head of department (or of house etc.) is regarded as a senior member of the
overall leadership and planning of the school. (p. 1)

We should, he holds, relish such a system. But, if we cannot make good use of the
opportunities it allows, then perhaps we would be better off 'with an educational
system that retains all significant decision making outside the school' (p. 2).

In this context, several writers suggest that how these 'opportunities' might be
construed is subject, in part at least, to interpretations which have varied over
time. Before turning to this issue it might be helpful to be clear about what is
entailed, logically, by the notion of a department and of a head of department.
Bailey (1981) is one of the few to attempt to do this. He holds that:

In principle, a department begins to exist (1) when two or more teachers begin to teach
a subject formerly taught by one; (2) when those teachers begin to co-ordinate their
work so that together they can perform tasks which no one of them could perform
singly; and (3) when, however informally, one teacher begins to lead and another to
follow. (p. 106)

Departments, then, may be said to exist only where deliberate *collaboration* takes
place, enabling an exchange of ideas and knowledge and facilitating some specialisation of task through various divisions of labour. By such criteria, the 'departments' and 'heads of department' of the pre-comprehensive era hardly qualify.
As Bayne-Jardine and Hanham (1972) point out, the circumstances of these
schools differed greatly from that of the modern comprehensive and in the
subject departments which developed within them there was little emphasis on
the notion of the 'team'. Heads of department tended to be appointed for their
seniority and their skills as a subject teacher, and not for any perceived managerial skills or aptitudes. Holt (1981) argues that while 'all this is far removed
from the assumptions of the contemporary comprehensive school . . . yet . . .
however noble our curriculum intentions might be, the formal structure of the

typical comprehensive school curriculum bears more than a passing resemblance to that of the grammar school from which it was derived . . . (and it is) still possible for the insular-minded department head to follow historical precedent, to run his own show, and leave the members of his department to run theirs'. As Best *et al* (1983) show, much the same kind of comment can be made of the pastoral head.

Bayne-Jardine (1981) stresses the necessity of analysing the ways in which heads of department have responded to 'match their *historical* role with changes in both organisations of schools and subject matter' (p. 38). He describes a number of *pathologies*, first identified by Hoyle (1969), which 'give an interesting insight into the way that the working of a subject department and curriculum development can be rendered difficult by the unquestioning acceptance of an ill-defined or inappropriate role'. These pathologies include the 'ritualist' (who hides behind detail), the 'neurotic' (who worries ineffectually about problems of carrying theory into practice), and the 'robber baron' (who is mainly concerned with 'increasing his territory', creating an image of efficiency and innovation, and achieving promotion rather than in developing the members of his 'team').

A number of attempts have also been made to present a history of pastoral care (Lang 1984; Ribbins and Best 1985) and Blackburn (1983b) identifies three main phases which he caricatures as follows:

> In phase 1 concern was for developing minds in healthy bodies . . . phase 2 was concerned with providing individual guidance to pupils as they passed through the system and with mopping up the casualties . . . phase 3 is concerned with involving pupils in a range of learning processes within groups designed to enable them to cope more effectively. (p. 20)

In attempting to meet this growing list of responsibilities:

> so the possibility of the pastoral head becoming the chief carer . . . has become unrealistic. He has to work through the team of tutors. From 'super tutor' he has to move to the role of managing the work of the members of his team. This transition has to take place very often without anyone declaring that there has been a change in expectations of what is to be achieved and without any in-service training being offered to help the pastoral head identify the skills and methods that he will now have to acquire for success.

In *Head of House, Head of Year*, Blackburn (1983a) offers a number of examples of the roles and responsibilities that particular schools (Altwood, Crown Woods, North Westminster, Sidney Stringer and Stantonbury) expect of their pastoral teams and pastoral heads which demonstrates just how wide-ranging and complex are the tasks and skills involved. He also quotes a list of *18* duties of a head of house or year taken from an advisory document produced by the Lancashire County Council. This formidable catalogue includes such tasks as:

> 4 To co-ordinate supervisory responsibility of staff and pupils on duty. 5 To know pupils in the year as well as possible, and to become accepted as a person to whom they can turn for guidance . . . 6 To have a watching brief over the academic progress of pupils . . . 7 To co-ordinate the keeping of written records of individual children . . .

10 To arrange meetings with parents . . . 11 To liaise closely with other services . . . (p. 18).

Finally, Blackburn (1983a) offers a useful diagrammatic representation of what he sees as the six main areas of responsibility to be exercised by the pastoral head (aims and roles; planning, organisation and evaluation; the pastoral curriculum; casework; parents; staff support) and the six main methods he or she must learn to use (one-to-one contact; staff meetings; induction; in-service training; record-keeping; work with pupils) in which 'each "area" interlocks with each "method" ' (pp. 39, 40).

Such intimidating catalogues of responsibility are not restricted to the pastoral task. The prescriptive literature dealing with the subject department and the head of department fully reflects Dunham's (1978) judgement that 'when a school is reorganised into the comprehensive system the role (of the head of department) is changed so much that it is probably misleading to retain the same name for it' (p. 11). This change was recognised by HMI in the early 1960s. What was taking place, they suggested, was a 'new concept of relationship' between heads and heads of department and between members of a department. These changes entailed a wide range of duties for the head of department which they listed under the following five headings: curriculum; supervision of staff; organisation of the department; communications; and finance (discussed in Siddle 1978). Siddle takes the view that:

> Although written for the guidance of HMIs during the 1960s, the general job specifications provided under the five headings appear from the observations of the author to be relevant today. (p. 6)

Many of these functions do, in fact, appear in more recent accounts. Hall and Thomas (1977) suggest a classification of the functions of the head of department under the headings of 'managerial' (related to the management and control of all aspects of the work of the department), 'representative' (the school to the department and the department to the school), and 'academic' (all aspects of teaching the subject). Ogilvie and Bartlett (1979), in the context of a comparison between departmental heads in Australia and England, suggest that despite superficial differences:

> Bailey's (1973) grouping of the traditional functions of the subject master is very similar to Hall and Thomas and might usefully be modified to: (a) academic (to know his subject, to keep himself up to date) (b) representative (to represent his subject in the school) and (c) managerial (to plan, teach and resource courses and evaluate pupils). (p. 3).

Bailey (1973) goes on to argue that the growth of the large comprehensive school has meant that heads of department have had to take on further responsibilities under the following *four* headings: staff control; pupil control; resource control; and communication.

The report by Hall and Thomas (1977) focuses primarily on the role of the head of the maths department and, as such, is one of a number of such studies which are concerned with the role of heads of particular subjects. Examples of these are

Siddle's (1978) wide-ranging monograph on the role of the head of science and Raleigh's (1983) book on the English department which, although 'addressed to every member of the English department . . . will be most useful to the new or inexperienced heads of department' (David 1983 p. 25). Yet other studies, although not focusing on the role of the head of department as such, have useful things to say about it. A notable example of this is the Cockcroft Report (1982) on the teaching of maths. In this report the role of the head of maths is given great significance:

> We consider that, among heads of department, the head of mathematics has a task which can be especially difficult and demanding . . . Unless he or she provides positive and sustained leadership and direction for the maths department it will not operate as effectively as it might do and the pupils will be correspondingly disadvantaged. (p. 154).

The list of duties for which the head of maths should take responsibility includes:

> the production and up-dating of suitable schemes of work;
> the organisation of the department and its teaching resources;
> the monitoring of the teaching within the department and of the work and assessment of pupils;
> playing a full part in the professional development and in-service training of those who teach maths;
> liaison with other departments in the school and with other schools and colleges in the area. (p. 154).

Finally, there are studies of the role of the head of department which, although they do not focus explicitly on a particular subject do, as a matter of fact, tend to offer examples drawn particularly from one subject. Perhaps the best example of this is to be found in Marland's (1971) early study of *The Head of Department*, in which the writer makes good use of his experience as a head of English in two large comprehensive schools.

Marland (1971; 1974; 1981; 1983) has written extensively on the role of both the pastoral and academic middle manager. To do justice to the range of his ideas is beyond the scope of this chapter, but since he offers his own summary of the *ten* tasks which may be expected of a head of department, we may quote that instead:

1 Structure a departmental team . . . to create a cogent internal structure
2 Take a major part in appointing teachers
3 Deploy teachers . . . consistent with their strengths and weaknesses and their career development – as well as fulfilling the needs of the school
4 Monitor teachers' work
5 Assist the development of teachers' professional skills . . .
6 Contribute to the initial training of student teachers
7 Take a part in the planning of the school's overall curriculum, and lead the planning of the curriculum within the department
8 Oversee the work of pupils . . .
9 Manage the finances, physical resources and learning methods efficiently
10 Assist in the overall leadership of the school.

                                                            (Marland 1981, p. 2)

Although the kind of view of the role of the middle manager discussed thus far has been very influential, it has not gone unchallenged. For a number of years Best *et al* (1977; 1980; 1983) have questioned whether such accounts too often tend to confuse what ought to happen with what does, in that despite the growth of interest in the topic, far too little systematic, empirical or theoretical research has taken place. Thus, in particular, there are very few ethnographies which focus on the activities of the middle manager in the context of particular schools. Other critics have suggested that we do not really know much about what expectations middle managers have of their roles or what others in schools expect of them (Lambert 1975). Yet others have argued that the kinds of expectations to be found in much of the literature are utopian and/or involve a conception of the middle manager as 'paragon' (Thomas 1983). To be fair, many of the accounts discussed thus far do contain reservations that acknowledge that things may not always be as they ought to be. What do these reservations amount to?

As long ago as the early 1960s, HMI recognised that 'there are wide variations in the extent to which department heads are exercising their responsibilities. In some cases inadequate action is the result of failure to appreciate the extent to which responsibilities have multiplied and increased in importance but this is often accompanied by a traditional reluctance to interfere with the professional work of one's colleagues' (quoted in Siddle 1978, p. 4). Many commentators emphasise the importance of control, supervision and the monitoring of the work of departmental staff as a key, even *the* key, function of the middle manager (Bailey 1973; Blackburn 1983 a and b; Marland 1981). This view is expressed particularly forcefully in Cockcroft (1982):

> We regard it as an essential part of the work of the head of department to be aware of the quality of teaching which is going on within the department . . . In our view it should be the normal practice for the head of department to visit lessons given by other members of department.

This may well be correct, but it is almost equally widely recognised that this is an aspect of their work which causes many heads of department great role strain. Bailey (1973) comments that heads of department 'have often to be persuaded to take charge of their departments', and Siddle (1978) concludes that:

> Heads of science are generally reluctant to supervise their departmental colleagues by assigning tasks, supervising their performance, recognising good performance and criticizing poor performance, correcting mistakes or resolving difficulties in the fashion of a good quality controller . . . They much preferred to adopt a laissez-faire attitude (p. 13)

The evidence available suggests that such attitudes are commonly shared by heads of other subject departments (Hall and Thomas 1977) and by pastoral heads (Best *et al* 1983). While this is an important source of role conflict, there are others as well.

Dunham's (1978) survey of 92 heads of department suggests that the middle managers of today face a greater possibility of stress and role conflict than did their historical predecessors. In a chapter in his latest book dealing with *Stress in*

Teaching, Dunham (1984) considers the pressures on middle managers in the contemporary secondary school as compared with those experienced by their predecessors:

> One major change has resulted in departmental heads becoming involved in management responsibilities . . . while still being required to carry a heavy teaching load . . . (and of) the pressures on Pastoral Care heads arising from their wide range of duties . . . as well as having to teach for some of the week. (p. 75)

The result was that some of his sample spoke of frustration leading to indifference, to depression, to demoralisation and to a withdrawal from responsibility, and others expressed real anxiety associated with considerable role confusion. The consequences of these stresses were manifest in tiredness, physical ailments, psychosomatic illness and sickness (Dunham 1978, p. 46). Bloomer (1980) summarises the findings of three series of workshops of teachers and others drawn from a wide range of institutions to investigate 'what sort of functions a head of department should have' (p. 1). Four sets of reasons why departmental organisation in schools is less efficient than it might be are distinguished as follows:

1 The organisational problems have become greater in the last twenty years . . .
2 Modern democratic styles . . . While they may well lead to an enrichment of school work also call for greater skills and adaptability in heads of department.
3 There is ambiguity as to the definition of the role of heads of department. Detailed contracts are rare, and most heads of department learn their role 'on the job' through their perceptions of what other heads of department do and the expectations of head teachers.
4 Training for the work of management in schools . . . is comparatively rare . . . (pp. 2–3)

While Bloomer (1980) found a 'considerable degree of consensus amongst workshop members', he also acknowledges that Lambert's (1975) research paints a different picture. Lambert set out to examine 'what heads of department and Heads saw as the role functions of heads of department, and to see if there was any evidence of potential role conflict between the perceptions of heads of department and the role expectations of heads' (p. 29). A four-fold typology of role functions is employed, based upon a division between *instrumental* (task-centred) and *expressive* (person-centred) functions and a second division between *academic* and *institutional* functions:

1 'Instrumental—academic' (e.g. the development and carrying out of school policy; the formulation of departmental policy; curriculum development).
2 'Instrumental—institutional' (e.g. choice of text books, deployment of staff).
3 'Expressive–institutional' (e.g. links with outside agencies and with parents; extra-curricular activities; departmental report for the head).
4 'Expressive—academic' (e.g. assisting new staff; supervising and monitoring staff).

Lambert (1975), summarises his findings on each of these role functions as in table 1.4.1

Only on the 'instrumental–academic' is there a high level of agreement between heads of department, between heads, and between the heads of department and heads. The overall index of agreement is particularly low on the set of items dealing with 'expressive–academic' functions but even these low figures mask the reluctance of heads of department to supervise and monitor their colleagues as against the high level of expectations shared amongst heads that this was a function that heads of department should perform. These findings are supported in a more recent piece of research by Howson and Woolnough (1982) in which it is reported that, when heads of department and heads were asked to rank in order of importance 15 representative tasks, heads of department placed 'assessing the teaching competence of staff in the department as low as 13th whereas heads ranked it 7th'.

Table 1.4.1 Summary of the four role-functional areas (from Lambert 1975, p. 36)

Area	Heads of Dept	Heads	Indices of Agreement
Instrumental–academic	85%	92%	0.93
Instrumental–institutional	66%	80%	0.82
Expressive–institutional	50%	62%	0.81
Expressive–academic	67%	89%	0.75

Lambert (1975) concludes that 'the expressive-academic area would seem to be the area which was likely to be the source of possible role conflict . . . that the expressive areas are the danger areas . . . In present practice there appears to be an assumption of a consensus of opinion on the role-functions of the head of department which the survey did not seem to justify' (p. 37). In commenting on these findings, Marland (1975) remarks that 'the conflict is not only between the Head and the head of department, but also between the subject teachers and their supposed leaders' (p. 38). He also suggests that 'by the early 1970s the expected duties of the holder of such a post were fairly well known, even if not always met' (p. 38).

Amongst the solutions to the problems which middle managers face, two are widely canvassed. First, that there 'is a need for an element of clearer role-definition within schools' (Lambert 1975, p. 37) from which it follows that 'every school must draw up an agreed job specification' (Marland 1975, p. 39) for its middle managers, a view shared by the Committee on the Curriculum and Organisation of Secondary Schools of the ILEA, in its report on *Improving Secondary Schools* (the Hargreaves Report, ILEA 1984). In the section dealing with the head of department two recommendations are made, one of which is that '*Headteachers* ensure that all heads of departments have clear job specifications' (p. 103). Ogilvie and Bartlett (1979) warn that although the potential for role conflict exists, necessitating clear role-definition, 'this might be achieved by more detailed job descriptions but is more likely to be achieved through regular professional discussions . . . so that expectations are clarified and consensus reached regarding these expectations' (p. 6). Second, that more attention should be given to the training needs of middle managers who have all too often in the past, had to learn 'on the job' or by 'trial and error'. Some areas such as the ILEA have faced special problems. Thus the Hargreaves Report comments that while 'most heads were unstinting in their praise of their effective heads of department . . . not all heads of departments were carrying out their functions as well as they should be.' This weakness at the level of middle management 'dates mainly from the early and mid-1970s when the steep rise in house prices and the near impossibility of obtaining adequate reasonably priced rented accommodation' drove aspiring young potential middle managers out of London and discouraged experienced teachers from coming to London. This meant that 'there are schools which are still suffering the effects of unsuitable appointments made at the time' (p. 102). Part of the solution is to offer more training opportunities:

> Since 1980 the ILEA has taken active steps to mitigate this state of affairs by offering a wide range of courses in management training. During 1982–83 115 teachers (from 79 schools) attended these courses, 74 of whom were heads of departments and 41 were pastoral heads. The course agendas now relate closely to the work of schools, and include school visits, the exchange of ideas and experiences between course participants, and practical work. (pp. 102, 103).

The training opportunities for teachers holding posts of middle-management responsibility have significantly increased over the last few years and there are now some very impressive short courses to be found, such as the DES Regional Course 'Middle Management in the Secondary School' run at the University of Nottingham with Derbyshire, Lincolnshire and Nottinghamshire. However, while there has clearly been some improvement in the training opportunities available it must still be said that, given the number of teachers who carry middle-management responsibilities, this has only just begun to scratch the surface of what is necessary. Such provision as is available is also unevenly distributed in various ways. Marland (1983) summarising the available evidence, suggests that as far as training opportunities are concerned, the pastoral head may be even worse off than the subject head:

> Whereas the aspiring head of department has had an initial training in the appropriate specialism, and usually had some inservice support or further training in the specialism, the aspiring head of house/year had usually been expected to 'pick it up' as she or he goes along. (p. 25)

Just how limited are the training opportunities available to those with pastoral responsibilities is confirmed by Maher and Best (1984). However, in his paper 'Preparing for Promotion in Pastoral Care', Marland (1983) does make a number of suggestions as to the kinds of knowledge and skills that the aspiring pastoral middle manager should seek to acquire and how to go about obtaining them.

Since the beginning of the 1970s the role of the middle manager within the secondary school has received increasing attention and we know a good deal more than we did about the kinds of conflicting expectations and ambiguities of role which confront those who take up such responsibilities. What we still know very little about is what middle managers actually do, how they account for their actions, and how they interact with 'relevant others' within particular schools. To explore these kinds of issues a quite different approach to the study of such middle management is necessary: one which adopts an interactionist conception of role and a broadly ethnographic methodology.

This is not to say that there have been no interactionist studies which have touched upon the activities of middle managers in the secondary school. Both Hargreaves (1967; 1972) and, especially, Lacey (1970) do consider this topic; and not all they have had to say is particularly reassuring. Lacey (1970), for example, suggests that many heads of department at Hightown regarded their duties as 'chores' or as stepping stones to further advancement. Like the work of Lacey and Hargreaves, Richardson's (1973) study of Nailsea is based on long and painstaking field research. As Siddle (1978) acknowledges, an issue such as, for example how far a head of department is free to make decisions without seeking the approval of a superior 'is impossible to assess without embarking upon the type of investigation undertaken by Richardson . . .' (p. 10). Certainly we can learn much from Richardson's report about the extent and nature of the power of different departments and heads of department and of the ways in which they act and interact. Her account of the modern languages, and especially the science, departments as 'the "giant" departments able to make their own conditions regardless of changes elsewhere in the system – almost, at times, to be holding the staff to ransom' (p. 90) is particularly revealing.

More recently, two in-depth case studies of comprehensive schools located in the South-East ('Rivendell' by Best *et al* 1983) and in the Midlands ('Bishop McGregor' by Burgess 1983) represent a welcome return to the traditions of the approach used so tellingly in the study of 'Lumley Secondary Modern' (Hargreaves 1967) and 'Hightown Grammar' (Lacey 1970) in the late 1960s. None of these studies focus primarily on the role of the middle manager, but they all examine the roles of various middle managers both in the context of the institutionalised sets of prescriptions and expectations that, taken as a whole, make up the formal structure of the school and also in terms of the interpersonal interactions of the individuals who sustain these structures. For as McGuiness (1984) recognises, such 'systems are not cold, clinical machines. The human beings who operate within them can make an inadequate system surprisingly effective – equally, the uncommitted or the incompetent can foul up the best of systems' (p. 152). What these studies also have in common, is a desire to offer detailed explanations of the various ways in which the patterns of the perception and actions of middle managers holding a variety of roles are determined by their personal needs and are shaped by the interactions of those who fill them with senior staff, other middle managers, and other staff.

In the nature of things it is difficult to offer brief illustrations of the kinds of insights into the role of the middle manager which such an approach provides, as the researcher focuses 'on the way in which the school *actually* worked in contrast to the ways in which different teachers thought it *should* work' (Burgess 1983,

p. 84). Best *et al* (1983) too, seek to explore a 'serious mismatch between *theory* and *reality* at a number of levels' with respect to the provision of care at Rivendell:

> at the level of what the 'conventional wisdom' says pastoral care is/ought to be and what is actually happening in schools; at the level of the school's official pronouncements about pupils' welfare and what a school actually does about it; and at the level of what teachers claim to mean by 'pastoral care' and the day-to-day practices in which they actually engage. (p. 29).

In both Bishop McGregor and Rivendell the researchers found major differences in the ways in which different houses and subject departments operated. As Burgess (1983) comments of Bishop McGregor, 'each house and department held a position within the school which had initially been defined by the headmaster. However, the staff in these houses and departments quickly established their own patterns of activity, their own characteristics, and their own relationships with each other and with their pupils'. These differences are explored at some length in Burgess's description of the 'Newsom' department and of the struggle for power that took place within it as its teachers attempted to operate with no formally designated head but with 'an "unofficial, self-appointed head of department" and at least two major competitors for the role' (pp. 182–190). Burgess also stresses the extent to which the houses at McGregor were different and the degree to which such differences were explicable in terms of the attitudes and practices of their heads of house:

> individual house heads defined the school's activities in different ways. When the school opened house heads had taken the opportunity to establish their own distinctive pattern of work and routine. In letters that were sent out to parents, house heads . . . indicated differences in their aims, objectives and activities . . . In Westminster house, the aim was simply to form a link between the home and the school . . . in Southwark house, it was emphasised there would be social, educational and fund-raising activities . . . In Arundel there were to be regular house masses together with a variety of clubs and societies for house pupils . . . in Hexham . . . it was intended that direct links should be established with (the) diocese of Hexham. (p. 58)

In these, and many other, ways each house 'developed a distinct set of aims, routines, practices and activities' (pp. 57–60).

Best *et al*'s (1983) study of Rivendell explores largely similar issues. Thus, much of a long chapter on 'Identities' (pp. 139–187) looks closely 'at the *styles* with which teachers interpreted their roles . . . and at some of the sorts of role-conflict which they experienced' (p. 142). In doing this, attention is focused mainly on the way in which three pairs of middle managers interpreted their roles and at the sorts of role-conflict they met. This analysis tries to show how different teachers respond 'in very different ways to the relationship between personal fulfilment and formal role-expectations, and the varying degrees of "attachment" and "commitment" which characterise their role play'. (p. 142) [As noted earlier,] the study also seeks to show:

> how role performance is to some extent dependent upon the 'perspectives' which

teachers adopt on their sub roles and the ideologies which seem to underlie them or which they are in the process of constructing as they work out the more or less tense encounters which make up their daily life.

It is in such a description of 'the various ways in which particular individuals sought to come to terms with such tensions and work them out in their inter-action with other members of staff in a way which was institutionally acceptable and personally meaningful and rewarding' (p. 186) that it is possible to convey something of the flavour of what role play for the middle manager can mean.

As McGuiness (1984) remarks, studies such as these 'journey into a world of great interest and enormous complexity' (p. 151) in which the perceptions and actions of those involved are subjected to close and sustained examination over considerable periods of time using a case-study approach. Not that such an approach is free of difficulty. Amongst its 'problems' are the fact that it is very time-consuming and, inevitably, limited to a very restricted number of settings. This calls into question the typicality of the generalisations that are identified. This is certainly a serious problem, but Bassey (1981) suggests that what he terms 'open generalisations' which offer reliable predictions beyond the particu-lar case although 'obviously useful . . . are also scarce in number and . . . once these few have been mastered . . . they appear obvious and no longer valuable'. For the teacher 'closed generalisations can stimulate his thinking about possible lines of action and can alert him to possible consequences; it can also assist him in deciding what to do, but it cannot tell him' (p. 84). This being so, 'an important criterion for judging the merit of a case-study is the extent to which the details are sufficient and appropriate for a teacher working in a similar situation to relate his decision making to that described in the case-study. The relatability of a case-study is more important than its generalisability' (p. 85).

By the kinds of criteria entailed in the sort of enriched conception of role outlined above, most published studies of the role of the middle manager (and of the head as well) are seriously deficient in so far as they *decontextualise* role. This decontextualisation takes two main forms, which can be illustrated using the case of the middle manager. First, such roles are decontextualised in so far as they are considered in isolation from the whole set of managerial and other roles with which they commonly interact and which shape and constrain what is possible or desirable for those who fill them. Second, these roles are decontextualised in so far as they are considered out of the context of the particu-lar institutions within which they are, in practice, enacted. Whatever the merits of approaches which decontextualise in this way, there is a strong case for the use of an in-depth, comprehensive, case-study approach to the study of middle management in the secondary school. As far as I know no such studies have been published to date and no funded research project using such an approach is taking place at present.

Summary and conclusions

Limitations of space have necessitated some hard choices as to the issues which could be considered in this chapter. A fuller treatment would have given attention to a number of themes not discussed here including, for example, the growing debate over whether comprehensive schools need, or can afford, both a pastoral and an academic structure and heads of house/year as well as heads of department (see Best and Ribbins 1983 for a discussion of the arguments involved in the debate on the 'pastoral/academic split').

What has been emphasised is an attempt to identify aspects of the role of middle management within the contemporary school which are often taken for granted in much of the literature and to treat some of these aspects as problematic in themselves. [. . .] Some attempt has [. . .] been made to treat the concepts of 'role' and 'role structure' in [a] sceptical way and much of this critique focuses upon the two main alternative conceptions of role derived respectively from 'functionalist' and 'interactionist' frames of reference. Finally, the literature dealing with the role of the pastoral and the academic middle manager is reviewed briefly and a case made out in favour of subjecting these roles to a more interactionist approach than has been the norm to date. It is suggested that, whatever the limitations of such an approach, it would have the merit of avoiding the kind of 'decontextualising' assumptions implicit in traditional studies.

Finally, are schools over-complex and over-managed? And is the role of the middle manager really necessary? HM Inspectorate have had something to say on both these issues. Thus the Welsh Inspectorate suggest that 'The status of heads of department in Welsh secondary schools has diminished in recent years at the same time as their responsibilities have increased' (Lodge 1984, p. 9). The report also concludes that 'Whether a pupil achieves or underachieves is largely dependent on the quality of planning, execution, and evaluation that takes place within individual departments' (HMI (Wales) 1984). There is little reason to suppose that what is true of Wales and the subject head of department is not also true of England and of the pastoral head. HMI (1979) are also on record as taking the view that: 'No institution which seriously tried to respond to differences of need, capacity and interest among large numbers of adolescents could be other than complex. It is still possible to question whether the existing complexities fulfil their purpose; whether complexity is often greater than it need be . . .' (p. 267). Their answer is unequivocal and might serve as an authoritative coda to this chapter:

> There is little evidence to suggest that schools of any kind of size are overmanaged or that teachers spend too much time outside the classroom. On the contrary, the indications are that they may need to give more time to a necessary range of non-teaching duties, particularly those of planning, consultation and assessment. Heads of department and teachers with guidance and pastoral responsibilities are often particularly short of time. (p. 267).

References

BAILEY, P. (1973). 'The functions of heads of departments in comprehensive schools', *Journal of Educational Administration and History,* 5(1).

BAILEY, P. (1981). 'Appraising the performance of departments in maintained secondary schools: concepts and approaches', in RIBBINS, P. and THOMAS, H. (ed), *Research in Educational Management and Administration,* 106–114, Coombe Lodge, BEMAS.

BASSEY, M. (1981). 'Pedagogic research: on the relative merits of search for generalisations and study of single events', *Oxford Review of Education,* 7(1), 73–94.

BAYNE-JARDINE, C. (1981). 'The qualities of a good head of department', in MARLAND, M. and HILL, S. (ed), (1981), *Departmental Management,* London, Heinemann.

BAYNE-JARDINE, C. and HANHAM, C. (1972). 'Heads of department', *Forum* 15(1).

BEST, R., JARVIS, C. and RIBBINS, P. (1977). 'Pastoral care: concept and process', *British Journal of Educational Studies,* **XXV**(2). 124–135.

BEST, R., JARVIS, C. and RIBBINS, P. (1980). *Perspectives on Pastoral Care,* London, Heinemann.

BEST, R., RIBBINS, P., JARVIS, C. with ODDY, D. (1983). *Education and Care,* London, Heinemann.

BEST. R. and RIBBINS, P. (1983). 'Rethinking the Pastoral Academic Split', *Pastoral Care in Education* 1(1), 11–18.

BLACKBURN, K. (1983a). *Head of House, Head of Year,* London, Heinemann.

BLACKBURN, K. (1983b). 'The pastoral head: a developing role', *Pastrol Care in Education.* 1 (1). 18–24.

BLOOMER, K. (1980). 'The role of the head of department: some questions and answers', *Educational Research,* 22(3), 83–97.

BURGESS, R. (1983). *Experiencing Comprehensive Education,* London, Methuen.

BURNHAM, P. (1969). 'Role theory and educational administration', in HOUGHTON, V. *et al* (ed), *Management in Education,* London, Ward Lock.

COCKCROFT, W. (1982). *Mathematics Counts,* London, HMSO.

DAVID. H. (1983). 'Team Spirit', *Times Educational Supplement,* 28 January 215.

DUNHAM, J. (1978). 'Change and stress in the head of department's role', *Educational Research,* 21(1), 44–8.

DUNHAM, J. (1984). *Stress in Teaching.* Beckenham, Croom Helm.

GOFFMAN, E. (1977). *Encounters.* London: Allen Lane.

GROSS, N., MASON, W., and McEACHERN, A. (1958). *Explorations in Role Analysis,* New York, Wiley.

HALL, J. and THOMAS, J. (1977). 'Research report: mathematics departmental headship in secondary schools', *Educational Administration,* 5(2), 30–37.

HARGREAVES, D. (1967). *Social Relations in a Secondary School,* London, Routledge and Kegan Paul.

HARGREAVES, D. (1972). *Interpersonal Relations and Education.* London, Routledge and Kegan Paul.

HMI (1979). *Aspects of Secondary Education,* London, HMSO.

HMI (Wales) (1984). *Departmental Organisation in Secondary Schools,* Welsh Office, HMSO.

HOLT, J. (1981). 'The head of department and the whole curriculum', in MARLAND, M. and HILL, S. (ed), (1981) *Departmental Management,* London, Heinemann, 9–25.

HOWSON, J. and WOOLNOUGH, B. (1982). 'Head of Department – dictator or democrat', *Educational Management and Administration,* **10**(1), 37–45.

HOYLE, E. (1969). *The Role of the Teacher*, London, Routledge and Kegan Paul.

(ILEA) INNER LONDON EDUCATION AUTHORITY (1984). *Improving Secondary Schools*. Report of the Committee on the Curriculum and Organisation of Secondary Schools in ILEA, chaired by D. H. HARGREAVES, London, ILEA.

LACEY, C. (1970). *Hightown Grammar: The School as a Social System*, Manchester, Manchester University Press.

LAMBERT, K. (1975). 'Research report: the role of head of department in schools', *Educational Administration,* **3**(2), 27–39.

LANG, P. (1984). 'Pastoral care: some reflections on possible influences', *Pastoral Care in Education,* **2**(2), 136–146.

LODGE, B. (1984). 'Department heads' drop in status', *Times Educational Supplement*, 11 May, 9.

MAHER, P. and BEST, R. (1984). *Training and Support for Pastoral Care*, London, National Association of Pastoral Care in Education.

MARLAND, M. (1971). *Head of Department*, London, Heinemann.

MARLAND, M. (1974). *Pastoral Care*, London, Heinemann.

MARLAND, M. (1975). 'Comment on LAMBERT (1975) "Research Report: the role of head of department in schools" ', *Educational Administration,* **3**(2).

MARLAND, M. (1983). 'Preparing for promotion in pastoral care', *Pastoral Care in Education,* **1**(1), 24–36.

MARLAND, M. and HILL, S. (ed) (1981). *Departmental Management*, London, Heinemann.

MCGUINESS, J. (1984). 'Review article: education and care', *Pastoral Care in Education,* **2**(2), 151–5.

MORGAN, C. and TURNER, L. (1976). 'Role, the education manager and the individual in the organisation', *Unit 14 Management in Education (E321)*, Milton Keynes, Open University Press.

NOLTE, M. (ed) (1966). *An Introduction to School Administration: Selected Readings*, London, Macmillan.

OGILVIE, D. and BARTLETT, V. (1979). 'Departmental heads in England and Australia: some comparisons', *Studies in Educational Administration, CCEA,* **15**.

PEEKE, G. (1983). 'Role Strain in the further education college', in BOYD-BARRETT, O. *et al* (ed.), *Approaches to Post School Management*, London, Harper and Row.

RALEIGH, M. (ed) (1983). *The English Department Book*, London. ILEA English Centre.

RIBBINS, P. 'The role of the middle manager in the secondary school' in HUGHES *et al* (eds) (1985), *Managing Education: The System And The Institution*, London, Holt, Rinehart and Winston.

RIBBINS P. 'Subject heads in secondary schools: concepts and contexts' in DAY, C. and MOORE, R. (eds) (1986), *Staff Development In The Secondary School*, London, Croom Helm.

RIBBINS, P. and BEST, R. (1985). 'Pastoral care: theory, practice and the role of research', in LANG, P. and MARLAND, M. (ed.), *New Directions in Pastoral Care in Education*, Oxford, Blackwell.

RICHARDSON, E. (1973). *The Teacher, The School and The Task of Management*, London, Heinemann.

SCHEIN, E. (1965). *Organizational Psychology*, New York, Prentice Hall.

SIDDLE, J. (1978). *The Head of Science and the Task of Management*, Herts, The Association for Science Education.

SILVERMAN, D. (1970). *The Theory of Organizations*, London, Heinemann.

THOMAS, H. (1983). Review of Marland and Hill (1981) *Departmental Management*, (London: Heinemann), *Pastoral Care in Education*, 2(1), 144–7.

TURNER, R. (1969). 'Role-taking: process versus conformity', in LINDESMITH, A. and STRAUSS, A. (ed.), *Readings in Social Psychology*, New York, Holt, Rinehart and Winston.

WOODLAND, D. (1979). 'Role; social role; role taking; role conflict', in MITCHELL G. (ed.) (1979), *A New Dictionary of Sociology*, London, Routledge and Kegan Paul.

Headteachers at work:
practice and policy

Valerie Hall, Hugh Mackay and Colin Morgan

[This chapter presents the authors' conclusions from their research – funded by the Leverhulme Trust – on the role of secondary headteachers in England and Wales. The investigation was based on detailed in-depth observation of four heads over an extended period. This methodology was chosen to obtain an accurate account of what heads actually do rather than what they, or theoretical analyses, say they do.]

In this [chapter] we aim first to draw together four distinctive approaches to the job of headteacher and its common elements; second, to consider secondary school headship from the perspective of present policy. We began [our report] by setting our description and analysis of the work of four headteachers in the context of our observations of the working days of fifteen heads. Like Wolcott (1973) we saw out task as providing descriptive data about the job of the secondary school headteacher. Our single day observation of fifteen heads showed their daily work to be fragmented, people-intensive and to encompass a range of tasks. Teaching emerged as the longest sustained activity for many headteachers and formal scheduled meetings constituted a low proportion of the job. The majority of the heads' activities were interpersonal, predominantly with individuals and groups within the school, although they gave vastly different emphases to the importance of building and maintaining interpersonal relations and motivating staff. They differed substantially in their levels of involvement in the tasks to be carried out as a result of their contrasting interpretations of the head's role. In general, they spent more time on teaching activities than on 'leading professional' matters of curriculum and other educational policy; more time on 'operations' and 'human management' than on 'educational policy'; and about ten per cent of their time daily in the school on 'external management' matters. Routine administration dominated the time spent within the 'operations management' category. Pupil issues claimed just over half of their 'human management' time.

The general features of the job (its fragmentation, people-intensive character and varied range of tasks) were reflected in our indepth study of four head-teachers. The striking characteristic of secondary headship is that the baseline of a formal description is missing, making it all the more important to know how it is actually done. In the course of the year the four heads all faced demands from staff, pupils, parents, and the LEA; the choices they made in responding to them and the constraints on proposed action varied considerably.

In observing four secondary headteachers we found that little had changed in the scope and character of heads' performance of the job since Lyons' (1974) description of its fragmentary quality. As then, the tasks of three of the heads we studied ranged over all the work of the school, although with differing levels of input. The preference of the fourth for considerable delegation made possible intense involvement in teaching and advising older pupils. While the managerial role of each of the heads was characterised by fragmentation, only Mr Shaw [*] took a predominantly proactive and strategic stance and appeared less at the mercy of events. In common with Wolcott (1973) we found a tendency among heads to respond to every problem as important, involving them in a multiplicity of 'little decisions'.

[. . .] We showed [. . .] how each head's style of working with staff was significantly tied to the kind of relationship they had with senior staff; and the extent to which they had consciously instituted systems into the school manage-ment structure for ensuring tasks were carried out. The emphasis of two heads was on creating and limiting opportunities for certain kinds of action, mainly through a vigilant watchfulness over what teachers were doing. In contrast, Mr Shaw and Mr Dowe were as much concerned about the ways in which teaching staff thought about their work. In general, three of the heads were uncomfort-able about instituting formal monitoring systems of teacher performance, per-haps reflecting some of their own feelings as former teachers rather than as heads. [. . .] Only Mr King, who had limited teaching experience and a non-collegial approach to his teaching staff, took pleasure in dropping in unannounced on teachers at work in the classroom.

In time of industrial action, each of the heads differed in their views of the teachers and their cause; and in the ways they chose to respond to a multiplicity of conflicting demands from the unions, the LEA, parents, governors and pupils. They had considerable freedom to choose individual responses, which were generally in keeping with their approach to managing staff relations in more harmonious times. Our interviews with heads prior to the onset of indus-trial action on the part of teachers showed that the rules governing heads' res-ponses to issues relating to collective bargaining were not defined. During the dispute that began in April 1984, we saw their uncertainty about how to act in unfamiliar circumstances, their reliance on each other for advice and example, and the influence of their own professional association and other allegiances on their response. Interviews with the larger sample of heads revealed [. . .]: a resistance to regular meetings with union representatives for fear of giving them

[*The four heads were given pseudonyms: Messrs. Shaw, Dowe, King and Mercer.]

too much status; a preference for being reactive rather than proactive towards union matters; and a primary concern that the interests of the pupils come first.

Richardson (1973) pointed to a growing stress among heads, relating to uncertainty about the boundaries and subsequent difficulties over the exercise of authority by those in leadership positions. Some fifteen years later, clarification of roles and responsibilities still remains elusive. [. . .]

In their work with pupils each head enacted a figurehead role in the school, responding differently to the possibilities it offered for teaching, counselling, and maintaining control. Among other features of their work within the school was the high proportion of time spent by three of the four heads on routine administrative tasks and their different systems for ensuring the completion of these. One mainly delegated this area of work; one chose to handle as many aspects as possible himself; two retained a high level of involvement whilst delegating substantial areas. Two were closely involved on a daily and often practical basis in the maintenance of buildings; one took a close interest without becoming practically involved; and the fourth delegated it almost entirely.

In responding to the situations and tasks associated with their leadership role, each head further acted to influence the style and behaviour of teaching staff in different ways. Mr King sought to achieve this through his presence and office. This accounted for his high visibility, allowing him to present a model of appropriate behaviour and ensuring constant supervision. He distinguished himself from his teaching staff by presenting himself as better than they were at the same tasks he expected them to accomplish. Mr Dowe also presented himself as a model for behaviour he desired from staff, but almost exclusively in the role of teacher and as a colleague rather than as a superior. Mr Shaw made his values and priorities clear in every working context, both as a colleague and a manager, though with greater emphasis on managerial aspects, Mr Mercer took upon himself an almost exclusive concern for ensuring desired outcomes to the school's immediate and longer-term needs. He was less apparently concerned to demonstrate through his own actions and behaviour the kind of stance he hoped teaching staff would adopt.

In their work outside the school [. . .] they differed in whether they saw parents as partners or clients and in the extent and ways in which they sought to involve parents in school activity. Their relations with the LEA were affected by the extent to which they saw the LEA as having a legitimate involvement in the organisation of their schools; and as taking action which was in the interest of their school as well as the Authority.

In common with the headteachers in Kogan's (1984) study, governing bodies were seen by the heads as agencies belonging to the school rather than the LEA. Mr Mercer and Mr King both demonstrated a preference for centralised decision-making, but their relations with their governing bodies differed. Mr King was secure in his knowledge that they supported the objectives and the values of the school and accepted his leadership style as legitimate. Mr Mercer was less confident in his governors' support for his centralised style of leadership or their agreement about the school's aims and objectives. He was more likely to try and control the information made available to them. Both Mr Shaw and Mr Dowe put a greater emphasis in their leadership style on consultation and sharing decision-making. However, while Mr Shaw's relations with his governing body demonstrated a recognition of the expectation that they would 'call the school to account' and express views on policy, Mr Dowe's relations were more passive, in response to the governing body's own passivity.

The approach of the heads to the media was similar: suspicion of media motives based on past experiences prompted a proactive rather than reactive stance to pre-empt media hostility. The community served by each school was seen and responded to by three of the heads as another potential ally in promoting the interests of the school. Each of these three, though not Mr Dowe, devoted some time to cultivating personal links with members of their school's community.

The freedom allowed in the job to interpret its demands differently was most apparent in each head's involvement in the educational world beyond the school. This was particularly extensive in one case and limited in another. One of the heads was unusual in not seeking out frequently the views and support of colleague heads in the Authority, which provided a frame of reference for the other heads' assessment of what they were doing.

LEA's views of headteachers in their Authority derived more from informal *ad hoc* sources of information than from face-to-face contact or hard documentary data. There was no evidence of attempts to systematise information on the performance of individual headteachers and criteria for judging heads as 'good' or 'bad' varied widely. Personal characteristics were cited more frequently than knowledge or skills, though the precise nature of each head's characteristics always remained elusive in their accounts.

Having summarised the heads' responses across different aspects of the job we now present a cameo of each of the four heads observed. [. . .]

Mr King was a lively, active head, highly visible though not always communicating easily with colleagues, as a result of the often critical stance he adopted. He started work well before the official start of the school day; and had a large number of interactions, especially with pupils, throughout the working day. In dealing with people he was loud and direct. His relations with staff were uneven; with a few he enjoyed friendly relations; with many – and this was highlighted during the teachers' industrial action – his relations were characterised by antagonism and conflict. He depended on vested authority rather than interpersonal skills, to achieve what he wanted from staff. There was a marked contrast in this respect between his interpersonal style within and outside the school. Decision-making was centralised and he was personally involved in the detailed aspects of administration – writing cheques and counting cash, for example. He was prominent in all matters concerning the physical fabric of the school, its condition and appearance. To this end, he cultivated and enjoyed friendly relations with cleaners, cooks and caretakers and even carried out minor repairs to the school buildings and plant himself. His omnipresence compelled him into involvement in matters demanding immediate attention.

He was in frequent contact with the LEA, often 'clearing' things before he proceeded with them. He got on well with senior officers in the Authority, who had a high opinion of him as a head. He worked closely with pupils on pastoral matters and expected staff to take his behaviour as a model, rather than his specifying rules for action. He usually attended an assembly; and was out of his room and around the school for the full duration of both breaks and the lunchtime; after school he personally supervised pupils boarding the buses. Much of this contact with pupils involved enforcing discipline, often by meting out physical punishment himself. He got on well with – and devoted much of his effort in this area to – older boys who were in trouble at school; he empathised with their position. He did not dwell at length or systematically on curriculum matters. He had close working relations with his governors, who strongly supported him in the school. He worked hard promoting his image and that of the school – in the media and in the community. He invited notables along to social events at the school and sat on a number of committees in the community. He had lived in this community since his own childhood. He attached considerable importance to the role and rights of parents, and particularly enjoyed his work with the PTA.

Mr Mercer most resembled those heads described in Lyons (1974) as being rarely 'able to plan their day in other than nominal terms, inevitably leaving a large part of it free in anticipation of the many minor crises that will occur' (p. 90). He combined high visibility through presence in assemblies and frequent tours of the school, with a degree of inaccessibility and non-availability, using his secretary as a gatekeeper. His approach to decision-making was more autocratic than participatory. His attempts to involve staff were tempered by his scepticism regarding their motivation, over which he saw himself as having little influence. Guidelines for desired behaviour were *ad hoc* rather than formalised or routinised. The organisation of the school over four sites involved him in many activities aimed at securing smooth school administration as well as the increased complexity of determining and implementing longer-term goals. He saw himself as mainly effective in influencing the school's appearance and its day to day operations (chiefly outside of the classroom). His preference was for an informal style of leadership, with few regular meetings though frequent *ad hoc* meetings. His approach was tactical rather than strategic, to take account of what he saw as the potentially negative consequences of the micro-politics of staff relations. He gave a high priority to interpersonal relations with non-teaching staff and to continued vigilance over the state of the buildings. While he often expressed his intention to manage time effectively and respond to a whole range of the school's activity, his days were spent more in assisting staff with routine tasks and responding to 'happenings' rather than planned events. The boundary between policy and administrative decisions was clear with a greater concentration of time on the latter. Mr Mercer encouraged in parents a confidence in the school's traditional approach to curriculum and pastoral matters, resulting in fairly limited contacts with them, occasionally as individuals and rarely as a group. His approach to the community served by the school was businesslike.

While remaining apart from it, he cultivated a network of contacts whose help could be enlisted to the school's advantage.

Mr Dowe's headship style emphasised the academic. He had a strong interest in curriculum, more in and around his own subject area than on a whole school basis. He taught nearly a half timetable of sixth-form classes, and dealt largely with pupils from this end of the school. He did not attend assembly and saw relatively little of other pupils. His main contribution to the school ethos was his academic emphasis, a result of his perception of the need for improvement in 'A' level results. He preferred a collegial rather than hierarchical approach to staff relations. The extent of his availability to staff, to whom he was always considerate and respectful, was curtailed by his extensive teaching and examining commitments, as well as his practice of going home to lunch. Beyond the school, he was actively involved in other work with several exam boards. He sought to demonstrate through his own professional competence as a teacher the ways in which he wanted staff to see their own teaching roles. Thus he played a large part in defining the school's instructional goals. Otherwise, he delegated running the school extensively. As a result he was required to spend relatively little time in dealing with matters requiring immediate attention; his teaching commitments dominated the space made available.

He encouraged participatory forms of decision-making, emphasising good interpersonal relations in the school, though not always clarifying on a systematic, 'whole school', basis the factors contributing to the achievement of school goals. On financial matters, Mr Dowe dealt with policy rather than administration. He respected the rights of parents as consumers, although on several occasions experienced the problems which are always potential with highly articulate parents, in defining the school's instructional objectives. He was not active in the local community, nor did he have much contact with his governors. He saw little of, and spoke rarely with, colleague heads in the Authority; and often failed to attend county heads' meetings, though was active in his regional heads' association. In a similar vein, he did not rate highly with educationalist officers of the Authority; on staffing matters, in particular, he came into considerable conflict with them. He was more concerned with the individual interest of his school than the broader policy concerns of the Authority; his relations with the LEA were sometimes antagonistic.

The main features of Mr Shaw's approach to his work as a head were his systematic involvement in the whole range of the school's activity, in spite of extensive commitments to activities outside of the school; his strategic view of school matters, ensuring continuing attention to longer-term planning; and his proactive stance towards innovation and change. He put great emphasis on being regularly visible and available to all the groups working in and with the school. In particular he approached systematically the task of building and maintaining interpersonal relations with staff, pupils and parents; as well as creating mechanisms for providing staff with the knowledge and skills to do their job effectively. He did this by involving staff consistently in the school's decision-making processes, making extensive use of his close working partnership with his senior management team to secure the staff's support. Having developed his preferred formula for running the school at its inception fourteen years previously, he remained wedded to these well-tried strategies which had, in his view, proved their worth.

He sought to combine an approach which encouraged staff to plan their goals (internalised rather than prescribed) with a view of the system as a whole, to be responded to as an entity, not just concentrated on in parts. In spite of its occasional, unanticipated (but not unfamiliar) fragmentation, his working day appeared organised, punctuated by regular events, with no gaps and considerable momentum. The control he was able to exert over the pace of his work, through the systems he had instituted to manage its demands, made it possible for him to include regular appraisals of longer-term issues, for which solutions were less well known, as well as to deal with matters requiring his immediate attention. He was active in the community served by the school although not a member of it.

Having shown in profile four distinctive approaches to the job of the head, we consider now the relevance of our analysis for policy development. The profiles show only one of the four heads as having made any substantial revision in the way comprehensive school heads arrange their working days since Lyons's work (1974). Unlike other managers, few of the headteachers that Jenkins (1983) or we studied had regular scheduled meetings or timetabled, extended blocks of time to study specific policy issues. In other words, they had created few opportunities to think out and develop strategies and instruments to meet the complexity of demands on them for the development of school educational policy and classroom practice. Much of the time of many of the heads was taken up by teaching and other pupil-related matters; in other words, in activities performed directly for the customers or consumers. In most cases the time taken for this can be seen as at the expense of attention to overall planning and executive tasks.

Practice-orientated management theory (e.g. Katz, 1974; Mintzberg, 1973) distinguishes between the tasks and responsibilities of top, senior and middle management, reflecting the balance between overall planning and executive tasks and direct contact with the customers or clients. An implication of this distinction for headteachers would be that they would not, for example, expect to have a high level of pupil contact. Rather, as a characteristic of 'top management' in schools, they would demonstrate little involvement in the more generic professional activites – for example, teaching – which have previously occupied them on their career path to headship.

We have shown that this is not a model which many headteachers practice. We have commented on the lack of prescription of the job of the head and the way in which this leaves individual heads considerable licence in their interpretation of it. Continuing with our example, we found a major attachment by heads to a personal teaching timetable. They argue that this is useful to enable them to know what life is like for their colleagues at the chalkface; and that it is necessary if they are to retain the respect of classroom teachers. Some choose to teach because they enjoy it or find it a therapy or welcome retreat from other pressures.

Clearly, with this choice as any other which they make, there will be opportunity costs, in that other activities may not be carried out while they are teaching.

In common with Jenkins (1983), we found similarities in the way in which heads do the job and differences from their counterparts in other occupational settings. We have also shown, in our detailed descriptions as well as our account of our single-day observation of fifteen heads, differences in how they view and perform the job. The four heads could be characterised by a particularly dominant feature of their style. Mr Dowe's emphasis, reflected in the proportion of time given to it, was on his involvement in teaching activities; his approach thus typifies that of the 'teacher educator'. A high number of scheduled meetings was a prominent characteristic of Mr Shaw's approach to the job, for whom attention to professional matters and to efficient procedures in the control of all organisational activity went hand in hand. In this respect he demonstrated the characteristics of what Hughes (1972) has called the 'leading professional' and 'chief executive' models of headship. Mr King's working day was characterised by a high number of contacts compared with the other three heads. His approach can be described as that of the 'pastoral missioner' because of its Arnoldian overtones in terms of the constant use of personal interactions to affect values and events. [. . .] The fourth head, Mr Mercer, combined features of the 'pastoral missioner' and 'leading professional' models.

The four heads studied in depth are therefore to be seen not as four exceptions in the spectrum of headship interpretation but as representatives of four recurring interpretations. What we cannot say, of course, is exactly what proportions they constitute in secondary headship interpretations as a whole; nor what the hallmarks are of other interpretations which may exist but which did not show up in our sample.

The problem facing policy makers, selectors and trainers is that variety remains the chief characteristic of how secondary headship is practised in England and Wales today. These varied performances need now to be set in the context of central government's increasing concern with the content of what schools do and the head's part in school success or effectiveness. Three recent publications carry explicitly or implicitly government expectations of secondary school headship. They are: 'Ten Good Schools' (DES HMI, 1977), 'Teaching Quality' (DES 1983); and 'Better Schools' (DES 1985). We consider each in turn.

'Ten Good Schools' argued the centrality of headship for school success and defined the elements of effective school leadership. While the problem of deciding what is to count as a measure of school success or effectiveness remains unresolved empirically it is interesting to link the criteria identified in 'Ten Good Schools' with our own observations of headteachers at work. We have summarised these links in Table 1.5.1.

'Teaching Quality', although primarily concerned with the initial training, supply and deployment of teachers, carried an important statement about the government's view of the core requirements for headship and its associated functions. It states:

Table 1.5.1 Four headteachers judged on the criteria of 'Ten Good Schools' (DES, HMI, 1977)

Ten good schools criteria	Shaw	Dauve	Mercer	King
Communication of specific educational aims to staff, pupils, parents	Systematic and comprehensive approach to all three groups	Communicates to all three groups but generally more concerned with the upper end of the school and more able pupils	Informs staff of developments from outside the school. Communicates specific educational aims on an *ad hoc* basis	Informs all three groups of developments from outside the school. Not a source of specific educational aims
Human management displays sympathetic understanding of staff and pupils; is available	Places a high priority on interpersonal relations with both. Not always available	Interacts well on a collegial basis with staff and the more able, senior pupils. Not always available	Variable sympathy and understanding towards staff. Availability restricted	Unsympathetic to staff. Highly sympathetic to some pupils, especially older delinquent boys. Readily available
Personal qualities good humour; sense of proportion; dedication to task	Committed educationalist and skilful manager. Good humour and a sense of proportion consistently present	Committed educationalist concerned about others' feelings. Good humour and a sense of proportion consistently present	Committed to the school's rather than staff's interests. Good humour and sense of proportion frequently evident	Totally committed to the school. Good humour and a good sense of proportion selectively demonstrated
Devolution of power Conscious of the corruption of power; power-sharing a keynote of the school	Extensive power-sharing combined with a high level of personal involvement	Extensive delegation and devolution of power, general lack of concentration of power on himself	Limited power-sharing Holds most of the power himself	Limited power-sharing Holds most of the power himself

Headteachers and other senior staff with management responsibilities within schools are of crucial importance. Only if they are effective managers of their teaching staffs and the material resources available to them, as well as possessing the qualities of effective leadership, can schools offer pupils the quality of education they have a right to expect.

(1983, para. 83, p. 25).

Effective management is thus added to the criterion of 'Ten Good Schools' as another criterion of leadership for school success or effectiveness. The document also identifies performance appraisal and staff development as key managerial functions:

> But employers can manage their teacher force effectively only if they have accurate knowledge of each teacher's performance. The Government believe that for this purpose formal assessment of teacher performance is necessary and should be based on classroom visiting by the teacher's head or head of department, and an appraisal of both pupils' work and of the teacher's contribution to the life of the school.
>
> (DES 1983, para. 92, p. 27).

There are currently no systematic school-based policies in these matters: we did not find headteachers undertaking teacher appraisal as an explicit policy, nor did they visit classrooms for that purpose. We did observe heads actively assisting individual teachers' aspirations for courses; but, altogether, what was observed did not constitute the implementation of a systematic policy for in-service training and staff development, involving subject updating, job rotation and other enrichment experiences. Of the four heads, we would judge only Mr Shaw to have demonstrated elements of a more comprehensive and systematic approach.

It is more difficult to judge the performance of the four heads in terms of what 'Better Schools' (DES, 1985) describes as the weaknesses and implicitly, strengths of secondary schools, since it is not easy to isolate the head's contributions to school effectiveness. Some of these weaknesses were: the absence of schemes of work; the concentration of teaching towards the middle band of ability; inappropriate teaching styles; lack of detailed assessment policies for pupils; mismatch between subject expertise and teacher allocation; lack of a systematic approach to career development; absence of policies for curriculum review; absence of regular and formal appraisal of all teachers; the need for more outreach work with parents; and inadequate attention to developing multi-cultural understanding.

Taking the first weakness, the absence of schemes of work: Mr Dowe, Mr Shaw and Mr Mercer discussed these with individual teachers on a number of occasions. Mr Shaw demonstrated a consistent concern with teaching across the whole ability range; Mr Dowe was more personally involved with the more able; Mr Mercer's focus changed at different points in the year; Mr King put most energy into promoting the interests of the low achievers.

Mr Shaw kept himself informed, mainly through consultation with others, about what teachers were doing in the classroom, the content and methods of their teaching. There were no systematic monitoring procedures, though heads of department were given time and scope to involve themselves closely in curriculum planning and optimising the use of staff. He welcomed the opportunity to try out the profiling system proposed by the LEA and actively encouraged staff to make maximum use of a multiplicity of non-staff resources. In contrast we rarely saw Mr Dowe discuss schemes of work with individual teachers and he had no formal way of monitoring what was happening in the classroom. Discussions with staff about career development were *ad hoc* rather than planned.

Mr Mercer dealt mainly with heads of department in considering schemes of work, discussing general principles rather than detailed proposals. His main concern was to promote the interests of the middle band of ability for whom he thought there was inadequate provision. He was satisfied that the provision for lower ability pupils was adequate and high ability pupils did not have a high profile in the school. Changes in the school's organisation as a result of projected falling rolls necessitated a more systematic approach (through interviews) to career development. He did not intervene with any regularity in departmental planning or the use of staff and non-staff resources. A recent HMI inspection had ensured that all staff had schemes of work available in Mr King's school and he monitored closely what was happening in the classroom, though on an impromptu basis. He actively promoted and supported a frequent, regular pupil assessment policy which was traditional in its approach. He was more concerned about the needs of low and underachieving pupils than those in the higher ability range. He was not concerned to develop a systematic approach to staff career development in the school.

Mr Shaw had instituted a system for curriculum review in the school; the other three heads approached the task on a more *ad hoc* basis. Profiling was most advanced in Mr Shaw's school, where teachers played an active part in agreeing the overall goals of the school. Mr Mercer in the same Authority was more cautious in his response to profiling. Mr King and Mr Dowe continued to use the traditional form of pupil reports in the absence of proposals for alternatives from the Authority. None of the heads had any system for the regular or formal appraisal of teachers.

They differed in the degree of proactivity of their work with parents; Mr Shaw and Mr King were most concerned about actively involving parents in the school's affairs; Mr Mercer and Mr Dowe only did so when necessary. In a mainly white school, Mr Shaw actively sought ways to enhance multi-cultural policies through the curriculum. We were not aware of Mr Dowe's specific promotion of a multi-cultural policy. Mr King and Mr Mercer both had multi-ethnic schools, and sought to secure multi-cultural understanding though in more traditional ways than advocated by recent ideas on multi-cultural education, such as the Swann Report (1985).

When reflected against the various policy declarations in the documents we have discussed above, our findings as a whole suggest two broad conclusions. First, many of the activities now being expected of headteachers in these three government documents are not presently being carried out: in particular, classroom supervision, performance appraisal, departmental evaluation and systematic curriculum review. Consequently these recent policy expectations imply the need for substantial investment in training to equip heads for these tasks. Second, the policy expectations which have been declared by the DES for schools imply the need for heads to re-interpret how they themselves carry out the job. All of the new policy requirements are demanding in time and imply detailed systematic policies under the head's constant supervision.

If all of the new policy expectations are to become a regular part of school management, a review of how heads spend their time will be necessary. Along with others in schools who are specifically paid for managerial responsibility, heads will have a great deal more of a specialist nature to do. If the full implications of the expectations expressed in these documents are to be met heads would face substantial and unavoidable challenges to their ways of working.

There are implications in an understanding of how headteachers do their work not only for policy makers, but for selectors and trainers too. As well as raising a range of issues when considered against current policy demands, our findings also raise the question of whether new policy is needed. Taken together these issues appear to us to fall into three, though not mutually exclusive, categories: (a) the implications of our findings for secondary headteacher selection: (b) the implications of our findings for headteacher training provision: and (c) school-centred issues that arise from the differences between the public policy expectations of headship and its observed performance.

[. . .] The complexity of the job and the degree of variance in interpretation have two important implications for headteacher selection methods. In a rigorous system, selectors need to assess overall competence across the whole range of job tasks and abilities, and to evaluate the appropriateness of the particular emphasis of interpretation which each candidate would bring to the job.

In respect of headship training, we see three main reasons why our findings imply complex and numerous issues of policy. First, there are the consequences of the complexity of headship in practice, that make it hard to believe that any deputy head, however competent and wide the experience in that post, could be ready for elevation to headship without prior formal training and management development. Whilst there are opportunities for deputies to receive training under Circular 3/83, the policy document for senior school staff management training, it is not obligatory for deputies to receive training before presenting themselves as candidates. In any case the current training provision places are overwhelmingly taken by heads. It could be argued therefore that the sequence is wrong; that a widespread training provision should be made first for deputies. Second, there are far-reaching training implications arising from the different interpretations we have observed across the tasks of headship. Heads describe themselves as having, and demonstrate, highly varying strengths and weaknesses. These both reflect and are reflected in the individual interpretation of the job. Any training and management development policy would need to be tailored to meet this variety of individual need: a bespoke rather than mass provision for heads' management development would seem to be required.

Third, there is the issue of who is to devise the policy to meet these detailed individual needs? LEAs at the present time have no techniques for evaluating the individual school or its head. Their methods are impressionistic rather than systematic, and the mismatch between the views of headship held in some LEA offices and the performance observed is not only unjust to the heads concerned but reveals an inadequate and shaky basis on which to found management development policies.

Finally, we turn to school-centred issues that arise from the differences between the DES expectations of headship and its performance as we observed it. First, there are what might be termed 'omissions' on the part of some or all heads: failure to carry out classroom supervision, performance appraisal, departmental evaluation, and detailed curriculum review, for example. Whereas at present these activities do not have the status of being mandatory, all of them – directly or by implication – would constitute obligatory responsibilities of headship if the detailed terms of salary restructuring proposals, as set out in the Joint Working Party on Salary Structure paper, come to be accepted (see Table 1.5.2).

Table 1.5.2 Joint working party on salary structure 1984 – proposals by employers

---

Headteachers:
The duties and responsibilities of a head shall include:

1 Formulate and gain approval for the school's overall aims and objectives and policies for implementation.
2 Establish and modify as required the school's internal organisation, deploying finance and staff so as to implement policies and maintain staff motivation and initiative, all within the requirements of LEA policies and of staff conditions of service.
3 Clarify to individual staff members the contribution required of them through the provision of job descriptions, consulting individuals as required.
4 Establish and maintain appropriate professional and performance standards for staff of all kinds including the conduct of performance appraisals and reviews.
5 Secure assistance and support from those whose activities and support can contribute to the attainment of the school's objectives.
6 Liaise and cooperate with governors, LEA members and officers and other heads.
7 Participate in arrangements for assessment of his or her own performance and identification and meeting of training needs.

Our description and discussion of how secondary school headship is performed has recorded how different individual role interpretations can be. This degree of variance raises the questions of whether government in England and Wales should set out some guidelines for school management. Minimum guidelines of this nature do not exist in England and Wales, although in Scotland central government has defined the minimum required management tasks for schools – for heads, deputies, middle and junior managers, as well as for subject and pastoral leaders in the school (SED 1984). The Scottish Education Department lists the responsibilities of these staff, and expects and assumes that such tasks are carried out in all secondary schools.

In England and Wales, current government expectations of headship challenge heads to review the responsibilities of all management role holders in their schools. The thrust of government policy is, as we have suggested, to achieve more systematic curricula and staff effectiveness policies within schools. They are likely to require sustained planning by heads. The time demands to carry out these could be incompatible with some interpretations of headship which we observed. The main issue raised for heads by the policy demands from the government, therefore, is how to find the time for these important developments within the constraint of the day to day traffic of school life. Our observation of the different interpretations of secondary headship suggest that analysis and synthesis of the current variety would offer options to resolve this dilemma; at the very least it implies the need for a review and explicit demarcation of the division of duties between heads themselves, their deputies, and their heads of years and departments.

References

DES HMI (1977). *Ten Good Schools: A Secondary School Enquiry*, HMSO, London.

HUGHES, M. G., (1972). 'The role of the secondary head', PhD thesis, University of Wales.

JENKINS, H. O., (1983). 'Job perceptions of senior managers in schools and manufacturing industry', PhD thesis, University of Birmingham.

KATZ, R. L., (1974). 'Skills of an effective administrator', *Harvard Business Review*, 52: 90–102.

KOGAN, M., *et al.* (1984). *School Governing Bodies*, Heinemann, London.

LYONS, G., (1974). *The Administrative Tasks of Head and Senior Teachers in Large Secondary Schools*, University of Bristol.

MINTZBERG, H., (1973). *The Nature of Managerial Work*, Harper & Row, New York.

RICHARDSON, E., (1973). *The Teacher, The School, and The Task of Management*, Heinemann, London.

SED HMI of Schools (1984). 'Learning and teaching in Scottish secondary schools: school management', HMSO, Edinburgh.

SECRETARY OF STATE FOR EDUCATION AND SCIENCE AND SECRETARY OF STATE FOR WALES (1983). 'Teaching quality', Cmnd 8836, HMSO, London.

SECRETARY OF STATE FOR EDUCATION AND SCIENCE AND SECRETARY OF STATE FOR WALES (1985). 'Better Schools', Cmnd. 9469, London.

WOLCOTT, H., (1973). *The Man in the Principal's Office*, Holt, Rinehart and Winston, New York.

How heads manage change

Dick Weindling and Peter Earley

[This chapter focuses on a major research project concerning the first years of secondary headship conducted at the National Foundation for Educational Research in England and Wales (NFER). The first section briefly reviews existing, mainly North American, research on the head's role in change; the second describes the findings of the NFER study which are relevant to this topic; and the third presents the main conclusions and draws broad comparisons between the NFER results and the North American findings.]

In his book *The Meaning of Educational Change* (1982) Michael Fullan points out that, 'While research on educational implementation is barely 12 years old, systematic research on what the principal actually does and its relationship to stability and change is (remarkably) only two or three years old – and much of this research is still in progress'.

The role of the head in change

In the UK, few studies have focused directly on the role of the head in change. Most of the research has taken the form of case studies of individual secondary schools and the part played by the head has been considered as only one aspect of the work (e.g. Bell 1979; Waddilove 1981; Gilbert 1981; Bailey 1982; Nicholls 1983; and Burgess 1983). A few studies have used interviews or questionnaires to look at heads and innovation in a number of schools (e.g. Dickinson 1975; Hughes 1975; McGeown 1979; and Collier 1982). Dickinson's study, although small-scale and limited to one LEA, revealed some interesting findings with regard to the current NFER project. He found that heads were the main originators of the innovations which were introduced to answer a perceived need in the schools. Each of the 15 head teachers spoke of all the innovations as being highly successful but, as Dickinson points out, 'real measures of evaluation in terms of learning outcomes, or understanding, appeared to be irrelevant, providing the innovation was successfully brought about'.

While a full review of the literature is not possible the next section outlines some of the work from North America, where the most detailed research on principals and innovation has been carried out. Fullan (1982) provides an excellent summary of the research and provides evidence to show that 'change is only one small part of the forces competing for the principal's attention and usually not the most compelling one'.

Wolcott's (1973) pioneering ethnographic study of one elementary-school principal and the research of Morris *et al* (1982) in eight elementary and six high schools, where the principals were shadowed for up to 12 days over a 2-year period, showed that most time was taken up with one-to-one personal interactions, meetings and phone calls. The main role of the principal seemed to be maintaining stability and little attention was given to programme changes.

The Rand project, by Berman and McLaughlin (1975), although not a direct study of the role of the principal, found that one third of the teachers surveyed thought that their principal functioned largely as an administrator who was uninvolved in change. In successful projects, the principals gave active support to the innovations. This was confirmed in case studies of the Teacher Corps projects (Reinhard *et al* 1980; and Rosenblum and Jastrzab 1980), where the most successful projects had principals who were intensely involved in the initial stages – what was done at this stage by the principal drastically affected later success or failure of the project. Active involvement by principals was important but active did not always mean direct; in some cases, the principals delegated day-to-day responsibility. As long as the principal was involved and interested in getting feedback and the staff were aware of the principal's commitment to the innovation, the project did not suffer.

A major study of innovation, the DESSI project (Dissemination Efforts Supporting School Improvement: Crandall and Loucks 1983; and Huberman and Miles 1984) looked at 61 innovations in 146 sites and conducted case studies at 12 sites. In the summary of their findings, Crandall and Loucks report, 'Forceful leadership is the factor that contributes most directly and surely to major effective changes in the classroom practice that become firmly incorporated into everyday routines.' The leadership could come from a central-office administrator or an influential principal: 'When the involvement is enlightened, forceful, resourceful and long lasting, highly significant changes are carried out.' From this it appears that the principals played a major role in change. But in the case studies reported by Huberman and Miles, we find that the prime advocates for change in 10 of the 12 sites were central-office administrators, who often reached directly into the schools to implement the innovation, thereby leaving the principals to play a secondary role. In 11 sites, central-office administrators were the key personnel in making the decision to adopt the innovation and 'principals had to get into line'. 'The principals were often as much the targets or consumers of the projects as were the teachers so initial commitment was not always high.'

The principal's role in innovation was examined by Hall *et al.* (1984) in their work with 29 elementary-school principals. They identified three types of change-facilitator style, which they termed Initiators, Managers and Responders.

(a) *Initiators* had clear, decisive long-range policies and goals, which transcended but included implementation of current innovations. Decisions were made in relation to these goals and in terms of what they believed to be best for the students. These principals had high expectations for students, teachers and themselves, which they conveyed through frequent contact with teachers. Initiators reinterpreted district programmes to suit the needs of the school.

(b) *Managers* demonstrated responsive behaviour to situations but also initiated actions to support changes suggested by the central office. They defended staff from what they felt were excessive demands and provided support to facilitate teachers' use of an innovation but did not move beyond the basics of what was imposed by the district administrators.

(c) *Responders* placed a heavy emphasis on allowing teachers and others the opportunity to take the lead. They saw the principal's main role as maintaining the smooth running of the school by concentrating on administrative tasks. Teachers were viewed as professionals who were able to work with little guidance from the principal. They stressed the personal side of their relationships with staff and, before making decisions, tried to allow everyone an opportunity to express their feelings. In most cases, the decisions were in response to immediate circumstances rather than in terms of long range goals. This seemed to be due in part to their desire to please others and in part to their more limited vision of how the school and staff should change in the future.

The three styles were found in a number of studies by the team of researchers, and independently Thomas (1978) identified three very similar roles for principals in managing innovations. Hall and his colleagues found that there was more quality of change in those school with 'Initiator' style principals than in schools with 'Manager' and 'Responder' principals.

Leithwood and Montgomery (1985) have reviewed previous work and carried out their own research to produce a 'profile of growth in principal effectiveness'. The study attempts to identify which principal behaviour is linked to school effectiveness. The profile involves four levels which, moving from less effective to more effective, are called the Administrator, Humanitarian, Program manager, and Problem solver. The higher levels represent an accumulation of skills, knowledge and attitudes from the lower levels, as well as some significant shifts in the principals' beliefs.

(a) *Level 1, the Administrator* – these principals believe it is the teacher's job to teach and the principal's job to run the school. Their main goal is to maintain a smooth ship. Change is a source of annoyance.

(b) *Level 2, the Humanitarian* – they believe strongly in the importance of interpersonal relations and that the effective school is a happy school.

(c) *Level 3, The Program manager* – they are particularly concerned about implementing the programme requirements as outlined by the central-office administrators.

(d) *Level 4, the Systemic problem solver* – a small group of principals whose philosophy of education involves high expectations for *all* pupils. This is used as a frame of reference to provide the best educational experience for students; they are receptive to changes that might achieve these goals. They use a wide range of strategies and are aware of the variety of factors that could improve classroom teaching.

Leithwood and Montgomery point out that only 10% of the 200 principals on whom they have data worked predominantly at the highest level. Most of the school systems involved in the study considered the lowest level in the profile to describe minimally acceptable, rather than unacceptable, principal behaviour.

The majority of the work in North America has been conducted in elementary schools and, although similarities exist between elementary and secondary schools, far more research is needed on the role of the secondary school principal or head. Gene Hall and his colleagues at the University of Texas, having previously worked with elementary-school principals, have recently begun a study of change at the high-school level. Their findings are similar to those of the DESSI study in that most of the changes originated from outside the school and local school administrators (who included principals) were the impetus for only a quarter of the changes. Working in 18 high schools, they found a number of different decision making and committee structures but 'the connecting link in all these patterns, however, is the principal, especially in terms of change. The principal may only say yes or no to change, may only provide sanction and support, or may be actively involved in some way. Yet in every instance the principal was a key figure . . . if only by virtue of his/her role as primary facilitator or in establishing goals for the school' (Huling-Austin *et al.* 1985). Nine of the selected schools were 'active' in change and nine were 'typical'. Many of the principals in the active schools had an 'initiator' style, which was also found to be the most effective in the previous work with elementary schools.

Fullan (1982) summarizes his review of the research by saying, 'a large percentage of principals (at least half) operate mainly as administrators and as *ad hoc* crisis managers. These principals are not effective in helping to bring about changes in their schools. Those principals who do become involved in change do so either as direct instructional leaders or as facilitative instructional leaders. Both styles of leadership can be effective.'

The NFER study

The research focused on newly appointed secondary heads and involved all 250 who took up their first headship in England and Wales during 1982–83.

Interviews were carried out with 47 heads at the end of their first term and 16 of these were followed over a two-year period. In the case studies, three visits were made to each school and interviews were conducted with the heads, all the deputies, four heads of department, four heads of year and eight Scale 1 and 2 teachers. (Over 350 interviews were carried out in the 16 schools.) Questionnaire data were collected from 188 of the cohort of new heads and compared with a sample of 228 'old' heads with 3–8 years' experience. A third national survey was used to obtain LEA officers' views on training and support for heads and senior staff.

The material which follows is largely drawn from the 16 case-study schools and examines the types of change made during the new heads' first two years. The full results of the research, which cover many aspects of the heads' work and have important implications for training and support are reported in Weindling and Earley (1987).

Organizational changes made soon after the new head's arrival were frequently concerned with *communication and consultation*. For example, regular meetings for heads of department and heads of year, and departmental and full staff meetings were calendared in most of the case-study schools. Daily or weekly staff briefings by the heads were established in 8 of the 16 schools and a weekly bulletin was introduced in 6 schools.

Another group of early changes was concerned with *promoting the school's image*, something of particular concern to the new heads, especially where the community had a low opinion of the school or in areas where the roll was falling. Changes in this category included building improvements, the introduction of school uniform, improved liaison with the feeder primary schools, new school reports and a newsletter for pupils and parents. A more controversial change was the abolition of corporal punishment, in 4 of the 16 schools. Most of the new heads were aware of the need for good 'public relations' and publicity, and had established links with local newspapers and community groups.

Curricular changes could not be implemented until the beginning of the second year, in September 1983, as the timetables were produced some time in advance, but a considerable amount of preparatory work was undertaken in the preceding year. This usually took the form of a curriculum review, where each department was required to set out their aims, objectives, schemes of work and, in some cases, methods of assessment. Twelve of the case study schools undertook full-scale reviews during the new head's first year. In three cases the request for such a review came from the LEA and in one other school it was required for a forthcoming inspection by the HMI (Her Majesty's Inspectorate). The heads in these schools welcomed these outside requests as a means of getting staff involved and of persuading their heads of department to critically examine the work currently undertaken. In the other schools where the heads instituted the reviews themselves, they met a mixed reception, with a few heads of department delaying as long as possible – 'it's like trying to get blood out of a stone' – while others welcomed the opportunity for a full-scale review.

The strategies used by the heads to introduce change were similar across the case studies. In addition to the curricular reviews, the heads discussed the proposed changes with their senior management teams and the relevant heads of department or heads of year, and produced discussion papers. Working parties were usually set up if the changes were cross-curricular or affected many staff. The aim of the working parties was to involve teachers in the consultation and planning process. In some cases, they were required to seek information about the topic, sometimes by visiting other schools, and produce a short report with recommendations. These were usually further discussed by the senior management team and the relevant committee (e.g. heads of department or heads of year) and then put to a full staff meeting. Once a decision had been made, a different type of working party was often established, whose purpose was to produce curricular materials for the new course. A variety of working parties was found in all the case study schools. However, industrial action by the teacher unions during the research meant that many meetings had to be cancelled and this particularly affected material-production groups.

The curricular changes introduced in the 16 case-study schools were similar to those reported by the cohort of new heads and consisted of various vocational and technical courses: computing, courses for the less able, integrated science and integrated humanities. Seven of the schools had introduced a timetabled form tutor period in the new head's second year and a further five schools planned to do so in the future. Seven of the 16 schools were also introducing personal and social education courses for their fourth and fifth year students.

Several hundred changes, both major and minor, had been introduced or were planned in the 16 schools and it was noticeable that only a handful did not originate from the new heads themselves. Some were initiated from outside by the LEA, either in response to national schemes (e.g. TVEI and the Lower Attainers Project) or to local schemes, such as profiling. Surprisingly, very few changes originated from the teachers in the schools. Some examples were school reports in one school and integrated science and integrated humanities in other schools.

It was clear that the new heads were the major initiators of the changes; but once the decision to adopt a change had been made, day-to-day responsibility was usually delegated either to a deputy head or a head of department. In some schools, the heads tried to chair several of the working parties, but found that it became too time consuming or that their presence inhibited some junior members of staff. In most cases, they maintained a watching brief, requesting regular feedback from the chairperson of the group and occasionally sitting in on meetings. One of the new heads said, 'the mark of a good head is to be able to facilitate things and then withdraw, but I find a problem in getting involved in too many things at once'. It was noticeable that most deputy heads were heavily involved in the change process, both during the initial discussion and planning stages and during implementation. The new heads clearly relied on their deputies to fully support the changes.

A problem of central concern to the new heads was the pace and timing of change. The majority felt it was best not to introduce major changes during the first year. But it was necessary to start planning and laying the groundwork for change almost immediately. Some of the heads arrived with the intention of waiting a year in order to settle in and have a 'good look' at what was required. However, this was not always possible: 'I wanted to wait a year ideally, but you don't start in a vacuum and so many things were wrong that I couldn't afford to hang around.'

Several of the heads deliberately chose to make early changes, which they called 'cosmetic', in non-controversial areas and recognized that 'it was important to be seen by the staff as someone who can get things done, as it shows you mean business'. Common examples of this concerned various building improvements. A balance had to be kept between 'making an impact, but not approaching things like a bull in a china shop'. Two of the heads said that ideally they should have moved a little slower but they specifically referred to the children and felt that they would suffer if the changes were left too long.

The heads recognized that some staff expected them to make changes, especially when the previous head had been in the post for a long time. 'The school has stood still, there was lots of teacher enthusiasm for change and I was able to tap the goodwill of the staff, so there has been no real opposition.' In fact, in 11 of the 16 schools, the previous head had been in the post for over 10 years and, in six schools, for more than 20 years. However, in some of the schools it proved harder for the majority of staff to accept some of the head's proposed changes. 'The changes I am trying to introduce are simply to make the school a very normal comprehensive, but the staff think some of the ideas are way out.'

As mentioned earlier, the heads established various committees and working parties in order to involve the staff. All the heads spoke about the importance of staff participation and consultation but also stressed that they reserved the right to make the final decision. Some also clearly recognized that staff wanted to see the heads do something positive: 'Consultation is very important but you have to show action after this – talk, talk with nothing happening is very demoralising.' However, several of the heads found it much harder than they expected to get the staff involved in discussions about change. One of the heads wrote an outline paper on the aims and objectives for the school but he was disappointed when 'it went through on the nod with no discussion.'

In-service training was an important factor in helping to prepare teachers for change. Heads used both school-based and course-based INSET to 'gear up' for the forthcoming innovations. One of the heads was able to use the annual LEA closure days to provide some school-based INSET for staff preparing for integrated science and integrated humanities. This head was clearly in favour of INSET and pointed out that 45 teachers had been on 95 courses in his first term.

Many of the heads felt it was important to demonstrate a personal commitment to the changes they were proposing. This was illustrated by one head attending an LEA course on active tutorial work with some of his staff. Another method used by several of the heads was to teach on some of the new courses, such as personal and social education.

In the later interviews the heads were asked how the various changes were progressing. It was noticeable that all the heads felt that most of the changes that had been implemented were going well (c.f. Dickinson 1975). If they had experienced a strongly negative reaction to a proposed innovation, the usual strategy was to postpone the introduction of the change. But this seemed to have happened quite rarely and the most noticeable examples concerned mixed-ability teaching in two schools. Although all the heads felt that the changes were going well, three felt that 'real change', by which they meant changes in how teachers and pupils interacted in the classroom – the 'quality of learning' – would take much longer to achieve.

Towards the end of their second year, the new heads were asked in the case studies and the questionnaires whether they felt they had been able to introduce all the changes they wanted to at that point in their leadership. The results from the survey showed that 60% felt they had *not* been able to achieve all the changes. The reasons for this varied considerably and included industrial action by the teacher unions; financial restrictions and falling rolls; 'no other change agents in the senior management team apart from me'; and obstructive staff in key positions – 'I am waiting for two staff to retire next year, they have Paleolithic attitudes'. (It is interesting that Doyle and Ponder, 1977, called one group of resistant teachers 'stone age obstructionists'.) The survey data showed that one of the most frequently mentioned difficulties for heads was 'persuading members of staff to accept new ideas'. About half the new and more experienced heads rated this a 'serious' or 'very serious' problem. In addition, about a third of the 47 new heads interviewed spoke about problems of inertia with some of the middle management. While some inertia and resistance to accepting new ideas obviously occurs in most schools, it must be stressed that so far we have only dealt with the heads' perceptions. Information presented later from the teachers themselves suggests that perhaps staff are not quite as resistant to change as is commonly believed.

How fast major changes could be introduced during the first two years was a factor that concerned most new heads. Some heads decided to move cautiously but realized that this could also cause problems:

> I had a clear programme before starting and concentrated during year one almost exclusively on getting to know the staff, buildings and matters of discipline. I'm glad I didn't venture very far into curriculum areas, as I now realize I would have made a lot of mistakes. Unfortunately, my priority list has probably given some staff the impression that I am only interested in toilets and ties!

Half the 16 case study heads felt that they had managed to introduce all the changes they had wanted to by the time of the researcher's third visit, towards the end of the second year.

Where the heads felt they had brought in all the changes they wanted, they spoke about the necessity for a period of consolidation as the introduction of change had been very time consuming and many of the staff were exhausted.

Teachers' views on change

When the teachers were asked about the changes taking place in the 16 case-study schools, the most noticeable finding was that virtually every one expected the new head to introduce change. The only exception occurred in the school with an internal appointment, where the head had previously been a deputy. About a third of the teachers interviewed at this school said they did not expect the new head to introduce major changes because 'he had been part of the senior management team and did not appear to be radically opposed to things under the previous head'. In all the other schools there was a clear expectation that the arrival of a new head meant that change was most likely.

The second general finding was that the vast majority of teachers interviewed felt that most of the changes were needed. The only changes that were seen as unnecessary were those termed 'change for change's sake'. An example of this was the new head's instruction that teachers' initials on the timetable were to be changed from their first and last names to the initial letters of their surname. The teachers at this school believed this was being done because it had happened at the head's last school – what advantages the change brought were not clear.

That almost all teachers expected change and thought that most were needed suggests that the traditional belief that teachers are simply opposed to change *per se* has been overstated. The research indicates that it is how change is introduced rather than the change itself that is most likely to upset staff.

Research in USA high schools, carried out by a team from the University of Texas, obtained similar findings which showed 'a clear picture of the teacher being primarily a *recipient* of change rather than an *initiator* of change'. Despite this, teachers reacted positively to most of the changes and the researchers concluded: 'In relation to school change, there seems to be a common assumption that teachers are quite resistant to change. These data do not support that assumption.' (Rutherford and Murphy 1985).

The teachers' comments about the changes in the NFER case-study schools showed that the overall reaction was largely favourable in six schools, largely negative in four schools and mixed in the remaining six schools. An analysis of the main reasons for this indicated that teachers were happy when the head did not come in like a new broom and sweep everything away: 'he didn't come in like a whirlwind. We expected change, the feelings were of the anticipation of summer after experiencing a hell of a winter.' (At this school, very little had happened under the previous head.)

A further point stressed by teachers was the need for the new head to recognize the good things that had happened previously at the school. Considerable change was seen to imply that nothing undertaken previously was any good. Teachers also wanted to be involved, be able to express their views about the proposed changes and see the head respond to these. Positive comments were made about heads who encouraged INSET and school visits and provided the necessary resources for an innovation.

It was difficult to please all the teachers about the pace of change. There was some indication that younger staff wanted more rapid change than their older colleagues but this was by no means a clear-cut distinction. Clearly, staff have different concerns at different points in their career, as the work of Hall and Loucks (1978) shows. While change can be threatening for some staff, for others it is highly motivating: 'He made haste slowly at first, but once the changes started, then wow! It was like having to hang on to a canoe as it was going over the waterfall. But it has been very challenging and I like that.'

In the four schools where the overall reaction to change was negative, the speed of change was the main reason. Interestingly enough, in two schools the pace was felt to be too slow while, in the two others, the pace was too fast. In those where the pace was too slow, teachers said 'We've talked a lot but done little.' Lots of papers were produced and numerous staff working parties had made their recommendations but nothing further had happened. In one of the schools, the teachers believed there was a desperate need for change, but felt they were not going anywhere and they wanted leadership and direction. The staff had high expectations of the new head initially, but towards the end of the second year they had become very disillusioned. In the other two schools, where the pace was seen as too fast, teachers said 'Nothing is the same, the school has been turned upside down, there is too much change too quickly.' It was noticeable that the turnover of staff in these two schools was particularly high (42% and 30%) over two years. Teachers who did not like the way changes were introduced and who were able to move elsewhere or take early retirement did so. For comparison, in three quarters of the 188 cohort schools the staff turnover in the new head's first two years was under 10%.

Various reasons were provided in the six schools where staff reaction to change was mixed. For some staff, their high expectations of the new head were not fulfilled: 'He is not a great innovator, more a tortoise than a hare.' In another school, the middle managers (heads of department and year) felt they simply rubber-stamped decisions already made by the senior management team: 'We are told, you are going to do it, and then asked what we think.' For some staff, there were too many working parties and meetings: 'We are sick to death of meetings, someone worked out there was a total of 75 in the year.' In one school, a joke circular was sent around, asking teachers to sign up for a working party on working parties! Many teachers spoke of the increase in the amount of paper circulating in the schools and one head was felt by some staff to have lost the personal touch by his over-reliance on memos.

Conclusion and discussion

A major difference between the current project's findings and the previous research outlined at the beginning of the paper concerns the amount of involvement by heads in innovation. Whereas most of the new heads played a major part in innovation and were the originators of almost all the changes, the North American work suggests that most principals had little involvement in change. Two main reasons appear to account for the differences: the fact that the NFER study focused on newly appointed heads rather than heads in general; and the cultural differences in the organization of schooling between the UK and North America.

The case studies showed clearly that teachers expected a new head to make changes and that the heads themselves were particularly concerned to improve the school in a variety of ways. The research suggests that new heads, especially those appointed from outside the school, initiate a series of organizational and curricular changes during their first years. Most of the major changes are probably implemented by about the third or fourth year and then require fine tuning. The NFER research poses some difficulties for the Leithwood and Montgomery model outlined earlier, as it appears that most of the new heads start at the higher levels of the profile. The authors do not consider new principals and it is not clear whether heads and principals move down the levels and become more administrative after implementing the major changes. There is some evidence from the current project that the more experienced heads, after being involved in the early discussions and deciding to proceed with an innovation, were happy to delegate the main responsibility to one of the senior management team or another member of staff and maintain a watching brief. In contrast, the new heads initiated almost all the changes and played a major role in seeing them through to implementation.

The design of the present project did not permit a study of the changes much beyond the implementation stage. Many of the factors listed by Fullan (1982) as those which affect implementation were found in the NFER research. For example, regarding 'need' and 'clarity', the majority of teachers interviewed believed that the changes were needed but many were unclear about exactly what they were expected to do differently. 'Mutual adaptation' – a change in the innovation and the person – appeared to occur, most changes being modified to fit the particular circumstances of each teacher. Although INSET was often used to help teachers, almost all of it took place *prior to implementation* and teachers were given little support thereafter. Fullan stresses that it is very important to allow teachers time for regular discussion meetings *after implementation*, as it is only then that they discover the real problems and suffer a period of anxiety about the innovation.

The pace and timing of change proved to be a major factor, requiring heads to move neither too quickly nor too slowly. Various meetings and working parties were used to allow teachers to express their views and opinions about the innovations. Having set up a working party with a clear brief, heads were expected to take full account of the recommendations and to do all they could to implement them wherever possible. The majority of teachers wanted heads to show through their actions that they were fully behind an innovation, even though day-to-day responsibility was delegated to a deputy or another senior member of staff. In addition, when advocating change, new heads had to be particularly careful not to imply that everything that had happened previously at the school was of little value.

A clear difference seems to exist between North America and the UK with regard to the power and autonomy of heads and principals. The American research shows that the majority of changes were initiated from outside the schools, largely by central-office administrators. While it may be argued that the autonomy of UK heads is being reduced, the NFER study found that almost all the innovations came from the new heads and that relatively few changes came from the LEA office or from national initiatives.

References

BAILEY, A. J. (1982). *Patterns and Process of Change in Secondary Schools*, D. Phil. thesis, University of Sussex.

BELL, L. A. (1979). 'The planning of an educational change in a comprehensive school, *Durham and Newcastle Research Review*, Spring, pp. 1–8.

BERMAN, P. and McLAUGHLIN, M. (1975). *Federal programs supporting educational change. The Findings in Review*, vol. IV, Rand Corporation, Santa Monica, CA.

BURGESS, R. (1983). *Experiencing Comprehensive Education: A Study of Bishop McGregor School*, Methuen, London.

COLLIER, V. (1982). 'The role of school management in the process of change', *Durham and Newcastle Research Review*, vol. 9, no. 48,, pp. 335–9.

CRANDALL, D. and LOUCKS, S. (1983). *A Road Map for School Improvement: Executive Summary of the Study of Dissemination Efforts Supporting School Improvement* (DESSI), vol. 10, The Network Inc., Andover, MA.

DICKINSON, N. B. (1975). 'The headteacher as innovator: a study of an English school district', in REID, W. A. (ed.)., *Case Studies in Curriculum Change*, Routledge & Kegan Paul, London.

DOYLE, W. and PONDER, G. (1977). 'The practicality ethic in teacher decision making', *Interchange*, vol. 8, no. 3, pp. 1–12.

FULLAN, M. (1982). *The Meaning of Educational Change*, Teachers College Press, New York.

GILBERT, V. (1981). 'Innovativeness in a comprehensive school: The head as Janus', *Educational Administration*, vol. 9, no. 3, pp. 41–61.

HALL, G. and LOUCKS, S. (1978). 'Teacher concerns as a basis for facilitating and personalizing staff development', *Teachers College Record*, vol. 80, no. 1, pp. 36–53.

HALL, G. *et al* (1984). 'Effects of three principal styles on school improvement', *Educational Leadership*, February, pp. 22–27.

HUBERMAN, M. and MILES, M. (1984). *Innovation Up Close*, Plenum Press, New York and London.

HUGHES, M. (1975). 'The innovating school head: Autocratic initiator or catalyst of cooperation', *Educational Administration*, vol. 4, no. 1, pp. 43–54.

HULING-AUSTIN, L. *et al* (1985). 'High school principals: their role in guiding change', paper presented at American Educational Research Association (AERA), Chicago.

LEITHWOOD, K. and MONTGOMERY, D. J. (1985). 'The role of the principal in school improvement', in AUSTIN, G. *et al* (ed.), *Research on Effective Schools*, Academic Press, New York.

McGEOWN, V. (1979). 'Organizational climate for change in schools', *Educational*

Studies, vol. 5, no. 3, pp. 251–264.

MORRIS, V. C. *et al* (1981). *The Urban Principal*, NIE Report, University of Illinois, Chicago.

NICHOLLS, A. (1983). *Managing Education Innovation*, Allen and Unwin, London.

REINHARD, D. *et al*. (1980). 'Great expectations: The principal's role and in-service needs in supporting change projects', paper presented at AERA, Chicago.

ROSENBLUM, S. and JASTRZAB, J. (1980). *The Role of the Principal in Change: The Teachers Corps Example* (ABT Associates, Cambridge, MA.

RUTHERFORD, W. L. and MURPHY, S. C. (1985). 'Change in high schools: Roles and reactions of teachers', paper presented at AERA, Chicago.

THOMAS, M. (1978). *A Study of Alternatives in American Education, Vol. II, The Role of the Principal*. Rand Corporation, CA.

WADDILOVE, J. (1981). 'Planning a curriculum change', *School Organization*, vol. 1, no. 2, pp. 139–148.

WEINDLING, R. and EARLEY, P. (1987). *Secondary Headship: The First Years*, NFER-Nelson, Windsor.

WOLCOTT, H. F. (1973). *The Man in the Principal's Office*, Holt, Reinhart and Winston, NY.

Section 2

School cultures and effectiveness

2.1

Cultural forces in schools

Charles Handy

Every organization is different. Each school is different from every other school, and schools, as a group, are different from other kinds of organizations. There is something natural and right about that, for organizations are living things, each with its own history and traditions and environment and its own ability to shape its destiny. It would be a very dull and uncreative world if there were only one way to design and run an organization just as it would be a very dull and uncreative world if all families were exactly the same. Nevertheless there are things that are true of all families and, in spite of their differences, there are some truths and theories that apply to all organizations, be they schools or hospitals or banks.

It was recognition of the essential rightness of differences that led to the development of the idea of organizational cultures. A culture, according to the Chambers Dictionary, is the 'total of the inherited ideas, beliefs, values and knowledge, which constitute the shared bases of social action' and 'the total range and ideas and activities of a group of people with shared traditions which are transmitted and reinforced by members of a group'. The French culture is different from the English one although physically only twenty miles of water separate the two peoples, and in the same way a bank is a very different culture from an oil refinery, and a hospital works on cultural assumptions very different from those of an insurance company or of a school.

In some organizations, and some schools, everything is very tight and tidy and precise. People wear uniforms, things run to precise timetables, individuals are addressed formally by their title - 'headmaster' - or by their surname - 'Mr Pierce'; there are rules and procedures for everything and things are expected to go 'by the book'. In other places life seems much more informal, less structured and less regulated. 'Anne' or 'John' get on with their own work - results are everything; provided they are good, no one seems to worry too much about how they are achieved. In some organizations there are clearly bosses and workers; in others the leadership seems more diffused, people can have three or even four superiors and can even work in a group led by one of their subordinates. In one place everything will be hurry and bustle, in another calm and precision. The things prized in one organization (music, or good sports results) will be discounted in another. Some organizations will boast that people never leave them, others thrive on a constant change of personnel. Do you speak your mind or keep your mouth shut, work as hard as you can or as little as you can? Are you motivated by the work itself, or by the security of belonging to a good institution? Do you feel that you have bosses, or only colleagues? It all depends on the culture of the organization.

A fourfold classification of cultures or 'ideologies' was first outlined by Dr Roger Harrison (1972), although earlier organization theorists had developed two-sided models (e.g. organic and mechanistic, or calculative and coercive). I developed this into a more comprehensive description of four cultural types, with indications of when and where each culture might be expected to thrive and how the four types blend together to form each individual organization's cultural mix.

The work on cultures, however, had been largely based on business organizations and public corporations. Would it have any relevance for school organizations? The 'conversations', which included opportunities to complete a questionnaire on the perceived culture of the school, suggest that all four cultures can be observed in schools, that each school has its own mix, and that the cultural dilemmas which effect other organizations are there in the schools as well. That does not mean that schools will necessarily find the same way out of those dilemmas that other organizations do. It means only that one way of looking at organizations *can* be used to understand some of the dilemmas of schools as organizations. Understanding is not enough, of course. It does not automatically help you to know what to do, but it is the first step towards sensible action. If one grows up in one system, one culture, knowing only that culture, then it is not always obvious that there are alternative ways to do things. The cultural traditions of the professions are sometimes so strong that their organizations (schools, hospitals, law courts, universities) seem to have grown up in different countries from the other organizations around them. They have invented their own organizational models, unaware that there was a range of models to choose from.

In this chapter I shall describe the four cultures in outline, and then show how the teachers with whom I talked saw their schools. It was clear to me, by the end, that the four cultures did apply to schools, for there was evidence of each culture in most of the schools. The problem for a school, as with any organization, is to choose the right culture when they are being pulled in four different directions at once. A description of the cultures will make this clearer. The four cultures are:

The club culture.
The role culture.
The task culture.
The person culture.

(A fuller description of the cultures is available in two books by the present author: Handy (1979) and (1978)).

It must be emphasized at the beginning that there are no wholly good cultures and no wholly bad cultures. All cultures are OK, in the right place, because each culture is good for some things, and less good for others.

The club culture

The best picture to describe this kind of organization is a spider's web, because the key to the whole organization sits in the centre, surrounded by ever-widening circles of intimates and influence. The closer you are to the spider the more influence you have. There are other lines in the web – the lines of responsibility, the functions of the organization – but the intimacy lines are the important ones, for this organization works like a club, a club built around its head.

The 'organizational idea' in the club culture is that the organization is there to extend the person of the head or, often, of the founder. If he or she could do everything themselves, they would. It is because they can't that there has to be an organization at all; therefore the organization should be an extension of themselves, acting on their behalf, a club of like-minded people. That can sound like a dictatorship, and some club cultures are dictatorships of the owner or founder, but at their best they are based on trust and communicate by a sort of telepathy with everyone knowing each other's mind. They are very *personal* cultures, for the spiders preserve their freedom of manoeuvre by writing little down, preferring to talk to people, to sense their reactions and to infect them with her or his own enthusiasms or passions. If there are memoranda or minutes of meetings, they go from Gill to Joe or, more often, from set of initials to set of initials, rather than from job title to job title.

These cultures therefore are rich in personality. They abound with almost mythical stories and folklore from the past and can be very exciting places to work *if* you belong to the club and share the values and beliefs of the spider. Their great strength is in their ability to respond immediately and intuitively to opportunities or crises because of the very short lines of communication and because of the centralization of power. Their danger lies in the dominance of the character of the central figure. Without a spider the web is dead. If the spider is weak, corrupt, inept or picks the wrong people, the organization is also weak, corrupt, inept and badly staffed.

These cultures thrive where personality and speed of response are critical, in new business situations, in deals and brokerage transactions, in the artistic and theatrical world, in politics, guerrilla warfare and crisis situations, provided the leader is good – for they talk of leaders rather than managers in these cultures. They are a *convenient* way of running things – although not necessarily the best – when the core organization is small (under twenty people perhaps) and closely gathered together so that personal communication is easy; once things get much bigger than that, formality has to be increased and the personal, telepathetic, empathetic style is frustrated. The key to success is having the right people, who blend with the core team and can act on their own; therefore a lot of time is spent on selecting the right people and assessing whether they will fit in or not. It is no accident that some of the most successful club cultures have a nepotistic feel to them: they deliberately recruit people like themselves, even from the same family, so that the club remains a club.

The role culture

It is all very different in a role culture. Here the best picture is the kind of organization chart that all these organizations have. It looks like a pyramid of boxes; inside each box is a job title with an individual's name in smaller type below, indicating who is currently the occupant of that box, but of course the box continues even if the individual departs.

The underlying 'organizational idea' is that organizations are sets of *roles* or job-boxes, joined together in a logical and orderly fashion so that together they discharge the work of the organization. The organization is a piece of construction engineering, with role piled on role, and responsibility linked to responsibility. Individuals are 'role-occupants' with job descriptions that effectively lay down the requirements of the role and its boundaries. From time to time, the organization will rearrange the roles and their relationship to each other, as priorities change, and then reallocate the individuals to the roles.

The communications in these cultures are formalized, as are the systems and procedures. The memoranda go from role to role (head of X department to deputy head) and are copied to roles, not individuals. The place abounds in procedures for every eventuality, in rules and handbooks. There are standards, quality controls and evaluation procedures. It is all *managed* rather than led.

Most mature organizations have a lot of the role culture in them, because once an operation has settled down it can be routinized and, as it were, imprinted on the future. All organizations strive for predictability and certainty – for then fewer decisions are needed, everybody can get on with their job, the outcomes can be guaranteed, and the inputs calculated. You know where you are and where you will be; it is secure and comfortable even if it is at times too predictable to be exciting.

These role organizations thrive when they are doing a routine, stable and unchanging task, but they find it very hard to cope with change or with individual exceptions. If it's not in the rule book, they really have to wait for the rule book to be rewritten before they can act. Administrative organizations, as in part of the social security system, *have* to be role cultures and they will prove very frustrating if you turn out to be one of those individual exceptions. On the other hand, if the social security system were administered by a host of club cultures, each responding as they saw fit, social justice would hardly be served. Efficiency and fairness in routine tasks demands a role culture.

The important thing in these cultures is to get the logic of the design right, the flow of work and procedures. People are, in one sense, a less critical factor. They

can be trained to fit the role. Indeed role cultures do not want too much independence or initiative. Railways want train drivers to arrive on time, not five
minutes early. Role cultures want 'role occupants', not individualists.

The task culture

The task culture evolved in response to the need for an organizational form that
could respond to change in a less individualistic way than a club culture, and
more speedily than a role culture.

The 'organizational idea' of this culture is that a group or team of talents and
resources should be applied to a project, problem or task. In that way each task
gets the treatment it requires – it does not have to be standardized across the
organization – and the groups can be changed, disbanded or increased as the
task changes. A net, which can pull its cords this way and that and regroup at
will, is the picture of this culture.

It is the preferred culture of many competent people, because they work in
groups, sharing both skills and responsibilities; they are constantly working on
new challenges since every task is different and thus keep themselves developing
and enthusiastic. The task culture is usually a warm and friendly culture because
it is built around cooperative groups of colleagues without much overt hierarchy.
There are plans rather than procedures, and reviews of progress rather than
assessment of past performance. It is a forward-looking culture for a developing
organization.

These cultures thrive in situations where *problem-solving* is the job of the
organization. Consultancy, advertising agencies, construction work, parts of
journalism and the media, product development groups, surgical teams – any
situation beyond the capacity of one person with minions to solve, and which
cannot be embodied in procedures, needs a task culture.

The problem is that they are expensive. They use professional competent
people who spend quite a lot of time talking together in search of the right
solution. You would not use a task culture to make a wheel because they would
want to reinvent it, or at least improve on it, first. It is a questioning culture,
which chafes at routines and the daily grind of 'administration' or 'repetitive
chores'. A task culture talks of 'co-ordinators' and 'team leaders' rather than
managers; it is full of budgets (which are plans) but short on job descriptions; it
wants commitment and it rewards success with more assignments. It promises
excitement and challenge but not security of employment because it cannot
afford to employ people who do not continually meet new challenges successfully. Task cultures, therefore, tend to be full of young energetic people developing and testing talents: people who are self-confident enough not to worry about
long-term security – at least until they are a bit older!

The person culture

The person culture is very different from the first three. All of the other three cultures put the organization's purposes first and then, in their different ways, harness the individual to this purpose. The person culture puts the individual first and makes the organization the resource for the individual's talents. The most obvious examples are doctors who, for their own convenience, group themselves in a practice, barristers in chambers (a very minimal sort of organization), architects in partnerships, artists in a studio, perhaps professors in faculties or scientists in a research laboratory.

The 'organizational idea' behind this culture is that the individual talent is all-important and must be serviced by some sort of minimal organization. They do not in fact like to use the word organization but find all sorts of alternative words (practice, chambers, partnership, faculty, etc.) instead, nor do they talk of managers but of 'secretaries', 'bursars', 'chief clerk' etc.; indeed the 'managers' of these organizations are always lower in status than the professionals. You may have a senior partner in a law office but if you ask for the manager you are likely to be shown into the chief clerk. Stars, loosely grouped in a cluster or constellation, is the image of a person culture.

The individual professionals in these organizations usually have tenure, meaning that the management is not only lower in status but has few if any formal means of control over the professionals. In a university, for these reasons, the heads of department or the dean of a faculty is usually a rotating job, often seen as a necessary chore rather than a mark of distinction.

In other words, a person culture is very difficult to run in any ordinary way. The professionals have to be run on a very light rein: they can be persuaded, not commanded, influenced, cajoled or bargained with, but not managed.

The culture works where the talent of the individual is what matters, which is why you find it in the old professions, or in the arts, some sports and some religions. Increasingly however some professions are finding that the problems are too complex for one individual's talents. Architects, city solicitors, even the clergy are grouping themselves into task cultures and submitting themselves to more organizational disciplines.

The mix of cultures

I have outlined the pure forms of the cultures, but few organizations have only one. They are more often a mix of all four. What makes each organization different is the mix they choose. What makes them successful is, often, getting the right mix at the right time.

That isn't easy, because organizations are people and people have their own cultural preferences and inclinations. Whatever we think, we are usually predisposed to one culture with another back-up culture as a possible alternative, but someone who is at home in the role culture will be incapacitated in the more intuitive free-form atmosphere of a club culture, and vice versa. Thus it is that role cultures, for example, find it very hard to change themselves into task cultures even if percipient leaders see that such a change is necessary. They often need a blood transfusion of new people if the culture is really going to change, and that, of course, is what tends to happen in the more cut-and-thrust world of business organizations. Where such dramatic transfusions are impossible, organizations tend to play around with the structure, partly to bring new people into prominence, partly to give themselves the freedom to set new norms of behaviour – that is, to introduce a new culture.

The mix that you end up with at any one time is influenced by the following factors:

Size: Large size and role cultures go together. The theorists are still arguing about which causes which. Is a bureaucracy a bureaucracy because it is large and that is the only way to organize a thousand or more people, or is it large because it is a bureaucracy, because that is the only way to manage a complicated task and it has to be large to justify all the overheads of bureaucracy? It is a pertinent question for the education system, which is happy to group children under 11 in small units but wants units of four to five times the size when they are aged 12–18. The other, non-role, cultures can only operate where the core staff number less than thirty or so.

Work flow: The way the work is organized has an important bearing on the culture you can operate. If it is organized in separate units or 'job shops' where a group or an individual can be responsible for the whole job, then club, task or person cultures can exist. But if the work flow is sequential or interdependent, in that one piece is tied in with another, then you need more systems, rules and regulations and the culture shifts towards a role culture. In other words, a lot depends on what the job of the organization is seen to be.

Environment: Every organization has to think about the raw material it receives and the products it turns out for society, whether those are bars of soap or educated human beings. If the environment does not give clear signals, if the institution is a monopoly and can therefore set its own goals and standards, or if the environment never changes, then the organization will tend to go for stability and a routine quiet life – a role culture. A changing or a demanding environment requires a culture that will respond to change – a task or a club culture.

History: Organizations are to some extent stuck with their past, with their reputation, the kinds of people they hired years ago, their site and their traditions. These things take years if not decades to change.

You have to start with what you've got, which is perhaps the hardest lesson for enthusiastic heads to learn, as they dream of what might be. A staff accustomed to a club culture with a strong central figure will find it very hard to adjust to the more participative task culture even if they all claim that this is what they want. Old habits, particularly of dependence, die hard.

The cultural mix in any one organization depends on the relative importance of each of those factors. Often you will find a role culture, topped by a spider's web, with task culture project groups round the edges and a few individuals of the person culture studded throughout like raisins in a cake. A consultancy group is different, however – a set of task cultures around a spider's web with a very low-level role culture doing the logistics and the accounts, while some organizations are really a federation of 'barons', separate club cultures loosely linked together by a role culture, each free to run their own little empires.*

What culture is a school?

The 'conversations' revealed that the cultures apply to schools no less than to other organizations.

Teachers, with few exceptions, saw themselves as task culture aficionados. A very few preferred the person culture and fewer still the club or the role cultures. Teaching it seems is seen as a group activity by competent people dealing with a constantly changing challenge – the education of the young. Ideologically, the idea that education can be reduced to the systems and procedures of the role culture, the world of 'management', is rejected.

When they look at their organizations, however, the ideal is not always there, but there is a big difference between primary and secondary schools. The primary schools were scored on the questionnaires as almost pure task cultures, although observation would suggest that in some cases a benevolent club culture would have been a more appropriate description. They were small enough for either. Each teacher had their own 'job shop' or year-group which, interestingly, was itself usually organized in task groups of children sitting in groups, not rows. Communication between staff in primary schools is very personal and informal, even telepathic across the classroom or in the passageway.

Secondary schools on the other hand were scored with a predominance of the role culture. They were big, the work flow was very interdependent with the timetable or operations plan a major feature, responsibility was divided up by function (academic and pastoral, year tutor or subject teacher) and there were arrays of systems, co-ordinating procedures and committee meetings. Only the very junior teachers saw the secondary school as a person or task culture in which they were left alone to get on with their own thing. Those in the middle ranks also perceived there to be a club culture on top of the role culture, the head and deputies: a web on top of the boxes.

The question has to be: does the role culture need to be so dominant in the secondary school? There are undoubtedly a large number of forces pushing it that way:

*For those who like to play around with Greek mythology it is interesting and sometimes illuminating to find patron gods for each culture. Zeus, a king of the gods, fits the club culture. Apollo, in his capacity as god of order and of sheep, belongs to the role culture. Athena, patron of that task-force leader Odysseus, might preside over the task culture. And Dionysus, the most existentialist of the gods, suits the person culture.

- Age-related, norm-referenced examinations push one towards standardization of teaching.
- The felt need to offer a wide choice of subjects requires large numbers of teachers and therefore large number of students.
- Promotion possibilities, if tied at first to increasing proficiency in a subject area, encourage specialization by individuals, and hierarchical organizations within the school.
- Unions press for the formulation of procedures and job demarcation.
- Authorities look for financial economies of scales through large institutions.

A large institution, divided up into special functions, with a requirement that the functions combine to produce a standardized product, is a recipe for a role culture.

On the other hand, Richard Matthew and Simon Tong (1982) describe a school as 'a series of interrelated independencies' and go on to suggest that 'the collegiate model will seem strange to many staffs and heads'. They see the school, in other words, as a *person culture* of individual professionals who have to be co-ordinated almost in spite of themselves. Within the role culture a person culture bubbles away.

Certainly the traditions of professionalism remain strong. Tenure, the privacy of the classroom, and the right to express one's own views in one's own ways, the sense of accountability primarily to one's profession – these are all hallmarks of a profession and of a person culture. They do not sit well with graded hierarchies, standardized curricula and the management ethos of a large institution, all of which call for a role culture.

The secondary school today seems afflicted by a sort of organizational schizophrenia – is it a bureaucratic factory delivering goods or is it a collective of individual professionals each doing their own professional thing? It is convenient for governments, local authorities and parents to see it as a factory. Then they can ask it to deliver particular types of goods, they can use the language of resources and outputs, they can impose quality control and other regulations, they can measure and compare effectiveness.

On the other hand, the ethos of education, the development of the individual, the crucial interaction between individual teacher and individual pupil, all argue for the maintenance of the professional tradition. Which should it be? It is not easy, perhaps not possible to run a role culture stuffed full of person-culture professionals. Primary schools do not try. They remain task or club cultures, which can tolerate professionals as long as they are not outrageously independent. It has been accepted that primary schools stay small and sacrifice the economies and variety offered by large size. Was it a conscious decision?

If the school is to be an efficient role culture, then the traditions of the individualistic professions may have to be abandoned. The alternative is to move the schools towards task cultures, the half-way house to professionalism. This will require different philosophies of management from the ones currently prevailing in most secondary schools. Interestingly, however, modern businesses are moving away from hierarchies to networks in response to the need for more flexibility and in order to give more room to the individual. It may be that in aping the bureaucracy of large businesses the secondary school has been adopting a theory of management that is already out of date.

Schools, like other organizations, are pulled four ways by the demands of the different cultures. Sometimes it must feel as if they are being pulled apart. It is the task of management to gather the cultural forces together, using the strengths of each in the right places. It is not an easy task. [. . .]

References

HANDY, C. (1978). *Understanding Organizations*, Harmondsworth, Penguin, ch. 7.

HANDY, C. (1979). *The Gods of Management*, London, Pan Books.

HARRISON, R. (1972). 'How to describe your organization', *Harvard Business Review*, Sept-Oct.

MATTHEW, R. and TONG, S. (1982). *The Role of a Deputy Head in a Comprehensive School*, London, Ward Lock.

2.2

Key factors for effective
junior schooling

Peter Mortimore, Pamela Sammons,
Louise Stoll, David Lewis and Russell Ecob

[This short chapter presents some of the major outcomes of the Junior School Project, which was conducted by the Research and Statistics Branch of the Inner London Education Authority (ILEA) under the direction of Peter Mortimore. The project was a four-year longitudinal study which followed nearly two thousand pupils through their junior schooling in fifty schools. Using a range of measures of pupils' background and progress and of school and classroom processes, as well as complex methods of analysis, the project aimed in part to identify which factors make some schools or classes more effective than others in promoting pupils' learning and development.]

[We investigated] the positive or negative effects that a variety of factors and processes had upon pupils' educational outcomes. Many of these factors had an impact on several different outcomes. Similarly, school and classroom processes were frequently related to each other. Thus, through a detailed investigation of these links, a picture evolves of what constitutes effective junior schooling.

This picture is not intended to be a 'blueprint' for success. Inevitably, many aspects of junior schooling could not be examined in the Junior School Project. Futhermore, schools are not static institutions. This survey was carried out between 1980 and 1984, and it has, therefore, not been possible to take full account of all the changes (particularly in approaches to the curriculum) that have taken place since that time. Nonetheless, this [chapter] identifies the key factors that were consistently related to effective junior schooling.

Initially, before examining factors over which schools and teachers can exercise direct control, consideration is given to less flexible characteristics of schools. It was found that certain of these 'given' features made it easier to create an effective school.

Schools that cover the entire primary age range (JMIs), where pupils do not have to transfer at age seven, appear to be at an advantage, as do voluntary-aided schools.[1] Smaller schools, with a junior roll of under 160 children, also

---

[1] On the whole, the latter tend to have more socio-economically advantaged intakes than county schools.

appear to benefit their pupils. Class size is particularly relevant: smaller classes, with less than 24 pupils, had a positive impact upon pupil progress and development, especially in the early years.

Not surprisingly, a good physical environment, as reflected in the school's amenities, its decorative order, and its immediate surroundings, creates a positive situation in which progress and development can be fostered. Extended periods of disruption, due to building work and redecoration, can have a negative impact on pupils' progress. The stability of the school's teaching force is also an important factor. Changes of head and deputy headteacher, though inevitable, have an unsettling effect upon the pupils. It seems, therefore, that every effort should be made to reduce the potentially negative impact of such changes. Similarly, where there is an unavoidable change of class teacher, during the school year, careful planning will be needed to ensure an easy transition, and minimise disruption to the pupils. Where pupils experience continuity through the whole year, with one class teacher, progress is more likely to occur.

It is, however, not only continuity of staff that is important. Although major or frequent changes tend to have negative effects, change can be used positively. Thus, where there had been no change of head for a long period of time, schools tended to be less effective. In the more effective schools, heads had usually been in post for between three and seven years.

It is clear, therefore, that some schools are more advantaged in terms of their size, status, environment and stability of teaching staff. Nonetheless, although these favourable 'given' characteristics contribute to effectiveness, they do not, by themselves, ensure it. They provide a supporting framework within which the head and teachers can work to promote pupil progress and development. The size of a school, for example, may facilitate certain modes of organisation which benefit pupils. However, it is the factors *within* the control of the head and teachers that are crucial. These are the factors that can be changed and improved.

Twelve key factors of effectiveness have been identified.

The twelve factors

1 Purposeful leadership of the staff by the headteacher

'Purposeful leadership' occurred where the headteacher understood the needs of the school and was actively involved in the school's work, without exerting total control over the rest of the staff.

In effective schools, headteachers were involved in curriculum discussions and influenced the content of guidelines drawn up within the school, without taking total control. They also influenced the teaching style of teachers, but only selectively, where they judged it necessary. This leadership was demonstrated by an emphasis on monitoring pupils' progress through the keeping of individual records. Approaches varied – some schools kept written records; others passed on folders of pupils' work to their next teacher; some did both – but a systematic policy of record keeping was important.

With regard to in-service training, those heads exhibiting purposeful leadership did not allow teachers total freedom to attend *any* course: attendance was allowed for a good reason. Nonetheless, most teachers in these schools had attended in-service courses.

2 The involvement of the deputy head

The Junior School Project findings indicate that the deputy head can have a major role in the effectiveness of junior schools.

Where the deputy was frequently absent, or absent for a prolonged period (due to illness, attendance on long courses, or other commitments), this was detrimental to pupils' progress and development. Moreover, a change of deputy head tended to have negative effects.

The responsibilities undertaken by deputy heads also seemed to be important. Where the head generally involved the deputy in policy decisions, it was beneficial to the pupils. This was particularly true in terms of allocating teachers to classes. Thus, it appeared that a certain amount of delegation by the headteacher, and a sharing of responsibilities, promoted effectiveness.

3 The involvement of teachers

In successful schools, the teachers were involved in curriculum planning and played a major role in developing their own curriculum guidelines. As with the deputy head, teacher involvement in decisions concerning which classes they were to teach, was important. Similarly, consultation with teachers about decisions on spending, was important. It appeared that schools in which teachers were consulted on issues affecting school policy, as well as those affecting them directly, were more likely to be successful.

4 Consistency amongst teachers

It has already been shown that continuity of staffing had positive effects. Not only, however, do pupils benefit from teacher continuity, but it also appears that some kind of stability, or consistency, in teacher approach is important.

For example, in schools where all teachers followed guidelines in the same way (whether closely or selectively), the impact on progress was positive. Where there was variation between teachers in their usage of guidelines, this had a negative effect.

5 Structured sessions

The project findings indicate that pupils benefited when their school day was structured in some way. In effective schools, pupils' work was organized by the teacher, who ensured that there was always plenty for them to do. Positive effects were also noted when pupils were *not* given unlimited responsibility for planning their own programme of work, or for choosing work activities.

In general, teachers who organized a framework within which pupils could work, and yet allowed 'them some freedom within this structure, were more successful.

6 Intellectually challenging teaching

Unsurprisingly, the quality of teaching was very important in promoting pupil progress and development. The findings clearly show that, in classes where pupils were stimulated and challenged, progress was greater.

The content of teachers' communications was vitally important. Positive effects occurred where teachers used more 'higher-order' questions and statements, that is, where their communications encouraged pupils to use their creative imagination and powers of problem-solving. In classes where the teaching situation was challenging and stimulating, and where teachers communicated interest and enthusiasm to the children, greater pupil progress occurred. It appeared, in fact, that teachers who more frequently directed pupils' work, without discussing it or explaining its purpose, had a negative impact. Frequent monitoring and maintenance of work, in terms of asking pupils about their progress, was no more successful. What was crucial was the *level* of the communications between teacher and pupils.

Creating a challenge for pupils suggests that the teacher believes they are capable of responding to it. It was evident that such teachers had *high* expectations of their pupils. This is further seen in the effectiveness of teachers who encouraged their pupils to take independent control over the work they were currently doing. Some teachers only infrequently gave instructions to pupils concerning their work, yet everyone in the class knew exactly what they were supposed to be doing, and continued working without close supervision. This strategy improved pupil progress and development.

7 Work-centred environment

In schools, where teachers spent more of their time discussing the *content* of work with pupils, and less time on routine matters and the maintenance of work activity, the impact was positive. There was some indication that time devoted to giving pupils feedback about their work was also beneficial.

The work-centred environment was characterized by a high level of pupil industry in the classroom. Pupils appeared to enjoy their work and were eager to commence new tasks. The noise level was also low, although this is not to say that there was silence in the classroom. Furthermore, pupil movement around the classroom, was not excessive, and was generally work-related.

8 Limited focus within sessions

It appears that learning was facilitated when teachers devoted their energies to one particular curriculum area within a session. At times, work could be undertaken in two areas and also produce positive effects. However, where many sessions were organized such that three or more curriculum areas were concurrent, pupils' progress was marred. It is likely that this finding is related to other factors. For example, pupil industry was lower in classrooms where mixed activities occurred. Moreover, noise and pupil movement were greater, and teachers spent less time discussing work and more time on routine issues. More importantly, in mixed-activity sessions the opportunities for communication between teachers and pupils were reduced (as will be described later):

A focus upon one curriculum area did not imply that all the pupils were doing exactly the same work. There was some variation, both in terms of choice of topic and level of difficulty. Positive effects tended to occur where the teacher geared the level of work to pupils' needs.

9 Maximum communication between teachers and pupils

It was evident that pupils gained from having more communication with the teacher. Thus, those teachers who spent higher proportions of their time *not* interacting with the children were less successful in promoting progress and development.

The time teachers spent on communication with the whole class was also important. Most teachers devoted the majority of their attention to speaking with individuals. Each child, therefore, could only expect to receive a fairly small number of individual contacts with their teacher. When teachers spoke to the whole class, they increased the overall number of contacts with children. In particular, this enabled a greater number of 'higher-order' communications to be received by *all* pupils. Therefore, a balance of teacher contacts between individuals and the whole class was more beneficial than a total emphasis on communicating with individuals (or groups) alone.

Furthermore, where children worked in a single curriculum area within sessions, (even if they were engaged on individual or group tasks) it was easier for teachers to raise an intellectually challenging point with *all* pupils.

10 Record keeping

The value of record keeping has already been noted, in relation to the purposeful leadership of the headteacher. However, it was also an important aspect of teachers' planning and assessment. Where teachers reported that they kept written records of pupils' work progress, in addition to the Authority's Primary Yearly Record, the effect on the pupils was positive. The keeping of records concerning pupils' personal and social development was also found to be generally beneficial.

11 Parental involvement

The research found parental involvement to be a positive influence upon pupils' progress and development. This included help in classrooms and on educational visits, and attendance at meetings to discuss children's progress. The head-teacher's accessibility to parents was also important, showing that schools with an informal, open-door policy were more effective. Parental involvement in pupils' educational development within the home was also beneficial. Parents who read to their children, heard them read, and provided them with access to books at home, had a positive effect upon their children's learning. One aspect of parental involvement was, however, not successful. Somewhat curiously, formal Parent-Teacher Associations (PTAs) were not found to be related to effective schooling. It could be that some parents found the formal structure of such a body to be intimidating.

Nonetheless, overall, parental involvement was beneficial to schools and their pupils.

12 Positive climate

The Junior School Project provides confirmation that an effective school has a positive ethos. Overall, the atmosphere was more pleasant in the effective schools, for a variety of reasons.

Both around the school and within the classroom, less emphasis on punishment and critical control, and a greater emphasis on praise and rewarding pupils, had a positive impact. Where teachers actively encouraged self-control on the part of pupils, rather than emphasizing the negative aspects of their behaviour, progress and development increased. What appeared to be important was firm but fair classroom management.

The teacher's attitude to their pupils was also important. Good effects resulted where teachers obviously enjoyed teaching their classes and communicated this to their pupils. Their interest in the children as individuals, and not just as pupils was also valuable. Those who devoted more time to non-school chat or 'small talk' increased pupils' progress and development. Outside the classroom, evidence of a positive climate included: the organization of lunchtime and after-school clubs for pupils; teachers eating their lunch at the same tables as the children; organization of trips and visits; and the use of the local environment as a learning resource.

The working conditions of teachers contributed to the creation of a positive school climate. Where teachers had non-teaching periods, the impact on pupil progress and development was positive. Thus, the climate created by the teachers for the pupils, and by the head for the teachers, was an important aspect of the school's effectiveness. This further appeared to be reflected in effective schools by happy, well-behaved pupils who were friendly towards each other and outsiders, and by the absence of graffiti around the school.

These are the twelve key factors that have been identified in the study. Some had a stronger effect than others on the cognitive and non-cognitive areas investigated, but all were positive. [. . .] These factors depend on specific behaviours and strategies employed by the headteacher and staff. It is essential to realize that the school and the classroom are in many way interlocked. What the teacher can or cannot do depends, to a certain extent, on what is happening in the school as a whole.

Whilst these twelve factors do not constitute a 'recipe' for effective junior schooling, they can provide a framework within which the various partners in the life of the school – headteacher and staff, parents and pupils, and governors – can operate. Each of these partners has the capacity to foster the success of the school. When each participant plays a positive role, the result is an effective school.

The management of school improvement

Ron Glatter

Introduction

This chapter is based on reflections arising from the author's participation in the International School Improvement Project (ISIP). ISIP was organized under the aegis of the Centre for Educational Research and Innovation (CERI) of the Organization for Economic Co-operation and Development (OECD). It was a collaborative project involving institutions and individuals from 14 countries which aimed, through seminars, publications and other means, to develop and disseminate useful knowledge about the process of school improvement.

The project was divided into six broad areas relevant to school improvement: school-based review; principals and internal change agents; external support; research and evaluation; school improvement policy; and conceptual mapping of school improvement. [. . .] The particular focus of this author has been on the area dealing with principals.

The chapter starts with a brief examination of the concept of school improvement, goes on to consider some current perceptions of management, and then attempts to relate the two ideas of school improvement and management by reference to various 'images' of schools as organizations. Finally, some implications of this analysis for the professional development of principals and others in leading positions within schools (who are subsequently referred to collectively as 'school leaders') will be mentioned.

A note of caution should be entered here. [. . .] The author is conscious that the concept of school improvement is North American in origin, that an impressive range of relevant empirical research has been conducted there and that there has been valuable and promising conceptual development (Clark, Lotto and Astuto, 1984). The European work is, by contrast, sparse (for a rare example, see Hopkins and Wideen, 1984). One of the outcomes of ISIP should be to initiate some correction in this imbalance. Meanwhile, this author has found it necessary – and educative – to draw mainly on North American sources.

The concept of school improvement

There is space to discuss only a small selection of aspects of this concept. We might ask first what are the distinctive resonances of the term 'school improvement' compared with those of its elder cousin 'innovation'? The tone of 'school improvement' is more comprehensive yet more incremental, implying a broader sweep over the school's activities but less radical in intent. There is also a clear focus on the attempt to achieve an outcome – improvement – rather than just to introduce something new. Thus, 'school improvement' is a term which reflects the current age in ways 'innovation' does not.

Meanings

The definition of 'school improvement' adopted by ISIP is as follows:

> A systematic, sustained effort aimed at change in learning conditions and other related internal conditions in one or more schools, with the ultimate aim of accomplishing educational goals more effectively.
>
> (Miles and Ekholm, 1985a)

Such a definition can clearly encompass many different varieties of change. The authors of the first ISIP book suggest three major variables – scope, size and scale. *Scope* refers to whether the boundaries of the change are broad or narrow, for instance a specific curriculum change compared with a broader reform aimed at several aspects of the school's functioning; *size* is the relative complexity of the change from the point of view of the persons implementing it; and *scale* relates to the number of units and levels of the educational system that the change involves. Quite modest changes (in terms of scope, size and scale) in 'related internal conditions' could fall within the definition. For instance, in the British context, a head teacher might feel that a strict policy on the wearing of school uniform by pupils would improve learning conditions and hence attainment. A sustained campaign to enforce the wearing of uniform would then constitute an attempt at school improvement. It certainly meets the authors' criterion of aiming at change in the school as a whole, not just in specific classrooms (van Velzen *et al*, 1985).

The example also highlights a theme familiar from innovation studies: the value-laden and political aspects of many attempts at school improvement. These aspects have probably grown sharper in recent years with, for instance, the decline in resources allocated to schools and expectations of a greater emphasis on vocationally oriented learning in secondary schools in many countries. The different connotations of a term like 'school improvement' in different national contexts are also striking. At a recent ISIP seminar such contrasting perspectives became very apparent. For instance, the Japanese view of improvement seemed to be in terms of the steady development of current activities: for them, as one Japanese speaker observed, 'School improvement is equivalent to better daily problem solving.' By contrast, in North America, improvement still frequently appeared in practice to be associated with specific curriculum (often single-subject) initiatives introduced by school districts. As a final example, in Sweden, the improvement attempt seemed to be concerned with altering the whole ethos of, and pattern of relationships within, the school. Attaching simple labels to each of these perspectives, we might select improvement (Japan), innovation (North America) and reform (Sweden).

Clearly, there are many qualifications to be made about such general perceptions. For instance, the reality at school level might look quite different and present far more common features than the sharp contrasts above imply. However, one conclusion in the first ISIP publication is that research suggests that the *process* which a school needs to go through when it improves is largely the same wherever it occurs (Ekholm and Miles, 1985). The validity of this conclusion must depend in part on how disparate are the meanings attached to 'improvement' in various contexts.

Improvement and maintenance

A relevant issue here is the connection between 'improvement' and routine operations. While the ISIP definition given above largely reflects the cultural shift from 'innovation' to 'improvement' outlined earlier, it nevertheless specifies that, to be classed as an 'improvement', a change must involve 'a systematic, sustained effort . . .' implying a sharp distinction between routine operations and attempts at change. Is improvement possible *only* through a 'systematic, sustained effort aimed at change . . .'? We have already seen that in the Japanese context such a distinction may not be wholly acceptable. March (1984), writing generally rather than with specific reference to education, has argued that administrative theory has been misleading in the emphasis it has given to this distinction, and that effective routine operations are often the main motors of organizational change. 'The theoretical rhetoric of change seems antithetical to routine, but I have argued that effective systems of routine behaviour are the primary bases of organizational adaptation to an environment' (March, 1984: 33). He urges us to recognize the impact of 'ordinary competence' and 'of the ways in which organizations change by modest modifications of routines rather than by massive mucking around' (March, 1984: 22). Change and improvement do take place through a large number of quite small adjustments, and we need to examine the ways in which this happens as well as the more overt and systematic attempts at improvement. For example, is the evolutionary adaptive process outlined by March capable of accommodating radical changes in environmental conditions or expectations?

If the old boundary between 'innovation' and 'maintenance' is becoming less firm, with the idea of 'improvement' acting to some extent as a bridge between them, this by no means implies that intervention and pressure will not accelerate change. As House observes, the nature of this pressure is a matter of debate on social as well as technical grounds: '. . . The school, being traditional, will be slow to change without pressures. How modernization should occur, through what legitimate means, and how fast, are the issues that divide people concerned about innovation' (House, 1981: 37).

The effects of school-level interventions during improvement processes have been studied by researchers, particularly in North America. In line with the trends outlined above, the activities involved appear to be more subtle and informal than is implied when as March puts it, 'we sing the grand arias of management' (March, 1984: 23). Hall and Hord (1984) developed an 'intervention taxonomy' based on their own studies of change processes in schools and from published case studies. Although there were significant interventions at various strategic levels, the most important type was the 'incident level intervention'; for example, a short interaction between two teachers concerned with a particular change or a memo from a school leader to all teachers involved in an innovation. 'From our studies to date, it is clear that delivery and understanding of incident level interventions is of crucial importance to successful implementation . . . The number of incident interventions is so large that their combined effect appears to "make or break" the effort' (Hall and Hord, 1984: 292). Another significant type of intervention was dubbed a 'mushroom' by the authors. A mushroom is an intervention that was not deliberately initiated to influence the course of an improvement process, but turns out to do so, for good or ill. 'Mushrooms can be flavourful and nutritious or they can be quite poisonous' (Hall and Hord, 1984: 295). Examples might include: a key person taking on an increased workload and missing meetings relevant to the improvement with negative, or possibly positive, effects on its progress; unexpected staff losses or gains, with their resultant impact (Miles, 1983); personality clashes within the staff group and their effects on the improvement attempt.

Such examples indicate not only the multiplicity of influences involved but also the importance of regarding school improvement as a process. For example, studies have found that staff commitment often grows during implementation: 'Changes in attitudes, beliefs and understanding tend to *follow* rather than precede changes in behaviour' (Fullan, 1985: 393). Of course, the ultimate object of a process of improvement is to stabilize a change in state, to establish new routines (Berman, 1981: Morris and Burgoyne, 1973), a point which emphasizes the close connection between improvement and maintenance processes.

Scope

Finally in this section, we return to the suggestion that 'school improvement' carries the implication of a process that will cover the whole of the school and affect it for the better. In the real world, however, there are always choices to be made and limited funds, time and energy to be allocated in certain directions rather than others. So the *scope* of a particular school improvement attempt is an important issue. 'Devoting resources and attention to one or two objectives is certainly a good way to improve performance in those areas. But if this is done without consideration of other domains, it is likely that the latter will suffer' (Fullan, 1985: 397). Since school improvement is an ambitious-sounding concept, it is well to ask of any particular scheme: 'Whether by accident or design, what is this proposal *not* intended to improve?' The answer should give guidance in assessing whether the plan might fairly be described as an attempt at school improvement.

Perceptions of the task of management

Recent writing on management, in education and elsewhere, has been reasserting the intuitive, judgemental aspects of the management task as distinct from the more technical scientific dimensions which were emphasized through much of the 1960s and 1970s. Schön, a leading exponent of this view, refers to 'the spontaneous exercise of intuitive artistry' and to managers becoming effective not mainly through studying theory and technique but through long practice 'which builds up a generic, essentially unanalysable capacity for problem-solving' (Schön, 1984: 41). (A somewhat similar assessment has been made by Griffiths [1979].) From these ideas, Schön develops his proposal for a 'reflective management science' based on the 'private inquiries' of reflective managers, supported by researchers whose primary tasks would be to facilitate and document these inquiries, synthesize their results and provide conceptual frameworks for them (Schön, 1984: 62).

The literature focusing specifically on studies of improvement and change is also increasingly stressing the less tangible, more subtle aspects of management. Glatter refers to 'the central role of imagination, judgment and a grasp of reality in management for adaptability' (Glatter, 1984: 34). Fullan identifies what he calls 'leadership feel for the improvement process' as a key variable, partly because 'processes of improvement are intrinsically paradoxical and subtle' (Fullan, 1985: 401).

Attempts to snare these elusive factors are proceeding apace. Rutherford and his associates have developed a model of 'change facilitator style' which includes not only 'behaviours' like providing for staff development and actively seeking resources but also 'attitude, motivations and feelings of adequacy for facilitating, knowledge of the task, beliefs about the role and philosophy of change' (Rutherford, Hord, Huling and Hall, 1983: 115). They consider that these factors may represent the 'inner states' to which Leithwood and Montgomery refer in their review of 29 studies of elementary school principals: 'These inner states explain much overt activity and are, in turn, affected by the consequences of that activity' (Leithwood and Montgomery, 1982: 320). Rutherford and his colleagues introduce a further 'intangible' factor as a component of their model of style: 'tone' similar to 'tone of voice'. They argue that it is not only the words in which a spoken statement is delivered which convey a message, but also the tone with which they are delivered (for instance, half listening compared with listening enthusiastically and asking an appropriate question). 'In fact, the tone of voice may carry a more powerful message than the words' (Rutherford, Hord, Huling and Hall, 1983: 116).

Setting directions

This is clearly difficult territory for researchers. There are, for instance, obvious problems in attempting to identify in any concrete terms the variables contained in this simple but striking sentence by Buckley, an experienced British head teacher and trainer who conducted a survey of European training provision for school leaders: 'A head must give a school a sense of direction and a feeling of confidence' (Buckley, 1985: 171). This conclusion is supported by a study of British primary school teachers' perceptions of, and degrees of satisfaction with, the leadership styles of their head teachers (Nias, 1980), which found that the teachers especially wanted their heads to provide a sense of purpose, direction and coherence. The style which was especially appreciated was one in which the head took the lead in goal-setting, but the teachers felt they were genuinely able to contribute to policy formation. This is resonant of the conclusion from North American research on effective principals that, in spite of often operating (as we have seen) in an informal manner, and in spite of involving their teachers extensively in decision making, their own preference is for a *task* rather than a relations orientation, emphasizing, for instance, the definition of goals related to student learning and monitoring their achievement (Leithwood, Stanley and Montgomery, 1984).

Change and stability

To try to ensure that this direction-setting task of management is adequately fulfilled, some have suggested that the 'routine' and 'improvement' aspects of management should be more clearly separated. This is related to the repeated finding that the frenetic and fragmented work pattern of school leaders (as of other managers) tends to drive out forward thinking, planning and goal defini- tion (Glatter, 1983). In fact, Buckley identifies as the *major* problem facing European secondary school leaders 'managing the present while preparing for the future at the same time' (Buckley, 1985: 22). He argues that this problem is made more severe when training programmes increasingly emphasize the school leader's role as a change agent which the individual is expected to fulfil while preoccupied with the task of maintaining day-to-day stability, and he considers that trainers should give careful attention to this dilemma. The strains imposed by this extension of the job in terms of *time* are additional to those resulting from its extension in terms of *space*, indicated by the school's increasing involvement in, and accountability to, society and its local community (Buckley, 1985; see also Morgan, Hall and Mackay, 1984).

Pressures of this kind and scale have led to suggestions like that made by
Handy, a British management specialist who undertook a close examination of
secondary schools in England. He concluded that '. . . there is not enough discussion of what we are trying to do and how we should be doing it and measuring
it and too much discussion of timetables, rosters and duties' (Handy, 1984: 35).
He makes a sharp distinction between 'leadership' and 'administration' and
argues that 'Professionals require one of their own to lead them but can, and normally should, use an outsider to administer things for them' (Handy, 1984: 23).
Handy himself recognizes that the two tasks are not divorced from one another
and in particular that 'An inefficient school is an ineffective school, and you
notice it straight away' (Handy, 1984: 35). The dichotomy is difficult to sustain
in practice, as March argued (even for timetables, rosters and duties) particularly in terms of the student's experience. Buckley's dilemmas are likely to
remain: school leaders are not solely change agents, nor can they avoid maintenance activity or functions which do not have an immediate and obvious connection with the process of teaching and learning. The detailed review of North
American research on the effective principal conducted by Leithwood and his
colleagues led them to the view that '. . . the principal must and ought to engage
in a wide spectrum of functions, that these functions all have some bearing
(positive or negative) on the quality of students' school experiences' and that the
objective in carrying out these functions is to give them coherence and purpose
'in order to realize the holistic image of the educated person to which students
and school aspire' (Leithwood, Stanley and Montgomery, 1984: 62). We now
need to focus collective attention on how such a demanding set of requirements
can be met, and on how the management of improvement and the management
of current operations relate to one another, rather than regarding them as largely
separate and unconnected activities.

Organizational images and school improvement

Underlying many of the trends which have been discussed in earlier sections is a
broader conceptual shift, from an over-reliance on rational, linear models of how
change occurs in schools towards acceptance of a far wider range of explanations. For instance, in their review of relevant American studies, Clark, Lotto
and Astuto (1984) criticize the 'model bias' of much work on school improvement because of its rational, bureaucratic view of organizations, goals, leadership and accountability and its assumption of a relationship of linear causality
between identified variables. Berman (1981) argues that the complex organizational sub-processes which make up the educational change process 'are loosely,
not linearly, coupled'. At the level of action in schools, a prime task for management is the identification of new problems and key opportunities which, as
Handy points out, 'is an activity that belongs more to the right or creative side of
the brain than to the left or logical and linear bit' (Handy, 1984: 27).

Images of schools

Several writers have recently developed useful schemes for classifying the different 'perspectives' on or 'images' of educational organizations found in the research literature (Cuthbert, 1984; Davies and Morgan, 1983; Ellström, 1983; House, 1981; Miles and Ekholm, 1985b). For instance, House (1981) refers to the technological, political and cultural perspectives, while Miles and Ekholm (1985b) identify five 'images' of schools as organizations: rational/bureaucratic, professionalized/collegial; social system; political; natural system. For House, the perspectives are 'ways of seeing' organizations and they function in a changing social and political world: 'The political and cultural perspectives are made more viable by the declining belief in technology and by less social consensus on goals' (House, 1981: 20). They are therefore more open to change than scientific paradigms and are more dependent on the particular context. Furthermore, they are not mutually exclusive. 'The same person may view innovation from one perspective, then from another for another purpose' (House, 1981).

Consideration has therefore been given to the relationship between the images. Davies and Morgan (1983) regard them as relating to distinct phases of a change process, whereas Ellström (1983) suggests that they should be seen not as phases but as *faces* or 'dimensions of the same organizational reality' and assumes that the different dimensions may be differently *salient* in different organizations (for instance schools and industrial firms), in different parts of the same organization or even in the same part at different points in time. Other writers are less specific than this, and simply stress the implications for our research and our practice of viewing schools through a particular 'lens': 'Regardless of the lens we use, the real life of any particular school may be more or less like the image' (Miles and Ekholm, 1985b). Schön argues that an overemphasis on the rational, technological aspects of management in the professional training of managers may create in them 'selective inattention' to the other aspects and the avoidance of 'situations – often the most important in organizational life – where they would find themselves confronted with uncertainty, instability or uniqueness' (Schön, 1984: 41). Sergiovanni (1984) advocates a 'multiple-perspective view' which does not involve a complete break with the technological perspective but locates it appropriately within a comprehensive theory of organization. Nevertheless, it is significant that, just when technological, 'rational' approaches to the management of school improvement are coming into increasing prominence in many countries, research-based analyses are increasingly questioning their validity and potency.

Implications for management

Some interesting contrasts between the behaviour of those attempting to manage improvements on the basis of the different images can be suggested (House, 1981; Miles and Ekholm, 1985b). The *rational image* emphasizes order and rules and assumes much consensus on interests and values. The tasks of management are then to clarify purposes and goals, to discover and specify ways of achieving them, to monitor performance and to ensure that teachers have the requisite skills and training. These managerial tasks can be carried out fairly aggressively since values and interests are not in serious dispute; structures tend to be hier-archical and authority is relatively unquestioned. This perspective is often asso-ciated with initiatives for improvement emanating from government agencies, and tends to be optimistic in its assumptions about what can be achieved by management action.

The *professional/collegial image*, as its name implies, emphasizes the professional competence and expertise of the teaching staff and their collegial collaboration in meeting the needs of the clients (students). The task of management in the improvement process is largely to support the work of teaching, perhaps even to 'fade into the wallpaper' and concentrate closely on administrative and support-ive activities while the professionals go about the real business. The collegial overlaps considerably with the *social system image*, but the latter stresses in addi-tion the idea of the organization as an interdependent collection of parts inter-acting with each other and with the environment, and also the development of open, trusting relationships and modes of communication. The tasks of manage-ment for improvement are to lead and to facilitate, especially in terms of the *process* aspects of improvement, involving everyone in thoughtful, collaborative work.

Some of the most interesting and least explored questions arise in connection with the 'newer' political and cultural images. The *political image* emphasizes the conflicting interests which individuals and groups have in organizations, and which they pursue through building factions and coalitions and through bar-gaining and compromise. In the *cultural image* (called 'natural systems image' by Miles and Ekholm [1985b]) schools and school systems are seen as composed of groups with separate and distinct cultures and their associated values interacting with one another: 'The fact that schools are often slow to agree to external initiatives suggests that they own *themselves*, and the so-called "demands of society" as filtered through governments and authorities are far away, in another world' (van Velzen and Robin, 1985). Handy (1984) has argued that one way to improve large secondary schools would be to strengthen their cultural aspects by, for instance, giving them federal structures and so making them 'cities of villages'.

The cultural and political images differ from the other three, as is often remarked, in that they do not assume consensus or clarity about goals. In consequence, these perspectives imply far less 'optimism' over the extent to which improvement can be 'engineered', although they can certainly accommo-date the possibility that organizations adapt effectively to their environment through routine processes, as suggested by March (1984) and discussed earlier in this chapter. Nevertheless, these perspectives seem, at least up to the present, to be more helpful in suggesting why attempts at improvement may fail – because they conflict with the values and/or interests of those who are intended to carry them through – than in indicating how such attempts may be made to succeed.

Thus, it has been suggested that the political perspective is 'essentially reactive' and is antithetical to participative decision making or group problem solving because political procedures are primarily 'a method for keeping order in institutions, not for obtaining the optimal solutions to problems' (Meier, 1985: 66). Equally, the cultural perspective has been characterized as harbouring a 'conservative, traditional view of change' because of the inherent difficulty of resolving conflict between cultures, short of political action by the stronger one (House, 1981). It is interesting, in this context, to note the increasing use of financial and other incentives in some countries to persuade schools and teachers to move in certain directions. Berman (1981) has drawn attention to US findings which suggest that innovation projects are often adopted opportunistically to benefit from external money or for political considerations rather than to solve pressing educational problems. Further data along these lines might lead us to conclude that the political perspective is rather more firmly based than the cultural!

Even in these perspectives, some tasks and requirements relevant to the management of improvement can be indicated. Conflict management is pervasive in both, though of a different kind in each, and in the cultural perspective it is akin to treading on eggshells. The political perspective implies the need for those managing improvements to have a close understanding of the interests and motives of those likely to be affected, to be willing to consider 'tailoring' the improvement to maximize political 'gains' and minimize 'losses' for key groups, and to be prepared to build coalitions and strike deals to secure support for the improvement. The notion of a 'market in political horse-trading' (March, 1974) may be remote from the conventional rhetoric of school improvement but it is clearly seen in the political perspective and widely recognized by those working in schools. The requirements for management in the cultural image include a tolerance for ambiguity and a strong sensitivity to the values and beliefs of different groups or 'sub-cultures': 'To interact effectively in a sub-culture means developing multi-cultural competence, learning what to expect' (House, 1981: 27). Although the political and cultural images of schools look somewhat different, their implications for management tasks and skills are related, in that both put a premium on factors such as sensitivity, ability to grasp situations, judgement and even intuition!

Towards integration

It is important to re-emphasize the point that 'perspectives are images of reality and not truths in themselves' and that their purpose is 'to enhance one's understanding and to illuminate one's view of the world' (Sergiovanni, 1984: 10). Much more work needs to be done to clarify and extend their usefulness for practice and research. For instance, as Miles and Ekholm (1985b) repeatedly stress, no single image is an adequate basis for understanding or action, hence the calls for 'multi-perspective' and 'integrative' views, 'comprehensive' strategies and so on. Yet it is far from clear what is entailed in such integration and how these or other 'images of reality' can most usefully be related to one another for different purposes (such as practice, training or research). Nevertheless, such classifications of perspectives seem potentially to have considerable heuristic value both to enhance understanding of our present practices and to provide a basis for further explorations into the mysteries of school improvement and its management.

Implications for professional development

There is space for only three brief concluding comments on the topic of professional development, which is taken up by others in greater detail elsewhere in this volume.

First, the discussion in the previous section would suggest some grounds for concern about professional development programmes related to the management of school improvement which are strongly focused on one or two of the images to the relative exclusion of the others. Certainly there may be contextual or other reasons to be advanced in support of the dominant focus, but legitimate questions can be asked about such a stance and the justifications might be closely examined.

Second, there are serious pedagogical and other difficulties associated with offering effective professional development relating to the political and cultural images in particular: for example, ethical dilemmas are involved in developing political capabilities. (Glatter, 1982). These problems need careful study.

Third, an important aim of professional development for those concerned with managing school improvement should be to help them realize what images they are using, both in specific situations and more generally, and to encourage them to consider whether these are either appropriate or sufficient.

References

BERMAN, P. (1981). 'Educational change: an implementation paradigm' in Lehming and Kane (1981).

BOYD-BARRETT, O., BUSH, T., GOODEY, J., McNAY, I. and PREEDY, M. *eds* (1983). *Approaches to Post-School Management* Harper and Row/The Open University, London.

BUCKLEY, J. (1985). *The Training of Secondary School Heads in Western Europe*, NFER-Nelson, Windsor, Berks.

BUSH, T., GLATTER, R., GOODEY, J. and RICHES, C. *eds* (1980). *Approaches to School Management*, Harper and Row/The Open University, London.

CLARK, D. L., LOTTO, L. S. and ASTUTO, T. A. (1984). 'Effective schools and school improvement: a comparative analysis of two lines of inquiry', *Educational Administration Quarterly*, **20** 3: 41–68.

CUTHBERT, R. (1984). *The Management Process* (Block 3, Part 2 of the Open University course *Management in Post-compulsory Education*), The Open University Press, Milton Keynes.

DAVIES, J. L. and MORGAN, A. W. (1983). 'Management of higher education institutions in a period of contraction and uncertainty', *in* BOYD-BARRETT *et al* (1983).

EKHOLM, M. and MILES, M. B. (1985). 'Conclusions and recommendations', *in* VAN VELZEN *et al* (1985).

ELLSTRÖM, P. (1983). 'Four faces of educational organizations', *Higher Education,* **12** 2: 231–41.

FULLAN, M. (1985). 'Change processes and strategies at the local level', *The Elementary School Journal,* **85** 3: 391–421.

GLATTER, R. (1982). 'The micropolitics of education: issues for training', *Educational Management and Administration,* **10**, 2: 160–65.

GLATTER, R. (1983). 'Implications of research for policy on school management training', *in* HEGARTY (1983).

GLATTER, R. (1984). *Managing for Change* (Block 6 of the Open University course E324 *Management in Post-Compulsory Education*), The Open University Press, Milton Keynes.

GRIFFITHS, D. (1979). 'Another look at research on the behaviour of administrators', *in* Immegart and Boyd (1979).

HALL, G. E. and HORD, S. M. (1984). 'Analysing what change facilitators do: the intervention taxonomy', *Knowledge Creation, Diffusion, Utilization,* **5** 3: 275–307.

HANDY, C (1984). *Taken for Granted? Understanding Schools as Organizations*, Longman for the Schools Council, York.

HEGARTY, S. *ed* (1983). *Training for Management in Schools*, NFER-Nelson for the Council of Europe, Windsor, Berks.

HOPKINS, D. and WIDEEN, M. (1984). *Alternative Perspectives on School Improvement* Falmer Press, Lewes, Sussex.

HOUSE, E. R. (1981). 'Three perspectives on innovation: technological, political and cultural' *in* Lehming and Kane (1981).

IMMEGART,. G. L. and BOYD, W. L. *eds* (1979). *Problem-Finding in Educational Administration*, D. C. Heath, Lexington, Mass.

LEHMING, R. and KANE , M. *eds* (1981). *Improving Schools: Using What We Know*, Sage, Beverley Hills, Cal.

LEITHWOOD, K. A. and MONTGOMERY, D. J. (1982). 'The role of the elementary school principal in program improvement', *Review of Educational Research,* **52** 3: 39–39.

LEITHWOOD, K. A., STANLEY, K. and MONTGOMERY, D. J. (1984). 'Training principals for school improvement', *Education and Urban Society,* **17** 1: 49–72.

MARCH, J. G. (1974). 'Analytical skills and the university training of educational administrators', *Journal of Educational Administration,* **12** 1: 17–44.

MARCH, J. G. (1984). 'How we talk and how we act: administrative theory and administrative life', *in* Sergiovanni and Corbally (1984).

MEIER, T. K. (1985), 'Leadership theories from industry: relevant to higher education?', *Educational Administration and History,* **17** 1: 62–69.

MILES, M. B. (1983). 'Unravelling the mystery of institutionalization', *Educational Leadership,* **40**, 14–19 (November).

MILES, M. B. and EKHOLM, M. (1985a). 'What is school improvement?', *in* VAN VELZEN *et al* (1985).

MILES, M. B. and EKHOLM, M. (1985b). 'School improvement at the school level', *in* VAN VELZEN *et al* (1985).

MORGAN, C., HALL, V. and MACKAY, H. (1984). *The Selection of Secondary School*

Headteachers, The Open University Press, Milton Keynes.

MORRIS, J. and BURGOYNE, J. G. (1973). *Developing Resourceful Managers*, Institute of Personnel Management, London.

NIAS, J. (1980). 'Leadership styles and job satisfaction in primary schools', *in* BUSH *et al* (1980).

RUTHERFORD, W. L., HORD, S. M., HULING, L. L. and HALL, G. E. (1983). *Change Facilitators: In Search of Understanding Their Role*, Research and Development Center for Teacher Education, University of Texas at Austin, Austin, Tex (mimeographed).

SCHÖN, D. A. (1984). 'Leadership as reflection-in-action', *in* Sergiovanni and Corbally (1984).

SERGIOVANNI, T. J. (1984). 'Cultural and competing perspectives in administrative theory and practice', *in* Sergiovanni and Corbally (1984).

SERGIOVANNI, T. J. and CORBALLY, J. E. (1984). *Leadership and Organizational Culture*, University of Illinois Press, Urbana, Ill.

VAN VELZEN, W. G. and ROBIN, D. (1985). 'The need for school improvement in the next decade', *in* VAN VELZEN *et al* (1985).

VAN VELZEN, W. G., MILES, M. B., EKHOLM, M., HAMEYER, U. and ROBIN, D. (1985). *Making School Improvement Work*, Acco Pub, Leuven, Belgium.

Section 3

The school and its context

Normative models of accountability

Maurice Kogan

The main models

[. . .] Three main models [. . .] of accountability [. . .] can be typified as:

1 *Public or state control* which entails the use of authority by elected representatives, appointed officials, and the heads and others who manage schools.
2 *Professional* control, that is, control of education by teachers and professional administrators. With this is associated *self-reporting evaluation.*
3 *Consumerist control* or influence which might take the form of (a) participatory democracy or *partnership* in the public sector; or (b) *market mechanisms* in the private or partly privatised public sector.

[. . .] All of the normative models, it should be noted, refer to the client, the teacher, the school and local authority rather than to the wider political system.

The account begins with the dominant existing mode which derives from the existence of a public sector of education, provided on the basis of law.

Public or state control and managerialism

The dominant mode of education accountability in the UK is that of public control. Its main formal characteristic is that of a managerial hierarchy. For example, the teacher is legally an 'assistant' who is required by contract to perform tasks set by the head, is subject to review by the head, whether overtly or implicitly, systematically or haphazardly, and whose present and future career prospects, whether in career grading or in the judgements made in references, are strongly affected by evaluations made by the head teacher.

If structures are hierarchical, teachers are held accountable by the head for their work. The head can use the sanctions applicable in many public sector institutions where tenure is the normal condition of work. The head cannot directly secure dismissal of a teacher for poor performance, but can institute a process to be implemented by others if there is gross malperformance. Otherwise the sanctions are somewhat more indirect and consist of the ability to affect a teacher's future career. In turn, the head is accountable for the work of the school and has authority to discharge that accountability.

Whilst heads are accountable for the running of the school and have authority over teachers, they may be both Chief Executives and Leading Professionals (Hughes, 1973) or colleague figures leading a collegium. [. . .] However, it must be asked whether the leading professional element can countermand that of the accountable manager. For purposes of formal analysis it is best to look to the dominant relationship rather than to the ways in which it is modified. A tiny number of schools might be collegial; Summerhill, Suffolk is a classic case and Countesthorpe in Leicestershire a less certain example, as a close analysis of the authority patterns stated by a former head reveals (Watts, 1976). It is safe to say, however, that British schools are hierarchical and managerial although some have moved towards 'modified hierarchical-managerial' structures.

The formal lines of hierarchy may be criss-crossed by collegial styles and non-hierarchical and matrix structures. In many schools, curriculum is considered and created by groups of teachers working within specialist groups such as departments or faculty meetings. Pastoral work is administered through the allocation of pupils to years or to all age tutorial houses, in which hierarchy may seem to be less explicit or in abeyance. Decisions and policies made by the executive and hierarchical system are also tested by representative systems. Staff meetings may be a regular feature of a school; the head may or may not be expected to attend, and if attending, would be likely to do so as a member of staff rather than as the hierarchical head of the school.

These second order structures of school, approximating to collegia rather than to hierarchies, are vital to the development of the curriculum and the running of the school. If they do not coincide in their values with the policies enunciated by the hierarchy, the school management will find it difficult to impose its policies and classic mechanisms for holding teachers to account will not work in terms of reasonable day by day encounter.

More fundamentally, the relationships are shaped in part by technology. A school relies on work by teachers who must put intellectual and moral commitment into their relationships with individual pupils and into their other tasks. Teacher professionalism is potent as a sustainer of norms and cuts across hierarchy (Lortie, 1969). Yet the tasks demand normative consistency between what the larger organisation – the school – demands and what the individual teacher believes he should be doing (Richardson, 1973; Packwood, 1980).

Power is further modified by teachers operating politically within associations against what they may believe to be unacceptable conditions of work and employment. Since 1961, when the first post-war strikes occurred in Britain, the unions have suspended hierarchical arrangements whenever they cause services to be withdrawn. Authority, then, which is weak in its power connections is likely to be unable to sustain well a structure of accountability.

There are few normative defences made of hierarchy and public control in British literature on education. For some of the components of an ideal model it is possible to turn to Jacques' (1976) description of what he calls bureaucratic accountability (which others in our field call variously contractual accountability or public accountability). It is on some such account that the normative model of traditional public control and managerial patterns of school accountability might be based.

Bureaucratic accountability has been typified by Jacques as deriving from employment contracts by means of which bureaucratic systems are established and employees recruited:

> the employment contract fixes the central feature of bureaucratic roles, namely the accountability of employees for the work they are expected to do . . . accountability calls for human judgements as to whether assigned tasks have been satisfactorily discharged; judgement in turn calls for authority – the authority of one person to assess another's competence.

Yet the authority to assess another's competence need not imply the authority to take action based on such an assessment. In the field of education, for example, inspectors or professional peers may evaluate but without the authority to hold those evaluated to account.

Jacques defines bureaucracy as:

> a hierarchically stratified managerial employment system which people are employed in to work for a wage or salary; that is to say, a stratified employment hierarchy with at least one manager who in turn has a staff of employee subordinates. [. . .]

Jacques' depiction of bureaucracy allows for a benign model of public control. [. . .] It depends upon a synthesis of values and institutional characteristics not available in the existing discussions of accountability and it is consistent with the main trends of thinking about welfare state institutions.

Current writing, indeed, mainly depicts public control as potentially harmful. It has largely emerged from research intended to help develop desirable practices. Elliott and his Cambridge colleagues [Elliott *et al.* (1981)] ascribe particular characteristics to structures that are managerial or bureaucratic or hierarchical. 'A control model of accountability [is one] in which calling to account is a power coercive strategy for changing teachers' behaviour in conformity with an externally imposed contract.' This is contrasted with a dialogue model where there is 'no implication of external compulsion . . . the only force is that of argument'. Elliott refers to the way in which the Assessment of Performance Unit 'represents part of the response from the DES for demands for greater accountability by the educational service for the resources it consumes'. The APU would also be part of an attempt to standardise a national curriculum in terms of the APU's operational categories and thereby 'make it possible for the central government to control, rationalise and evaluate the provision of educational resources'. *The School Curriculum* (DES, 1981) recommended a national core weighted towards maths, English, science, modern languages and technology.

> One might indeed describe this core as 'the industrialists' curriculum' and infer that from the standpoint of the Department of Education and Science (DES) the chief

function of the educational service today is the revival of our nation's industrial base.
    The goals of education become synonymous with the goals of the state; namely 'to
promote industrial efficiency.'

(Elliott *et al.*, 1981).

In Elliott's view, the APU was tacitly intended to subordinate educational
practice in schools to state goals. 'The idea which is increasingly used to justify
this transference of power from the professionals to the state is that of public
accountability.' In this, Elliott shares Ernest R. House's interpretation of similar moves in the USA as responding to the 'dominant bureaucratically controlled "productivity" model'.

Elliott thus [associates] particular normative intentions with a managerial or
hierarchical model. He assumes that attempts to increase lay control, and particularly that embodied in ministers or, presumably, councillors, mandated perhaps remotely by public elections are necessarily 'product oriented'.

This assumption would not, however, be supported by a reading of documents such as the Taylor Report which certainly advocated a shift from professional to lay or 'public' accountability. Nor would it emerge from a study of the
Inner London Education Authority's attempts to assert greater public control
over the curriculum in order to improve the educational opportunity of the ethnic
minorities or the female majority. Notions of what underlies 'public' control
need to be disaggregated and considered in their specific context and from their
specific origins. The purposes are as various as the political orientation of the lay
or public controllers. Indeed, current criticisms of public bureaucracy berate it
for failing to be related to the ethos of production, rather than the opposite.

Elliott also makes assumptions about the internal organisation of the school.
His picture of the bureaucratic-managerial pattern is as follows:

> Intra-professional accountability must be distinguished from hierarchical accoun-
> tability. In the latter, the information flow is strictly one way, up the chain of
> command. The more one moves up the hierarchy the more people know about the
> activities of those below, and the more one moves down the less people know about the
> activities of those above them. Hierarchical accountability facilitates social control
> over an organisation by a powerful elite at the top of the pyramid. It is indicative of a
> bureaucratised school organisation and is concerned with achieving the goals of the
> organisation most effectively and efficiently.

Elliott continues that scientific management in schools produces rigid
standardisation, specialisation and the subordination of tasks and roles to hierarchy. These, again, are conclusions to be arrived at empirically and could be
contested by examples to the contrary. For example, it is often assumed that
those at the top of the hierarchy know less rather than more of what is happening
below.

The Sussex Report [Becher *et al.* (1979)], too, draws a distinction between
intra-professional and hierarchical accountability. A managerial system
involves a considerable specialisation of responsibilities for different tasks which
are strongly hierarchised. A professional system is grounded in a collegial sense

of responsibility for the formulation and execution of the school tasks. But, again, it could be argued, professionally led institutions can be hierarchical rather than collegial. Conversely, a managerial system can endorse a matrix rather than compartmentalised ways of working.

Jennifer Nias, one of the Cambridge Team, noted that there was some conflict within the school between the head teacher's attempts to institute open management which might imply intra-professional accountability, and the preference of some of his staff for a hierarchical chain of command. It was not clear that the staff wanted a policy of dispersed responsibility or participation in decision making. And, going further than her colleagues in specifying institutional arrangements, she concluded that:

> trust . . . depends upon the predictability of personal and institutional behaviour and of technical competence, and upon awareness of school goals. . . . There is bound to be conflict over the aims of education. . . . To claim that this conflict can be resolved by mutual trust rather than by 'formal procedures' is to be guilty of circularity. It is also to ignore the part played in the establishment of trust by forms of organisation. In a world which is 'crooked as cork screws', accountability must be expressed in part through formal order. . . . Formal procedures facilitate the growth of trust and help ensure it survives.

And she recognised, too, that the public will not take for granted the teachers' own sense of their responsibility.

A further issue is the effect of internal organisation on relationships with client groups. Elliott feels that where there is a top-down system of social control over the activities of individual teachers it is 'increasingly difficult for client groups within the local community to influence what happens in the schools, and for the schools to be responsive to their clients' needs'.

Both the Cambridge and Sussex writing implies that calling teachers to account should not be to secure conformity to externally prescribed rules of conduct but to enable professional decisions and judgements to be responsive to public criticism. The Sussex account in particular goes to great pains to specify the several different modes in which the school works. The emphasis is, however, on forms of evaluation which will enhance trust and self-confidence rather than ensure that schools comply with policies legitimated by the electoral system.

Managerial models of accountability, called variously 'hierarchical', 'bureaucratic', 'public contractual or coercive' are thus seen as producing a range of outcomes which vary according to the perspective of the observer. Drawing on these it is possible to draw up a balance sheet of the perceived merits or otherwise of managerial accountability. Unlike the accountability of professionals to each other, the managerially accountable school within a local authority is legitimated by the electoral process. That may mean, however, that it is tied into the political-administrative system of the local authority and less capable of being influenced by its immediate clientele. It reduces ambiguity about objectives and accountability because those in charge are identifiable. A managerial hierarchy may produce more certainty for teachers who then know the limits within which to work. They may also be more secure in the face of external criticism. At the same time, however, managerial arrangements may work less well across boundaries because too much authority at the top of the system gives insufficient discretion below. A managerial structure can be less ambiguous but also less capable of sanctioning the development of multiple cultures. Accountability may be so focused that the corresponding authority and discretion may not be well distributed among staff.

Assumptions about 'public accountability' or managerial models can reflect conflicting assumptions about value and affect and they can represent strikingly different derivations of liberal democracy.

The professional accountability model

If managerial hierarchy is the dominant mode in British schools, much recent writing about accountability in education puts the argument for a 'professional' model of accountability in order to meet two objectives. The first is to protect schools from demands for product orientated outcomes. For accountability not to be determined by external determinations of products or outputs, self-evaluation and self-report by teachers are argued as essential. Upon the basis of professional self-control, the laity might then form a judgement. The second objective is that of responsiveness to clients. It is assumed, for example, by Elliott (1981) that the stronger the professional autonomy of teachers and schools the more responsive to their clients they will be.

> The 'responsively accountable school' . . . enters into free and open communication with a variety of interest groups about the aims and nature of the education it provides. It works through dialogue rather than power and must operate at the local rather than the more remote bureaucratised level of the state. The responsive model also suggests that schools ought to be self-accounting. This can be contrasted with the 'control' or 'productivity' model where the accounting is done by some external monitoring agency.

Elliott's description is allied to House's notion of responsive accountability which is itself similar to Barry MacDonald's 'process' model which he outlined (1976) as an alternative to 'the technocratic product model'.

The same general assumptions are implicit in writing about the best ways of evaluating schools (for example, Parlett, 1974; Simons, 1979, and others associated with the University of East Anglia's Centre for Research in Applied Education).

Sockett (1980) moves the issue further forward by specifying the constitutional relationships which would make free standing professionals contractually committed to ethical practice. This professional model of accountability would be an alternative to a results based model. It would expect teachers to be accountable for their modes and actions and not for their results. It would have the following 'characterising differences':

1 Accountability would be for adherence to principles of practice rather than for results embodied in pupil performances.

2 Accountability would be rendered to diverse constituencies rather than to the agglo-merate constituency of the public alone.

3 The teacher would have to be regarded as an autonomous professional, not as a social technician within the bureaucratic framework of a school and the educational system.

4 The evaluation through measurement of pupil performances (the 'how' of account-ability) would be replaced by a conception of evaluation providing information for constituents allied to a system of proper redress through a professional body.

Groups of professionals should establish detailed codes of conduct in each branch of professional activity. The professional model of accountability would include the drawing up of a 'contract' or 'covenant', i.e. discussion with the interested parties on what the schools and individual teachers ought to be doing, and the delivery of an account, that is producing the kinds of justifications and explanations which are relevant to the concerns of these very different parties. In these actions the teacher aspires to the status of an autonomous professional.

The professional has self-government but must give an account of what aca-demic freedom means in the context of compulsory schooling, as well as devise positive codes of conduct, not warnings, in a range of areas including relation-ships with parents.

Sockett's model is consistent with the standard definitions of the professional which refer to those who have 'a body of knowledge and skills, a prolonged period of training to acquire them, societal acceptance of the legitimacy of the expertise, and a professional culture containing ideas relating to organisational modes and ethics and standards' (Greenwood, 1966). [. . .]

Sockett's model of professional accountability is consistent with Elliott and his colleagues' accounts of 'responsive' schools. The main authorities tend to assume a correspondence between professional autonomy and self-reporting and responsiveness to clients. Sockett also assumes that a public or 'bureaucratic' system must reduce teachers to the role of 'social technicians' and that, indeed, evaluation of 'principles of practice' rather than of 'results' is only possible in a non-hierarchical school. These assumptions do not depend upon any argued logic of organisation. Hierarchical schools are capable of endorsing good prac-tice or process rather than striving after narrowly conceived results; that is the well proclaimed achievement of many British primary schools. Equally, hier-archy may be associated with dispositions towards conservative educational practice. But there is no definite and mechanistic association. [. . .]

The Cambridge project (Elliott *et al.* 1981) used the notion [. . .] of the Neighbourhood School. Here Ebbutt drew implications for accountability from the existence and acceptance of the neighbourhood as a psychological entity, from the school's proximity and visibility to instant evaluation by the neigh-bourhood, and from the expectations exerted by the neighbourhood that the school should 'fit in' with their values. Plainly the quality of the neighbourhood school as opposed to that of an 'extended catchment school', to use Ebbutt's term, is that it fits more closely notions of 'responsiveness' than 'public accoun-tability', at least as earlier described.

Professional accountability and self-reporting

The notion of the professionally led, 'responsive', school is closely tied to the notion of self-reporting or self-evaluation. There is already an impressive literature on this subject. According to one survey (G. Elliott, 1980) which listed over 300 British and American references to the subject, by the end of 1980 sixty seven local education authorities in England and Wales had initiated discussions on self-evaluation with teachers. The objectives, accountability connotations and techniques varied widely. Some, for example, were overtly tied to accountability intentions and were linked to inspection by LEA staff. But

> throughout all the documents the tone is one of partnership and co-operation. Even where the schemes are linked to external inspection the emphasis is on devising means to improve education through a consultative process which is open and collaborative. There is no hint of a return to more traditional forms of inspection of the type usually associated with HMI.

By the end of 1980 at least 5000 schools were estimated to have been supplied with guidelines on self-evaluation by local authorities.

Another more limited but intensive study (Open University, James, 1982) was able to identify distinct organisational strategies within self-evaluation. Not all were 'collegial', sharing decision making among colleagues. Collegially organised evaluations, however, were more likely to be conducted by staff at all status levels for purposes of professional or curriculum development. But in both types insiders constituted the principal audience for any report. The accountability was interpreted as being to colleagues rather than to parents, employers or political masters. Accountability to colleagues, however, involved the same justifications and explanations that teachers owed to their superiors for how they earned their money and spent their time. 'Moral' and 'implicit' modes of accountability most usually characterised evaluation organised on a collegial basis whereas 'legal', 'formal' and 'explicit' modes of accountability characterised evaluation of the rational management kind. The Open University team concluded that 'there is a strong element of strict accountability in some in-school activities' as well as 'an implicit element of answerability or moral accountability to self and colleagues, as well as to parents and pupils and others'.

In their judgement, therefore, the East Sussex classification over-simplified what was happening at school level because it linked modes of accountability (moral, professional, strict) too tightly to particular audiences (clients, colleagues, employers).

> it is surely not the case that moral, professional and strict accountability are necessarily mutually exclusive.
> This is a conclusion which we have reached from the logic of accountability rather than from the empirical evidence used by the Open University.
>
> (James, 1982)

Anxieties about the authority connotations of reporting are expressed in studies of schools but also in one of the few British works on higher education evaluation. Adelman and Alexander (1982) consider the relationship between moral accountability and externality in writing of the Council for National Academic Awards (CNAA) validation process. They believe that internal validations resulting from CNAA activities

> may tend to exist not so much because they are seen as educationally desirable but because they are a proven device for chances of success in external validation. This may disturb the judgemental criteria so that they are less about the educational quality of the proposal than about its chances of being externally validated. . . . They may display disproportionate concern with documents and claims (rather than activity) and the ability to present a convincing . . . performance . . . may well account for more than the case itself.

There is concern lest the freshness and developmental potential of self-evaluation is spoiled by external validation or links with inspection or other arrangements with connotations of accountability. Rochdale local authority (Nuttall, 1981) hoped 'by deliberately avoiding a reporting document . . . to avoid regression to a norm and allow flair and ambition to remain effective'. Yet difficulties arising from self-evaluation are also noted (Smith, 1980). Pressure from outside for accountability might not be satisfied if self-evaluation is related only to the school's self-determined objectives. At the same time, it is difficult to prove to staff that self-evaluation is not really back-door inspection. Hence Smith argues for some element of external monitoring of self-evaluation.

More detailed accounts can be found in the ILEA statement about self-assessment of schools which was devised by their Inspectorate (ILEA, 1977; Varnava, 1979; Simons, 1979 and Becher *et al.*, 1981). *Keeping the School Under Review* was intended to be used, with separate sections for primary and secondary schools, as a check-list to support self-evaluation. The booklet constituted a set of indicators of quality, ostensibly for use in the context of teacher autonomy 'but "outsiders" are brought into evaluations by the use of their criteria – and perhaps also by their physical presence' (McCormick, 1982).

The guide advises that in coming to a view the school 'will be affected by the general climate of opinion in society at large by their contact with governors, parents, fellow teachers, educational journals and other professional influences'. But the implication is that the process will be that of self-assessment rather than that of evaluation in order to render account. Data should range from statistics showing the number of parents choosing the school to a curriculum analysis displaying the deployment of staff teaching and non-teaching time. The school environment can be evaluated subjectively by staff, including not only physical characteristics but also, for example, the manner in which pupils move around the school. Decision making and communications will be evaluated. Other sections depict the arrangements for learning, departmental or faculty self-assessment. And there is 'the acid test'. 'Would I recommend a colleague to apply for a post at the school? Would I recommend the school to friends for their children?'

The principal intention was clearly to enable the school to evaluate itself for purposes of professional development. As such it has been found to be valuable by some (for example, Varnava, 1979) in order to identify strengths, weaknesses, particular needs and to explain any fall in level of achievement; to stimulate dialogue between teachers, pupils and parents and, above all, to ensure that the individual and the school know just where they stand. 'Since the school must be accountable for standards to its public and its clientele it must be ready to initiate change for the sake of progress.'

Both the ILEA and the HMI Primary Survey (1978) employ check list approaches which have been criticised (Becher *et al.*, 1981) as lacking guidance on evaluative strategy. 'The important issues of focus and methodology are glossed over.' Also they are thought to have 'a strong management orientation' and contain questions imposed from above. That surely depends, however, on how the instrument is used, and by whom. Nor does self-reporting necessarily entail any particular methodology. For example, the use of indicators for monitoring purposes has been advocated by Shipman (1979) as being usable by schools themselves as well as for purposes of external evaluation. A similar approach to higher education has been adumbrated by Sizer (1979).

The arguments in favour of self-report are made by Helen Simons (1979) who prescribes for 'the democratic approach to evaluation'. This stresses the need to recognise 'democratic' principles in school self-evaluation programmes, in that they recognise the interests of the particular groups of participants involved. Self-evaluation on democratic principles enables schools to respond to demands for external review whilst extending and protecting their professional autonomy. Schools might present accounts of their work to the public but control should be shifted to those within the school. 'Giving teachers control over their own evaluation respects their autonomy, protects their right to privacy and, paradoxical though it may seem, provides a process for making the policies and practices of school more public.' Evaluation should be free of bias and this must be ensured by internal checks. The evaluator and the evaluation must be protected against co-option by particular groups within or outside the school. The credibility of the evaluation must be established. 'Self-reports, as is so often said, have low credibility.'

Participants must control their own data and there should be controlled release of information that is already public knowledge so that participants will not be made vulnerable by co-operating and contributing. Negotiation is a central principle in democratic evaluation. It protects participants from evaluators taking total control over the data and using it for their own purposes. The balance between the public's right to know and the individual's right to be discreet is then maintained.

Simons proposes how schools might take the initiative for reporting to the public by first accounting to themselves. Having facilitated self-reflection within their own school teachers might also produce accounts which meet accountability demands. 'But such reports would be defined in the school's own terms and their distribution to any other group controlled by them'. She is chary of linking self-reporting to external accountability 'at the present time'. 'Honest accounts of one's practice could be construed as evidence of weakness and positively used as a basis for alleging incompetence' (1981).

The Simons formula aims to keep faith with participants in an evaluation. It is responsive to their policy concerns and to criticisms made within the school. It is not clear, however, how those who feel that the school is inadequate, or that teachers are irresponsible or worse, might get access to evaluations. In the Simons evaluations these are not external or summative but internal and formative. Moreover, as with the use of the word 'responsive' her particular use of 'democratic' assumes the democracy to consist of the publicly employed practitioners in schools and not those who receive services from them. The exercise is devoted towards making teachers more sensitive and self-confident. It does not say how the laity's views on policy or performance can be brought into the school. A less selective view of democracy would allow inputs from those authorised by the ballot box and from parents.

The East Sussex Project gives methodological, economic, political and developmental arguments for school based accounts. It can take the form of internal self-assessment, externally reported self-assessment and audited self-assessment. But the difficulties of making an adequately comprehensive assessment for external audiences might then be insuperable. And even self-reporting, that is, teachers reviewing their performance for the sake of their own colleague group, can create tension between teacher autonomy and a coherent school policy.

> if accountability is used to create more central control by the head, the relationship between the report and the reality may become increasingly tenuous as teachers find ways of disguising their departures from detailed prescriptions to which they feel little commitment.

Yet Becher *et al.* concluded that giving parents information did not allow them too much power and influence. More information might in fact reduce criticism. But that might depend on the nature of what is given and received. The time spent on communicating with parents could be regarded as an important part of the educational task of the school. It is possible to provide six types of evidence: personnel, milieu, curriculum, teaching process, progress of individual pupils and general performance. By personnel, Becher meant the responsiveness of teachers to parents in their dealings with the schools. On milieu, the school could explain how it maintained good order and reasonable behaviour. This might occur through open assemblies or meeting the head for a conversation or by quick visits to the working classroom. Some schools developed written accounts of curriculum policy and parents welcomed them. On teaching process, parents who gained access to the classroom showed increased confidence in teachers. And on the progress of individual pupils, teachers could inform parents about what their child had learnt, give some indication of the child's aptitude and motivation and discuss any matters which either the teacher or the parents regarded as 'problematic'. This is, therefore, a more open model than that proposed in Simons' self-reporting scheme where the cautions against exposure are emphasised.

In general those who favour schools self-reporting are cautious about such evaluations becoming the basis of full reports on a regular basis to the outside world. They fear that such a process will make teachers defensive and non-cooperative (Becher and Maclure, 1978(a)). There is reluctance about the institutionalisation of procedures which could help self-development but might become formalised and therefore less useful and accurate if converted into public report. Implicit in these anxieties is, however, a political and normative belief as well as a technical judgement of the effects of different procedures. Public accountability in the sense of rendering an account to a governing body or the local authority is not seen as a favoured option for the schools.

Consumerist control: partnership

The metaphor 'partnership' was frequently used in the Report of the Taylor Committee and has been elaborated most clearly by one of the committee members, Joan Sallis (1979). The relationship between schools and parents must go beyond the metaphors and thinking of the market place. Clients should participate in a partnership and not in a relationship where the client is dependent on the professional. Joan Sallis in fact eschews the metaphors both of client and of consumer as failing to express the collaborative equality which should exist between teachers and parents. Parents did not sufficiently expect to be consulted on ways in which the schools should be improved and thought they would be 'totally bewildered' if asked 'does the school make sure you understand and consent to what it proposes to do for your child?' Their expectations in these respects must be strengthened.

Relationships with professionals should involve parental consent to what is being provided. They should contain three components rarely present in education: consensus about objectives, an exchange of information about methods, their limitations and implications, and some dialogue to discuss the success of what has been done. To Sallis they are

> components of accountability, and the most important is information. Without it we cannot judge whether the objectives are realistic, even if we support them, we cannot approve the programme, we cannot assess the outcome. Nor, which is the most important part of all, can we play our vital part unless we understand what is to be done, how it is to be done, and what can be expected at the end.

Education is different from other professional activities and the differences require a partnership between parents and teachers if there is to be a properly accountable relationship. In the school there may be a conflict between accountability in a collective sense, through parent bodies and governors and accountability to individual parents as partners in the education of their own child.

Sallis argues for a recognised status for individuals in the process because collective mechanisms to explain or justify or monitor 'will be dominated by minorities of parents whose confidence is greater than their fellows'. Parents must share responsibility with the school for the education of children. Schools and parents must be accountable to each other for their contributions to a shared task. Hence the vocabulary of consumerism is too limited.

The Sallis model takes the argument some steps forward. It notes well that accountability has to be spelled out in terms of its unit of analysis if an accurate statement of relationships is to be made. It firmly predicates parity between providers and client. It could be criticised for not adequately stating the differences between the role of the teacher and parent. Nor does it tie in with the working of the larger, election-legitimated system.

Consumerist control: free market analogies for accountability

British arguments for different measures of accountability have all rested within the fairly conventional, if broad, framework of legitimate public authority. Even the most participative doctrines, such as partnership, or responsive accountability, or professional accountability, continue to assume that the ballot box and those appointed by it will ultimately rule, although as we have seen, some formulations are largely silent on the links between schools and local authorities.

It is American cases which provide examples which go either to the extremes of popular control, or recommend movement beyond systems of public control altogether. One such possibility is the use of vouchers which has been tried out in some American districts (Cohen and Farrar, 1977).

Vouchers would break the monopoly of public institutions. Voucher schemes argue that the state should provide resources through which parents can operate equitable rules enabling them to seek places in privately run schools through the use of vouchers. Parents will then be able to exert accountability by use of the right of exit, whereas at present parents whose children use a monopoly public system have nothing more to use than voice (Hirschman, 1970). At present, it is argued, public authorities possess a monopoly which the majority of parents cannot break. There is thus public control over schooling; the controls should be those of the family (Coons and Sugarman, 1978). Schools are given no encouragement to compete in providing better standards of education because their trade is guaranteed.

Voucher schemes are designed to put pressure upon schools through market style mechanisms rather than through publicly maintained systems of control. Almost all of these schemes, it should be noted, are 'social' market rather than economic or free market models. They assume that consumer preference will be elucidated and met through schemes which enable public authorities to pursue public goals whilst giving maximum play to private wishes. [. . .].

The values underlying the model are clear but also wide. The uniqueness of the individual, his right to choice of life style, the doctrine of self-help, the role of the family, posit individualism. But at the same time, the authors maintain that they will be advancing social ends of more efficient and equal education for all citizens. Essentially, however, the case for family control rests on the assumption that there is not, and perhaps should not be, other than minimum consensus over the goals of education and that consensus is not to be entrusted to professionals. It turns away from the assumption that the schools can accommodate desirable traditions, norms, skills and ways of delivering services that society as a whole wants. Such schemes thus dismiss the powerful institutionalist tradition of British social policy and would force the school back to a residualist mode. In this mode, the state holds the ring between contenders rather than leads in the formation of the public interest. Teachers will indeed become accountable but not to publicly appointed bodies or other professionals in public authorities. The head and staff will have their behaviour conditioned by the degree of success that they achieve in attracting pupils.

The objections to these schemes are clear. The effect on teachers' professionality of being part of a competitive scramble for students has not been assessed through any empirical studies. The best of independent schools, which respond to market demands, may be fully set on achieving good examination results and securing places in the most favoured universities, but also manage to provide good and broad education. Others can be narrowly instrumental seeking measureable results in order to keep up trade.

Paradoxically, the free market schemes share some of the assumptions of both the professional accountability and partnership modes. They reject the power and the legitimacy of the wider political-administrative system. They look for negotiative relationships between professionals and clients but with different distributions of power and authority to be decided through different mechanisms.[. . .]

References

ADELMAN, C. and ALEXANDER, R. J. (1982). *The Self-Evaluation Institution: Practice and Principles of the Management of Educational Change*, Methuen.

BECHER, T. and MACLURE, S. (1978b). *The Politics of Curriculum Change*, Hutchinson.

BECHER, T. *et al.* (1979). *Accountability in the Middle Years of Schooling*, Working Papers and Final Report to the Social Science Research Council, (Sussex Report).

BECHER, T. *et al* (1981). *Policies for Educational Accountability*, Heinemann.

COHEN, D. K. and FARRAR, E. (1977). 'Power to the parents? The story of education vouchers', *The Public Interest*, no. 44, Summer, pp. 72–98.

COONS, J. E. and SUGARMAN, S. D. (1978). *Education by Choice. The Case for Family Control*, University of California Press.

DES and WELSH OFFICE (1981). *The School Curriculum*, HMSO.

ELLIOTT, G. (1980). *Self-Evaluation and the Teacher. An Annotated Bibliography and Report on Current Practice*, Part 1, University of Hull with the Support of the Schools Council.

ELLIOTT, J. (ed.) (1981). *Cambridge Accountability Project*, University of Cambridge, Institute of Education.

ELLIOTT, J., BRIDGES, D., EBBUTT, D., GIBSON, R. and NIAS, J. (1981). *School Accountability: The SSRC Accountability Project*, Grant McIntyre.

GREENWOOD, E. (1966). 'The elements of professionalisation', in H.M. Vollner and D.C. Mills (ed), *Professionalisation*, Prentice Hall.

HIRSCHMAN, A. O. (1970). *Exit, Voice and Loyalty: Responses to Decline in Firms, Organizations and States*, Harvard University Press.

DEPARTMENT OF EDUCATION AND SCIENCE (1978). *Primary Education in England: a survey by HM Inspectors of Schools*, London HMSO.

HOUSE, E. R. (1978). 'An American view of accountability', in T. Becher and S. Maclure (ed), *Accountability in Education*, SSCR and NFER Publishing Co.

HUGHES, M. G. (1973). 'The professional as administrator: the case of the secondary school head', *Education Accountability Bulletin*, 2(1).

ILEA, (1977). *Keeping the School Under Review*: A Method of Self-Assessment for Schools Devised by the ILEA Inspectorate.

JAMES, M. (1982). *The Open University, Educational Evaluation and Accountability Research Group, A First Review and Register of School and College Initiated Self-Evaluation Activities in the United Kingdom.*

JACQUES, E. (1976). *A General Theory of Bureaucracy*, Heinemann Educational Books.

LORTIE, D. C. (1969). 'The balance of control and autonomy in elementary school teaching', in A. Etzioni (ed.), *The Semi-Professions and Their Organization*, Free Press of Glencoe.

MacDONALD, B. (1976). 'Evaluation and the control of education', in D. Tawney (ed.), *Curriculum Evaluation Today: Trends and Implications*, Schools Council Research Studies, Macmillian.

McCORMICK, R. (1882) (ed). *Calling Education to Account*, London, Heinemann.

NUTTALL, D. L. (1981). *School Self-Evaluation: Accountability with a Human Face?*, Schools Council.

PACKWOOD, T. (1980). 'The school as a hierarchy', in T. Bush *et al.*, (eds.), *Approaches to School Management*, Harper & Row.

PARLETT, M. (1974). 'The new evaluation', *Trends in Education*, vol. 34.

RICHARDSON, E. (1973). *The Teacher, The School and the Task of Management*, Heinemann Educational Books.

SALLIS, J. (1979). 'Beyond the market place: a parent's view', in J. Lello (ed.), *Accountability in Education*, Ward Lock Educational.

SHIPMAN, M. (1979) 'The school assessment programme: externally referenced by public examination results', in *In-School Evaluation*, Heinemann Educational Books.

SIMONS, H. (1979). 'Suggestions for a school self-evaluation based on democratic evaluation', *CRN Bulletin*, no. 3.

SIZER, J. (1979). *Performance Indications for Institutions of Higher Education Under Conditions of Financial Stringency, Contraction and Changing Needs*, Address to Annual Conference of Society for Research into Higher Education, reproduced in R. McCormick (ed.), Calling Education to Account, Heinemann Educational Books, 1982.

SMITH, K. R. (1980). *Development Towards Financial Processes for School Self-Management*, Sheffield City Polytechnic.

SOCKETT, H. (ed.) (1980). *Accountability in the English Education System*, London, Hodder and Stoughton.

VARNAVA, G. (1979). 'Self-assessment at a London comprehensive', *Forum for the Discussion of New Trends in Education*, vol. 22, no. 1.

WATTS, J. (ed.) (1976). *The Countesthorpe Experiment*, George Allen & Unwin.

Models of governing bodies

Tim Packwood

With the revival of interest in governing bodies in the 1970s, and their subsequent increase in numbers, governors became suitable subjects for instruction. Some local authorities provided training courses and interpreted their Articles and Instruments of Government in handbooks of guidance. Governors who wanted to find out more for themselves were increasingly able to turn to a variety of references,[1] including, eventually, a course of training from the Open University.[2] Yet despite the attention that their role has received in recent years, our research with governing bodies confirmed the findings of Bacon[3] in presenting a picture of considerable uncertainty. Governors were unsure what they should be doing and consequently doubtful if they were spending their time on the right things and, in particular, whether they were being as effective as they might be.

Much of this uncertainty stems from the structural position that governing bodies occupy within the local educational system. They are placed at the intersection, and under the shadow, of two strong institutions, the school and the local authority, both of which have a continuous and visible role in the system.

Further, as Baron and Howell indicated,[4] they also stand at a point in the system where different forms of authority – professional, administrative and political – meet. Thus governing bodies are surrounded by a constellation of values and purposes from which they must select a role of their own.

[. . .] The institutions and forms of authority that surround governing bodies are themselves structurally interrelated and seek to influence one another. Some of these influences are transmitted through, and mediated by, governing bodies. A considerable portion of their time, for example, is spent in making approaches to the LEA on behalf of their schools. By their nature such relationships contain a large element of uncertainty and their quality cannot be determined in advance. Rather, they develop from practice. Governing bodies forge their own patterns of relationship and the result is likely to be quite distinctive; a product of past experience, the issues that have to be handled and the skills of individual governors. Here then, in the reliance of governing bodies on relationships with other bodies, lies a further cause of uncertainty.

A second implication of the position occupied by governing bodies in the local educational system is that unless they make strenuous efforts to the contrary, they spend much of their time in reacting to the concerns of others. Their business is fashioned by the traffic which surrounding institutions, schools and LEAs or groups in the community, send their way. As a result their work has an unpredictable character. It is outside the governors' control; ebbing and flowing according to the needs of others.

Uncertainties about relationships and work are exacerbated by the absence of any common view as to what governing bodies are about. The institutions and forms of authority that surround them are likely to hold very different expectations of what governing bodies can be expected to do. Not only is there variation between institutions, as when schools see governing bodies as a way of promoting school interests and LEAs see them as a way of enforcing authority policy, but also within institutions. Local councillors, for example, may see governing bodies as an extension of the political system, determining that professionals follow the wishes of the public. Officers of the same local authority, however, may hold the view that the governors' role is essentially advisory and serves to link the school to local interests.

To summarise the argument so far, governing bodies experience uncertainty because they face different expectations and demands and need to create different relationships with the surrounding institutions and interests in the local education system. However, because of their own differentiated composition with members who are appointed by the very institutions and interests

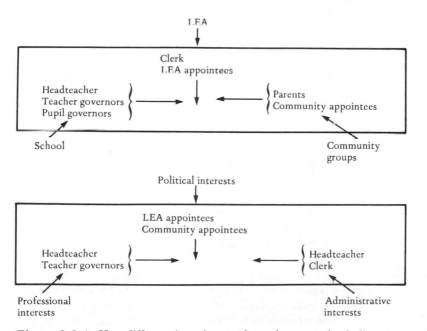

Figure 3.2.1 *How different viewpoints are drawn into governing bodies*

concerned, these differences become sucked in to the governing bodies themselves. This is shown diagrammatically in Figure 3.2.1.

In these circumstances it is hardly surprising that members of a governing
body differ widely in the way they see their role and are uncertain whether they
are concentrating on the right things.

[. . .] Articles of Government indicate the areas of concern for governing
bodies but cannot determine how they work. Governing bodies have to shape
their own role, or have it shaped for them, through their interaction with surrounding institutions and interests. Much, then, depends on what is seen as
important at any one time, who sees it as important, and the strength of particular interests within the governing body.

Looked at in context, the uncertainties and variety are a realistic response to
what governing bodies face. This makes it meaningless to suggest any single
description of a governing body as a model for general application. Obviously
there is value in comparing and categorising governing bodies in a number of key
dimensions, [. . .]. The results may explain the variety, but they do not define
what is or is not a governing body. Any such model could only be based upon its
author's normative conception of what governing bodies should do. The governing body that would have emerged if the recommendations of the Taylor Report[5]
had been fully implemented would be only one such normative model. If, however, it is accepted that it is legitimate for governing bodies to serve a number of
purposes, any interpretation of their role similarly requires a number of models.

Our study of governing bodies enables us to suggest different models, each
based upon a different conception of what a governing body has as its purpose.
Further, we can draw upon the knowledge of the factors which condition the
work of governing bodies, [. . .] to suggest desirable properties for each model.

The governing bodies depicted in these models contain elements which do not
accord with current practice. The models are presented to show the implications of
pursuing different purposes, not as an account of reality or as a prescription
for the future.

Four such models are presented in the following pages:

1 The accountable governing body.
2 The advisory governing body.
3 The supportive governing body.
4 The mediating governing body.

The purpose of each is described and then its associated properties are suggested
under the headings of: authority, representation, resources, public relations,
style of work, and demands of the work. The first three (authority, representation, resources) concern inputs that are necessary for the governing body to
achieve its purpose, while the latter three (PR, style and demands of work)
specify aspects of its process of working. A final section for each model considers
how it is related to ideas of government, to models of governing bodies suggested
by other commentators, and to current practice as experienced in our research.
Table 3.2.1 (p. 158–9) summarises the main features of each model, and thus
provides for easy comparisons.

The accountable governing body

This type of governing body centres its efforts on its school. Its purpose is to ensure that the school is working satisfactorily within the policies and prescriptions of appointing authorities, normally LEAs but in the case of voluntary aided schools religious foundations. Where the appointing authority is willing to delegate decisions and tolerate variety, the governing body is able to concentrate upon the school's ability to meet the needs of the community it serves. For this role to be effective its properties would be as follows.

Authority

The range and scope of authority exercised by this form of governing body depends upon the discretion allowed to the governors.

With minimum delegation of authority the governing body would function as a sub-committee of the LEA or foundation, enforcing the decisions of the appointing authority. It provides a safeguard for the authority in checking that its policies and requirements for the school are being observed and alerting it to any deviations or special needs.

With maximum delegation of authority the governing body, while still ensuring that prescribed policies are followed, is delegated some authority to shape the school on behalf of the various interests with a stake in its work – the LEA or foundation, parents, teachers, community groups. This could mean that it is involved in determining the objectives of the school and in taking primary decisions, such as the selection of staff, the nature of the curriculum and the allocation of money. The extent of the governing body's authority is a matter for negotiation, between the appointing authority and the governing body, on the one hand, and the governing body and headteacher on the other. The governors cannot realistically expect to manage the day-to-day work of the school.

At a minimum, then, the governing body would require the authority to ensure that the LEA or foundation provided it with the relevant information to monitor the school's activities. The school, for its part, must accept the authority of the governing body in the restricted version of accountability developed by Elliott *et al.*, to 'call it to account'[6] in dimensions of its work specified by the appointing authority and must abide by the rulings it receives.

If, however, discretion is extensive, the authority of the governing body is wider. Taking the LEA or foundation first, the governing body would be likely to see it as accountable for providing the school with adequate resources. The governors could naturally expect to be provided with information on policy guidelines for the school and, since the governors express community needs, that the LEA or foundation would consult with them regarding the substance of policies. The school could be 'called to account' in respect of any aspect of its activities; anything involving the school might potentially involve the governors. This would mean providing the governing body with such information as it might require, taking part in consultation regarding past, present and future

Table 3.2.1 Models of governing bodies

	Accountable	Advisory	Supportive	Mediating
Focus	School	School	School in the local education system	Local education system
Purpose	Ensure that school is operating satisfactorily within prescribed policies. *Minimum* Reflects interests of local stakeholders. *Maximum*	Legitimate and test professional activities. Safeguard against professional malfunction.	Support the school with other interests.	Bring together and negotiate different interests in education. Safeguard against malfunction in any part of the system.
Authority	Ensure that prescriptions of the appointing authority are followed.	Decide how to shape the school within prescriptions of the appointing authority.	Learn what the school is doing and have governing body views considered by the school.	Decide how to promote school interests.	Learn how the system is working and have governing body views considered by other parties.
Values	Appointing authority.	Interests in the local education system.	Interests concerned with the school.	School.	Interests in the local education system.
Representation	Representation of the appointing authority.	Delegates or trustees from major interests concerned with the school.	Trustees for major interests concerned with the school,	Individuals connected with major interests valued by the school.	Delegates from major interests concerned with the school.
Resources	Information regarding limits to be observed by schools and	Information regarding policies affecting schools	Information on all aspects of school management.	Information on needs of the school. Clerk/officer presence helpful.	Information regarding policies affecting schools and community, on school policies and

Table 3.2.1 Continued

	Accountable		Advisory	Supportive	Mediating
	whether these are being adhered to. Information on needs of the school.	and all aspects of school management. Require clerk/officer presence.			needs, on community needs. Require clerk/officer presence.
Public relations	Unimportant.	Governing body known in school and by the appointing authority.	Governing body known to school.	Governing body known to valued interests.	Governing body known in local education system.
Style of working	Political or foundation leadership. Professional report.	Lay leadership. Importance of articulating different viewpoints and achieving agreement.	Professional leadership. Importance of rational argument.	Professional or managerial leadership. Importance of individual contribution.	Professional or lay leadership. Importance of articulating different viewpoints and achieving agreement.
Demands of work upon the governors	Undemanding.	Demanding.	Moderately demanding.	Undemanding, except in crisis or for key members.	Demanding.
View of educational government	Classical, democratic.	Pluralist.	Neo-pluralist.	Élitist.	Pluralist.

activities and implementing the decisions that are made. Naturally, if the governing body felt that its authority was being disregarded by the school it would have the sanction of referring the matter to the LEA or foundation as the responsible authority.

The governing body could, itself, be called to account for the way in which the school was performing. With the minimal delegation this would only be likely if there was a crisis, or the school was persistently failing to meet the specified criteria laid down by the appointing authority. Where greater discretion is allowed it could be argued that the appointing authority needs to be familiar with the way in which the governing body applies its delegated authority. There would thus be a case for the governing body to present an annual report, or for its chairman, together with the headteacher, to meet with the chairman of the education committee and senior officers for a review of school performance along the lines of regional and district reviews in the NHS.[7] Groups within the local community might also regard the governing body as accountable for ensuring that the school was serving community needs. There might thus be a case for the governing body holding an annual public meeting to give an account of its stewardship to interested parties.

Representation

Clearly, the governors must be aware of both the values of the appointing authority and of the policies it has laid down. In voluntary aided schools this knowledge is provided through the requirement that the majority of governors are appointed by the foundation that established the school. In LEA-maintained schools the requirements of the 1980 Education Act do not prohibit the LEA-appointed governors providing a majority of the membership, although the Secretary of State hoped that this category would also be used to appoint members from the local community or from industry and commerce.[8] In any event, it would seem appropriate that the LEA appointments should include members who can speak to, and interpret, authority policies. This means appointments from the ruling political party, with some councillors and ideally a councillor from the education committee or one of its sub-committees. If the governing body has little delegated authority other sources of membership are largely irrelevant. However, if it is expected to exercise local discretion, additional members must be provided who can express the values of all those other interests with a stake in the satisfactory operation of the school – teachers, older pupils, parents and local community groups. If the governing body is to represent these interests in running the school, members should serve as delegates, mandated to follow particular lines of action, or at the least as trustees, with the capacity to accurately reflect the general opinion of their particular constituency.

Resources

These depend upon the authority exercised by the governing body. At a minimum the governing body requires information from the LEA or foundation, in order to be aware of the requirements which the school must follow. From the school, the governing body will require information, which may well be standardised in report form, regarding those aspects of school management which are considered important by the appointing authority. Where the governing body is delegated wider authority it requires all this, together with advice from the LEA or foundation on the pros and cons of alternative courses of action and their implications. The presence of a clerk and perhaps a senior officer from the appointing authority would seem essential. Demands will be heavy on the school, since the governing body requires information on any aspects of school management and is likely to be particularly concerned with ways of evaluating what is being achieved.

Public relations

The need for the governing body to be visible to the public depends upon its authority. If it is the expectation that it does no more than check that prescribed policy is being followed and pass demands to the appointing authority, public relations are relatively unimportant: the governing body can remain anonymous. If, on the other hand, it is expected that the governing body has some freedom to shape the school, public relations take on an enormous importance. The governing body requires to be known, and recognised as such, by the appointing authority, in the school and in the local community.

Style of working

The accountable governing body would be led by the lay governors. If it is a subcommittee of the appointing authority, leadership would come from the politicians, or members of the foundation, who would require a report from the headteacher and use the meeting to acquaint him with, or stress, relevant requirements. Much of the meeting time would probably be taken up by hearing what the school needed in the way of resources from the appointing authority. If the governing body has delegated authority the leadership is more open. The governors would require a wide range of inputs, from the headteacher, from other staff of the school, and from their own number. Since the authority of the governing body gives it the power to benefit some interests and disappoint others, meetings would be likely to prove contentious and party politics would probably play a more prominent role than is currently experienced in many governing bodies. The chairman would have a particularly crucial role in securing consensus and in coordinating and progressing the breadth of work involved. There is obviously a suspicion that he or she would become the *de facto* chief executive of the school, and the development of a close and trusting relationship with the headteacher would be essential.

Demands of the work

If the governors have little discretion, their role is primarily symbolic of the LEA or foundation. The governing body becomes a route for communication between the school and the appointing authority, with decisions being taken at each end by the school and authority, respectively.

Were governing bodies to be delegated greater authority, there would be considerable demands, although without doubt the governing body would need to delegate a good deal of authority to its headteacher and guard against becoming drawn into the day-to-day running of the school. The demands of the work would exceed the current norm and this might well prove a constraint in attracting members, particularly members who were already engaged in other public activities. The governing body would require a deeper and more continuous oversight of the school and its affairs than is possible through termly meetings and would need to work through sub-committees and working parties. The relationship with the teaching staff would be highly sensitive, so governors would need to know, and become known in, the school. They would need to feed back information to their particular constituencies and arm themselves with constituency opinion. They would need to be familiar with the policies that impacted upon their school and be aware of their implications.

Basis of the model

This model, with either limited or extensive discretion, is based upon the premise that the governing body exists to control the activities of the school. At a minimum this is according to the prescriptions of the appointing authority. With greater delegation of authority it could include the views of the interests represented on the governing body, within a framework defined by the appointing authority. The former, then, is explained by traditional democratic theory, in which authorities represent the public, or sectional, interest in determining the activities of the institutions they provide.[9] The latter contains elements of this in its delineation of a clear line of accountability from school to governing body and from governing body to LEA or foundation, but also owes something to ideas of pluralism [. . .] in so far as authority is delegated to local interests to shape their school as they see fit.

Accountability with minimum delegation was common, as Baron and Howell illustrated,[10] with the education committee or its sub-committees putting on different 'hats' and becoming the governing body for all their schools. Dissatisfaction with this practice and the narrow role that it allotted to both governors and professionals, was one of the forces leading to change that culminated in the Taylor Inquiry and the 1980 Education Act. The Taylor Committee, itself, advocated the accountable governing body with greater authority, recommending that there should be a clear line of delegated responsibility from the LEA through the governing body to the school, and that the governors should be responsible for the life and work of the school as a whole.[11]

From our experience, the accountable model is not found widely in current practice, although a few LEAs are deliberately delegating more authority to their governing bodies. However, our research certainly provided examples of governing bodies, or groups of governors within them, seeking to exercise accountability for their schools. This was apparent in such activities as deciding on pupil suspensions, or appointing teaching staff, but also included attempts to formulate objectives and monitor performance. Nevertheless, such efforts were intermittent, and were liable to be treated as recommendations rather than decisions. The research indicated just how formidable are the obstacles to governors exercising full accountability for their schools: domination of professional interests; reluctance of LEAs to allow or afford governing bodies a stronger role; resistance of many governors to greater involvement; and doubts as to whether the local educational system has the space for strong governing bodies.

The advisory governing body

This type of governing body also centres its efforts on the school. Its purpose is to provide a forum in which school activities are reported to the laity and tested against their ideas of what the school should be doing. It thus provides some safeguard against professional malfunction.

For this role to be effective it is necessary to satisfy the following conditions.

Authority

With this model the governors possess the authority to 'call the school to account'.[12] The school, through the headteacher, is obliged to inform the governing body of its actions, explain the reasons behind them, and consider the governors' viewpoint. The authority of the governing body is advisory, but this is more substantial than common usage of the word implies. The governors must be told what is happening and provided with reasoned explanations. Their suggestions or responses must also be given due consideration. In other words, there must be a degree of give-and-take, for an advisory relationship rapidly becomes meaningless if the advice is never taken. As a last resort, if the governing body feels that it is never being given the true picture, or that its suggestions or criticisms are consistently disregarded to the detriment of the children's education, it has the sanction, as borne out by the Tyndale Inquiry,[13] of pressing the issue with the LEA, as the higher authority responsible for the school. This could also serve to make the issue public and the power of public criticism can be potent.

Representation

This type of governing body benefits from broad membership, with members who can speak as trustees for local interests that have a concern with the school's work. Appointees are in a position to know the values of the various interests, and what they want from the school, through their own contacts; they do not come to the governing body as delegates committed to promote particular policies. In making its appointments, then, the LEA is less concerned with nominating councillors or ensuring that the membership reflects party political strength, but is more interested in matching its appointments to the particular needs of the school. If, for example, appointments are to be made to the governing body of a special school, it could be helpful to select one or two individuals with experience of working with handicapped children.

All governing bodies of this type might benefit from the presence of one or two members with educational knowledge, who can help their colleagues make sense of what they are told and provide a source of comparison to the school. A LEA that wished to work to this model might usefully frame its Instruments of Government to allow a sizeable proportion of appointments to be coopted. The governing body could then consider its own membership in the light of the needs of the school and deliberately seek out individuals with desirable attributes. It might, for example, approach someone living in a part of the school's catchment area that was unrepresented, or someone who had always shown an interest in the school, or seek a member from the main source of local employment.

Resources

Such a governing body would require little from the LEA. It might even be unnecessary for the authority to provide an official clerk, for governors could provide one of their own number to service their meetings and, providing he is briefed by the authority, the headteacher could keep the other governors informed of policy developments. An officer presence would, however, provide the LEA with an early warning of any dissatisfaction and, where a major change in authority policy was envisaged, it would naturally help the governors if an officer or adviser attended to explain the issues.

Far more would be required from the school. If the governing body is to act as an advisory forum for the school, the governors need to be familiar with all aspects of school management – the objectives of the school, the primary decisions such as staffing and curriculum that give effect to the objectives, and the secondary activities that make up the school's day-to-day life. If, moreover, the governors' advice is to influence school objectives, the governing body must be drawn into discussions at an early stage, when ideas are fluid, not presented with a *fait accompli*. The governors are also likely to be concerned with how objectives can be measured and evaluated. If the governors are to influence the primary decisions of the school, they must have a presence at the appropriate events. Governors should thus have a voice, although not the decisive voice, in staff selection. They should similarly be able to comment upon curriculum proposals and financial allocations. Governors must also hear of the daily life of the school: its triumphs and its failures. In this context it may be helpful for them to receive regular reports on the activity of particular aspects of the work, such as the arrangements for pastoral care, careers work or transfer of children to the secondary school, from the responsible staff, or individually to associate themselves with particular departments or sections of the school.

If the governing body does its job well, it will generate its own demands for information. This imposes additional demands upon the school, but should be regarded as potentially useful in providing fresh insights and generating wider support.

Public relations

The prime requirement is that the governing body is known to all directly concerned with the school. Teachers and parents, in particular, need to recognise it as an interested party in the educational process and accept that it has a contribution to make in respect of school activities. The governors need to meet the staff, collectively and individually, see them at work and generally demonstrate their interest in the life of the school.

Style of work

This type of governing body is professionally led. It provides a public witness and sounding-board for professional activity. The model assumes a rational world, in which people do listen to reasoned argument and may alter their behaviour as a result, and that it is possible for the laity and professionals to reach agreement on the appropriate course of action. The governor working to this model thus requires the abilities to listen and consider the arguments of others and of articulating his or her own. The governing body functions through debate and discussion, and the member who cannot present ideas, or finds argument threatening, is unlikely to make much of a contribution.

The chairman needs considerable skills. In meetings he or she must ensure that adequate professional explanations are forthcoming and can be understood, encourage a wide range of lay contributions and formulate an agreed view to present to the school. In meetings and without, the chairman must work to sustain a climate of trust between the lay governors and the professionals.

Demands of the work

Being a governor under this model is moderately demanding. Governors need to know their school, and be known in it. Their work is done better if they keep in touch with local interests or gain some knowledge of the education system as a means of assessing the performance of their school.

Basis of the model

For the lay governors this model is based upon the necessity, or some would argue the sound sense, of trusting the professional. Lay governors lack the expertise and time to run the school, hence they must leave the job to the specialists. However, their trust is not unconditional but depends upon the achievement of satisfactory results. This means the laity must be able to learn what the professionals are doing.

For the professional, the model is based upon the recognition that professional authority requires public support. Indeed professional activities will be strengthened from knowing the feelings and demands of the consumers.

The model thus fits with the neo-pluralist conception of government. Governments today have no choice but to delegate a considerable amount of freedom to professionals, but they, for their part, have the responsibility of listening and responding to the public interest.

In evidence to the Taylor Committee, Glatter suggested that governing bodies could perform a role more suited to their capabilities if they were placed, like Community Health Councils, outside the executive structure.[14] Their function would thus be advisory, representing views to those who have the authority to take decisions.

Aspects of this model can be widely found in current practice. Our research suggests that governing bodies do focus a lot of attention upon their schools, are commonly professionally led in their work, as evidenced by the central importance of headteachers' reports, and provide a witness and second opinion for professional performance and intentions. They are predominantly reactive bodies, and therefore, provide schools with feedback on their activities as advocated by Howell.[15] Further, it was also apparent that governors introduce their own viewpoints and concerns for consideration; suggesting, for example, a different means of achieving an objective, or questioning the resources allocated to a particular activity. However, it was also our impression that professional acceptance of the right of governing bodies to hear about any or all aspects of school performance and of their own obligation to consider and respond to lay inputs, was not so common. Lay advice on issues concerned with school management, such as the maintenance of the estate, was legitimate. Concern with educational practice, such as with the curriculum, teaching methods or class control, proved more contentious.

The supportive governing body

Although this type of governing body also centres its activities on the school, it is looking outwards to influence the activities of other bodies, rather than inwards on the activities of the school. Its purpose is to provide support for the school in its relationship with other institutions and interests in the local educational system. For this role to be effective the essential properties are as follows.

Authority

With this model, the school gives an account of its activities to the governors rather than being called to account, selecting those items that it feels are relevant for them to know.[16] These mainly concern matters where it is thought that the governors can provide some help. Thus governors are more likely to become involved in the area of primary decisions which determine the resources that are available to the school, or with problems of management, than with the objectives of the school, which will be seen as a professional matter. Indeed, unless there is a crisis, the attention of the governing body is focused on resource inputs and the management of educational processes, rather than the nature of the processes themselves, or the ends they serve.

The needs of the school will usually be presented to the governors by the headteacher. However, while headteachers are leading professionals, they are primarily concerned with school management and may seek to use their governors to confirm their own managerial role. But if the school is under threat, the governors may be drawn into its defence in any area of activity. The requirement by the LEA that a school undertakes a process of evaluation may thus cause the head-teacher to discuss objectives with the governors as a defence against possible criticism from the authority.

The LEA may well be seen by this type of governing body as accountable for providing the school with the resources it needs. Becher and his colleagues noted how some governing bodies are used by the professionals to hold the LEA to account in this way.[17]

Representation

Since the LEA is an important source of authority and resources for the school, it is important that the LEA appointments to the governing body should provide some councillors, including members of the ruling party. Such appointments provide the school with a route for transmitting its demands directly to the centres of power and influencing key decision-makers. Other appointments could usefully be made by co-option, or after consultation with the headteacher, in order that they provide a link with those interests that can help the school. Active parents, local employers or prominent local residents serve as examples.

With this model the value of representation lies in the members themselves and what they can contribute to the school through their own contacts. Members are required to take on the values of the school. They thus serve on the governing body as individuals, speaking for themselves, rather than as trustees or delegates for particular interests.

Resources

The supportive role will be strengthened if the LEA keeps the governing body informed of decisions relevant to the school. Since much of the supportive role is inevitably going to concern the LEA, it will help the governing body if the authority provides a clerk and/or senior officer to attend their meetings to process their concerns and report on progress. From the school, the governors require information on needs and some guidance as to how they can help in their promotion.

Public relations

The governing body needs to be visible to the LEA and other interests valued by the school. Thus the LEA must recognise that governing bodies will act as a pressure-group on behalf of their particular schools. Similarly, the governing body should be known as representing the school in relationships with interests in the local community, such as parents or employers. The governors' supportive role is made that much harder if their existence is unknown.

Style of work

This form of governing body is led by the professionals from the school or, and the concerns may be different, by school management. The governing body exists to help the school and needs to be shown what to do. The chairman must ensure that the skills of individual members are drawn upon as appropriate and can have a time-consuming job in progressing and coordinating any action taken by the governing body.

Demands of the work

For most governors the work is undemanding, their presence is largely symbolic and where they do provide support this is frequently passive, expressed in the form of resolutions supporting the action taken by the headteacher. However the chairman and other key members are likely to be more actively involved and this can involve considerable time and effort. It also presents the governors with a dilemma in calculating the appropriate strategy to adopt. This is particularly the case in seeking to influence the LEA. Is it, for example, more productive for governors to leave it to their clerk to express their opinions, or to take personal action? If the latter, how do they proceed: by letter or by personal visit? By trying to influence officers, or councillors, or both? By keeping issues within the educational system, or publicising their dissatisfaction in the local paper? The difficulty in receiving any response, let alone satisfaction, from the authority is a frequent grumble of governing bodies. It helps, therefore, to have governors who are familiar with the local government environment.

Basis of the model

This model is based upon the premise that the governing body exists to help the school, whose professionals are to be trusted and supported. It thus fits the élitist conception of government. According to this argument school government is dominated by professional interests and governors are coopted in their defence. However, there is probably more substance in the view of educational government as dominated by a managerial élite, comprising headteachers, education officers and advisers, and educational politicians and which thus extends across the local educational system from the school to the LEA. Members of this élite serve on and service governing bodies, the latter being coopted to serve the interests of the managers. This was the role of governing bodies defined by Bacon in his Sheffield study.[18]

Again, aspects of this model are widely found in current practice. Most governors we interviewed suggested that one of their reasons for joining a governing body was to help their school; many mentioned the importance of backing the headteacher. LEAs, too, appeared to expect that governing bodies would act as a lobby for their particular school. The supportive role is primarily deployed *vis à vis* the LEA as the major resource provider for the school, but the research identified many other examples, as where parent governors were given fund-raising responsibilities, or governors made contacts with the press or with employers on the school's behalf. It appeared to be a characteristic of their supportive role that the governing body supplemented what was already being done, albeit along a different route, by the school. Indeed, much supportive activity was stimulated by head-teachers presenting problems or requesting help, although governors also volunteered their efforts spontaneously. The supportive role provides governors with something definitive to do but, as we frequently observed, can prove time-consuming, complicated and frustrating.

The supportive purpose is frequently combined with other functions, but the largely unquestioning support and external promotional forms which characterise this model do not sit easily with the more critical scrutiny of the school, which is a characteristic of other purposes.

The mediating governing body

This type of governing body is concerned with the local educational system. Its purpose is to express the interests of the various parties and promote a consensus that can be taken up in action by those concerned. It thus provides some safeguard against things going seriously wrong in any part of the system – the LEA, the school or in the negotiation of particular interests with the school. For this role to be effective the following properties are required.

Authority

The governing body requires the authority to be informed and consulted by all the major interests in the local educational system regarding matters affecting the school. Thus the LEA may be called to account[19] for the effect of its policies upon the school and/or the local community, as well as for its provision of resources to the school. The school may similarly be called to account, and the governors could require information on any aspect of school performance, and expect the professionals to consult and indeed allow the governing body a voice in the determination of objectives and primary decisions for the school. If the governing body is dissatisfied with the response to its authority, it has the sanction of publicising its lack of effect to the interests it represents.

However, the precise delineation of authority is not the essential feature of this model. The governing body is concerned with creating and maintaining relationships between different parts of the local educational system. At a minimum it provides a channel for communication. However, it is successful if its advice leads to the various parties becoming aware of wider viewpoints and altering their actions as a result. The governing body serves as an 'early warning system' for discontent and new demands, while at the same time attempting to filter such inputs to secure an outcome that is productive.

Representation

It is obviously important that the governors are able to express the values of and speak for the various constituencies they represent, or their mediating role becomes impossible. This suggests that governors serve as delegates for particular interests, with the means of contacting their constituents and learning their opinions. Parent governors, for example, should be linked to a parental organisation, such as the PTA. LEA appointments would need to include some councillors, and some of these should include members of the ruling party and the education committee, or its sub-committees, who could be expected to speak for the authority. If they cannot be provided any other way, LEA appointments must allow for representatives from relevant community interest groups – ethnic or residents' associations, or the local churches, for example.

Not all interests, however, will be formally recognised or incorporated into the local educational system. Working to this model, governors must be prepared to take up worries and demands from all sections of the community.

Resources

From the LEA, the governing body requires information regarding relevant policy and its implications for both the school and the local area. It is important, then, that the LEA provides a clerk and/or senior officer or adviser to attend meetings.

From the school, the governing body requires information regarding its objectives and the primary decisions that have to be satisfied if these are to be achieved.

From the community, the governing body requires information on the impact of both LEA policies and school activities and of the needs and demands of the various interests in respect of education.

Public relations

This form of governing body needs to be visible within the local educational system: to the LEA, to the school and the local community. The governors might hold an annual meeting with all of the school staff, a similar meeting where they could meet parents, and be prepared to hold *ad hoc* meetings with other interested parties as seems desirable. Chairmen of such governing bodies, at the least, might meet regularly with the Director of Education and Chairman of the Education Committee.

Style of work

Leadership of the governing body is shared by the professionals and the laity, changing with the issues under discussion. Indeed, governing bodies adopting this model can expect to cover a wide area of work; at one point in their meeting concerned with the effects of the lack of nursery provision on the community and in the next breath with the state of the floor in the school hall. Since this type of governing body expects to hear and test different viewpoints, it is important that its members have the confidence to articulate their concerns. The governing body also expects to be able to reach a consensus and present an agreed viewpoint to the body concerned, so it is important that members are prepared to accept the conventions of collective working.

The chairman needs the skill both to ensure that different viewpoints are aired and that some agreed position, even if it is that the governors find it impossible to reach a decision, emerges from the discussion. He or she will probably have to devote considerable time to developing and maintaining relationships across the educational system.

Demands of the work

Working to this model is demanding. Governors need to gather the viewpoints of their own particular constituencies regarding the outputs of the local educational system and also assimilate the impact of LEA and school performance. Naturally, the amount of work is dependent upon the issues that arise, but termly meetings will probably prove insufficient, and governors will need to meet more frequently and/or make use of sub-committees.

Basis of the model

This model is based on the premise that a number of different interests have a stake in education and that they should have a voice in how it is provided – the members of the authority, the officers and advisers who work for it, the professionals in the schools, parents, and community interests. Governing bodies provide a forum in which the various interests can be expressed and negotiated. The model thus fits with the pluralist conception of government. Educational policy emerges from a process of negotiation between organised interests.

Aspects of this model are widely promulgated. The Taylor Committee recommended that the governing body should devote attention to developing good relationships between the various constituencies represented by its members, although they saw governors as trustees for particular interests rather than delegates as advocated here.[20] LEA handbooks of guidance to governors regularly stress the importance of the governing body in bringing community interests to the attention of the school. Howell suggests that governors' links with other parts of the local educational system reinforce their ability to provide their schools with feedback and that they can act, as suggested in this model, as demand regulators to protect schools from stress.[21]

Aspects of this model were apparent in our research, where groups of governors were able to articulate the views of ethnic minorities and the reservations of the teaching staff regarding a proposal to become a community school, or were able to speak with some confidence for the parents. However, it was clear in the contexts we studied that the various bodies and interests in the local educational system develop their own relationships and do not have to relate through the governing body. LEA officers and advisers will, for example, develop close and influential links with schools that never reach the governors. Parents, too, may similarly enjoy a close relationship with the school, both individually and collectively through friends' organisations or the PTA, which remain completely divorced from the governing body. From our experience, governing bodies do not, as might have been expected from their remit and membership, act as a focus for issues circulating on the community grapevine.[22] Indeed, community interests may make their own links with the LEA through the party political system and never seek to use governing bodies for transmitting their demands. This 'underemployment' may be attributed to invisibility in the system, to the weakness of governors' links to any constituency, or reflect judgements of relative power. However, in practice, it means that the governing body is by-passed. The relationships it provides are 'B roads' with the important issues passing direct between the parties concerned.

Problems are also associated with the purpose of mediation. It could be argued that promoting consensus between different interests rules out any but minor adjustments to the *status quo*. For example, could such a governing body sustain a major challenge to the way in which the professionals were running the school? What sanctions could it bring to bear if it was at odds with the LEA? In the final analysis, the power of this type of governing body depends entirely on the willingness of the interests represented first, to make use of it and, second, act upon its mediation.

Models and reality

Attempting to model human interaction is one thing: reality quite another. As has been suggested, our research found that in their current operation governing bodies and even more so groupings within them, exhibited characteristics from all of the models presented in the preceding pages. Indeed, the models themselves represent a spectrum of activity ranging along the two dimensions of focus of attention and type of authority. The position on this spectrum occupied by any governing body at any one time is a product of what is brought to its attention and the power it is allowed to exercise by the school, the LEA and other interests. It is also a product of past traditions and of the preferred ways of working of the headteacher, the chairman and the governors themselves.

Although none of the governing bodies we studied corresponded precisely with what are ideal types, it is possible to generalise. Over the fifteen-months study period the majority (five of eight) of our governing bodies approximated closest to the advisory model. These governing bodies spanned all four LEAs and we concluded that local factors such as professionalism and the respect it is accorded by governors, the absence of dissatisfaction with the schools, and the weakness of governors' links with any constituency were relevant in explaining the dominance of this model.

One governing body could be characterised as occupying the mediating model. This was made possible by the LEA seeking to involve governing bodies in consultation on educational matters, and by the presence of governors with strong links with external institutions and interests.

The other two governing bodies we characterised as predominantly supportive in their approach. In both cases it was significant that the schools had recently experienced a change in headteacher. The former incumbents had not encouraged external interference and both governing bodies were in the process of renegotiating their role with the new heads. In one case, too, serious problems with school buildings, which necessitated support from the governors, dominated the agenda.

None of the governing bodies in our case studies could be characterised as occupying the accountable model. They were not seen in this way by appointing authorities, by schools, or indeed by the majority of their own membership, and lacked the authority, resources and, for the most part, inclination for such a role.

However, in their practice governing bodies resist tidy categorisation. Their various purposes are not clearly differentiated and they swing between them according to the situations and demands that present themselves. The variation in the work of governing bodies that was discussed at the beginning of this chapter is thus also due to pursuing multiple purposes, even although, as the preceding analysis should have shown, these require different approaches and relationships to succeed. Indeed, [. . .] it is plausible to suggest that different ideas of purpose reflect quite distinct conceptions of the role of lay authorities in educational government. Howell wondered whether governors 'will manage to meet and reconcile all the diverse and possibly conflicting demands being presented for them'.[23]

No doubt flexibility is a great virtue, but it is expecting a lot of the members of any institution that they should operate as rulers, advisers, mediators and assistants at one and the same time, and doubly difficult when they belong to an institution as spasmodic in its operation as a governing body. In these circumstances the 'woolly' definition of the governing body's role lends itself to manipulation by those interests that happen to be the most powerful – school or LEA, professional or political.

It is suggested, then, that the promotion of a number of potentially conflicting purposes combines with the structural position of governing bodies in the local education system to cause uncertainty in their work. The models of purpose represent ideal types and would no doubt require major changes in practice if any were to be implemented as set out. The emphasis on the contribution of local authority members, for example, reflects both the increasing importance of the LEA in defining the activities of schools and the increasing importance of party politics within local government.[24] Clearly, however, it is difficult to provide a councillor presence when each school has its own governing body. Such involvement might only be possible by such means as returning to grouping schools; providing one governing body to each secondary school and its feeder primaries or making governing bodies responsible for all schools in a given locality, as is the case with school boards in the United States.

Similarly, some of the models would require LEAs to devote considerable resources to governing bodies in terms of attendance of officers, provision of information, and time spent in negotiating decisions. This runs counter to current feelings in a number of authorities that withdrawal from governing body work is one of the least harmful ways of securing educational economies.

Such difficulties aside, the crux of our argument is that governing bodies have a number of possible roles open to them. Identification of a range of models may aid governors and those associated with their work in deciding what they really wish to do and what resources they require to apply their efforts effectively.

Notes and references

1 See Bullivant, B., *The New Governors Guide*. Home and School Council Publications, 1974; Burgess, T. and Sofer, A., *The School Governor and Managers Handbook and Training Guide*, Kogan Page, 1978; Sallis, J., *The Effective School Governor*, Advisory Centre for Education, 1980; Wragg E. and Partington, J., *A Handbook for School Governors*, Methuen, 1980; Brooksbank, K. and Revell, J., *School Governors*, Councils and Education Press, 1981; National Union of Teachers, *Teacher Governors*, 1982; Socialist Educational Association, *Handbook for Labour Governors*, 1982.

2 Open University Governing Schools Course Team, *Governing Schools: Training Manual*, Open University, 1981.

3 Bacon, A., *Public Accountability and the Schooling System*, Harper & Row, 1978.

4 Baron G. and Howell, D., *The Government and Management of Schools*, Athlone, 1974.

5 Taylor Report, *A New Partnership for our Schools*, HMSO, 1977.

6 Elliott, J. Bridges, D., Ebbutt, D., Gibson, R. and Nias, J., *School Accountability*, Grant McIntyre, 1981.

7 DHSS, *Health Care and its Costs*, HMSO, 1983.

8 DES, *Circular 4181. Education Act 1980: School Government*, June 1981.

9 Kogan, M., *The Politics of Educational Change*, Fontana, 1978.

10 Baron and Howell, *op. cit.*

11 Taylor Report, *op. cit.*

12 Elliott *et al.*, *op. cit.*

13 *Report of the William Tyndale Junior and Infant Schools Public Inquiry* (The Auld Report), ILEA, 1976.

14 Glatter, R., 'Reforming school management: some structural issues', *Educational*

Administration vol. 5, no. 1, Autumn 1976.

15 Howell, D., 'Problems of school government', in Simon, B. and Taylor, W. (eds), *Education in the Eighties*, Batsford, 1981.
16 Elliott *et al., op. cit.*
17 Becher, T., Eraut, M. and Knight, J., *Policies for Educational Accountability*, Heinemann, 1981.
18 Bacon, *op. cit.*
19 Elliott *et al., op. cit.*
20 Taylor Report, *op. cit.*
21 Howell, *op. cit.*
22 Becher *et al., op. cit.*
23 Howell, *op. cit.*
24 Alexander, A., *Local Government in Britain Since Reorganisation*, Allen & Unwin, 1982.

Section 4

Curriculum and resource management

4.1

The school and curriculum decisions

Malcolm Skilbeck

School-based curriculum development may be thought of as a set of inter-related ideas about, or proposals for, how whole curricula are to be designed and how the related teaching and learning are to be planned and organized. It includes the roles and relations of the various parties and interests who are or might be involved in curriculum decisions. This is to approach the matter reflectively and critically, as a way of thinking about and organizing action to be taken. On the other hand, we may conceive of school-based curriculum development as a very loosely applied, descriptive label for a varied and perhaps miscellaneous collection of activities in schools. Whatever schools do that is in some measure related to the curriculum, whether in whole or part, and their ways of deliberately changing the curriculum, would fall under this definition, as would the shifting balance of control over the curriculum, as between schools and other agencies. Studying school-based curriculum development, trying to understand it in order, perhaps, to improve or perfect our actions, requires us to adopt both of these approaches. On the one hand, we need clear and strong organizing ideas: robust concepts that help us in the tasks of observation, analysis, appraisal and generalization that are essential in planning and in theory building. But, on the other hand, we need to be open to the diversity, variety and the ordinariness of a great deal of practice that arises through the actions and interactions of people in specific situations. It is indeed one of the characteristic features of curriculum theory that it serves as a bridge between the concreteness and variability of practical activities in teaching and learning, and the systematically analysed research data and constructs of the several branches of educational knowledge.

A question of definition

[. . . In] talking about curriculum development in any form we must give our main attention to plans, designs and ideas for action: our theory is a theory of action and its tests must go beyond the canons of discourse, evidence and logical argument to the arenas of teaching and learning and the test of experience in classrooms, workshops, field centres, libraries, laboratories and so forth. This requirement is all the greater in [. . .] school-based curriculum development, as is immediately apparent if we consider in a preliminary way a definition of that term: 'the planning, design, implementation and evaluation of a programme of students' learnings by the educational institution of which those students are members'. To extend this definition a little further, the educational institution may be a school, a study circle, a college or university, and so on, but what we have in mind is that the institution should be a living educational environment, defined and defining itself as a distinct entity and characterized by a definite pattern of relationships, aims, values, norms, procedures and roles. The curriculum in school-based curriculum development is internal and organic to the institution, not an extrinsic imposition. The institution also has a network of relationships with other institutions, groups and bodies, as for example a school is part of a local education authority and a national educational system and it relates to community bodies. The curriculum should not be parochially conceived. A further point to note is that it is not only the teachers that we have in mind when referring to what the institution determines and decides. [. . .] School-based curriculum development ought not and indeed cannot be reduced by professional sleight of hand to teacher-based curriculum development, important as teachers' roles are at every stage. Decision making in the curriculum should be shared, participatory, with students involved in determining the pattern of experiences they are to undergo.

A final observation to make on this preliminary definition of school-based curriculum development is that it will not prove very serviceable if we think of it as conferring upon individual institutions powers and prerogatives – and resources – that they do not and arguably ought not to command. As we shall see a little later in this chapter, [. . .] the school must apprehend its role in curriculum development as a close yet ever-changing partnership with other institutions and agencies in society. It no longer makes sense, if ever it did, to treat the school as the sole and exclusive determiner of the curriculum. That is not how our educational and social systems work, so we need to be especially sensitive to the relationship issue. In defining the school's role, however, we must also be prepared to define, or redefine, related roles: the school is not merely a reflexive agent of other institutions or forces in society. By drawing attention to the school's role we are bringing to its notice the problematic nature of its social relations. If, as some sociologists have claimed, the school unconsciously (or perhaps at times deliberately) reproduces existing relationships of power and control (Apple 1982) it needs to learn ways of constructive social criticism in order to perform its educative role of social reconstruction (Skilbeck 1975, 1982).

Turning for a moment to the aims and processes of curriculum development, to give to the school a central role is to raise challenging questions about the source and authority of the aims and values it adopts, the manner in which it selects and arranges curriculum content and its capability as an organization to handle the time-consuming and often difficult tasks of planning, designing, implementing and evaluating curricula. Changes in school management, organization and climate are required if schools are to be effective in their curriculum roles. We cannot, perhaps on ideological grounds or as a matter of administrative convenience, simply confer roles. Consequent changes in the life of the institution and its need for resources and support must be addressed.

A context for school-based curriculum development

The central ideas in school-based curriculum development may seem quite straightforward, but in order to see them clearly, to understand their implications and to know how to act upon them we have to study and think about a wide assortment of issues and developments in modern education. Like all simple yet profound ideas that get caught up in institutional life, they have become surrounded by a complex array of beliefs, values, theories, practical arrangements – and ambiguities and misunderstandings. Because the role of the school and the task of the teacher in curriculum development cannot be understood in isolation, we need to be prepared to take a broad overview of other agencies and forces at work in curriculum. School-level decisions inevitably affect and are affected by other kinds of curriculum decisions outside the school. Not to try to relate the one to the other is to risk parochialism and indeed a failure of effort.

Paradoxical as it may seem, approaching school-based curriculum development as a practical and potentially effective approach to educational change requires that we give particular attention to structures and processes which lie at the heart of the national educational system. There are several reasons for this. First, in most educational systems around the world, policy is centrally determined and funds centrally allocated even where they are regionally and locally administered. By central, we do not necessarily mean the political and bureaucratic apparatus of the nation state. Within federal systems, for example, policy may be – and usually is – centralized at the state or provincial level and control may be divided. However, whether the concentration of power and decision making is state, provincial or national, for school-based curriculum development to work or to be seen to have a role to play, its relationship with that central apparatus of policy and resource allocation needs to be explored.

A second consideration is that, significant among the factors affecting local decisions about the curriculum are the general outlines, guides or frameworks, voluntary or mandatory, which are an increasingly common feature of central educational administrations. Even among countries traditionally identified as decentralized or having strong and seemingly durable local decision-making structures, such as Britain and the United States, there have for long been influential curriculum proposals emanating from central bodies.

Thirdly, in most parts of the world since the Second World War considerable sums of central government money for education have come to be directed towards the achievement of curriculum values and objectives identified at the national level, whether these be in the form of government sponsored curriculum development projects and agencies, or government funding of local initiatives within the broad framework of these values and objectives. [. . .]

A fourth reason for approaching the subject of school-based curriculum development through its relationships with the structures, policies and programmes for curriculum that are external to the school is that it is now accepted that neither the independent initiatives of the school nor those larger external forces in the curriculum are by themselves sufficient for achieving the system-wide kinds of changes that are needed. Imposed change from without does not work, because it is not adequately thought out, or it is not understood, or resources are not available to carry it through, or because it is actively resisted. Within-institution change is, by its nature, situation specific, often piecemeal, incomplete, of mediocre quality and so on. Each process requires the other, in a well worked out philosophy and programme of development.

It is the interrelationship, including the quest for better communication, a more concrete kind of partnership and shared decision making, between the school and the larger educational environment that has to be the focus of our efforts in future. This is shown both in the experience of those all too numerous curriculum development projects that have failed to engage significant proportions of teachers and in those many school projects that have remained partial, parochial and inconclusive. The theory of curriculum has had to be revised in an effort to comprehend these problems, provide explanations for them and suggest better and more effective designs, structures, models and processes for the future. By way of illustration, one of the best known of the curriculum development design models is the so-called 'Tyler rationale'. Formulated in the late 1940s, by Herrick and Tyler, the rationale was intended to show that there are four fundamental elements of a curriculum design: decisions about the educational purposes the school seeks to attain; experiences provided to attain these purposes; organization of these experiences; and assessment and evaluation to determine whether the purposes have been attained (Herrick and Tyler 1950; Tyler 1949). The design is, in fact, more elaborate and sophisticated than this, for example in its incorporation of data about society, subject matter and student learning needs, but these four stages, related as a linear sequence, are how the Tyler rationale has come into curriculum discourse, as a design model.

In a discussion with one of his critics, John Goodlad, Ralph Tyler some years later conceded that his rationale needed to be changed in significant ways, to give a definite role to teachers in curriculum design, to avoid an oversimplified linearity whereby all designs were supposed to commence with a statement of purposes to be attained, and to give a more definite place to local and personal assessment of student needs than the rationale allowed (Klein 1976). [. . .] For the present, let us notice that the 'concessions' Tyler had in mind all take us towards a more open, school-focused modification of the rationale. Here is an example of one of the most influential of modern curriculum theorists acknowledging the need for a revision of theory in the light of the results and experience of large-scale sponsored curriculum research and development which frequently by-passed schools except for purposes of 'trialling' materials and 'implementing' change.

Conversely, in Britain since the late 1960s, school-based or school-focused discussions of the curriculum have had increasingly to come to terms with a new national dynamic, itself embodying social and economic forces of far-reaching effect. [. . .] I refer to this emerging policy response as the *national framework*, or *national curriculum framework*. This is a complex of general aims, proposals for curriculum content – whether subjects or areas of knowledge or experience – and changing patterns of student assessment. However inadequately as yet, the national framework is helping schools and educationists to relate their activities to changes in our society and its culture which pose a dramatic challenge to the older notions of schooling. [. . .]

It is evident that a quite fundamental change in the balance of educational forces is taking place, nor only in Britain but in many other countries and, looking forward rather than to the past, we must now take the discussion of school-based curriculum development out of the localist context in which it emerged as a distinct philosophy of curriculum in the 1960s and earlier, and try to relate it to the changing circumstances and needs of schools, the newer perspectives in curriculum theory and the changes in national curriculum policies, structures and practices.

Schooling has lost much of its isolation or distance from the larger society, and the development of the curriculum is now rightly regarded as a matter of public policy not an exclusive professional preserve. Although we cannot [. . .] hope to treat the social and cultural phenomena of curriculum development in any kind of detail, some effort has to be made to bring the analysis of curriculum issues into the arena of changing social and cultural realities. It is these as much as our improved understanding of curriculum dynamics that oblige us to rethink school-based curriculum development. [. . .]

The case for school-based curriculum development

We have been proceeding in this chapter on an assumption which now needs to be examined: the assumption that the school is properly to be regarded as an agency – a principal agency – of curriculum *development*. Because school-based curriculum development as a philosophical stance in education expresses some profound truths, it is not for that reason self-justifying. It is now more than ever necessary that practitioners in education, whether in or out of the classroom, should be able to explain and justify their curriculum ideas and decisions to a wider public. Just why the school ought to be singled out as the arena for special attention in curriculum making is a question that is not answerable by comfortable assumptions and traditionalist assertions of school and teacher autonomy. Those assumptions are under challenge and the assertions can very easily sound defensive. Nor can we accept the pinchpenny argument that curriculum development as a whole can simply be left to schools, as a means of economizing, with no recognition or provision of the essential resources. We need, in short, a rationale for the school's role in curriculum development, an understanding of the school's place in the wider field of curriculum, a sure grasp of the principles and procedures of curriculum review, evaluation and development, and well-reasoned arguments for essential resources – notably, adequate staffing and professional expertise. If we lack these, our moves to promote and seek support for school-based curriculum development will seem like special pleading by interested parties – the teachers.

It is frequently assumed that schools have a fundamental right to determine their own curricula and there have been many declarations of teachers' professional responsibility for curriculum decisions. In England, particularly, school control of the curriculum has had the status of an article of faith which has been rephrased and reiterated over the generations not only by individual teachers and schools but by philosophers, committees, civil servants, development agencies, teachers' unions and local and central government (Board of Education 1943; Morrell 1963; National Union of Teachers 1981; Whitehead 1932).

Like other articles of faith, school and especially teacher control of the curriculum [has come] under question. That control never has been unconditional and changing circumstances in school and society require its reappraisal. While there are rights for teachers which need to be affirmed and worked out in practice, it is not clear that they extend into all aspects of the curriculum. Nor are teachers the only people in or related to the school with curriculum rights. For example, would we concede that the decisions of the school teacher as to what the student should be taught ought to be made in all cases independently of parents' views and the preferences of students themselves? Would we accept that the teacher's role in curriculum decision-making is in any way constrained or needs to be moderated by such wider social requirements as the needs of the employment market for trained personnel, the State's interest in responsible citizenship, or the views of people in higher and further education about appropriate areas of knowledge for young people to study and standards for them to attain? It is because teachers are but one of the groups and schools but one of the agencies with a stake in the school curriculum that the issues of how far and in what manner schools can or should seek to determine the curriculum have become so much a matter of public, political and professional concern in recent years (Becher 1984; Department of Education and Science (DES) 1981; Weinstock 1976).

The question, 'Who should control the curriculum?', inevitably raises philosophical and political issues about rights and participation. These can be endlessly debated; in addressing them we need to keep a sense of balance about the school's legitimate rights over the curriculum as they exist and have evolved. If we look at the matter historically and go far enough back in time, schools were set up as places where, among other things, decisions would be taken corporately about what to teach and how to teach it. There were no other agencies for this purpose. The school was formally established, as an institution, just because there was felt to be a need for these decisions to be taken in respect of moral, aesthetic and physical as well as intellectual training or because individuals and groups, such as the teachers of Athens in the classical period, believed they had something to teach – a curriculum – for which there would be a ready demand (Butts 1955, pp. 9ff.; Freeman 1907; Marrou 1956, pp. 39–45 et seq.).

The overlaying in modern times of this concept of the school as itself the place where the curriculum would be decided, by the massive apparatus of local and national educational bureaucracies, examining and accrediting bodies, the publishing industry, teacher education institutions, professional associations and so forth, although now so well established is, historically speaking, of relatively recent origins. We need to appraise it in the course of reviewing school roles. Yet it would be a mistake to suppose that schools ever were or are, except in a very small minority of cases, just places where a group of teachers get together to organize learning for others. A closer analysis shows that school policies, including curriculum policies, embody and express the preferences and decisions of community groups, and of governments both local and national: the school never has been entirely shut off from the larger society as a specialized 'teaching shop'. [. . .] Allowing for these relations between school-community-society, we can say that the very establishment of the school casts the teaching staff into the role of curriculum makers in some quite basic but not unrestricted ways.

It is all too easy to lose sight of the intimate interplay of school-community-society relations in everyday school life when so much of the contemporary discussion of curricula is dominated by the larger issues of government policies, the state of the economy, society's changing needs, the future prospects for young people and other macro concerns. To an extent this is inevitable, reflecting as it does the scale of public schooling. We are reaping the fruits of the setting up of State-supported or controlled systems of elementary education, mainly in the eighteenth and nineteenth centuries in the nations of Europe and the USA, and in the twentieth century in the developing countries and in revolutionary societies. Throughout the world, these movements have resulted in State dominance of schooling, with a great deal of curriculum decision making centralized in bureaucratic structures and reflecting broad social policies or contributing to the implementation of State plans (Connell 1980, part 3).

It is only exceptionally, in countries such as England and Wales (but not Scotland), that there has persisted, as if in an unbroken chain, a belief that the curriculum in some quite fundamental respects is the school's responsibility, independent of central government. The historical authenticity of this view has been debated (Gordon and Lawton 1978; White 1975) and it is true that the English Elementary Code during the nineteenth century imposed quite specific constraints on teachers' freedom of action, but the tradition – or myth – has persisted in spite of that and it is certainly the case in the twentieth century that the teacher in the school has been widely accepted – and proclaimed – as a kind of prince regent in curriculum making (Central Advisory Council 1967; Morrell 1963).

There is another sense – additional that is to this historical train of events, or myth if you like – in which it is scarcely disputable that the teacher's role in curriculum making is crucial, regardless of whether the educational system is centralized or decentralized. This point is well expressed by the American educator, J.J. Schwab, one of the sharpest critics of those mid-twentieth-century curriculum development projects and programmes which, in the USA, bypassed teachers and led to unenlightening squabbles amongst curriculum theorists. Schwab wrote:

> There are a thousand ingenious ways in which commands on what and how to teach can, will, and must be modified or circumvented in the actual moments of teaching. Teachers practise an art. Moments of choice of what to do, how to do it, with whom and at what pace, arise hundreds of times a school day, and arise differently every day and with every group of students. No command or instruction can be so formulated as to control that kind of artistic judgement and behaviour . . .
>
> . . . teachers *must* be involved in debate, deliberations, and decision about what and how to teach.
>
> (1983, p. 245)

This sense of the indivisibility of the teacher's classroom decisions was often submerged in the great surge of curriculum development through national projects that occurred in many English-speaking countries starting in the USA in the 1950s and then spreading to the UK, Canada, Australia and others. Hence there arose the notion of the 'teacher proof' curriculum – a course of studies so well structured, so tightly integrated, so well sustained by rich and stimulating materials that teachers either would not wish to or could not stand in the way of a direct transaction between the learner – the student – and the learning resources – the curriculum package.

Easy as it is to dismiss this as an aberration of the technological imagination, or as academic imperialism, not all teachers are inspirational, creative, effective. The projects in some cases went too far but their mission was to support teachers. Moreover, these exuberant curriculum designers and developers were quite reasonably concerned primarily with children's learning – not with the teacher's sense of propriety or views about curriculum ownership. Nevertheless, the aspiration sometimes had unfortunate consequences in practice for the reasons Schwab and many other critics of the 'teacher proof' curriculum advanced.

Some of the large-scale curriculum development projects involved considerable numbers of teachers in school trials of new materials and methods of teaching; others stimulated school developments which continued beyond the project; others again more nearly constituted loose networks of collaborating schools and teachers than tightly controlled national development schemes (OECD/CERI 1979; Stenhouse 1980). But they were still regarded by some educationists as an alternative to either school-based curriculum development on the one hand or commercially published textbooks on the other. Their role as sources, agents and guides of school initiative in curriculum was not consistently worked out across the whole curriculum. The history of the Schools Council for Curriculum and Examinations for England and Wales, from its inception in

1963 to its closure in 1984, is a good illustration of this point, as there was no consistency of policy in respect of school roles and only a handful of whole curriculum projects (Skilbeck 1984).

Thus far in this chapter it has been suggested that school-based curriculum development is but one of the various styles or modes of curriculum development, such as the national project team, the State committee or commission and the commercial publishing venture. Despite its attractions for some educators, it is by no means universally accepted or even understood either outside or within schools. Even in an educational system where schools have traditionally enjoyed considerable autonomy in curriculum decision making, other factors and forces in education itself and in the wider social and cultural environments shape or constrain the exercise of this autonomy. Even were it possible, it would not be desirable for schools to attempt a major role in curriculum making except by relating their ideas and activities to other educational institutions and agencies and by drawing upon the resources and talents available in curriculum development projects and other external bodies. In Britain, the transformations occurring in the roles and relations of central and local government, not only in education but right across the field of social and economic affairs, necessitate a rethinking of the concept of school-based curriculum development and the procedures to be deployed. It is as well to mention here another problem, which is a common misunderstanding about school-based curriculum development – that it is assumed to require of schools a significant curriculum materials production role. There was a period when, with school resource centres being widely sought, and new means of reproducing print materials being installed, the vision of the school as a centre of materials production was proclaimed. [. . . But] the central task of the school in respect of resources is *management* for educational purposes, not wholesale production. This is entirely consistent with and, I shall argue, necessary for effective school-based curriculum development.

All of this is, as it were, a reminder of the need to see the school situationally and to understand its actions in curriculum in appropriate contexts. None of it, however, is to be construed as a reason for the abandonment of the long-held progressive principle, that the curriculum of learners should be determined in an important measure by and through the agency of the educational institution of which they are members. [. . .] It may be useful for us to identify the major arguments for school-based curriculum development and to set against them several of the recurring doubts, criticisms and difficulties schools need to address in curriculum development.

In a project of OECD/CERI, which extended over several years and incorporated case studies, seminars, reviews and reports, the case for school-based curriculum development has been extensively debated and refined (OECD/CERI 1975, 1975a, 1978, 1979). I was closely involved in the project and will draw freely on its conclusions. In the light of such constraints – which operate differentially in the member countries of OECD – as legal, financial and administrative powers over school decision making, the capabilities of the teaching profession, and the need for school-based curriculum development to relate itself to other modes of development and the various types of organization of schooling, a case was ultimately made out on the following grounds:

1 Demands for the increased autonomy of the school in curriculum making are part of a wider movement in modern societies for greater participation in the control and management of all sectors of public life: the democratization of decision making and policy through direct involvement and not only via representative or legitimate bureaucratic structures. Schools, as a part of society where intellectual and professional freedom are a crucial concern, participate in this movement and must be expected to provide leadership at least to their own members including students, parents and local communities.

2 Descending models of control, such as centrally constructed (and non-participatory) curriculum policy or legislated or decreed changes in curriculum content and organization, have created dissatisfaction or resistance, or have resulted in indifference to the underlying ideas and values of the proposed changes. In addition, projects based on a centre-periphery model have usually been underresourced or inadequately designed as comprehensive innovations, and their limited impact has generated a widespread (if not entirely justifiable) belief in the 'failure' of large-scale project development. This argument holds true even of traditionally centralized systems like France where central governments have failed to enforce most of the large-scale postwar educational reforms (OECD/CERI 1983; Skilbeck 1984).

3 The school is a social institution comprising people in active relationships with one another: it is a living organism which needs to organize and manage its affairs in such a way that its primary purpose, the education of children and youth, can be achieved in the best possible way. It engages in complex, not one-way, relations with its environment, exchanging and interchanging ideas, people and resources; it communicates with that environment and both is influenced by and influences it. The conduct of its affairs including its responsiveness to that environment requires freedom, opportunity, capability and resources. We cannot expect a school to be a vital centre of education if it is denied a role of self-determination and self-direction: the curriculum is the central structural component of schooling upon whose reasonable control the educational vigour of the school and the success of its educational mission depend.

4 The content of the curriculum consists of learning experiences – planned, resourced, structured, organized, undergone, assessed and evaluated. These learning experiences have to be charted, drawing upon the fundamental resources of the broad, consolidated areas of human experience that we term culture, the knowledge structures that we term subjects, and the themes and topics of everyday life. In charting these experiences we have to draw inferences or make claims about individual learners' needs and this requires a close knowledge and appreciative understanding of them individually and collectively. The planning and designing of the curriculum, for given groups of

students in particular institutions, is what schools can do best: the construction of and the teaching and learning of a specific programme or course are its essential curriculum tasks.

5 The necessity for adapting, modifying and adjusting plans, programmes and designs for the curriculum to meet unforeseen circumstances, or just the particular exigencies of teaching and learning, requires that at the very least, schools should be in a position to adapt curricula to local circumstances. Since learning includes variable types of group and individual activity, involving different rates and types of learning task and the differential use of resources, equipment and so forth, flexibility in managing the curriculum is essential for efficiency in school organization. These are minimal roles in curriculum; they can be more effectively carried out where schools have freedom and opportunity, in the form of designated responsibility, to design and construct as well as to vary and modify – a condition which, for example, external examination syllabuses make it difficult to satisfy.

6 The role of the teacher as a free and responsible professional person, cannot be fulfilled unless there is scope for direct participation in significant aspects of the curriculum including its planning, designing and evaluating. Teacher self-actualization, motivation and sense of achievement are integrally bound up with curriculum decision making which is the staple of teachers' professional lives. They are important qualities to cultivate in education and have a contribution to make to the maturity, freedom and sophistication of society at large. (OECD/CERI 1975, 1975a, 1978, 1979; Skilbeck 1974.)

7 With hindsight, we may now regard the school as a more stable and enduring institution for curriculum development than those regional, statewide and national research and development bodies which played so prominent a part from the 1950s to the 1970s in creating the modern movement of curriculum development. In the USA, few of the regional laboratories and university Research and Development (R and D) centres remain; the Schools Council has collapsed; many professional and teachers' centres in Britain have closed; the Australian Curriculum Development Centre has lost much of its independence; and many other national agencies are struggling for resources, under review or devoted very largely to producing syllabus materials within single subjects. The capacity of the educational system to sustain curriculum development as an institutionwide process embracing the whole curriculum is a function of several different parts of the system: teacher selection and training, in-service education, further professional development, well-framed national policies earmarked resources and so forth. However, we have a most valuable resource for curriculum development in the school itself. Structurally (despite many organizational changes) it is stable and enduring; as a community it is characterized by a high degree of expertise and professionalism; substantial resources are concentrated in and can be mobilized through it.

These are, as it were, premises of the argument. All have been put to the test if not fully evaluated; but they have in general a hypothetical and

forward-reaching character, since they are propositions for a policy and a programme, incorporating values. The aim is to define, strengthen and support
schools in the role projected for them. Some schools, accepting the challenge and
enjoying the freedom and resources, have responded, but we still know too little
in any detailed, systematic way about how they have done so, including the difficulties they have encountered. Research has been relatively sparse, although
there are studies available including one which analyses research findings partly
in the light of the present author's concepts of and proposals for school-based
curriculum development (Knight 1983).

Difficulties and challenges

The evidence of such research studies as have been made of school-based curriculum development [. . .] makes it perfectly clear that we cannot simply accept
at face value a case for school-based curriculum development but have also to
reflect upon the problems – and the possible alternatives. We should, then, note
the kinds of difficulties that have been experienced or may be anticipated. These
can be broadly grouped as follows:

1 *Capabilities and skills of teachers and others involved.* The assumption of school-
   based curriculum development, that teachers will play a major (but not an
   exclusive) role in planning, designing, implementing and evaluating
   curricula, must be tested against what is known about the competence of the
   profession as a whole and in particular institutions. In one sense, this will
   always be found deficient in some respect; however, a policy for school-based
   curriculum development would identify this and indicate how, for example
   through programmes of professional development, in-service training etc.,
   the need is to be met. This is a responsibility not only of educational systems
   but also of individual schools. [. . .]
2 *Teacher attitudes, values, motivation; alternative value orientations.* It cannot be
   assumed that the teachers of any system are predisposed to favour shouldering
   the responsibilities and demands of school-based curriculum development or
   that they will not have had experiences, perhaps of failed in-school projects,
   which have had a negative effect. [. . .] There is a responsibility falling upon
   school principals to foster a suportive climate for in-school initiatives. There
   may be more serious difficulties, including the active resistance of groups of
   teachers – for example some of those who are working towards examination
   syllabuses or who have been long settled in their ways – to becoming involved
   in review, evaluation and development groups, or covert scepticism about the
   likely results. [. . .]
3 *Organization, management and resources.* School organizational structures which
   are hierarchical and conservative in respect of decision making can easily
   inhibit or frustrate curriculum innovation. The organizational framework
   both inside and outside the school is a major factor in the take up and success of
   development roles (Lindblad 1984). [. . . It is difficult to establish] sound

organizational and managerial procedures to sustain and reinforce initiatives that might be started off with enthusiasm. One of the greatest resources for local development work is time, a precious commodity in the heavily time-tabled school day. Skilful management of time is crucial [. . .]. Deployment of clear and well-tried procedures, such as GRIDS (Guidelines for Review and Internal Development for Schools) . . . [(McMahon (1984)] is another useful managerial contribution. But such problems as staff turnover, conflicting or demanding alternative priorities, the pressures on school management arising from such 'non pedagogical' demands as handling insurance, health, safety and other regulations, negotiating office routines and maintaining relations with local education authorities – these are a potential inhibitor of significant local development work.

4 *The efficiency and effectiveness of school-based curriculum development as a general strategy.* Perhaps the most serious difficulty of all is the often unvoiced but very real administrative and policy scepticism about school-based curriculum development as a strategy for managing curriculum development. Costs have never been adequately calculated although in the OECD/CERI studies already referred to efforts were made at least to identify cost factors. The scale and variability of local development work do not lend themselves to systematic evaluation but in some informal evaluations school principals and administrators have questioned whether the wider and more ambitious functions of school-based curriculum development – notably in relation to whole curriculum planning and design – can be performed other than in a small minority of schools or in quite exceptional circumstances. Combined with the common and rather superficial – criticism that school-based curriculum development by its nature will lead to varying standards and lack of uniform educational provision, this scepticism has been a powerful constraint in the extension of school-based curriculum development, at least in centralized educational systems.

5 *Localism, parochialism and conservatism.* Much that goes under the name of school-based curriculum development, while it may well be a kind of highly practical and adaptive small-scale innovation in a particular part of the curriculum, lacks any significance for the overall curriculum of a school or a system of education. Sometimes, school-based curriculum development may simply mask a conservative resistance to a much needed general review, or serve as a diversionary measure to avoid challenge on more basic issues (Hargreaves, A. 1982). For these reasons and because of a feeling that schools cannot be expected to mastermind large-scale, comprehensive development of the curriculum, school-based curriculum development is sometimes regarded as an adequate device for tinkering with bits of the curriculum but quite inadequate in respect of policy planning. Consequently, in the minds of many, common or core curricula should be adopted by all schools, or we should ensure that there is a wide range of national, large-scale projects under way to serve as a constant stimulus and source of new ideas and practices. The challenge to the school is twofold: to show how it can plan and organize far-sighted,

whole-school review, evaluation and development and not only limited theme or subject-based projects; to accept a role for itself in curriculum making which acknowledges a national or systemwide curriculum policy and process and specific curriculum-making school tasks that are related thereto.

These and other arguments against school-based curriculum development continue to be advanced. Better reporting by schools of their own experience, and more substantial comparative research studies will help in the clarification and analysis of problems which, in some form or another, are an inevitable outcome of innovation. The question must be whether we have the willingness and ability to respond constructively to difficulties, assuming that there are good grounds for wishing to extend and enlarge the school's curriculum role. [. . .] By building in school-based curriculum development as a crucial component of a systemwide style of curriculum review, evaluation and development, we may find that the school's role in the curriculum becomes clearer and more manageable than it has appeared to many of its critics in recent years.

Summary

School-based curriculum development has a potential for the reform and improvement of education which has been only partly explored, either in the practice of schooling or in studies of educational R and D and strategies of change. It is not the same as teacher-controlled development – although teachers have a central role – since the school is a community in which many partners and interests interact. The school is an organic community, and curriculum is the comprehensive range of student learnings for which the school takes responsibility in the pursuit of educational goals and values. Accordingly, development must be a partnership and must focus on the whole curriculum and the whole child or youth. The case for school-based curriculum development rests on a mixture of arguments which include both the need for educational freedom and responsibility, and the inadequacy of top-down strategies of change. There are, however, problems and difficulties to face before the school can take its rightful place as a major curriculum centre. The processes of review, evaluation and development of the whole curriculum are not straightforward and impose demands which many education systems have yet to meet adequately. In performing its role as a central agent of curriculum construction, the school must seek new ways of understanding and relating to profound changes in national educational policies and structures, in the culture of modern society and in educational research and theory. Building up each school's capability to respond creatively to these challenges and to play its part in these larger movements is increasingly being recognized as a necessary condition for the growth and reform of schooling.

References

APPLE, M. W. (1982). *Education and Power*, London, Routledge and Kegan Paul.

BECHER, T. (1984). 'The political and organizational context of curriculum evaluation' in Skilbeck, M. (ed), *Evaluating the Curriculum in the Eighties*, London, Hodder and Stoughton.

BOARD OF EDUCATION (1943). *Curriculum and Examinations in Secondary Schools*, Report of the Committee of the Secondary School Examination Council (Norwood Report), London, HMSO.

BUTTS, R. F. (1955). *A Cultural History of Western Education*, New York, McGraw-Hill Book Company.

CENTRAL ADVISORY COUNCIL FOR EDUCATION (1967). *Children and their Primary Schools*, London, HMSO, (The Plowden Report).

CONNELL, W. F. (1980). *A History of Education in the Twentieth-Century World*, Canberra, Curriculum Development Centre/London, Harper and Row.

DEPARTMENT OF EDUCATION AND SCIENCE (1981). *The School Curriculum*, London, HMSO.

FREEMAN, K. F. (1907). *Schools of Hellas*, London, Macmillan (Concluding Essay: The Schools of Hellas).

GORDON, P. and LAWTON, D. (1978). *Curriculum Change in the Nineteenth and Twentieth Centuries*, London, Unibooks.

HARGREAVES, A. (1982). 'The rhetoric of school-centred innovations', *Journal of Curriculum Studies*, 14, 3, pp. 251–266.

HERRICK, V. E. and TYLER, R.W. (eds) (1950). 'Towards improved curriculum theory', *Supplementary Educational Monograph* no. 71, Chicago, University of Chicago Press.

KLEIN, M. F. (1970). 'Tyler and Goodlad speak on American education', *Educational Leadership*, May.

KNIGHT, P. (1983). 'English school-based curriculum development', unpublished MA Thesis, University of Lancaster.

LINDBLAD, S. (1984). 'The practice of school-centred innovation: a Swedish case', *Journal of Curriculum Studies*, 16, 2, pp. 165–172.

MARROU, H. I. (1956). *A History of Education in Antiquity*, London, Sheed and Ward.

McMAHON, A. et al. (1984). *Guidelines for Review and Internal Development in Schools* (GRIDS), *Primary and Secondary School Handbooks*, Longman for the Schools Council, York.

MORRELL, D. (1963). 'Curriculum study: the freedom of the teacher', *Educational Research*, V, Feb.

NATIONAL UNION OF TEACHERS (1981). *Curriculum and Examinations* (Memorandum of evidence submitted by the National Union of Teachers to the Education, Science and Arts Committee on curriculum and examinations for the 14–16 age group), London, National Union of Teachers.

OECD (1975). *Educational Development Strategy in England and Wales*, Paris, OECD.

OECD/CERI (1975a). *Handbook of Curriculum Development*, Paris, OECD.

OECD/CERI (1978). *Creativity of the School*, Paris, OECD.

OECD/CERI (1979). *School-based Curriculum Development*, Paris, OECD.

OECD/CERI (1983). *International School Improvement Project: Contributions to the Discussion on Strategies of Change in a Centralized Educational System, the Case of France*, Paris, OECD, Mimeo.

SCHWAB, J. J. (1983). 'The practical 4: something for curriculum professors to do', *Curriculum Inquiry*. 13.3, Fall, pp. 239–265.

SKILBECK, M. (1974). *School-based curriculum development and teacher education policy*, Paris, OECD, Mimeo.

SKILBECK, M. (1975). 'The school and cultural development', in Golby. M. *et al, Curriculum Design*, London, Croom Helm and the Open University Press, pp. 27–35.

SKILBECK, M. (1982). 'Three educational ideologies', in Horton, T. and Raggatt, P. (eds), *Challenge and Change in the Curriculum*, London, Hodder and Stoughton and the Open University Press, pp. 7–18.

SKILBECK, M. (1984). 'Curriculum development: from R-D-D to review, evaluate, develop (R-E-D)', in Nisbet, M. (ed), *World Yearbook of Education 1984–5*, London, Kogan Page.

STENHOUSE, L. (ed) (1980). *Curriculum Research and Development in Action*, London, Heinemann.

TYLER, R. W. (1949). *Basic Principles of Curriculum and Instruction*, Chicago, University of Chicago Press, (also 1969).

WEINSTOCK, A. (1976). 'I blame the teachers', *The Times Educational Supplement*, 23 January.

WHITE, J. (1975). 'The end of compulsory education', in *The Curriculum: the Doris Lee Lectures*, London, University of London Institute of Education.

WHITEHEAD, A. N. (1932). 'The organization of thought', in *The Aims of Education and Other Essays*, London, Ernest Benn.

Research into educational innovation

Michael Fullan

[*Editor's note*: The essential activity that is managed in educational organizations is the curriculum. Sometimes curriculum is perceived as little more than syllabuses, more often it is perceived as the whole teaching-learning activity that makes a school a school and a college a college.

Because educational institutions tend to consolidate and conserve whatever practices have grown up around curriculum, changes tend to occur as lurches and sudden bursts of energy between long periods of quiescence. Yet in [recent] years, there have been many attempts to change curriculum, a number of great movements of educational innovation. The nature of such changes must be understood by educational managers and consultants though it is only in recent years that a questioning of previous optimism has come about.

In this chapter, Michael Fullan describes the matter of the implementation of educational change and indicates how much further we have to go if we are to help people in educational institutions to deal with effective innovation, so that there is a true institutional dynamism rather than a cosmetic change in appearances.]

Over [recent] years research on educational innovation has moved from a preoccupation with general theories and uncritical advocacy of the latest fads to a concern with what is actually happening *in practice*. This article focuses on current knowledge and directions in research on implementation of educational innovations. The vast majority of the research on which it is based comes from Canada and the United States, although many of the basic findings are similar to those in other western countries. It is divided into four main sections: I. What is Implementation; II. What Factors Affect Success or Failure; III. Principles and People in Implementation; and IV. Reflections on Implementation Research.

I What is implementation?

Effective implementation or changing practice at the classroom and school level in regard to a new program or policy was rare enough in the 1970s to be called a 'non-event' (Charters and Jones, 1973) – it was so rare in the 1960s that it wasn't called anything. Understanding the meaning of implementation and associated problems is not as straightforward as it seems at first glance. In fact, one of the basic reasons why so many innovations have failed is that implementation tasks have been underestimated and misunderstood. Implementation is *changing prac-tice* (with the emphasis on actual rather than assumed use). More fully, implementation is the process of altering existing practice in order to achieve more effectively certain desired learning outcomes for students. The terms inno-vation, change, and revision are all frequently used in the context of describing implementation. Change is the generic term with innovation usually referring to a more radical or thorough change than does revision. In either case, imple-mentation is involved when a person or group of people attempt to use a new or revised program for the first time.

What does 'changing practice' mean? In examining any proposed curriculum or policy document the initial implementation question is, 'What aspects of current practice would change if this document were to be used effectively?' The complexity of implementation begins to surface in that there appear to be at least three aspects or dimensions of change involved. Implementation is multi-dimen-sional. To take a curriculum guideline or document as an illustration, we can immediately discern that at least the following three kinds of changes are at stake – possible use of new or revised *materials*; possible use of new *teaching approaches* (e.g., teaching strategies), and the possible incorporation of new or revised *beliefs* (e.g., philosophical assumptions and beliefs underlying the parti-cular approach). All three aspects of change are hypothetically directed at achie-ving more effectively some new or existing educational goal (see also Leithwood, 1981).

Virtually every curriculum change states or implies the three aspects of change whether we refer to language, arts, geography, history, science, special education, etc. Thus, for each of these programs there may be a set of materials (guidelines, textbooks, local curriculum documents, audio-visuals) which, if used in the classroom, represent one indicator that implementation is taking place. But these same curricula also contain implications for what teachers and others might do differently; those skills and actions which would engage a teacher if he or she were putting the curriculum into practice. Teaching students listening skills, problem-solving skills or an understanding of Canada and its peoples, for example, involve the use of certain pedagogical approaches, meth-ods of diagnosing student learning, planning, and evaluation which, if not carried out by the teacher, result in failure to achieve desired objectives for students. I am not suggesting that curriculum documents do a good job of identifying and presenting ideas for teaching strategies, only that teaching behaviour is a fundamental component of change which must go along with replacement or revision of materials.

Finally, curricula are based on certain assumptions, philosophies, or beliefs about education. These beliefs are often critical to effective implementation (because they shape the teacher's thinking and subsequent actions). They are also extremely difficult to change. To take a simple example, the teacher who believes (whether or not explicitly recognizing it) that acquisition of facts and individual student memory work is basic, will think and behave much differently from the teacher who believes that students should be exploring knowledge, formulating and testing ideas, and interacting with fellow students. Implementation of a new curriculum, therefore, may necessitate changes or adjustments in the belief system of teachers as they work through it (see Werner, 1980). In summary, an innovation or a revised program consists of potential alterations in materials, approaches and beliefs. Implementation refers to whether or not these alterations occur in practice.

Given at least the three dimensions within which curricular change may occur (materials, teaching approach, and beliefs), it is clear that any individual may implement none, one or two, or all three dimensions. A teacher could use new curriculum materials in the classroom without using related teaching strategies (e.g., teaching inquiry oriented materials in a lecture oriented format). Or a teacher could use at least some of the teaching strategies and materials without coming to grips with the underlying beliefs. We should also make it clear that we are making no assumptions at this stage about who decides on or formulates the beliefs or other aspects of what should change. Teachers for example, can participate fully in defining beliefs and teaching approaches. This depends on the process (Section II) but, whatever the process, one of the main aspects of implementation consists of beliefs.

The three dimensions have also been presented in increasing order of complexity for implementation. Materials, most visible and tangible of the three, are the easiest to produce and to use literally. Alterations in teaching approach or style present greater difficulty when significant new skills must be acquired or additional time to plan must be found. Changes in beliefs are yet more difficult to bring about: they challenge the core values held by a person regarding the fundamental purposes of education and they are often not explicit or recognized, but rather buried at the level of unconscious assumptions. The relationship between behavioural change (e.g., teaching approach) and changes in beliefs is complicated. Logically one might think of beliefs changing first which, in turn, lead to new behaviour associated with the belief. Practically, however, there is considerable socio-psychological evidence to support the view that beliefs are learned through experience (see Elliott, 1978, McLaughlin and Marsh, 1978). Perhaps it is sufficient for our purposes to recognize that the relationship between beliefs and behaviour is reciprocal – trying new practices sometimes leads to questioning one's underlying beliefs; examining one's beliefs can lead to attempting new behaviour.

Why worry about all three aspects of change? Why not be satisfied to produce better curriculum materials and encourage their use in classrooms. The answer is simply that such a limited change would be unlikely to result in the kind or amount of student learning usually aspired to by a curriculum program or policy change. Curriculum materials alone focus the student on particular types of content. The teacher's behaviour shapes the learning experiences of students as they confront that content. And the teacher's belief system provides a set of criteria or a screen for sifting valuable from not so valuable learning opportunities that inevitably arise spontaneously during instruction.

What implementation is, can now be restated. *Implementation consists of alterations from existing practice to some new or revised practice (potentially involving materials, teaching, and beliefs) in order to achieve certain desired student learning outcomes.* The logic of implementation is depicted in Figure 4.2.1.

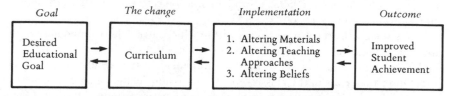

Figure 4.2.1 *The logic of implementation*

There are three main observations to be made about Figure 4.2.1. First, implementation is the hypothesized means of accomplishing improved student achievement. If implementation does not occur or only partially occurs (as when materials change but teaching approach does not), it is, of course, unlikely that the desired outcome will be achieved.

Second, the implementation process represented in the figure is not necessarily linear. The two-way arrows denote that curriculum change frequently gets defined or redefined in practice. This point is extremely important because it relates to the complicated question of what the role of the classroom teacher is in implementation. There is widespread agreement that the teacher has a role in defining and adapting curriculum. In fact, some researchers such as Connelly caution that the very use of the concept 'implementation' tends to cast teachers in the role of adapters rather than full partners (see Connelly and Elbaz, 1980, and Connelly and Ben-Peretz, 1980 and Roberts, 1980). For my part, I use the term 'altered practice' to mean that it could occur *either* through minor adaptations by teachers *or* through significant individual teacher development in working with new curricular ideas or programs. I stress this issue because there is a tendency to read Figure 4.2.1 from left to right, while not giving equal weight to the possibility that the reverse process occurs and may be equally important in bringing about improved prâctice. It is useful to keep in mind the two-way nature of implementation as I describe in the next section the factors that affect whether or not altered practice comes about. [As I take up in Section II, there are at least two different research perspectives on implementation. One is called the 'fidelity' or 'programmed' approach in which researchers attempt to assess the degree of implementation in terms of the extent to which actual use corresponds to the developer's intentions; the other is called the 'adaptive' or 'mutual adaptation' approach in which the researcher attempts to identify the interaction of the innovation and the setting in order to determine how they influence or alter each other (see Fullan and Pomfret, 1977; and Berman, 1980).]

The third point I would make about Figure 4.2.1 is that it is not always possible to measure or prove that a certain student learning outcome has been achieved, especially if it involves some of the more complex cognitive (e.g., decision-making skills) or affective (e.g., valuing Canada's multi-culturalism) educational objectives. Whether or not, and how, to measure student achievement raises some difficult philosophical and practical questions which I cannot adequately explore in this article. Some educators would be content to establish specific new activities and experiences, that is, to alter practice and to presuppose that learning outcomes will be accomplished without actually measuring them. On the other hand, assessing achievement levels can raise important questions about what program improvements and altered practices may be needed.

In concluding this section, I should like to mention that the ideas of implementation also apply to broader program or policy changes as well as to curriculum revision. For example, special education legislation is one of the more complex educational reforms on the current educational scene, and as such it highlights the dimensions of implementation – the need for new or revised specialized curriculum materials, alterations in teaching practices of special education teachers and of regular classroom teachers, changes in the relationship between regular classroom teachers and special education teachers, an examination of beliefs about the education of children with special characteristics, and a whole host of assessment and decision-making procedures involving parents, teachers, and administrators (for one description of the implementation of special education reform, see Weatherley, 1979).

As we turn to identify and discuss those factors which affect whether or not implementation happens, I might anticipate the overall problem by saying that most efforts at curriculum and policy change have concentrated on curriculum development and on 'paper' changes. Put more forcefully, the implementation process has frequently overlooked people (behaviour, beliefs, skills) in favour of things (e.g., regulations, materials) and this is essentially why it fails more times than not. While people are much more difficult to deal with than things, they are also much more necessary for success.

II What factors affect success or failure

Now that we have some idea of what is involved in changing practice, we can ask, 'Why are some proposals for change implemented and others not? Why do some curricula receive effective implementation in some classrooms, schools, and districts, and fail to be implemented in others?'. While more research is needed to unravel the complexity of the implementation process, existing evidence consistently emphasizes twelve factors as especially critical to changing practice (see Table 4.2.1). In addition to these twelve factors we could discuss other possible causes pertaining to personality (e.g., dogmatic resistance to change) or demographic characteristics (e.g., age), but I do not see this as fruitful. These factors cannot easily be altered. Moreover, much of what appears to be resistance may be a result of lack of planning, inadequate incentives and resource support for implementation, and thus not intrinsic to individual personalities, although the latter certainly can make a difference.

Table 4.2.1 Factors affecting implementation

A. *Characteristics of the Innovation or Revision*
    1. Need for the change
    2. Clarity, complexity of the change
    3. The quality and availability of materials
B. *Characteristics at the Local Education Authority (LEA) Level[*]*
    4. History of innovative attempts
    5. Expectations and Training for Principals
    6. Teacher input and Technical Assistance for Teachers (in-service, etc.)
    7. Board and Community Support
    8. Time line and Monitoring
    9. Overload
C. *Characteristics at the School Level*
    10. The Principals' actions
    11. Teacher/Teacher relations and actions
D. *Factors External to the School System*
    12. Role of the Government Departments of Education, and other Educational Agencies

---

A close examination of the factors listed in Table 4.2.1 leads to the conclusion that they operate in a dynamic fashion as a *process* over time, and that they form a *system of variables which interact*. If any one, two, or three factors are working against implementation, the process will be less effective. Put positively, the more factors supporting implementation, the more effective it will be. In the next several pages I discuss how these twelve factors operate to influence implementation. The purpose of this description is to explain what causes practice to change.

A *Characteristics of the innovation or revision*

The first three factors influencing implementation are related to the nature of the change itself. Teachers, for example, frequently do not see the need for a change that is being advocated, are not clear about what they ought to do differently in their classroom, and find the materials inadequately developed, impractical, or unavailable. These three factors – need, clarity/complexity, and quality and availability of materials – affect the likelihood that implementation will occur (see Gross *et al*, 1971, Charters and Pellegrin, 1973, and Ponder and Doyle, 1977–78).

[*Editors' note*: The LEA characteristics listed in this table and discussed below refer particularly to the North American context of school districts. However, most of the factors discussed are also applicable to the UK context.]

In regard to need, any given change may not be needed or valued in some situations. Even when there is a potential need, as when teachers want to improve some area of the curriculum, the change may be presented in such a way that it is not an obvious solution. Or the change may not be sufficiently well-developed to be 'implementable'. Whatever the case, we do know that lack of clarity about what teachers would actually do when implementing a curriculum or policy change frequently discourages them from using new curricula. The more complex and unclear the change appears, the more likely it will be avoided (see Robinson, 1980).

Materials that are vague or not practical to use, contribute to this complexity and lack of clarity. But it is possible to have 'false clarity' in which the change is interpreted in an oversimplified way (in other words, the proposed change has more to it than people perceive or realize). For example, an approved textbook may easily become *the* curriculum in the classroom, yet fail to incorporate significant features of the curriculum guideline on which it is based. Such reliance on the textbook may detract attention from behaviours and underlying beliefs critical to the achievement of desired student outcomes. The dismissal of proposed curriculum change on the grounds that 'we are already doing that', provides a somewhat different illustration of the same problem. Frequently, this assertion refers only to content aspects of a curriculum, ignoring suggestions for change in teaching approaches and beliefs. [On the problems of false clarity and superficial change, see Goodlad and Klein, 1970, Bussis *et al*, 1976, and Berman and McLaughlin, 1979).]

In summary, the need for change, the lack of a clear, practical picture of the discrepancy between current practice and what is proposed, and the development or acquisition of quality materials constitute one major set of barriers to implementation. The solution is frequently not to present ready-made, highly specific curricula, but to set up a process through which the need for change and its implications for concrete action can be developed with a group of people over time. As with other aspects of change, clarification should be seen as a process with people, not something that can be achieved on paper at the development stage.

B Characteristics of the LEA

Implementation of the same curriculum is often relatively successful in one school system, and relatively fruitless and discouraging in another. What factors are operating differently across these systems that account for this? A substantial amount of evidence (both large scale studies and case studies of successful and unsuccessful school systems) points toward six such factors or variables as indicated in category B, Table 4.2.1. (see Berman and McLaughlin, 1977, Emrick and Peterson, 1978, Fullan and Pomfret, 1977 and Yin *et al*, 1977). The first variable concerns previous experience – the history of innovative attempts in the system (Sarason, 1971, ch. 13). The more that previous attempts at change have been painful and unrewarding, the more sceptical people will be about the next change that comes along. This variable operates relatively independently of the innovation, because it stems from a general belief people have acquired through experience; the belief that subsequent changes will follow the same ineffective pattern as previous ones. We might wish that this belief did not exist, but it does for many people because of their [past] experiences [. . .] This factor helps explain why so many people initially view proposals for change in a highly sceptical light.

The effects of the next five factors depend substantially on the quality of the school district or Local Educational Authority plan guiding the implementation process. Many LEAs do not have a well worked out plan at all; others have plans which omit or underestimate key elements. Implementation has worked more effectively when LEAs have explicitly planned for factors 5 through 9 in Table 4.2.1. [The reader should be reminded that the specific formulations are based on research evidence in North American settings.] Specifically, the chances of changing practice are enhanced when LEAs: 1. have had clear expectations and provided training and follow-up that permits and encourages *principals* to take responsibility for facilitating implementation in their schools (Fullan, 1980); 2. have set up a system for obtaining *teacher input* about the need for a given change and have provided technical assistance on a continuous basis during implementation (technical assistance includes provision of good materials and resources, in-service training, and some opportunity for one to one assistance) – teacher input means that teachers are giving and receiving help and helping to define the change in practice (Berman and McLaughlin, 1977); 3. have obtained *parent and board support* for the direction of change, including the willingness of boards to allocate budget for implementation activities (some boards allocate substantial money to in-service education and other resources for principals and teachers, while others allow only minimal amounts); 4. recognize implementation as a process which takes some *time*, and which requires a *monitoring or information system* during the implementation period – an implementation plan should permit work associated with a new guideline to take place over a period of time (two, three or more years) and should incorporate an information gathering system which can be used by teachers and administrators to address implementation problems; and 5. take some steps to address the *overload* problem which occurs when teachers are attempting to implement several curricula simultaneously – effective LEA plans include the determination of priorities and their sequencing over time (this does not eliminate the overload problem, but it makes it more manageable).

It takes considerable planning skill to influence the record of innovative experiences and the other five school system factors just mentioned. Obviously, the role of the chief LEA administrator is crucial. Effective implementation is much more likely when he or she works with system and school staff to put together a comprehensive, broadly endorsed and understood plan for implementation than when implementation is left to the chance of curriculum products, written directions, one-shot workshops, and infrequent meetings.

C Characteristics of the school

What happens at the school level finally determines whether implementation occurs effectively. The actions of the principal and teacher interaction are the two key factors. There is very strong evidence in North America that principals who play a direct *active* role in leading the process of change influence the extent of implementation much more so than principals who carry out more of an administrative role leaving implementation to the individual teacher or department (see Fullan, 1980 for a review of the evidence). We need more detailed descriptions of what constitutes effective principal behaviour. The evidence we do have suggests that principals who provide leadership for change at the school level are not necessarily experts in the content of the curriculum. Rather, their leadership is in curriculum planning and implementation – becoming familiar with the general nature of what a guideline implies for a program, and working with staff to set up and carry out a plan for change at the school level. Of course, if the LEA administration expects and helps principals in this role, it is much more likely to happen. If the system does not do this, the influence of the principal will depend on the individual interests and skills of principals – some will become involved and others will not. Involved or not, the principal has a major impact on change.

Teachers also vary in their interest in working on a new curriculum. In those school situations where, for whatever reasons, teachers interact with each other on some ongoing basis, implementation is much more likely (Berman and McLaughlin, 1979, Rosenblum and Louis, 1979, and Miles *et al*, 1978). When teachers in a school have, or create, the opportunity to assist each other in addressing and attempting to resolve the many issues raised in the implementation of a significant change in the classroom, change in practice will more likely occur. Implementation, as I have said, involves the development of new teaching approaches and examination of underlying beliefs. Teachers as a group in a school are likely to have the collective ability to help one another acquire many of the skills and understandings associated with a change. Teachers' colleagues are a preferred source of knowledge and skill. One of the greatest obstacles to effective implementation is that teachers do not have the time to interact with each other about their work, and changes therein. Again, the LEA and the school through the principal can help create the conditions for teachers to interact with other teachers in the division, with the department head, the principal, and with system consultants and other resources external to the school. While pre-implementation orientation sessions are necessary and useful for certain purposes, it is *during* attempts at implementation that most specific issues arise and must be addressed. In brief, effective implementation requires some ongoing, systematic face-to-face *small scale interaction* among teachers and between teachers and others.

D Factors external to school system

While a number of societal forces affect educational change, government departments of education at the regional and national levels represent the main vehicle
through which specific policies and programs are proposed. What changes are
presented, and how the government does this, have a major impact on the
likelihood of success. Implementation has received varied and inconsistent
attention by government agencies over the past fifteen years during which time
our knowledge of implementation was only gradually emerging. As a result,
many new programs were produced for implementation in too short a time, with
little support provided. Many of these changes were not implemented adequately. There will always be problems arising from the fact that government
proposals for change reflect a political reality; an expectation from 'society' that
policy changes get implemented fully and in short order. Variations in how
many changes are proposed at one time, how rapidly they are expected to be
implemented, how clearly the need for change and the nature of the change are
developed and specified in comparison to current practice, how carefully the
orientation is carried out, and how supportive the government is in providing
guidelines and resources for implementation all affect the chances of success.

III Principles and people in implementation

Principles

The previous two subsections have said, in effect, that implementation or
change in practice is not a thing, a set of materials, an announcement, or a
delivery date; rather, *it is a process of learning and resocialization over a period of time
involving people and relations among people in order to alter practice.* Socialization
requires interaction and support, especially among peers and between peers and
others close to their situation. Change in practice may also be thought of as a
process of learning in which adults are the main learners; all the main principles
derived from knowledge about socialization or learning theories apply.

In reflecting on principles of change one should recognize that the three
aspects of implementation (materials, teaching approach, and beliefs), and the
twelve factors affecting implementation interact in any given LEA as a *system* of
variables. Although I will not attempt to present additional research evidence for
the following ten principles, I present them in order to make more explicit what
seems to be the underlying thinking or assumptions behind current implementation research.

  1 *Implementation is a process not an event.* It is self-defeating to think of implemen-
    tation as completing one task or event, forgetting about it and proceeding to
    the next one. Implementation occurs gradually or incrementally over
    time – usually two or more years for most significant innovations, during
    which time all twelve factors must be *continuously* addressed.

2 *The innovation will get adapted*, further developed and modified during use – this may be either a good or bad thing depending on the adaptation and the solution, but it will happen. Adaptation can be a good thing if it improves the fit of the innovation to the situation, or if it results in further development, specification or other improvements in the innovation.

3 *Implementation is a process of professional development and growth*. It is at once a highly personal and a social experience. It is personal because it is the individual who finally makes change (in practice and thinking). It is social because effective personal change occurs in the context of a socialization process.

4 *Implementation is a process of clarification* whereby individuals and groups come to understand and use a change involving new materials, behaviour, and thinking.

5 Because implementation is a socialization and clarification process it follows that *interaction and technical assistance are essential*. Regular opportunites for professional interaction, mutual help and external assistance are required.

6 There are many practical obstacles to implementation which occur naturally. *Planning at the school and at the system level is a necessity if obstacles are to be addressed*. Systematically identified strategies have a noticeable effect in overcoming obstacles.

7 *The LEA and school plans to guide action must incorporate several features*: (a) they must be based on and be true to the principles listed here; (b) they must systematically address the three implementation outcomes (materials, teaching, approaches, and thinking) and the twelve factors which affect implementation by employing coordinated strategies; and (c) they must monitor and otherwise gather information during the process which is used to assess progress and to address problems which are encountered. There is no one best plan, but all plans should include the above features.

8 *Developing and using a plan is itself an implementation problem*. As with any innovation it cannot be laid on. People must learn to use it, modify, it, etc. over a period of time.

9 *One hundred percent implementation is probably not desirable, and in any case is impossible*. An effective plan is one in which the implementation process and outcomes are better for more people than they would be if it were done another way or left to chance. Another version of this is that the new plan brings about more improvements than the previous plan. Thus, effectiveness of a plan can be measured in terms of the progress that has been made compared to previous approaches, not in terms of whether it solves all the problems – the latter will never occur.

10 *The ultimate goal of implementation is not to implement X or Y particular innovation, but to develop the 'capacity' for LEAs, schools, and individuals to process all innovations and revisions*. The goal is to have this implementation capacity built into the LEA as a normal, regular procedure. Implementation of any specific innovation will probably get easier as this basic capacity gets established.

People

The one common factor underlying effective principles and plans is the recognition that the success of change is dependent solely on what people do and are prepared to do. It is necessary to consider the role of some of the main participants at the school and LEA level, although in the short space available it is not possible to provide more than a good glimpse of the main issues.

Teachers are legitimately preoccupied with coping with the everyday demands of classroom and school life. Discipline, extra-curricular duties, meetings, marking tests, planning the next day or next week's lesson, covering the curriculum can easily take all the teacher's energy. There is little normal time and opportunity for reflection and serious interaction with fellow teachers on instructional matters. Moreover, norms promoting individualism and non-interference with fellow teachers have reinforced the likelihood that teachers will grapple with their professional instructional concerns pretty much alone (or at best with one close colleague). There are some exceptions to this (particularly if the principal and staff have set out to do it differently) but, by and large, teachers do not carry out regular, ongoing discussion with fellow teachers about curricular matters (see House, 1974, Sarason, 1971).

Adding new demands (i.e., implementing a new curriculum) creates further problems. We need more practical research about what teachers consider or ask themselves when they examine a proposed change. There is some evidence that they ask at least two questions: 'Will it benefit the students (including whether it is procedurally clear and practical)?' and 'What are the costs in terms of my time, energy, and anxiety in learning to use it?'. Teachers usually choose not to change when the answers to these two questions are not positive – a very rational choice (what Ponder and Doyle (1977–78) call 'the practicality ethic of teachers'). A teacher who is preoccupied with the demands involved in maintaining the existing program, cannot be expected to change readily when the change does not seem needed, is unclear or unrealistic in timeline or resource support, is not understood by the principal, may seem politically motivated, and is likely to be reversed or altered in the near future based on new political pressures.

Implementation will occur to the extent that *each and every teacher* has the opportunity to work out the meaning of implementation in practice. Involving teachers on curriculum development committees is helpful, but not sufficient. Once the curriculum is produced, it is just as new or foreign to those teachers who have not been involved (the majority of teachers) as when it comes from any external source. Because every teacher cannot participate in development, it is essential that the implementation process permit and encourage involvement of every teacher. The teacher is a professional who should be learning from fellow teachers and external resource people as well as contributing to learning by his or her peers. The process should allow adaptation, further development and specification of any new or revised curriculum by teachers as individuals and groups.

In sum, the very substantial demands faced by teachers, their perspective on those demands, and an opportunity to discuss and address the needs and meaning of practices new or revised, must be recognized in any effective plan.

Principals are also faced with pressure to keep up with the daily demands of their work, demands which have become greater in range over the past twenty years (see Fullan, 1980). One of the many new responsibilities added to their role is the expectation (written in role descriptions) that the principal should be a leader or facilitator of implementing curriculum guidelines. There seem to be three basic problems in doing this. First, there is not enough time. It is quite easy to spend all of one's time handling conflicts, administrative matters, and going to meetings. Second, some school systems do not *really* expect or help their principals to be agents of change, but rather to be administrative managers who keep things running smoothly. Third, it is not at all clear what principals should do to be effective leaders of change. Generalities that the principal is the gate-keeper of change or the instructional leader do not provide any practical clarity about what to do. Moreover, principals normally do not receive pre- or in-service training for their roles as curricular change leaders (although some in-service programs have now been developed).

The principal's problems are compounded by the multiplicity of curriculum changes being introduced. It was noted above that some of these proposed changes will not meet a high priority need from the teachers' point of view, will not be clear, and will be introduced in a way which does not provide resources to support implementation. In short, many principals find themselves in an over-loaded and ambiguous situation. If the LEA administration keeps its own house in order and provides training opportunities to help principals in their roles as curriculum facilitators, problems for the principals can be greatly reduced. The principal is facing not only many new program changes, but also changes in his or her role, namely, to provide more effective assistance in guideline implemen-tation. This involves planning at the school level to address and manage the factors associated with change. The principal is the critical person for better or worse, when it comes to school planning.

Trustees, Parents, Students: Very little research is available on the views of trustees, parents and student groups about curricular change. Evidence that does exist indicates that board and individual parent support is essential for effective implementation. School boards which are relatively successful in bringing about curricular implementation also have established good relation-ships between the community and the Board. These latter groups are not nece-ssarily actively involved in implementation, but the successful board maintains a good information flow about new programs. It is possible for some implemen-tation to occur without the community (e.g., when the community is content to leave everything to the professional educators). However, implementation benefits from the more active knowledge and support of parents. The commu-nity and board can force adoption of a new policy or program, but not change in actual practice if they are not willing to listen to teachers, and to provide support for a process of implementation that will allow for further modification or development of new ideas.

The little that is known of relevance about these three groups can be summarized as follows: the board needs to receive enough program information in order to know what new activities are going on and to make judgements on the goals of change. It is particularly important that the board become more sensitive to the requirements of implementation so that they will support (financially and otherwise) the training and resource needs during that period. Individual parents often experience great difficulty in understanding the purpose, meaning, and quality of new programs. One can surmise (and there are a few studies which confirm it) that the more knowledgeable and involved parents become, the more effective implementation is likely to be (see Armour, 1976). As for students, they are almost always thought of as passive recipients of change in terms of achievement, job market, etc. It is worth reflecting on the possibility of treating students as *participants* when it comes to implementing new programs. What would happen if a teacher spoke to students in his or her classroom about the purpose and meaning of new activities, especially if that involved a new role (e.g., problem solving, independent study) for students? We do not have a firm basis for answering this question, but it is worth exploring.

The LEA administration is the last group to be considered. They are referred to as a group consisting of the director, superintendent, area or zone superintendents, coordinators, and consultants. This group receives many conflicting demands from a variety of sources including the government, the trustees, parents, principals, teachers and teacher groups. What administrators can do about these demands is not the subject of this paper (see Fullan and Leithwood, 1980). Suffice it to say here that there are large variations among LEA administrations in the effectiveness with which they consider, select, and implement program change. The way in which they do this can make a great difference in the realities of change of all other district staff.

IV Reflections on implementation research

There are two broad implications which I would like to consider: one concerns the notion of implementation outcomes or success, the other relates to problems of how to do implementation research given the fidelity versus variation possibilities.

What is implementation success in terms of outcomes? Hypothetically, implementation is the *means* to attaining a desirable educational goal. One of the most serious problems in research on innovations is that the extent of implementation is frequently not examined (see Charters and Jones, 1973). However, one of the larger questions is whether more thorough implementation is always a good thing. Clearly it is not. Figure 4.2.2 depicts four logical possible implementation outcomes.

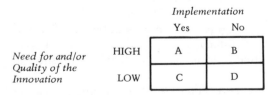

Figure 4.2.2 *Implementation outcomes*

Implementation 'success' can be seen as outcomes A and D, while situations B and C can be thought of as 'failures'. Thus, non-implementation (rejection) of a bad or unwanted idea (case D) gives school systems protection against questionable program decisions. On the other hand, non-implementation of a needed policy (case B) represents a major problem. Of course, it is not very easy to gain consensus on whether an innovation is needed and possesses quality, but the heuristic idea of conceptualizing outcomes as in Figure 4.2.2 seems to be a necessary perspective.

The second major problematic area concerns the uniformity versus variation dilemma. If innovations get adapted (vary), and should be adapted as they are used in a variety of situations, how can one assess implementation? This is a complicated research question, but the general response is that it is possible to approach implementation in a programmatic way or in a more open-ended manner. The methodological issues are too detailed to discuss in this paper, but need to be considered carefully in designing any implementation research (see Berman, 1980, Fullan, 1981, Murphy, 1980, Shipman, 1974, and Elmore, 1980).

Problems in implementing many policies and programs may be less those of dogmatic resistance to change (although there is no doubt some of that) and more those of the difficulties related to planning and coordinating a multi-level social process involving hundreds of people. It is up to research on implementation to identify, unravel and in general to enlighten what is happening, and with what results, as new or revised policies and programs are developed and tried.

References

ARMOUR, D. (1976). *Analysis of School Preferred Reading Programs in Selected Minority Schools*, Santa Monica, California, Rand Corporation.

BARDACH, E. (1979). *The Implementation Game: What Happens After a Bill Becomes a Law*, Cambridge, Mass, MIT Press.

BERMAN, P. (1980). 'Thinking about implementation design: matching strategies to situations', in MANN, D. and INGRAM, H. (eds), *Why Policies Succeed and Fail*, Berkeley, California, Sage Publications.

BERMAN, P. and McLAUGHLIN, M. (1977). *Federal Programs Supporting Educational Change, vol. VII: Factors Affecting Implementation and Continuation*, US Office of Education, Dept. of Health, Education and Welfare.

BERMAN, P. and McLAUGHLIN, M. (1978a). *Federal Programs Supporting Educational Change, vol. VIII: Implementing and Sustaining Innovations*, US Office of Education Dept. of Health, Education and Welfare.

BERMAN, P. and McLAUGHLIN, M. (1978b). 'Federal support for improved educational practice', in TIMPANE, M. (ed.), *The Federal Interest in Financing Schooling*, Cambridge, Mass., Ballinger Publishing Company.

BERMAN, P. and McLAUGHLIN, M. (1979). *An Exploratory Study of School District Adaptation*, National Institute of Education.

BUSSIS, A.M., CHITTENDEN, E.A. and AMAREL, M. (1976). *Beyond Surface Curriculum*, Boulder, Colorado, Westview Press.

CHARTERS, W.W. and JONES, J. (1973). 'On the risk of appraising non-events in program evaluation', *Educational Researcher*, 2(11).

CHARTERS, W.W. and PELLEGRIN, R. (1973) 'Barriers to the innovation process: four case studies of differentiated staffing', *Educational Administration Quarterly*, 9, pp. 3-14.

CONNELLY, F.M. and BEN-PERETZ, M. (1980). 'Teachers' roles in the using and doing of research and curriculum development', *Journal of Curriculum Studies*, **12**(2): 95-103.

CONNELLY, F.M. and ELBAZ, F. (1980). 'Conceptual bases for curriculum thought: a teacher's perspective', in FOSHAY, A. (ed.), *1980 Yearbook, Association for Supervision and Curriculum Development*, Alexandria, Virginia, Association for Supervision and Curriculum Development, pp. 95-119.

ELLIOTT, J. (1978). 'How do teachers learn?', Cambridge Institute of Education, prepared for OECD.

ELMORE, R. (1980). *Complexity and Control: What Legislators and Administrators Can Do About Implementing Public Policy*, National Institute of Education, Washington, D.C.

EMRICK, J.A. and PETERSON, S. (1978). *A Synthesis of Findings Across Five Recent Studies in Educational Dissemination and Change*, San Francisco, California, Far West Laboratory.

FULLAN, M. (1980). 'The role of human agents internal to the school districts in knowledge utilization', in LEHMING, R. (ed.), *Improving Schools: What Do We Know*, Berkeley, California, Sage Publications.

FULLAN, M (1981). 'The relationship between evaluation and implementation in curriculum', chapter in LEWY. A. (ed.), *Evaluation Roles*, United Kingdom, Gordon & Breach Publications.

FULLAN, M. and LEITHWOOD, K. (1980). *Guidelines for Planning and Evaluating Program Implementation*, prepared for Ministry of Education, British Columbia.

FULLAN, M. and POMFRET, A. (1977). 'Research on curriculum and instruction implementation', *Review of Educational Research*, 47(1): 335-97.

GOODLAD, J.I., KLEIN, M.F. and Associates (1970). *Behind the Classroom Door*, Worthington, Ohio, Charles A. Jones Publishing Company.

GROSS, N., GIACQUINTA, J. and BERNSTEIN, M. (1971). *Implementing Organizational Innovations*, New York, Basic Books.

HOUSE, E. (1974). *The Politics of Educational Innovation*, Berkeley, California, McCutchan.

LEITHWOOD, K. (1981). 'Dimensions of curriculum innovation', *Journal of Curriculum Studies*, 13(1), January-March.

McLAUGHLIN, M.W. and MARSH, D. (1978). 'Staff development and school change', *Teachers College Record*, 70(1).

MILES, M.B., SIEBER, S., WILDER, D. and GOLD, B. (1978). *Final Report, Part IV: Conclusions – Reflections on the Case Studies and Implications*, New York: Project on Social Architecture in Education, Center for Policy Research.

MURPHY, J. (1980). *Getting the Facts*, Santa Monica, California, Goodyear Publishing.

PONDER, G. and DOYLE, W. (1977-8). 'The practicality ethic in teacher decision-making', *Interchange*, 8, pp. 1-13.

ROBERTS, D. (1980). 'Theory, curriculum development and the unique events of practice', in MUNBY, H., ORPWOOD, G. and RUSSELL, T. (eds), *Seeing*

Curriculum in a New Light: Essays from Science Education, Toronto, OISE Press.

ROBINSON, F. (1980). 'Superordinate curriculum guidelines as guides to local curriculum decision-making: an Ontario case study', in LEITHWOOD, K. (ed.), *Studies in Curriculum Decision-making*, Toronto, OISE Press.

ROSENBLUM, S. and LOUIS, K.S. (1979). *Stability and Change: Innovation in an Educational Context*, Cambridge, Mass., Abt Associates.

SARASON, SEYMOUR (1971). *The Culture of the School and the Problem of Change*, Boston, Allyn and Bacon, Inc.

SHIPMAN, M. D. (1974). *Inside a Curriculum Project*, London, Methuen.

WEATHERLEY, R. (1979). *Reforming Special Education: Policy Implementation from State Level to Street Level*, Massachusetts, MIT Press.

WERNER, W. (1980). 'Implementation as belief', Faculty of Education, University of British Columbia.

WILLIAMS, W. (1980). *The Implementation Perspective: A Guide for Managing School Service Delivery Programs*, University of Berkeley, California, University of California Press.

YIN, R., HEALD, K. and VOGEL, M. (1977). *Tinkering With the System*, Lexington, Mass., Lexington Books.

The conduct of the curriculum: the roles and deployment of teachers

The Education, Science and Arts Committee, Third Report

[This chapter is an extract from *Achievement in Primary Schools*, the Third Report from the Science and Arts Committee of the House of Commons (a Select Committee), published in 1986. The Report comprised three parts, dealing with 1 the nature of achievement in primary schools; 2 the curriculum and its management; 3 issues of teacher training and supply. The extract below is from the section on the management of the curriculum, and discusses the role of curriculum co-ordinators (paras 9.1–9.29). The priority that the Select Committee gave to "whole school development plans" and the part to be played in them by co-ordinators is illustrated in Paragraph 13.41. Paragraphs 14.76–14.84 come from the committee's concluding recommendations, and identify the extra resources considered necessary for co-ordination and collegial planning to become effective.]

9.1. Nearly all primary school teachers are class teachers, or headteachers, or both. A small minority are neither heads nor class teachers; these may spend most of their time teaching in one school or working in a number of schools; they may concentrate their efforts on one part of the curriculum or on a narrow band of children, for example slow learners.

The class teacher

9.2. A class teacher is, typically, responsible for all or most of the work of one class of children. He or she may take that group of children for one school year only or may continue with them for a second or more years. It is rare in England for a teacher to take a group of children all the way through a school unless the school is very small. If the school is vertically grouped[1] the teacher probably takes children for two or more years, with some entering and some leaving the class each year.

9.3. The HMI survey of 1978[2] referred to a number of potential advantages of the class/teacher system. The teacher has time to get to know the children well and to know their strengths and weaknesses. The one teacher concerned can readily adjust the daily programme to suit special circumstances. It is simpler for one teacher than for a group of teachers to ensure that the various parts of the curriculum are co-ordinated[3] and to reinforce work done in one part of the curriculum with work done in another.

9.4. In secondary schools it is rare for one teacher to be wholly responsible for the work of a group of children, or even nearly so, and more likely that he or she will take a group for at least two or three years in a curricular subject. The advantages available to the primary school class teachers are at least diminished and there may be fragmentation of the curriculum.[4] On the other hand, the secondary school teacher has the advantage of developing a continuous course over a number of years, and the opportunity to concentrate his or her in-service training and reading on one aspect of the curriculum.

9.5. The nature of the role of a class teacher and its importance brought comments from very many of our witnesses. They were concerned with three main issues. First, to what extent do primary school children need only one teacher so that teacher and children can get to know each other well, that the group has stability, and that the work and approach are consistent? Second, is it possible for one teacher to cope with the full range of the modern curriculum and the methodologies required? Third, if the answer to the second question is "no" what should be done?

9.6. The answers to the questions depended, not surprisingly, on the ages of the children being considered. An NAHT witness, Mrs Leeke, a primary school head, told us that young children do not like other teachers coming into their classrooms, but accept this as they get older.[5] The Association of Chief Education Social Workers thought it best for young children to have one teacher but favoured there being more than one for a class at the top of the primary school.[6] The IAPS told us that some specialisation occurs in preparatory schools from the time children are nine years old but pointed to the need for each child to have one teacher, in some cases the headteacher, to whom he or she might turn.[7]

9.7. A number of witnesses stressed the advantages of the class teacher system. The National Association of Teachers in Further and Higher Education[8] (NATFHE) saw the primary teacher's role as essentially and predominantly that of class teacher. The NUT[9] thought it had "overriding importance". The Mathematical Association saw primary teachers as generalists.[10]

9.8. There was wide agreement, though, that the curriculum has become so enlarged that it is too much to expect the class teacher to cope unaided.[11] When he gave evidence, the Senior Chief Inspector[12] made it clear that he was not advocating the secondary school model when he expressed the view that the class/teacher basis of primary schools should not be so absolute as it is. Professor P. Taylor[13] pointed out that teachers are taught to cover a variety of subject areas, but "we have come to require primary schools to do more and more and more, to take on a wider curriculum with increased density."

9.9. We may fairly summarise the answers our witnesses gave to the first two questions as follows. It is advantageous to maintain the class/teacher system as far as possible; but it is unreasonable to expect one teacher to cope with the depth and width of the modern primary curriculum. We are satisfied that our witnesses are right. We are satisfied that the work of a primary school class, particularly but not only classes of nine-or ten-year olds, is more extensive and has more depth than one teacher can be expected to cover unsupported, and it is unreasonable to require one teacher to keep abreast of all parts of the curriculum through the necessary reading, attendance at courses, and learning what is happening in the best schools. Without implying comment on any other possible causes of low morale, we believe this heavy load to be one reason why so many primary school teachers feel dissatisfied with what they are doing. It is urgently necessary to find a way of reducing the demand upon them. The third question requires an answer but our witnesses were clearly less agreed about what it should be.

Co-ordinating and specialist roles of primary school teachers

9.10. There are two possible ways of going forward when a class teacher is in difficulty with regard to a part of the curriculum. One is to provide the teacher with the advice and support that will enable him or her to proceed. The other is to arrange for someone else to take over the teaching. Obviously these procedures cannot be used at the same time, though they can be used with the same teacher on different occasions. We found many witnesses in favour of the first solution. The terminology varied from witness to witness: some referred to the advantage of having co-ordinators[14] and others to consultants,[15] curricular leaders[16] or advisers;[17] still others to the use of teachers' specialisms[18] or expertise,[19] or posts of responsibility.

9.11. It would be an advantage if there could be a common terminology. "Co-ordinator" appears to be the most popular. It has the advantage that it cannot be confused with "specialist" in the secondary school sense. It suggests that the person carrying out the function has a positive role to play and does not wait to be asked, as a consultant might. It implies that one works with others rather than on them. It does not necessarily have links with salary scales as "post of responsibility" often does. We shall use "co-ordinator" and hope that others follow suit.

9.12. If co-ordinators are potentially useful in primary schools to support class teachers who are unsure what to do, two matters arise: where can co-ordinators be found and what should they do?

Who might be co-ordinators?

9.13. The answer to this question depends at least in part on how many there should be. The answer, to judge by our witnesses, seems to be rather more than there are aspects of the curriculum. We include a selection. The Assistant Masters and Mistresses Association[20] thought co-ordinators would be useful in planning English and mathematics syllabuses and would be of even more use for science, music, physical education, art and craft. The Association for Science Education[21] and the ACC[22] agreed about science. Professor Taylor, Mr Riley[23] and the Incorporated Society for Musicians[24] did so for music and the PE associations[25] for physical education. The National Association for the Teaching of English,[26] following the Bullock Committtee, also proposed English, and the Mathematical associations,[27] following the Cockcroft Committee, promoted the case for mathematics. Both of these subjects also received strong support from the National Association of Headteachers.[28] Professor Blyth[29] wanted a co-ordinator for social knowledge and awareness; the Historical Association[30] for history; and the Geographical Association[31] for geography. The Professional Council for Religious Education[32] saw the need for a co-ordinator for religious education. Other claimants went beyond aspects of the curriculum. The Library Association[33] wanted someone in charge of the library. The National Association for Remedial Education[34] wanted a special needs co-ordinator. Interestingly, the paper from the National Primary Project[35] of the Microelectronics Programme saw it as right that coordinators for the use of micro-computers should gradually be phased out at school and LEA levels as the apparatus became more familiar to teachers and children.

9.14. Some co-ordinators might oversee a combination of these aspects of a school's work. On the other hand we might have added more requirements such as English as a second language, assessment and testing, links with other schools, drama, craft, design and technology.

9.15. Various estimates have been made of the number of teachers that might reasonably be expected to cover the range. The Education Officer of the Association of County Councils[36] drew attention to the idea that a primary school may not be viable with fewer than eight teachers and indicated that work by the inspectorate of a member authority tended to support this idea. The National Association of Inspectors and Educational Advisers[37] appeared to express a preference for one member of staff for each of the nine areas of experience suggested by HMI.

9.16. It is impossible to be precise in a matter of this sort because different teachers can offer different groups of expertise. Any estimate must be based on assumptions about what it is reasonable to expect of teachers and what levels of expertise are required. We do not need to accept the suggestion that a primary school lacks viability if it has fewer than eight teachers to agree, as we do on present evidence, that the range of expertise required by a class teacher is likely to necessitate access to about seven other teachers. One or more of these might be a part-time teacher, or a peripatetic teacher, or a teacher in a nearby school. Neither the number of co-ordinators nor the aspects of learning they represent must necessarily be reflected in the way the curriculum is divided for teaching purposes.

9.17. If, as we agree, the class/teacher system has advantages that should be retained, it is certain that the overwhelming majority of co-ordinators must also be class teachers, as is the case in schools where co-ordinators already operate. Furthermore, if the co-ordinating role is to be as common as we – and others – think necessary, there is no prospect of restricting it to teachers paid above the basic salary scale and nor would we think it right to do so. The Burnham Salary Scale for teachers at present provides for a basic salary scale known as Scale 1. Scales 2 and above are paid to some teachers who are appointed to posts that carry them. The number of posts in any one school and the levels of post are arrived at by applying a formula that takes acccount of the number of children in a school and their ages. There is some local discretion in the application of the formula. It is common for teachers on Scale 2 and above to be expected to carry out duties additional to being a class teacher. In a small school there may be no posts above Scale 1 except for the Head's post, which is on a separate scale. The proportion of primary school teachers on salary scale 1 in January 1986 was about one-third.

9.18. We are of the view that it should be part of the ordinary duties of virtually every primary school teacher to act as a co-ordinator in some aspect of primary school work. In larger schools it should be possible for the co-ordinator's work to be carried out within the school. In small schools arrangements are required to allow co-ordination to operate within a cluster of schools. Some LEAs[38] employ advisory teachers who work within a group of schools and this can be a partial solution. Clusters of schools already exist and the teachers employed within the cluster share their expertise;[39] arrangements of this sort need further development and monitoring. It is probably more necessary to share between schools in some parts of the curriculum, for example science[40] than in others.

What should co-ordinators do?

9.19. Many of our witnesses thought the two principal functions of co-ordinators were to advise other teachers[41] and, occasionally, to work with children alongside their class teacher.[42] We were strongly warned against specialist teaching on a secondary school model[43] mainly on the grounds that to introduce it would disadvantageously fragment the children's work and reduce the quality of personal relationships, but also because the introduction would be organisationally difficult in small schools. Others warned that any change of practice should be limited[44] to the older children or to certain subjects. Some wanted any changes carefully monitored, taking into account the effects on parents as well as on schools.[45]

9.20. We accept unreservedly that primary schools should not adopt a practice whereby each aspect of the curriculum is taught by a teacher specialising only in the teaching of that subject. We regard such a practice as likely to be disadvantageous for children between three and 11 or 12, as well as being unnecessary, extremely difficult to operate in large schools with anything like present staffing levels and quite impossible in medium sized or small schools.

9.21. Nor have we met anyone who wishes otherwise, though there does seem to be some misunderstanding among witnesses about what others think. Our impression is that the confusion comes in part from an indiscriminate use of the term "specialist". We have heard the word or derivatives of it used to describe a teacher's knowledge or interest; to describe a form of teaching organisation of the kind outlined in the previous paragraph; to describe a partial form of that organisation; and to describe the narrowing of a pupil's curriculum so that he or she concentrates on some subjects and omits others. The confusion may also arise from real differences of opinion about the balances of advantages between: (a) ensuring the coherence of the curriculum and (b) the provision of sufficiently high teaching expertise; or between (x) progression and development in learning and (y) pastoral concern and care for a child as a whole. Unfortunately the discussion is too often about only one side of the various issues to be balanced.

9.22. We hope that what follows goes some way towards clarifying the issues and may even provide a basis for consensus.

9.23. We begin from the assumption that most teachers in primary schools can teach most aspects of the curriculum to most of their pupils. We are satisfied that this view is supported by the evidence available to us, including what we saw on our visits to schools. It is particularly important that the younger children are provided for in ways that do not present them with frequent changes of teachers, though we are sceptical of the point of view that they are worried when other adults occasionally come into their classroom. In our experience a good many were delighed with the chance to show what they were doing or to ask about us. Moreover, in North-Rhine Westphalia where there is much "half-time" teaching, two teachers often share a class with no sign of ill effects on the children.

9.24. As we have already said, it is too much to expect every teacher to keep up with changes in knowledge and methodology in every field. Each would be helped by having a colleague nearby to turn to for information and help from time to time, and especially so if the roles of adviser and advised could be exchanged on other occasions: i.e. that there was no question of hierarchy.

9.25. We envisage that the colleagues giving help should do so in two main ways: by taking the lead in the formulation of a scheme of work; and by helping teachers[46] individually to translate the scheme into classroom practice either through discussion or by helping in the teaching of the children. Much the most frequent method would be discussion. Direct teaching might often take place with the class teacher present, not least so that the class teacher can manage on his or her own next time. But sometimes it might be better to teach the children away from their own teacher because that is easier for the co-ordinator to manage, or because to do so makes it possible to avoid distraction, or because the class teacher could use the time to do something else. If the teaching is done separately, the class teacher should be responsible for ensuring that the work done fits with the rest of the child's programmes. Linkage with the rest of the programme is what matters, not where the teaching takes place. Children near the end of the primary stage are more likely to need access to additional teachers than are those near the beginning.

9.26. We believe this scenario represents the highest common factor of what various witnesses have put to us and is consistent with what we have seen and been told by teachers in schools. We consider it to be quite unlike the forms of specialist teaching commonly found in secondary schools, though it does allow the possibility of movement between teachers. The most extreme cases we postulate are, on the one hand, a class is taught by the class teacher alone; and on the other, a whole class is taught for a minority of subjects by teachers other than the class teacher, who may or may not be present. In between, and most commonly, a class teacher will be advised by another teacher from time to time; or the coordinating teacher will help with the teaching of the class or group of children in the presence of the class teacher; or will take a group of children elsewhere for some aspect of their work.

9.27. All of these arrangements occur in primary schools and some have done for many years. The late Mr Elsmore,[47] HMI, said that primary schools have always practised a degree of specialist teaching, mainly for music and physical education. When they are treated in this way, these subjects are usually taken with the whole class and away from the class teacher. The IAPS and others mentioned specialist teaching for children requiring remedial teaching,[48] or enrichment,[49] both of which are commonly arranged for a group of children from a class; as is instrumental tuition by a peripatetic music teacher. Two aspects of the curriculum that we were told were particularly troublesome to some teachers are science and mathematics and perhaps older primary school children in the classes of these teachers would benefit rather than lose if these subjects were more often taught by the relevant co-ordinators. There is no good reason to suppose that a teacher in difficulty with some aspect of mathematics or science will be in difficulty with all, and no reason to arrange for teaching by the co-ordinator for those parts of the subject in which the class teacher is competent. Any change of practice should be decided wholly on grounds of general effectiveness. [. . .]

Exchanges between class teachers

9.28. As we saw in schools, specialist teaching for music and physical education are often arranged by the simple practice of teachers exchanging classes. The critical factor is whether the "other" teacher can take the music or the PE; what the non-musician or the [non-PE] teachers can do is regarded as less important. They do whatever they can that fits into the time available. The specialist's class[50] is obviously likely to suffer, particularly if the specialist is required to take every other class in the school, which may amount to more than a quarter of a week for music in an eight class school. This practice cannot be regarded as satisfactory, though it may be unavoidable if every teacher has responsibility for a class. Remedial teaching, work with enrichment groups and the teaching of English as a second language depend on the availability of a teacher not in charge of a class, working either part-time or full-time. Provision for these groups or for other children with special educational needs were, we were told[51] likely to be threatened if the education budget is cut.

9.29. The least developed practice is the one that so many witnesses argued for: the co-ordinator working alongside the class teacher. This practice also requires more teachers than there are registration classes. We accept the arguments that have been put to us for extending the practice and for four reasons: first, it provides an opportunity for in-service training of the class teacher; second, it offers the opportunity to concentrate available teaching skill on the group of children who for the time being require it; third and fourth, because the co-ordinator will acquire knowledge of what is happening in other classes than his or her own, it should be easier to develop continuity from class to class, and to adapt the programme more nearly to the needs of the children and the capacities of the staff. [. . .]

Some priorities

13.41. We believe that the most urgent and demanding task is to redirect a proportion of resources so that they meet the immediate needs of schools as identified by staff, governors and LEAs as a result of the formulation of school development plans. *It is not practicable to expect all schools to produce and operate school development plans immediately, but a beginning should be made soon and we recommend that all schools should be drawn into a phased national scheme within five years.* We regard the support and development of co-ordinators as best encompassed in the work directed at the implementation of school development plans, that is to say *we recommend that the provision of the necessary staffing resources and INSET to allow a school to adopt a collegiate form should be associated with the formulation and operation of an agreed school development plan. The meeting of national curricular priorities should for the most part be incorporated into this aspect of training, though we recognise that some advanced courses are required to build up the group of people who may themselves take on the role of training co-ordinators.* [. . .]

The demand on the class teacher

14.76. It is advantageous to maintain the class/teacher system as far as possible; but it is unreasonable to expect one teacher to cope unsupported with the depth and width of the modern curriculum. (para 9.9)

Co-ordination – the class teacher

14.77. There are two possible ways of going forward when a class teacher is in difficulty with regard to a part of the curriculum. One is to provide the teacher with advice and support that will enable him or her to proceed. The other is to arrange for someone else to take over the teaching. Obviously these procedures cannot be used at the same time. (para. 9.10)

14.78. We suggest that teachers who provide the advice and support or take over some of the teaching are called "co-ordinators". (para 9.11)

14.79. Virtually every primary school teacher should act as a co-ordinator in some aspect of primary school work. The role should not be restricted to teachers paid above the basic scale. In larger schools it should be possible for the co-ordinator's work to be carried out within the school. In small schools arrangements are required to allow co-ordination to operate within a cluster of schools. Some LEAs employ advisory teachers who work within a group of schools and this can be a partial solution. The clustering of schools needs further development and monitoring. It is probably more necessary to share between schools in some parts of the curriculum, for example science, than in others. (para 9.18)

14.80. We accept unreservedly that primary schools should not adopt a practice whereby each aspect of the curriculum is taught by a teacher specialising only in the teaching of that subject. (para 9.20)

14.81. Most primary schoolteachers can teach most of the curriculum to most of their pupils. The younger children especially should not be faced with frequent changes of teachers (para 9.23)

14.82. Since the roles of adviser and advised are exchanged on different occasions there should be no question of hierarchy. (para 9.24)

14.83. We envisage that the teacher giving help should do so in two main ways by taking the lead in the formulation of a scheme of work; and by helping teachers individually to translate the scheme into classroom practice either through discussion or by helping in the teaching of the children. Much the most frequent method would be discussion. The class teacher should be responsible for making the work as a whole cohere. (para 9.25)

The extra teachers

14.84. We were very pleased to be assured by the former Secretary of State that he regarded it as necessary to increase the number of primary school teachers by 15,000 in addition to the number required to maintain the present pupil: teacher ratio for primary schools. These extra teachers are required mainly to facilitate the use of all teachers' expertise outside their own classrooms and not to reduce the sizes of registration classes, any change in which should be considered separately. The 15,000 is roughly one tenth of the number of primary school teachers (both as full-time equivalents) other than heads. We regard the provision of this teaching time as the most urgent resource need in primary schools [. . .].

Notes

1 See [chapter 8 of the report from which this extract is taken.].
2 "Primary Education in England".
3 Ev, p. 208 (ACC), Ev, p. 305 (Miss D S Jackson, School Natural Science Society).
4 Ev, p. 211, (ACC).
5 Q56.
6 Ev, p. 365.
7 Appendix 27, pp. 66, 68.
8 Appendix 39, p. 118.
9 Ev, p. 129.
10 Ev, p. 243.
11 eg Ev, p. 21, (NAHT), Ev, p. 229 (AMA).
12 Q3–4.
13 Q175.
14 Q516, Association of Teachers of Mathematics: Ev, p. 243 and Q463. (Miss Shuard, The Mathematical Association); Ev, p. 229, Ev, p. 145 (NAS/UWT).
15 Appendix 36, p. 111, (NAGC): Ev, p. 23. (NAHT)(who also spoke of co-ordinators).
16 Appendix 6, p. 13. (British Association of Advisers and Lecturers in PE); Ev, p. 57 (NAPE).
17 Appendix 5, p. 10. (Professor A. Blyth) (who also used the word "consultant"); Appendix 25. p. 63 (The Historical Association).
18 Q180, (Professor P Taylor); Ev, p. 127, (NUT).
19 Ev, p. 191. (National Association for the Teaching of English).
20 Ev, p. 85.
21 Q252.
22 Ev, p. 211.
23 Q178.
24 Appendix 28, p. 91.
25 Appendix 6, p. 12 (BAALPE), Appendix 45, p. 134 (PE Assn of GB and NI).
26 Ev, p. 191.
27 Q516, Q460, Q463.
28 Ev, p. 23.

29 Appendix 5, p. 10.
30 Appendix 25, p. 63.
31 Q1388.
32 Appendix 49, p. 145.
33 Ev, p. 334–5, Q668.
34 Appendix 38, p. 116.
35 Appendix 32, p. 97.
36 Ev, p. 207; The 1978 HMI survey suggested, in para 8.48: "where the staff is eight or more strong, it may be possible to provide the necessary range and level of specialisation from within the staff especially if the requirement is taken into account when teaching appointments are made".
37 Ev, p. 270. "Each school must now be able to review and develop its provision on a continual basis in each of the nine areas. This calls for a high degree of expertise, preferably each school having the services of a suitably qualified teacher for each of the 9 areas."
38 eg Oxfordshire, Cumbria.
39 Ev, p. 244, Mathematical Association; Ev, p. 290, SEO.
40 Q599, School Natural Science Society.
41 eg Ev, p. 145. (NAS/UWT).
42 Ev, p. 243. (Mathematical Association).
43 p. 190–1. (National Association for the Teaching of English); Appendix 36 (NAGC); Q600, Q606, (J Williams Sch Nat Science Soc); Ev, p. 211, (ACC); Ev, p. 127 (NUT); Ev, p. 258, (Association of Teachers of Mathematics); Appendix 49. (Professional Council for Religious Education); Ev, p. 290, Q574, (SEO); Appendix 19, (Council for Subject Teaching Associations); Appendix 35, (Modern Languages Association); Appendix 50 (Mr G R Roberts), Q461, (Mrs W Moore Mathematics Association).
44 Q 252, (Association for Science Education); Ev, p. 23, (NAHT); Q178, (Professor P Taylor and Mr Riley).
45 eg Q179, (Professor P Taylor).
46 The National Association for Primary Education drew our attention to an important difference between a co-ordinator in a primary school and a head of department in a secondary school: the former is responsible for helping teachers who are not expert in the subject under discussion and so may need considerably closer and more prolonged help. Ev, p. 57.
47 Q4.
48 Appendix 67.
49 eg Ev, p. 349 (NFER).
50 Ev, p. 229 (AMA), Ev, p. 208 (ACC).
51 eg Q431 (Councillor Mrs Harrison, AMA).

Conflict and strain in the postholder's role

Jim Campbell

[This chapter is an extract from a research study of curriculum development and curriculum postholders in the primary school. The study was based on Campbell's investigations in eight primary schools in a Midlands county. The following extract looks at the issue of role conflict for curriculum postholders.]

Conflict and curriculum development in school

> The one thing I won't do is to go into other classes to see how it's (the new policy) working . . . I started to do it at the beginning, you know, in the time I was given to see what was happening throughout the school, but I didn't get much further than asking Donna who's got a first year class just like me. I could tell straightaway, even in the staff room not in her classroom I mean, that, well, she didn't really want me in. It's a bit silly because we're in and out of each other's classes quite a lot but if I was going in like, well, officially to see how she was putting the policy into practice – well it would be too inspectorial, as if I was checking up on her . . . and anyway think what it would be like in the staffroom – resentment and bad feeling. I don't think it would be worth it and I told the head so. I'd rather leave it to them to make the first move, ask my advice or something and then perhaps I could go and talk about how it's going.

This is how one of the postholders described the strain imposed on her relationship with one of her close colleagues when she tried to monitor the implementation of a school-wide policy they had developed together. It illustrates an aspect of school-based curriculum development only infrequently alluded to, namely that conflict and strain are generated by it. In [my] inquiry seven of the [ten] postholders reported encountering some conflict or strain arising from their role as curriculum developers. By 'conflict' I mean 'disagreement over professional issues' and by 'strain', 'unease about professional relationships with colleagues'. Another way of putting it is that 'conflict' refers to actual disagreement whereas 'strain' refers to potential disagreement. There is no implication that teachers engaged in curriculum development activities were constantly quarrelling or arguing with each other: on the contrary, [there was a great deal] of staff collaboration. [. . .] What the case studies revealed was that the process of curriculum development itself often exposed facets of those subterranean differences of value and of professional judgement that normally remained undisturbed beneath the surface of routine relationships in school. Although these differences occasionally erupted into the open, they more normally took the form of an underground rumble of ambiguity.

Another illustration may be helpful. In [one school,] a group of four teachers planned and agreed upon a team teaching arrangement called combined studies. In the first year of its operation they met regularly but informally to monitor how the scheme was progressing and to plan new units of work in detail. One of the problems that emerged concerned the relative inflexibility of the curricular sequence they had planned, which meant that the individual teachers could not control the pacing of their pupils' learning according to their perceived individual needs, but had to go along with the common team pacing. The four teachers seem to have experienced what has commonly been said of team teaching arrangements, namely that although designed to create some flexibility, they sometimes turn out to be less flexible than the educational needs of the pupils demand. The four did not agree about how far this problem had been resolved, and at an early stage in the year it had been a matter of great concern and some frustration for them.

> You know that you've got three sessions with them – and half way through the second session you think, 'Oh I'll have to get them moving on quickly so that they've got things finished in time.' Whereas you really would like to consolidate the skills they've started. For example I did lino-cuts with them and really there are a lot of developments of lino-cutting that it's good for them to work on but I only had time to teach them the techniques, give them some practice and then let them produce and display a simple lino-cut design.

Likewise, one of the teachers felt that in order to progress through the agreed topics he was not able to give enough time initially to what he regarded as a very important study skill: note-making. He believed very strongly that note-making from documentary sources, from class lessons and from audio-visual sources such as radio and TV programmes was a study skill fundamental to the approach of learning built into the scheme of work. The teacher also stressed that for the relatively few children slow at learning, it was important to have more than the allotted time on it. For this reason, in the first term particularly, this teacher reported his sense of frustration, and to some extent disillusionment, with the curriculum development programme. The postholder said of the situation:

> He got very fed up, he was really down about it, and we used to say 'Look it'll be alright, we'll find time for it' and we'd listen to what he was saying and we knew he cared about it. We discussed his frustrations about it (note-making and the problems of the slower pupils) and we tried to take them on board.

This kind of conflict and strain amongst teachers was reported by Evans and Groarke (1975) in a substantial language development programme in a junior and infant school, involving the authors, eight teachers from the school and three from other schools. They experienced two forms of conflict: opposition to the programme itself and disagreement about the priorities within it. About the former the authors say, with a frankness rare in the literature on school-based curriculum development:

> There was dissatisfaction and this showed itself in a variety of ways. Sometimes we felt a cold disillusionment and one teacher confessed she felt all her previous teaching had been a waste of time. Other teachers reacted strongly against the exercise itself, handling the uncertainty with a show of scepticism and amused malice. (p. 127).

According to Evans and Groarke, their development also produced disagreement of a professional nature – about curriculum priorities:

> members of staff felt that discussion of language development was pushing out other priorities, and staff often felt slighted by the scant attention paid to other cherished curriculum objectives they were working towards with children. (p. 134)

Another study where conflict is explicitly discussed is by Hargreaves (1980), in what is essentially a report of the suppression of staff disagreement about educational values, with the head and deputy head of a middle school (8–12) effectively dominating a staff workshop/discussion, with the consequence that educational alternatives to their own position could not be explored.

That conflicts of one kind or another are experienced by teachers engaged in school-based curriculum development is not entirely surprising. Its inherent difficulties had been suggested by Skilbeck (1972):

> the task is complex and difficult for all concerned. It requires a range of cognitive skills, strong motivation, postponement of immediate satisfaction, constructive interaction in planning groups, and emotional maturity.

It would be unrealistic, and potentially counter-productive, to pretend that school-based curriculum development is easier, smoother or more trouble-free than it may turn out to be. For this reason, if for no other, a fuller analysis of such conflict needs to be offered, and the one that follows is based upon the seven cases in which conflict and/or strain for the curriculum postholder emerged.

Three sources of uncertainty in the curriculum development role

In general, conflict was derived from the fact that the role of the 'teacher as educationalist' (Keddie, 1971) is fairly novel in primary schools, and so by definition is not clearly specified. It was therefore experienced as a role suffused with uncertainty, not because postholders themselves were necessarily uncertain, but because the activity itself was an ambiguous enterprise; it was often difficult to be sure, while it was being carried out, that the effort involved would be worth while. Furthermore, responsibilities are not clearly demarcated in primary schools, so although the postholder might have successfully initiated a new curriculum policy, individual class teachers were the ultimate arbiters of the curriculum practice in their own classes. So the postholders in the research schools were, as curriculum developers, very much 'making' their role rather than 'taking' it, improvising a role for themselves rather than stepping into a fully scripted one; achieving a role rather than having one ascribed to them. Since they were feeling their way, negotiating the rules and roles as the developments proceeded, differences and disagreements were encountered, and occasionally some professional nerve-endings were set on edge. Three sources of such uncertainty were identifiable:

1 Ambiguity in relationships with class teachers.
2 Conflicting priorities.
3 Strain in the 'teacher as educationalist' role.

Relationships with class teachers

Perhaps the most distinct source of ambiguity in the postholders' role as curriculum developers was the mismatch between their formal status and their actual power, as perceived by themselves and by their colleagues. Curriculum postholders were given the responsibility for developing their subject throughout the school, for implementing developments and for monitoring progress. However, alongside such formal responsibilities, there existed a set of informal perceptions and relationships – how the postholders' responsibilities were perceived by their colleagues – which did not necessarily fit with the official specification. Her Majesty's Inspectors (DES 1978) appear to have conflated these distinctive aspects of the postholder's status in their proposition (para. 8.45) that the status should be improved. In the Inspectors' view the standing of postholders:

> is a product of the ways in which teachers with special posts regard themselves and also of the attitudes that other teachers have towards them.

This appears to be too simple a view of a very complex network of formal and informal statuses, for the relationships within it embodied a particularly pervasive strain. In every case the postholders talked of their anxiety about appearing to 'dictate' to the class teachers, or 'impose' the curriculum on them. One postholder made the situation quite explicit. She had developed a school-wide scheme in environmental studies and after staff discussion it had been accepted as the school's official scheme. The new scheme had been a development of existing work.

> We didn't sweep away everything that we'd been doing. We took what we thought was working well and extended it, and built it into an overall scheme so that there was more progression in it.

Nevertheless, in the postholder's words, there had been considerable 'hostility' to the scheme from many class teachers on the grounds that it reduced their autonomy. They had claimed that the scheme contained 'too much to get through', and that if you were always a first-year teacher you would always be doing the 'same old topics' year in, year out. The interesting thing is that neither of these objections was particularly valid: the scheme and the postholder encouraged teachers to be selective, and to develop their own versions of topics to be covered, so long as they did not cover work or topics designed for other year groups. (The headteacher had a somewhat different perspective on the issue. He regarded 'hostility' as an inappropriate term for the response of some of the teachers. He described it as 'some resistance initially' to the new scheme, but reported it as short-lived and limited.)

We have seen something rather similar in the description of the team teaching programme earlier.[. . .] What was happening in this and the other cases was a clash, or a revealed tension between 'institutional' interests (i.e. the development and implementation of a school-wide policy to secure overall progression in the pupils' work) and 'individual' interests (i.e. the perceived freedom of teachers to control and implement the curriculum in their own classes). There were clear echoes here of the 'zones of authority' issue highlighted by Taylor and his colleagues (1974).[. . .]

It is not being suggested that there was a constant curricular guerrilla warfare between the postholders and the class teachers as people. Instead, what did emerge from the case studies was the tension between these roles, a tension compounded by the fact that postholders were usually class teachers as well. Thus, paradoxically, from the point of view of curriculum development, the concept of the class teacher's 'autonomy' in curricular matters was to some extent shared by the postholders themselves, despite the fact that the consequence of their curriculum development activities was to bring such a concept into question.

Language and participation: styles of ambiguity
Two aspects of school-based curriculum development reflect this tension in a particularly clear and interesting light. The first concerns the language of the curriculum documents in the schools, and the second concerns the participatory style of the curriculum decision-making.[. . .] In both, the essential ambiguity in the roles of postholder and class teacher was made palpable.

In respect of the language in which school curriculum documents were couched – the terminology of curriculum change, so to speak – there was a resolute tentativeness, apparently designed to avoid at all costs the impression that policies would be imposed if they were not implemented. This comes through in the vocabulary adopted, in that syllabuses are not syllabuses but 'guidelines' or 'frameworks' or 'policies', and curriculum content is not content but 'concepts' or 'conceptual areas'. Moreover, the documents themselves were written in a style notable for its delicacy. For example, a review of curriculum practice in a school would have to suggest the need for change, and at the same time refute the implied criticism of class teachers' existing practices. A report written specifically for the research by [a] postholder [. . .] is a good example of such sensitivity:

If adhered to, the original Environmental Studies Scheme would have ensured progre-ssion of content and avoided repetition, but generally speaking staff devised their own themes. The result was (to state the extreme case): i) lack of progression, ii) repetition of content, iii) imbalance of work, iv) skills developed unsystematically, v) no effective record keeping, vi) difficulty in providing resources and materials, given the unpre-dictability of coverage.

Nevertheless, it was generally thought that in spite of these problems the school staff taught Environmental Studies using a topic approach rather well. There was variety of approach, techniques and methods, the children were well motivated, and the work produced was generally worthwhile and attractively presented. This was attributed chiefly to the fact that the staff had freedom to develop the topic from the beginning and make their own decisions about content, methods, aims, objectives, progression, etc. As a result (it was believed) the teacher communicated an enthusiasm for learning through the topic.

In short, the autonomy of the class teacher was seen as a contradictory source, both of problems and of pride. The postholder's language retains its curricular cake, having first consumed it.

Similarly, with the detail of the revised policies themselves, there was a clear reticence about appearing to direct class teachers. Where there were indications of work appropriate for children to cover, the policies offered them as 'sugges-tions'. In one case, where the policy had been agreed upon and accepted by the whole school staff, the preamble made explicit its respect for the class teacher's professional autonomy, even though providing a statement of agreed intentions and practices:

the policy has been divided into sections covering the aims and ideals of each skill and providing suggested reading for the teacher. Much of what is included here is designed as an aid to the individual teacher, rather than a list of inflexible rules. As well as this the policy exists to lend some cohesion and continuity to our approach.

A feature of the policy's format was that interspersed among the sections were lists of curricular experiences to be practised with the children, headed 'Sugges-tions for Development'. Indeed the policy made a point of stressing those few issues that could not be regarded as 'discretionary' for class teachers. In this, therefore, as in most other policy documents, the language made explicit the uncertainty of the postholders' relationship with the class teachers: the former were not directing the latter to teach given content, but were responsible for offering a framework within which it could appear that both individual auton-omy and institutional consistency would be safeguarded.

[A] collaborative and participatory style [was characteristic] of the curriculum decision-making [in the schools.] This style – usually involving a working group of staff whose deliberations were disseminated through whole staff meetings – may also be interpreted as evidence supporting the essentially ambiguous relationship between postholders and class teachers. The style can be seen as a response by postholders to their relative lack of power in order to ensure the implementation of changes in the classes throughout the school, for a revised scheme produced by active staff participation in discussion and workshop sessions would embody ideas likely to be acceptable to class teachers. It also followed that class teachers could not logically or legitimately complain that they were being dictated to, since they either had participated in the production of the scheme or had agreed to its final version. In either case, it ensured 'that the postholders would not have to have recourse to power they did not possess, in order to implement or sustain the innovation. Thus, although the widespread practice adopted by postholders, of encouraging a participatory style in the production of new schemes or programmes, may be justified by a rhetoric stressing its superiority as a strictly educational process, it can also be seen as a symptom of the ambiguity in the power position.

Monitoring progress throughout the school

A further problem of relationships and status arose when innovation was monitored, even if very indirectly, by the postholder. She was not a superior to some of her colleagues, and in her relationships with most of them she saw herself, and was seen, as an equal. And yet the postholder was expected to visit classrooms to see work in progress, and in three of the seven relevant case studies she had timetabled time available for this purpose. The quotation at the opening of this chapter typifies the ambiguity, in that the postholder was anxious that her relationships with her colleagues should not be adversely affected by her performing a role that could be interpreted as 'inspecting' their work.

The case studies where problems associated with monitoring progress were absent, or not referred to, in a limited sense provided evidence supporting the general analysis of ambiguity. In [a] school where the headteacher was the initiator of change, such ambiguities did not emerge, probably because the headteacher's role and status are defined more clearly as superior to other teachers'. The other two cases were the only ones where the postholders were used as specialist teachers. In one case, [. . .] the innovation did not actively involve other teachers, and there was therefore no basis for ambiguity in her relationships with other teachers. In the case of [an] art/craft [teacher,] it may be that the postholder's status as 'specialist' provided her with a stronger base from which to monitor work in progress.

The postholder concerned certainly saw it in these terms. As she said when asked to comment on her role as specialist:

> Well one thing that's very important is that the pupils see me as 'the Art teacher' and they get sent to me with their work if it's very good . . . of course I am responsible for Art in the school but really it's more how they see me – the teachers as well as the pupils. I've got two periods on Friday morning to, you know, go and see the class teachers and their Art work but it's not the official time that matters it's well if the teacher needs some help with say needlework, they automatically come to me about it – they accept that I'm supposed to help them. It's rather like the pupils, really, as I said, seeing me as 'the Art teacher'.

If she was right, it looks as though there was a better match between her formal and informal status than in some other schools, and that this followed from her specialist teacher role. It is something of a paradox that she also adduced the 'good personal relationships' in the school as one further basis for her being able to monitor work in progress, since these were precisely the reasons given by the postholder at the opening of this chapter for not engaging in such activity.

Passive resistance to change

In the last resort, in these primary schools, the postholders were brought up against the realities of their relative lack of power when faced with teachers who responded to initiatives for innovation by the tactic of passive resistance. A minority of teachers in the schools were uncommitted either to the particular programme or to curriculum development activities in general. One head explained to me that:

> There is a hard core in this school, and in most schools I've known, who are just 9–5 teachers. They don't want to change what they do. In a curriculum development programme it's the teachers who don't need to change who take part in it, and the ones who do need to change, who never attend. It's like the parents of children really – the ones you need to see on open evenings don't come and the ones whose children are doing OK always turn up.

Heads and postholders agreed that as things stood there was little that could be done to bring about change in the classroom practice of teachers uncommitted to it, or disinclined to become involved. Even allocation of formal staff meetings for discussion and decision-making could not ensure participation by the uncommitted, let alone guarantee change in their classroom practice. Faced with passive resistance to innovation, the postholder was impotent.

Conflicting priorities

Promoting curriculum change within the school was not an exclusive or even the main responsibility of the postholders in the schools in which the inquiry was carried out. All but the two postholders used as specialist teachers had a number of other major responsibilities to fulfil. [. . .] This characteristic spread of obligations might be designated 'role diversity', which is a term sociologists use to describe a position in which there is too much for its occupier to do. This diversity was a source of conflict for postholders because it raised questions of priority in the allocation of their time and energy. There is, for all primary school teachers, a limit to how much time and energy can be allocated to one activity, if several others make equally legitimate claims over the same period. There was a sense, therefore, in which, for at least some of their time, curriculum development had to be seen as a relatively marginal role by postholders.

It is not being proposed that curriculum development activities were seen as marginal by the postholders or other staff, in the sense that they regarded them as unimportant. However, the importance of the activity has to be put into the context of the overall role demands made upon teachers as staff members, not just as postholders with responsibility for designated areas of the curriculum.

These other demands make equally strong, and in some senses stronger, claims upon the postholders' time and energy. This can be illustrated by referring to the other most widely held responsibility: class teaching.

On the face of it, class teaching should make only routine demands of time and organisation upon experienced teachers, although this is not to underestimate the workload involved. However, at the time of the inquiry, there was evidence that class teaching was itself creating more demands upon teachers. Falling rolls in the schools had led to the introduction of some classes of mixed age composition. Class teachers were also under pressure nationally to give more consideration to ways they could cater for the needs of the more able pupils in their classes, and for those of pupils with other special needs. And in schools where a teacher left, the post was filled, if at all, by a teacher on temporary contract. The consequences were unfavourable to development.

In one of the schools this kind of pressure had limited the nature of the postholder's commitment to curriculum development:

> It's not that I'm not interested in it (curriculum development) – of course I am – but my class have had two temporary teachers last year – it's nobody's fault, it couldn't really be helped, it's just the case that you know they had the two of them who've been cut, and now they've got me and I think I've got to build up, well er, to give most of my effort this year to giving them stability, and getting them to know the standards I expect . . . and really I think that's more important, right now, for these kids than having another go at the curriculum policy . . . Perhaps I should do both but I've got a personal life of my own as well you know . . . and the time it takes to do it properly, I just think I've got to concentrate on the class this year.

Four postholders had responsibility for co-ordinating work across a year group. What this involved in the different schools, or indeed in different years within a school, varied, but the general responsibility could be a substantial one because of its 'pastoral' aspect. In one of the schools it included the responsibility of getting to know the children in the year group individually, maintaining general disciplinary levels, and organising the use of equipment, resources and facilities within the year group. In relatively small schools, of course, a year group co-ordinator will be one of only two teachers working with the year group, but in three-form entry schools and above the demands will be substantial.

In one of the smaller schools in the inquiry, a two-form entry school, the demands of year co-ordination were particularly pressing and had led to a slower pace of curriculum development than would otherwise have occurred, according to the headteacher. The postholder for art/craft in the school had been attempting to introduce a substantial component of craft, design and technology (CDT) into the classroom practice of teachers throughout the school. He had the advice and support of the recently appointed deputy head, who had developed CDT in his previous school, where the quality of the work had attracted some national and regional attention. There was therefore in the inquiry school both the interest and expertise to develop CDT, and appropriate policy documents had been created. But enabling the development to take root in the classroom practice of the teachers had been restricted by other demands, especially the need to provide support and consistency across the year groups, for one of which the postholder was co-ordinator. The head explained:

> It's been very difficult (to move faster). We've had staff cuts that reduced flexibility, so that the postholder can't work alongside the class teachers and that's the crucial thing. And then we've got three teachers on temporary contracts, so I've had to ensure that the experienced permanent staff take a major role in the year groups, to make sure that there's good general work, that the temporary teachers get to know the ropes, and that the normal work is consolidated. There's a limit to the amount of curriculum development you can do in the present situation – our rolls are stable, it's not from falling rolls, it is that we've lost staff and new staff aren't permanent. In this situation, innovation isn't necessarily the most important priority, and may not even be a good thing.

To demonstrate the other main claims upon the postholders' commitment is not in itself to demonstrate the perceived marginality of curriculum development for them, but it does suggest on the face of it that if postholders are satisfactorily to fulfil the range of regular and routine demands made upon them by the various school roles they occupy, curriculum development activities cannot make a predominant claim upon their time, or can only do so intermittently. It also suggests that if an unusual burst of energy is necessary to plan, launch and evaluate a new programme, the less dramatic but no less important commitment to *sustaining* the innovation may be what is adversely affected by the other legitimate role demands.

There was support for this interpretation from a follow-up discussion held with the head and postholder in [one particular development.] In the school concerned a new approach to science had been planned, implemented and evaluated, with the consequence that a number of areas where the development could be consolidated and improved had been highlighted. For example, the postholder saw the need to produce, index and store sample collections of pupils' work in science, and to give class teachers concrete illustrations of the kind and quality of work they should expect from pupils at given stages in the scheme. Class teachers had also asked for the production of more resource packs to support the development and some consideration of appropriate language work. Talking of these demands upon the postholder, the head commented:

> He needs time to think a bit more about it, to reflect about the stage it's reached. He needs a term free of his other jobs to consolidate what's been achieved. Perhaps some time at the university, and visiting some other schools; some time to work with the other teachers in the school and then some time to produce materials and resources. He can't do what is necessary without time – he works all the hours God gives him already, and he's also in charge of boys' games as well as his own class. He won't be able to do what needs doing now, or at least he won't be able to do it as well as he could do, if he has to do all his normal teaching and other things as well.

This kind of problem may be inevitable in primary schools, for the teacher's role is already extremely diverse even before the demands for school-based curriculum development are met. The postholder at Abbotsmead Junior School, Susan Timms, expressed the position neatly, in Donoughue et al (1981):

I would like to say a little more about another aspect of the time factor . . . like most schools we have Harvest, Christmas, drama and musical evenings, sports days, swimming galas, school reports and consultation evenings, to name a few. In school we have displays to feature children's written work, art and craft, Christmas parties, Halloween, Bonfire night, sports matches with other schools, clubs for chess, nature, drama, dance, gymnastics, a school choir and instrumental groups. While I fully appreciate the need for an up-to-date curriculum, no one would suggest that it be at the expense of the above activities. So, while in one sense curriculum progress seems to be slow, anyone contemplating in-school curriculum development must be aware and considerate of the competition which already exists for the time of the teacher.

The educationalist context

Keddie (1971) saw the educationalist context as an ideological arena in which teachers confronted value issues in a school through the discussion of educational ideas:

> The educationist context may be called into being by the presence of an outsider to whom explanations of the department's activities must be given, or by a forthcoming school meeting which necessitates discussion of policy of how things ought to be in a school. (p. 135)

The dominant feature of the context is a requirement for teachers to give an account of their educational policies and practices. In [my] inquiry this feature – a matter, quite literally, of accountability – encompassed a wider range of activities than appears to have been the case in Keddie's school. It included activities such as drafting aims and objectives for a new scheme of work and introducing its rationale to a staff group, justifying an approach to curriculum planning through defining the conceptual structure of a subject, organising, preparing and presenting material for a staff INSET programme, discussing curricular policies with local-authority advisers and/or secondary school staff meetings, displaying pupils' work as examples of the quality and standard to be expected by other staff, and teachers familiarising themselves and their colleagues with aspects of educational research and theory.

This kind of activity was relatively novel for most postholders; indeed the head-teachers of six of them saw the curriculum development programme as one way in which the postholders could gain experience of leading a group of staff for the first time. [One head,] for example, said:

> The need to provide opportunities for staff development is understood and considered important within the school and the invitation (to the postholder to develop a staff INSET programme) was seen as a chance for her to extend and develop her already strong interest in language work. It was also an opportunity for her to practise and develop a leadership role in influencing the thinking and practices of her colleagues.

The role was also a source of strain even where it was most clearly seen by the staff group as having been exercised effectively. It is possible to analyse this kind of strain by looking at both the contexts in which the teacher acted as

educationalist and the nature of the acts themselves. The contexts were all ones
in which the postholder was highly *visible* to her colleagues; the nature of the acts
themselves required the postholder to give *accounts* of curriculum policies and
practice; and it is under these two headings that role problems are described and
illustrated below.

Role visibility

One feature that particularly distinguishes the 'teacher as educationalist' role
from that of the 'teacher as teacher' is that the former tends to be carried out in
front of colleagues and other professionals, whereas the latter tends to be performed in front of pupils. As 'educationalist' the postholder is highly visible to
professional peers; as 'teacher' she or he is mostly invisible. There are some
qualifications to this distinction, for example where teaching is carried out as
part of a team or when postholders do some private reading and research to
update themselves in their subject. But in general it was true of the postholders in
[my] inquiry that a characteristic of their role as curriculum developers was its
high degree of 'visibility', that is, its tendency to be carried out at crucial times in
front of colleagues and other adults, or under their scrutiny.

In [one school,] it took the very limited form of giving staff involved examples
of how an option for pupils should be described, whereas in [another] it was a
more 'public' business of displaying work done by pupils in the postholder's
class for other colleagues to see. On the face of it, displaying work done by pupils
is a routine part of every teacher's activity; display is used in corridors, foyer and
classrooms both to illustrate the nature of the school work to visitors and to
transmit to pupils a sense of the value placed upon their work by the teachers.
However, samples of pupils' work carried out under the tuition of the postholder
had to serve a further, different function in five of the case studies. In them, the
quality of work done by pupils taught by the postholders was offered as *exemplary*,
as setting standards for other teachers and pupils to emulate. In short, it became
a requirement placed upon the postholders publicly to demonstrate professional
excellence in their curriculum area to their colleagues.

In one case, display took on almost a 'demonstration lesson' form. The postholder had been asked by a class teacher to help her with screen-printing techniques in her class. Although he had given some advice outside the classroom to
the teacher, she was still unsure about the practical work and skills involved. The
postholder's class was taken by the head for two sessions so that he could work
alongside both teachers in the year group and demonstrate the skills with their
own children. After this the teachers were able to develop the work in following
lessons and one in particular expressed greater confidence about her own skills.
The postholder used this example to illustrate the importance for 'non-
specialists' of having a specialist working with them on practical skills even if for
an apparently limited amount of time.

> The important thing is to see it in practice with your own pupils – there's no other way
> in which you can get the feel for what they are capable of – standards if you like. The
> most useful thing is if I can go in and teach their class, or some of their class, with them

and together we can actually see the skills involved, how to demonstrate them, how to help the children when they get into difficulties, and what to expect from them . . . of course it means it's got to work or there's no point to it. No amount of discussion outside the classroom is going to be a substitute if you can't show what you mean in practice.

Another aspect of visibility, and a more common one, was the practice of running discussion groups, or staff workshops, in which the postholder's organisational ability and specialised knowledge were simultaneously under the scrutiny of colleagues.

In the case study discussed more fully in an Open University course (1987) the significance of the post holder's handling of the staff working group was highlighted by the teachers involved who made the point that the sessions 'didn't just happen'. They had needed to be structured and led by someone who could provide overall direction. One of the staff involved said:

> There would be problems if the discussion sessions had just been started cold. They needed someone who is familiar with the material, and who knows the background to it . . . The last thing I'd want would be where we'd get to the stage where we'd say 'What shall we talk about this week?'

In the particular case, on the face of it, this role appeared effective and relatively trouble-free, to judge from the comments of the teachers involved. However, discussion sessions in other cases often brought into question the underlying values of the curriculum development project, with which the postholder was, of course, particularly associated. When this happened the postholders' knowledge and expertise were very much put to the test in that they had to provide justification for the project, and this is not an easy matter at the best of times.

Another kind of arena in which postholders were subjected to scrutiny was the kind of meeting in which they had to represent their subject to people other than their colleagues in school, usually teachers in other schools or local-authority advisers. In one of the case study schools the headteacher and the postholder had attended a liaison meeting with the 'academic board' of the nearby secondary school in order to give an account of the overall curriculum development plan. The official minutes of the meeting recorded the wide range of accounts that were required of the head and postholder in the meeting, but they did not bring out its daunting atmosphere. The head said afterwards of it:

> This was a formal and somewhat forbidding experience: while I could not say I detected open hostility (to the curriculum design overall) at least the meeting began in a cool and somewhat critical manner. As it progressed and people were able to voice their worries, the tension eased and Jane (the postholder) and I felt at the end that it had been a very worthwhile exercise.

The illustrations that have been presented above have been selected to show the varieties of *context* in which the postholders were subjected to peer-group scrutiny. But within those contexts, postholders had to provide accounts of the curricular policies they were promoting, and an examination of the nature of the accounts themselves suggests further sources of strain, for the accounts needed to address problems of educational theory and research, themselves far from unproblematic areas.

Giving accounts of the curriculum to professional peers
Teacher accountability has been discussed mainly in terms of teachers' accountability to non-professionals, to governors, parents and other members of the community. For example, Taylor (1977) raised the need for school staff to explain curricular policies in prospectuses and other documents for parents, and to give an account of curricular achievement to governing bodies. The kind of account that flows from such an obligation is a carefully prepared document, privately scrutinised in advance, with a perceived audience of non-professionals. Documents produced for this purpose tend to be, quite properly, essentially *descriptive* accounts. The kind of accounts that postholders provided for their colleagues and other adults were both more complex and qualitatively different. Accounts were commonly oral and unscripted, because they were given in response to questions that were not known in advance, and were directed at a professional audience, sometimes including people perceived to be 'experts', such as local-authority advisers. In addition, even where there were prepared curriculum documents, they were not merely descriptive accounts but were normally *justificatory* ones: they did not simply explain a policy or programme, but attempted to justify it by reference to educational values and principles of one kind or another.

An illustration of the nature of a justificatory account in written form is the following statement from a curriculum policy document [. . .] where the aims and scheme of work in part of the school's environment studies were elaborated.

HISTORY

Why teach History?
It enables one to see one's own life as part of a steadily unfolding narrative. It provides a sense of perspective. It provides examples for comparison. It arouses sympathy and understanding of people of other times and other countries. It allows one the opportunity to draw conclusions from available evidence.

What can we teach between 8–12?
In a sense there is no limit but as only the most able children wil have developed an appreciation of historical time by the age of 12, then we should try to give them a general understanding of (a) the recent past 19th century and onwards, (b) the Middle Ages and (c) the ancient and classical worlds from which our civilisation has sprung.

How can we teach History at this age?
Our aim should be two-fold: (a) to give an opportunity for the children to study an earlier Society in some detail and (b) to give them the opportunity to discover for themselves and to learn to sift and weigh evidence.

Some history teaching must be didactic. The teacher tells a story and there is no better method for introducing say the Greek Myths: provided that there is opportunity for discussion, interpretation and possibly dramatisation, then this is a good approach at all ages.

Some teaching will depend upon television and radio programmes. Again it is the quality of the discussion that determines the success with which the material is used. It is not sufficient to regurgitate the facts. The children should be provoked to ask 'Why?' and to keep on asking until they have reached a satisfactory conclusion.

Other topics may depend upon a combination of methods involving a wide use of reference books and audio visual material. Again it is not sufficient to simply repeat the information from the book. Children should use a reference book to find the answer to a particular question. If it is a question that they have raised themselves, then so much the better. The teacher's role is to guide the child to the relevant material and this can be done only if the teacher has a wide knowledge of the sources of the information available. We have a wide selection of charts, slides, transparencies and pictures that can be used by children and teachers. Close observation can often reveal a wealth of information.

There is no better method of developing a sense of history than examining the artefacts that previous generations have left behind. Houses, clothes, weapons, utensils, jewellery, paintings, journals, letters – the list is endless. Some can be brought into school while others necessitate visits but always the emphasis should be on questioning to attempt to fathom the place of this particular article in the historical pattern.

Look with caution on textbooks.

They tend to over-simplify and to repeat hoary myths, long disproved by scholarship. Teach children to be sceptical. In many cases we really do not know exactly what happened, let alone why someone acted as he did.

Characters in history were not necessarily more logical in their actions than we are ourselves. Given the benefit of hindsight, we can develop reasons that the participants may never have considered let alone acted upon. I recall a boy in my class looking at a picture of David Livingstone's wife and advancing his own original theory as to why Livingstone travelled so far into the wilderness. He may have been right at that!

Teach children to challenge evidence. 'How do we know that?' should be a constant question and one that can rarely be answered by saying 'Because it's in the book!'

Use drama and role play. It may not reveal the truth but it can help children to appreciate that Duke William did not know the outcome of invading England or indeed whether Normandy might not have been attacked during his absence.

What topics shall we teach?
Broadly speaking, I should like to feel that by the time a child leaves this school, he or she will have some knowledge of the following:

1 Pre-history.
2 The Ancient World. Egypt, Greece, Rome.
3 The Vikings and Normans.
4 Medieval society.
5 The Tudor Age.
6 The industrial and agricultural changes of the period 1750–1830.
7 The Victorians.
8 Britain in the 20th century.

In addition, I should like to see an understanding, at least, of the development of technology and some idea of Man's understanding of the Universe.

It is instructive to put aside one's own ideas about history in the curriculum, and about whether or not one agrees with the views being advanced in the policy (as well as one's reaction to sexist humour) and to reflect upon the nature of the account itself, which is presented, as most such accounts must be, relatively briefly, and in jargon-free language. The aims in the first paragraph include both cognitive and affective dimensions; there is in the second paragraph recognition of the psychological constraints of concept development in young children; and in terms of pedagogical styles, paragraphs 3 to 12 advocate the adoption of variety rather than uniformity. The Brunerian idea, that problem-solving will aid discovery learning, is also adumbrated in these paragraphs, as is the notion that children's learning should be disciplined by evidence, preferably of a first-hand kind.

Oral accounts, called for in staff discussions, have the same justificatory style, but tend to be more wide-ranging. For example, [in one school,] a staff meeting was called to evaluate the first year's operation of a new science scheme, and the postholder's role in it. The meeting was good-humoured and positively constructive, but there were a number of occasions when some fundamental issues were raised which the postholder was required to confront. These included: the apparent curricular priority given to science at the expense of other subjects (geography, for example); the extent to which an agreed content area as a set of concepts was necessary, if the aim was to develop scientific methods of observation, recording, hypothesising etc.; the extent to which subject teaching of science in the fourth year was hindering integration with topic work, for example; and the issue of transmitting a gender-differentiated image of science.

The issues were not raised in the formal terms that have been used to summarise them above and did not lead in the particular case to the postholder's being personally or professionally threatened. But because they were genuinely felt problems, and because they were expressed as value issues, the postholder was being required publicly to confront them with, for example, his own account of the advantages of the use of subject teaching. (As a matter of fact it was the head at this stage who drew attention to some of the arguments for specialist teaching.) The point that needs to be stressed is that despite the context – an atmosphere entirely devoid of personal antipathy – the postholder was being required to give an account of, a justification for, educational practices, if the programme were to continue its development. And the account was subjected to, and arose from, professional scrutiny that was as probing as it was public. Perhaps this kind of role context is part of Goodacre's (1984) reason for suggesting that postholders need 'assertiveness training'.

Thus, as curriculum developers, postholders were brought up against the need to enter into forms of educational discourse and rapidly acquire fluency in its use. Perhaps the most difficult area was a directly practical one: the need to specify, organise and explain the major conceptual and skill structures of a subject. To do this at all requires considerable time and knowledge: to do it and feel that it has been done with authority is a formidable undertaking. It is not being suggested for a moment that postholders were required, or should have been required, to undertake a substantial formal 'course' in educational theory before engaging in school-based curriculum development, but once they had engaged in it, they were confronted with the need to adopt ideas and forms of discourse with which, initially at any rate, they were unfamiliar and insecure. Such insecurity was only intensified if familiarity had to be acquired in haste and alongside more routine but exacting demands of everyday teaching.

In part uncertainty in the role derives from the nature of the activity itself. The school curriculum is essentially problematic, and its developers had to live with and tolerate ambiguity for the most part. But the degree of uncertainty was reduced by two postholders, who had been able to gain access to highly special-ised advice. In [one case] this had happened by the postholder following a post-experience course before the development activity was planned, and in [the other] the postholder gained access to an authoritative source, a local lecturer who happened to have specialised in the field concerned. Most postholders, however, had to operate in contexts in which such sources were either not avail-able or not available when needed.

Tolerance of ambiguity: the postholder's virtue

[It has been argued elsewhere (Campbell, 1985)] that national policies encour-aging postholders to establish a role for themselves as curriculum developers in their schools have underestimated the complexity of the task. This chapter has attempted to illustrate a further point, that conflict and ambiguity in the role have also been underestimated. Some sources of this conflict have been illus-trated in order to show how pervasive a feature of school-based curriculum development it was in the inquiry schools.

There is evidence that some aspects of this kind of conflict and ambiguity in the schools in this study are not unique to them. Other studies of the teacher's role in primary schools by Coulson (1978) and by Leese (1978), as well as the analyses already referred to by Lortie (1969) and by Taylor, Reid, Holley and Exon (1974), have exposed the structural problem of the autonomy of the teacher in relation to school-wide policies. Similar sources of ambiguity were reported by Ginsburg and his colleagues (1977), who noted the relative influence of the head, deputy and year heads, as against that of the 'subject adviser', in middle schools, and commented that innovatory schools provided for teachers 'considerable ambiguity and confusion as to the most appropriate way to per-form their role'. The wide spread of responsibilities also exists in other schools, as studies by Bornett (1980), Ginsburg et al (1977) and Blyth and Derricott (1977) have shown about middle school teachers and Rodger et al (1983) have shown amongst postholders in primary schools.

Thus, in an indirect way, the analysis of the postholder's role offered [here] is congruent with other studies, even though direct empirical examination of the role of postholders in curriculum development has been made only rarely. Where it has, as in Donoughue et al (1981) and Goodacre and Donoughue (1983), the picture of conflict and uncertainty is supported. It follows that the ambiguities and uncertainties identified are not exclusive to the schools studied, but are probably typical of general teaching roles in primary and middle schools. Indeed, it is highly likely that school-based curriculum development simply focuses in a specific and palpable way conflicts and dilemmas inherent in contemporary teaching generally. The conflicts are, so to speak, particularly sharp symptoms of a general condition.

It would be wrong, however, to leave an impression of curriculum postholders as permanently and unmitigatedly angst-ridden individuals, poised ambivalently between the contradictory demands of curriculum renewal, class teaching and collegial goodwill. Although such conflict has been identified in the postholder's role, the term 'conflict' is itself a term to which sociologists have perhaps too ready recourse. There was potential conflict in school-based curriculum development, and postholders bore the brunt of the ambiguity, dilemma and uncertainty. The ambiguities were not personal or professional defects: they arose from the ambiguity of the curriculum development enterprise itself, and from the uncertain role relationships built into the schools, shored up by both the conventional wisdom and the intellectual isolation of the primary school staffrooms. This is not the same thing, however, as saying that postholders were unable to promote curriculum development because of the role conflict, or that where it was promoted it had little impact. It is to say that the task of school-based development was difficult, stressful, and had little in the way of tangible or immediate measures of success, other than the intrinsic sense of achievement. Despite the difficulties, the case studies revealed the postholders making active attempts, in less than ideal contexts, to renew the curriculum in the schools, mostly in a participatory style. All these attempts were perceived as effective by the headteachers, the postholders and the participant teachers, although in varying degrees. Apparently it was possible for the postholders simultaneously to promote such curriculum renewal and to tolerate the ambiguity and conflict that it brought to the surface.

References

BLYTH, W. A. L. and DERRICOTT, R. (1977). *The Social Significance of Middle Schools*, London, Batsford.

BORNETT, C.(1980). 'Staffing and middle schools', in HARGREAVES. A. and TICKLE, L. (eds), *Middle Schools: Origins, Ideology and Practice*, London, Harper and Row.

CAMPBELL, R. J. (1985). *Developing the Primary School Curriculum*, Ch. 3, London, Holt Rinehart & Winston.

COULSON, A. A. (1978). 'The politics of curriculum reform', in RICHARDS, C. (ed), *Power and the Curriculum*, Driffield, Nafferton Books.

DES (1978). *Primary Education in England*, London, HMSO.

DONOUGHUE, C. *et al* (eds) (1981). *In service: the Teacher and the School*. London, Kogan Page/The Open University.

EVANS, P. and GROARKE, M. (1975). 'An exercise in managing curriculum development in a primary school', in TAYLOR, P.H. (ed.), *Aims, Influence and Change in the Primary School Curriculum*, Windsor, NFER.

GINSBURG, M. B. *et al* (1977). *The Role of the Middle School Teacher*, Aston Educational Monograph 7, Department of Educational Enquiry, Aston University.

GOODACRE, E. (1984). 'Language postholders and assertiveness', *Education 3–13*, 12(1), pp. 17–21.

GOODACRE, E. and DONOUGHUE, C. (1983). *LEA Support for the Language Post-holders in the Primary School*, School of Education, Middlesex Polytechnic.

HARGREAVES, A. (1980). 'Teachers, hegemony and the educationist context', paper presented to 4th Annual Sociology of Education Conference, Westhill College, Birmingham.

KEDDIE, N. (1971). 'Classroom knowledge', in Young, M. (ed.), *Knowledge and Control: New Directions for the Sociology of Education*, London, Collier Macmillan.

LEESE, J. (1978). 'Politics and power in curriculum reform', in RICHARDS, C. (ed.), *Power and the Curriculum*, Driffield, Nafferton Books.

LORTIE, D. (1969). 'The balance of control and autonomy in elementary school teaching', in Etzioni, A. (ed.), *The Semi professions and their organization*, New York, Free Press.

OPEN UNIVERSITY (1987). E325 *Management and the School*, Block 3, Managing Curricular and Pastoral Processes, Part 2 Primary school case study: Cashmore School, Milton Keynes, The Open University.

RODGER, I. *et al* (1983). *Teachers with Posts of Responsibility in Primary Schools*, University of Durham, School of Education.

SKILBECK, M. (1972). 'School-based curriculum development', mimeo, University of Coleraine, quoted in Eggleston, J. (ed.), *School-based Curriculum Development in Britain*, London, Routledge and Kegan Paul.

TAYLOR, P. *et al* (1974). *Purpose, Power and Constraint in the Primary School Curriculum*, London, Macmillan.

TAYLOR Report (1977) *A New Partnership for Our Schools*, London, HMSO.

4.5

Pastoral needs in schools

Michael Marland

Introduction

[Some] years ago I declared that 'the pastoral need' is 'the central task of the school' (Marland 1974, p. 12). Clearly most of the rest of the educational community have not thought so – at least if published and public manifestations are any indication. Pastoral care remains a desperately under-considered aspect of education, whether one is thinking of colleges and departments of education, the DES, the HMI, in-service courses, writers and educational journalism, or the research community. All are caught in a vicious spiral – so little is known that less is taught; few questions are thus formulated, and fewer researched.

True, some sharp researchers have thrown spotlights on a number of key questions. However, most of those have been concerned with the unusual pupil – the truant, the delinquent, the maladjusted, or deprived pupil. The central task of the school to give 'personal, educational and vocational guidance' to *all* has been put to one side by most of those who support schools by intellectual, procedural, philosophical, or research work.

In this paper, I consider the current state of research into pastoral care issues; the difficulties faced by teachers in making use of the research studies that do exist; and the potential value of research to the work of teachers in school. The paper looks in detail at four areas where we lack basic knowledge and research evidence which could help schools to improve the quality of their pastoral care provision: the needs of the child (as daughter or son, as pupil, as student and as information-user); the structures of pastoral care systems; the needs of the tutor; and key aspects of the pastoral curriculum. [. . .]

Research, pastoral care and the school

'Research' is often belittled by teachers, but little read. Even the most famous research is normally mediated by the press – often not even the specialist press.

Neville Bennett and his colleagues at the University of Lancaster have checked this gap between opinions on research and the reading of it in a study of the impact of *Teaching Styles and Pupil Progress* (Bennett 1976). His research showed that of those teachers claiming knowledge of and expressing opinions on the work, the majority were basing their views on television references or the newspaper.

In many years of participating in discussion towards in-school decision-making I have come to distrust phrases such as 'Research shows . . .' or even worse 'Everyone knows research shows . . .' as being rhetoric to support prejudice with only rarely an actual reference to a research study. Similarly, in papers prepared for staff debate or as preparation for major decisions, it is very rare to find any use of the relevant research studies. I fear one must add that those with specific responsibility for pastoral care leadership appear to be amongst the least well-read professionally. Their colleague heads of departments are far more likely to have studied the relevant research literature.

Yet the UK has the most autonomous educational decision-making pattern in the world. Power is disseminated eccentrically and unpredictably from the Secretary of State to the class tutor or teacher. The node of power is in the teacher team (e.g. junior school staff, secondary school pastoral team or department), and most decision-making takes place there. If these local decisions are to be well made, the teachers must be able to draw on (and ideally commission) the research that will illuminate the matters on which they will be making decisions.

All aspects of the pastoral care of schools, primary and secondary especially, need research attention. In the teaching of reading, science, mathematics, language, and many aspects of the academic curriculum, research enquiries and even sometimes answers are available for schools to use for their consideration of in-school planning. In the pastoral aspects of schools far too much is hunch at its best, and habit more often. There has been some important work, but it is rare. [. . .].

Part of the task, of course, is making more accessible the research that has been done. For those of us working from 8.30 to 5.30 inside a school without a moment to sit and read, the available research suffers from a number of problems:

1 Most of it is into aspects which relate to our pastoral care work, but is from the specialised point of view of a particular discipline and needs re-focusing for in-school use.
2 The primary reporting is in a wide variety of journals; most schools cannot afford or do not organise access to this material.
3 A researcher often quite properly includes in a report a literature review, a description of method, and a great deal of supporting data. Not all of this is necessary for school use.

Just as 'pastoral care' is a synthesising concept, some synthesising of the relevant research is also required.

Some part of the research needed should be school-initiated and based.

Although the difficulties of such work are great, many aspects of pastoral care research would lend themselves to such modes of research. The contributors to Jon Nixon's *Teachers' Guide to Action Research* (Nixon *et al* 1981) have shown that the teacher-researcher has especial strengths drawn from the insider's perspective. My ambition is to see a family of schools or a large school on its own, supported by LEA advisers and local university staff, methodically analysing their needs and relating these to the research community. This would improve the quality of decision-making, help the career development of the teacher – and produce a more helpful feedback and stimulus to researchers. (I have described one modest contribution to this, which is a school·'journal club', in *Preparing for Promotion in Pastoral Care* (Marland 1982).)

The busy day of a tutor, junior school class teacher, secondary head of house/ year, or deputy head leaves the teacher reeling from the buffets of the incidents. As teachers, we bring to each encounter and each decision an implicit 'theory', but rarely have we made ourselves conscious of the theories underlying our multifarious decisions and actions, and still more rarely are our theories and approaches supported by research findings. It is up to the pastoral care community, especially at this moment in its growing professionalism, to articulate some of its questions for the consideration of researchers.

The child

The child as daughter or son

The relationship between school influences and home ones has not to my knowledge been as carefully explored as one would think. The indicators of 'home' are usually the surely too crude ones of socio-economic class. Researchers considering school outcomes, whether overall such as Rutter or more specific such as Galloway, make statements about the similarity of areas that do not fully ring true. They often talk of schools 'drawing from the same area'. However, as I walk to school in the morning I can see groups of secondary school children separating out, with some schools apparently attracting a noticeably more 'respectable' type of child. When schools in urban areas are fairly close together, the parental selection/rejection of certain schools produces an 'amplifying' effect – that is, once the proportion of difficult pupils reaches a certain threshold, certain parents fight against sending their children there and then the proportion becomes further exaggerated. When this happens, the peer-group pull changes the school and its effect on all pupils. [. . .]

The child as pupil: 'Taking up the pupil side'

[. . .] The power of the deceptively ordinary and simple phrase, 'the child as pupil', is that it helps us all to see that the child in school has a task, and that this task, like every other task in life needs learning – and thus teaching. Paradoxically, how to be a pupil is the hardest thing a child has to learn in school. (If she or he has learnt that, the school is a storehouse of riches.) Bitterly, it is amongst the rarest things teachers set about teaching. How much easier for the tutor to admonish or console the failed pupil than to prepare a course to avoid such failure!

One of the central pastoral tasks is to help pupils learn to be pupils. The whole school in all its aspects will have to be marshalled to help and the pastoral curriculum (Marland 1981) will be the articulation. Within that, there is little doubt that the pastoral programme will need to carry the major burden. The essence of 'being a pupil', or, rather, being able to 'fill the role of pupil', is undoubtedly, an attitudinal matter. To 'be a pupil' is to have expectations about what schools can offer, and optimism that one can draw on those offers. It is to believe that if the role is well played there will be gains for the role bearer. However, if a pastoral curriculum is to be planned to enable the child to fill the role and gain what is to be gained, some attempt to break down the broad role of pupil is necessary. Only then can the school help the pupil build up the model.

The pupil as student

Much of the school day takes place in classrooms and is ostensibly devoted to 'school work', and even the vaguest pupil has some idea that 'you go to school to learn'. Yet as one researcher put it: 'We have no direct studies of what this phenomenon "work" means to teachers and pupils' (Woods 1978). Certainly my impression is that the tutor, whose task of 'educational guidance' involves at the very least helping pupils cope with their work, has very few specific ideas of the most hopeful ways of inducting pupils into secondary school studies. Indeed in the masses of educational research in the last quarter of a century, so much of which has considered the pupil as a member of a social 'class' rather than a school 'class', there is little research I know that considers what ways pupils may be helped to come to grips with their schoolwork demands. The studies of the *difficulties* of subject matter and texts, for instance, have been deeply illuminating and influential to those who have studied them, e.g. the SSRC-funded 'Concepts in Secondary Mathematics and Science Programme' at Chelsea College from 1974 (Shayer and Adey 1981). The tutor needs to look at the process from the other direction, and across the subjects. She or he needs to know, more than instinct and the rushed feed-back of the tutor room will offer, what the obstacles are and what form of group and individual pastoral work will help convert the pupil into a student.

Peter Woods appears convinced that ' "Work" has undergone a metamorphosis, scarcely any longer involving the totality of the person. It is by and large a nagging necessity, to which people have adapted over the years, developing new meanings which are filtered through to their children direct from their first-hand objective experience of work and participation in work cultures, which help perpetuate "the cycle of inequality". No amount of teacher advice and persuasion can scratch the surface of this massive influence.' (Woods 1978, p. 325). This is not quite how it feels to me in school, but that last sentence rings true: some students come to school already able to understand schoolwork (and this is *not* simply an artefact of socio-economic class), but for those who do not, our pastoral care is vague and unfocussed.

It is generally agreed that induction into the school is an important pastoral task (e.g. Hamblin 1978, and Marland 1980b). Yet how well do we do it? How much do we know what is done? How much research has been carried out into possible ways? Some researchers have considered the start to secondary school, and the work I have seen is interesting: John Beck, in his unpublished PhD thesis, has found little of the trauma expected (Beck 1972), nor has a more recent study in the Camden/Westminster division of the ILEA (Division Two, 1984). However, this looks at the pupil and does not consider ways of effective induction.

'Induction', though, is not required simply 'to the school', but throughout schooling to new courses, aspects, stages. Narrowly-focussed but significant action research has been carried out by Jean Ruddock and her colleagues at the Centre for Applied Research in Education, at the University of East Anglia. The starting point was the observation that innovating programmes in schools are often inhibited by the ways in which 'the pupil group may act conservatively with regard to attempted change, or may misconstrue the aim of new approaches and so behave in ways which are conservative in their effect' (Hull *et al* 1981, p. 1). The team accordingly set up action research to test in practice the hypotheses:

1 That pupils' understanding of the form of an innovation would be increased if they were given access to concrete representations of it in practice (i.e. through video-tape recordings).
2 That such access would foster the development of a mutual commitment to the work sufficiently strong to counter the pull of existing conventions. (*ibid*, p. 4)

For the range of pastoral 'educational guidance' responsibilities their choice of examples (which was made for other purposes) was limited as they had to be innovations: (a) new sixth forms in schools, (b) a new history project in a high school, and (c) a new humanities course using discussion-based learning in a middle school. However, the action research to some extent at least demons-trated their claim that:

> It seems that even children of middle-school age can develop an articulate critical awareness of classroom procedures which facilitates the explicit and collaborative management of learning in the classroom. . . . Pupils' achievement may be enhanced by their capacity to distinguish, understand, and be critical of the particular form of learning they are engaged in. Pupils' command of the structure and convention of the learning process is a topic we consider rich in research potential.
>
> (*ibid*, p. 129)

Here we are moving powerfully from the specific induction of a new subject or a new teaching style, to that pastoral task of educational guidance which is well-phrased in the title of another paper from the project: *Pupils' Grasp of Classroom Process* (Ruddock 1981).

A related aspect which has similarly been under-considered is the tutor's educational guidance task in relation to homework. In a review of the research Frank Coulter comments accurately: 'What teachers actually say or do to prepare their students for home study remains something of a mystery.' (Coulter 1979, p. 27). However, both he and the Mortimores in a thorough but brief survey (Mortimores 1981) consider the issue almost entirely from the point of view of the subject teacher – that is the setting of assignments, the briefer and the responder, and not at all from the pastoral viewpoint.

The student as 'information-user'

One aspect of the 'child as pupil' deserves special emphasis. We know from research into library-user education (Irving and Snape 1979), that there is very little effective groundwork done in what used to be called 'library use'. More recently, however, the concept has been deepened, and the student seen as someone who has processing information as one of her or his central activities – an activity which also has a key place in the adult working world. Ann Irving has reviewed [. . .] research carried out [. . .] in aspects of either 'library-user education' or 'study skills' in a study with a deeply significant title, *Educating Information Users* (Irving 1983). Her title has established a key phrase. [. . .]

Douglas Hamblin has stressed 'how pastoral care can help make the processes through which pupils learn become part of a continuous dialogue between teacher and taught' (Hamblin 1981, p. 1), and he, properly in my view, brings the question of study skills into the focus of pastoral care. However, his view of study skills is not as wide or as related to information handling as it perhaps could be. A group of specialists, under the auspices of the Schools Council and the British Library, met in 1980 to try to pin down the essential skills, and to relate them to the pastoral curriculum in general, and the tutorial programme in particular (Marland 1981). However, even armed with Hamblin's *Teaching Study Skills*, the Schools Council/British Library's *Information Skills in the Secondary Curriculum*, Ann Irving's *Study and Information Skills across the Curriculum* (Irving 1985), and possibly the best students' text *Effective Learning Skills* (Healy and Goodhand 1983), the tutor or the pastoral team leader still seems to me to have been left uncertain about how best to divide the task of educating information users between contextual subject teaching and the tutorial programme. Research has hardly touched this central question.

Motivation

A key aspect of the pupil role is making use of the feedback from teachers. Thus a central part of the pastoral role of 'educational guidance' is helping pupils make the best of themselves by *using* the responses of teachers. I do not know much about the content of initial training psychology courses, but I doubt if they move very close to the tutor or primary classteacher's needs to understand motivation.

The typical tutor engages, I suspect, in a large amount of exhortation ('try harder') and encouragement ('you really can do it'). All of this is very unsystematic. I have found no UK equivalent of the fascinating US studies into achievement and motivation. Apart from its importance for the issues of equal opportunities, which I discuss later, the work of the American psychologist Carol Dweck, now Professor of Human Development at Harvard, seems to me to be of startling importance to our pastoral work in schools. Essentially she has shown that 'deterioration in quality of intellectual problem-solving performance is generally independent of proficiency at the task' (Dweck 1977, p. 44), and has developed in a series of papers the concept of 'learned helplessness' (e.g. Dweck 1977, Dweck and Bush 1976, Dweck, Davidson, Nelson and Enna 1978, Dweck and Goetz 1978, Dweck and Elliott 1983).

Years ago I remember it being said that 'a good form master is worth another couple of ''O'' levels a boy' (that was a boys' grammar school!), and we should all agree that part of the tutor's pastoral task is to help the pupil succeed to the best of her or his ability. We should also, I hope, agree that this helping is not solely for the sake of the successes thus gained within schooling, nor even entirely for the value in later life of the examination tickets thus achieved, but that the very process of learning how to succeed is one of the big lessons for all future life. It is this central pastoral task that has had, as far as I know, no research attention in this country, and we just do not know how to set about it.

Carol Dweck's studies point the way. She reports: 'Our research shows that the variable that consistently predicts response to failure is the child's interpretation of failure – what he thinks caused it and whether he views it as surmountable.' (Dweck 1977, p. 4) More recently, her research has focussed on the relationship between childrens' motivation and their theories of intelligence. From field research she has shown that children tend to polarise into those who have what she calls an 'incremental' theory of intelligence, and those who have an 'entity' theory. The former see tasks as manageable and failure as a useful lesson; the latter fear failure. A few sentences cannot do justice to what I find of immense power in pastoral care: a research-based theory of motivation that can be used for the pastoral curriculum (we should teach about learning), and for group and individual counselling (for she shows attitudes can be changed).

What we need to find out is whether this research is valid in this country and whether there are ways in which attribution research, understanding of motivation, and the theory of 'learned helplessness' can be researched to find pastoral procedures.

The structure of pastoral care systems

Best has criticised, to some extent, the concern of writers like myself with the 'structure' of pastoral care in schools (e.g. Best *et al* 1980), but he and his colleagues could have pointed to a flaw in the data we have used for our concern: we have been obliged to use anecdote and personal observation as remarkably little is known about the details of pastoral care structures. The DES surveys of teachers omit 'form period' and 'tutor period', and DES statistics are thus weak from the start (*cf* Secondary Schools Staffing Survey 1984). Amongst the plethora of facts displayed about secondary teachers, we just do not know about tutorial times. It is highly significant that the phrase 'contact ratio' is used as 'a measure of the assigned average load per teacher,' and the glossary defines this as 'teaching contact with pupils as distinct from administration, preparation, marking, etc.' (HMI 1979, p. 272). This does *not* include tutorial time!

Similarly, many national surveys have been concerned about training and qualifications, e.g. English teachers ('and so it would appear a third of those teaching English have no discernible qualification', Committee of Enquiry 1975) and Mathematics (the Cockcroft report). *Aspects of Secondary Education* analyses the qualifications of heads of departments (HMI 1979, p. 48) and their teaching experience (*ibid*, p. 49). Similarly, careful analyses were done of the staffing of Remedial, Religious Education, English, and French (*ibid*, pp. 41–56) and inadequacies commented on – but there is no consideration of the qualifications of pastoral care team leaders.

We know nothing of the basic statistics of allowance points to case loads, despite the huge national investment in pastoral care leadership. The range of Burnham points invested by LEAs, through schools, in formal pastoral care is amazing. The NAPCE survey (Maher and Best 1984, p. 1a) of a sample of eighteen secondary schools shows the staff invested into pastoral care leadership. If, for the sake of simplicity, deputy heads are omitted from the calculation, and the scale posts computed as the points used, it is possible to calculate the number of pupils per scale point. This I suggest is a rough-and-ready computation of the investment in pastoral care. The mean is 62, with a range from 32 to 131! Ten of the eighteen fall beneath the mid-point of 81. Some of the sample are schools with more than one site, and one might have expected a greater investment in these schools. The schools with more than one site include the highest investments.

Sites	Scores
2	63
2	32
3	55

Even that though does not explain the range. The remaining fifteen single-site schools range from 38 pupils per point to 131!

Very little research consideration has been given to the structure and responsibilities for pastoral care within the school. I and others have outlined our ideals, but they have not been put to the test of comparative research. Reynolds and Murgatroyd in the South Wales absentee study (1977) have interesting comments on the tutor/middle management responsibility, and David Galloway, one of the rare research writers on pastoral care, discusses his and others' evidence on managing disruptive pupils in the light of responsibilities. He comments that although studies have emphasised the variables within the school, 'none, though, has focussed in much detail on the schools' pastoral care systems' (Galloway 1983, p. 245). He goes on: 'Research on the relationship between pupils' behaviour and the organisation and practice of pastoral care is conspicuously lacking' (*ibid*, p. 246). His observations are very much from the point of view of the disruptive pupil, but I suspect it would be true of all pupils, (Galloway *et al* 1982).

In the meantime, getting the team leader/tutor balance of responsibilities right in schools is hampered by this lack of research. *How* does the team leader lead an untrained group (HMI 1982, p. 33: 56% of probationers considered that they were not well prepared to undertake pastoral duties), who have little support (Maher and Best 1984), and for whom the main call on their time and loyalties, and therefore most career prospects, are elsewhere?

The tutor

Many writers in recent years have stressed the role of the tutor, perhaps first outlined in the chapter 'Roles and Responsibilities' of my own *Pastoral Care* (Marland 1974, pp. 74–80), and more fully developed by Douglas Hamblin (1978), Keith Blackburn (1975 and 1983), and Leslie Button (1981). I declared that:

> The role which is most often taken as read is that of the teacher in charge of the pastoral base-unit. The first-level pastoral figure is arguably the most important person in the school: the definition of his or her task is one of the school's most important planning tasks. (Marland 1974, p. 74).

Best and his colleagues in their SSRC-funded case study research (Best *et al* 1983) and Peter Lang in his Warwick-based research (Lang 1983 and 1984) have shown that what is intended in those 'how to do it' accounts simply does not always happen. Indeed many pupils just did not realise what tutors were intended to be for (Lang 1983), and he comments:

> Individuals other than teachers, particularly parents, relatives, and peers were much more frequently mentioned than teachers, and teachers with specific pastoral roles were mentioned infrequently. (1984, p. 7)

We need to discover the various elements of this partial failure: to what extent is it the result of, for instance:

1 Lack of professional training of tutors?
2 Lack of a school's definition of the role and briefing?
3 Lack of leadership for tutors?
4 Lack of induction and education of *pupils* into how to use the school?
5 Lack of opportunity in terms of time and suitable setting in the school?

The fact is that we know very little about how tutors work at all!

[. . .] the oft-quoted concern for social and personal development seems a sham: we simply do not know how often tutors talk to their tutees, for how long, or in what circumstances. We do not know what happens in tutor periods – indeed the ordinary observations of advisers, inspectors, team leaders, visitors, and senior staff seem much less frequent in tutor periods than subject lessons.

Even the important NFER study of *The Teacher's Day* (Hilsum 1971) does not appear to distinguish group pastoral time from other teaching. Indeed pastoral work is, typically, regarded as 'work with individual pupils' (*ibid*, p. 140). However, a detail in this study hints at what could be revealing, e.g. a mean time of 21.6 minutes per day (4.3% of working day) was computed to be devoted to 'pastoral tasks (*ibid*, p. 91); included in their definition of 'pastoral' were: 'individual pupil, special occasions, extra-curricular activity' (*ibid*, p. 28). The 1978 follow-up specialising on secondary teachers (Hilsum and Strong 1978) is more precise, and has found a category 'Registration' – a phrase I hate as 'taking the register' indicates such a limited view of the tutorial role. This study looked at a sample of 201 teachers. It found that of the 35 minutes devoted to registration and assembly those teachers who carried out both duties spent 0.8 minutes mean time on 'pastoral' (2.2%) and 4.9 minutes (14.0%) on 'teaching' (*ibid*, p. 17). Those taking only registration had higher figures of 1.2 minutes (3.4%) and 7.9 minutes (23%). A closer look was taken at 38 teachers' 'registration' time. The researchers found that about five minutes was spent 'on clerical registration work', and they comment with surprising apparent ignorance of pastoral ambitions: 'As may be seen from the actual durations taken by registration procedures compared with the time set aside for this purpose, the allocated time was in general more than sufficient' (*ibid*, p. 173)!

A proper consideration of pastoral care is bound to involve enquiring how much time is currently available and how that time is spent. If the mis-match between 'the rhetoric of pastoral care' (Best's depressing but illuminating phrase, Best 1980) and the reality is to be removed, we need to know what is happening.

As well as the quantitative aspects outlined so far, we need to know about the apparently intangible questions of personal interaction. What has been researched and written on this agenda appears to be subject-lesson based (e.g. Hargreaves 1972, chapter 6). In most cases, the guidance we offer is to be given by tutor to tutee regardless of the personalities or feelings of the two. A few schools complement this by a more personality-based 'personal tutoring' system. For instance, at North Westminster Community School all potential HE students are given a 'personal tutor' halfway through their lower-sixth year, to complement the work of the 'group tutor'. This tutor is chosen by the person organising the scheme in an endeavour to match interests and to some extent personalities. The experience is that very happy personal relationships develop in these cases.

A colleague at North Westminister, Oliver Sterno, has suggested that we need to know more about the inter-relationships between tutor and tutee, and he argues for a research project on this:

1 The inter-relationship between tutor and tutee is fundamental to the tutorial system working effectively. What are the factors which affect this inter-relationship? This is a crucial consideration and yet it is either assumed that this concept is of little consequence, or it is set up fairly easily through institutionalisation.

2 This research thesis aims to analyse this inter-relationship of tutor/tutees:

   (a) do tutees use their tutors as 'confidants' in similar ways regardless of individual differences between them? These differences could include gender, ethnic background, age, subject specialism and interests, social class, banding?

   (b) if there are anomalies, who do tutees go to as 'confidants' instead and for what kinds of matters?

   (c) are these anomalies due to family influences, e.g. is there only one parent present?

   (d) is the primary school experience influential?

   (e) do tutors perceive differences in their role which affects these inter-relationships?

3 The emergent issue here is one of trying to improve the effectiveness of pastoral care. This may be through attempting to reduce negative anomalies. Or it might be through devising a more specialist form of tutoring. The former might require more in-service education courses for tutors; the latter might require that tutors develop specialisms and tutees would confide in particular tutors for specific reasons: in other words, the view that the tutor can have a holistic caring approach for their tutees could be misplaced.

Very little work that I can find relates to how the pastoral aspect of a teacher's role is seen in terms of maladjusted behaviour. We have a tendency to explain anti-social behaviour within a school by such broad categories as 'poor home background', 'unsuitable curriculum', or 'restrictive school rules' (the fashions change). Our repertoire of ways of helping these pupils is instinctive or traditional, rather than drawing on a methodology derived from research. The maladjusted child has always interested psychological researchers, but the relationship to possible strategies of help by the pastoral care of a school are rarely explored. For instance, one can see potential in studies such as that on 'Knowledge of Strategies for the Expression of Emotion among Normal and Maladjusted Boys' (Taylor and Harris 1984). Tests were given to 7–8 year-old and 10–11 year-old boys from normal and 'maladjusted' schools 'to asssess their knowledge of strategies of control for both facial and overt behavioural expression of a negative emotion (*ibid*, p. 145). The main findings seemed to indicate that 'normal and maladjusted boys differ in the strategies they propose for reacting to provocation but not in the emotion that they expect to feel'. It is interesting from the point of view of those of us working with young people to note the researchers' caveat: 'It is tempting to conclude that maladjusted boys lack knowledge of control strategies. However, it could also be argued that while they know of such strategies, they find them difficult to apply in practice or choose to adopt counter-aggression instead' (*ibid*, p. 144). Why? And how can they be helped to deploy their knowledge of control strategies actually to use other responses? The 'personal guidance' of pastoral care work would be substantially helped by further research in this way. Even less research, that I know of, has been devoted to the ordinary pupil, that great under-researched species, and her or his needs from a tutor. It is said of students in USA high schools with separate 'guidance and counselling departments', 'if you haven't got a problem, then you've sure got a real problem' – because the student with no recognised problem tends to get overlooked. Is not the same true here? We do not know, but I fear that the personal and social growth of the undemanding pupil gets little help from tutorial work. In England and Wales the guidance and welfare of pupils is embedded not in specialist 'guidance and counselling departments' as in the United States, but in a system which is normally built round the tutor. Those of us organising pastoral care in schools, producing job descriptions, briefing, observing, and supporting just do not know enough about the actual or the possible.

Finally, one of my greatest problems in school is helping colleagues develop pastoral skills. The NAPCE pilot survey has shown the startling inadequacies of [. . .] in-service provision (Maher and Best 1984, pp. 4–12), and we know from NAPCE papers of the economical but effective programme of professional development in Clwyd (Weeks 1984). However, we have little knowledge of the best ways to produce effective in-service work in pastoral care, especially for the thousands of tutors. The [. . .] very valuable book on *School-Focussed In-Service Training* (Bolam 1982) recognises the problem but is, yet again, far less full on school focussed training for pastoral care than other aspects. [. . .]

The pastoral curriculum

From a time only a few years ago when to use the words 'pastoral' and 'curriculum' in the same session, never mind the same sentence, produced anger, the paired words are now in fairly common use. The most common meaning, to me regrettable, is merely to cover the activity of the tutor period. Indeed for some people the title of Jill Baldwin's and Harry Wells' *Active Tutorial Work* (Baldwin and Wells 1979, 80 and 81) is abbreviated, 'ATW', as the generic title for any tutorial work! I prefer to use the phrase 'pastoral curriculum' in the wider sense I defined in an essay of that title (Marland 1980), to mean 'the school curriculum looked at for the moment solely from the point of view of the personal needs of the pupil resolving his individual problems, making informed decisions, and taking his place in his personal world' (*ibid*, p. 157).

My argument is that the individual 'personal, educational and vocational guidance' of a school's pastoral work has to be prepared for by a 'pastoral curriculum' which is devised to teach the underlying facts, concepts, attitudes, and skills required by the individual for personal and social development, and also for any individual guidance. This whole-school pastoral curriculum is then divided amongst subject and pastoral teams. That which is reserved for the latter is called the 'pastoral', and within that is the scheme of work for tutors in their group sessions, and this is the 'tutorial programme'. Up and down the country many schools are struggling to produce this 'tutorial programme', usually without working out a whole-school pastoral curriculum first. Most schools are finding it very difficult indeed, and we all lack the external work which we can make use of in other aspects of the curriculum. With the exception of Button (1981), Baldwin and Wells (1979, 1980 and 1981), Bulman (1984), and Pring (1984) we are on our own.

Kenneth David in a Schools Council Study *Personal and Social Education in Secondary Schools* (David 1982) has considered 'the requirements within a school for such a coherent programme to be developed, and what can prevent the implementation of such work' (*ibid*, p. 29). He charts the stages of identification, review, and implementation, and, not surprisingly finds that 'the traditional school system of management through subject departments can be a major constraint' (*ibid*, p. 34). His ingredients for 'a co-ordinated approach' (*ibid*, p. 36) are sensible; however, the study, like others, is far from a research-based approach.

HMI considered in Chapter 9 of *Aspects of Secondary Education* (HMI 1979) 'the extent to which the curriculum, the content of learning, the teaching methods employed, the knowledge, ideas and skills made available and the intellectual frameworks provided as an aid to the ordering of experience, appeared to match the needs of all pupils' (*ibid*, p. 208). They add that 'it is clear that there are considerable intellectual and organisational difficulties in this approach' (*ibid*, p. 209), and certainly everything I have heard from colleagues in other schools as well as my own personal experience confirms that whole-school curriculum planning is extraordinarily difficult, and the whole-school planning of a pastoral curriculum the hardest part of that. (See also Bulman and Jenkins 1988) Where is the *research* on this aspect of the curriculum?

Occupations

Consider, for instance, the aspect of the pastoral curriculum concerned with 'careers', or as I prefer to call it, 'occupations', which is bound to be part of a pastoral curriculum, stretching far beyond tutorial periods to virtually all 'subjects'. [Many] years ago the DES expressed the view which is still unusual and over-ambitious in the reality of most schools that 'for all boys and girls careers education should be a continuous and important element in the curriculum' (DES 1973). By the 1979 secondary survey there appeared to have been little change: 'In general the potential for careers education within the subjects of the curriculum was not being exploited'. (HMI 1979, p. 232). I have myself argued that this is the way to plan curriculum, both as an understanding of the adult world and for specific 'careers guidance', much of which is too late, too little, and too narrow, trying to graft occupational counselling onto a tree of ignorance (Marland 1974, pp. 214–221; 1980, pp. 164–165). More recently, Catherine

Avent has argued the case in *Careers Across the Curriculum* (Avent, forthcoming). However, it is probably fair to say that the curriculum implications of this background to guidance have not been explored. We do not know the details of what is required, and our efforts in school are limited by the lack of research, despite the politicians' complaints about the need.

Sex education and health education

Take another element of the pastoral curriculum, sex education (itself a limiting phrase normally taken to mean education about reproduction and not about sexuality). Bridget Brophy (Brophy 1977) and Stevi Jackson (Jackson 1978) have made devastating criticisms of schools' education about sexuality, the first based on a survey of the texts and the second on field research amongst girls. Jackson's book on sexuality in childhood is also relevant (1982). However, it does not seem that we have done the research-based groundwork of what could and should be taught and learnt about sexuality to inform adequately our curriculum planning of this aspect of the 'personal' part of the pastoral curriculum.

One might have thought that 'health education' had been better covered, with Schools Council projects and a national Health Education Council. However, the publications from that combination (Schools Council 1983) have a gross gap between aspiration and the majority of the teaching/learning material. Community Service Volunteers have produced a teachers' pack, *Health*, which is good on the organisational side of health services, but still does not relate sufficiently to young people's needs (CSV 1982).

Option choice

A special facet of the pastoral curriculum which I should like to highlight is option choice. This process both serves the rest of the curriculum, by helping pupils make wise choices, and is part of the key content of the pastoral curriculum, by helping pupils choose wisely.

The United States school pupil faces 'electives' yearly from at least what we should call first-year secondary (grade 6). The professional help is typically given by 'guidance and counselling' *departments*, specialists with no teaching timetable. In this country it is usual to face the first 'option' choices at fourteen, leading to a two-year examination course. In both countries the choosing of subjects has a double importance: on the one hand the choices affect the student's future, both by encouraging or inhibiting success at school and by keeping later study and occupation possibilities open or not. On the other hand, these are also the most important choices an adolescent makes largely within the school's influences and teaching. Choosing options is a paradigm for all choices. As part of the pastoral curriculum the teaching of 'choosing' is central. Choosing options is thus a *real* experience to be used by the school to help the pupil learn about choice.

There has clearly been recognition of this importance and a continuing debate about the so-called 'compulsory core' since Jim Callaghan's 'Ruskin speech' in

1977, and in particular the agonised curriculum arguments in, e.g. *A view of the curriculum* (HMI 1980, especially Propositions 13 and 14) and the ILEA's *Consultation Paper on Curriculum in Schools* (ILEA 1980), which has as its first 'suggested principle': 'Children must have freedom to play a major part in determining their own lives.' (p. 15). It is therefore surprising that there has not been a major series of research studies on pastoral care and curriculum choice. In the USA the professional separation of the guidance task and its annual requirement has encouraged specific research. In this country, however, there have been only narrowly-directed and limited studies. [. . .]

In 1982, the Schools Council published *Options for the Fourth* (Schools Council 1982), the result of a low-cost, exploratory study involving staff in schools, LEAs, and the Council in an extension of their normal work' (*ibid*, p. 7). There is some information about a small exercise on 'How pupils reach decisions'. It rated the influence of 'Parents' as first, 'School Option Information' as second, and 'Teachers' as third (*ibid*, p. 15), and rated 'Subject Teachers' as vastly more important than 'Form Teachers' (*ibid*, p. 16). However, the study is essentially taking a *curriculum* viewpoint, and, indeed, the Foreword puts the study firmly in 'the continuing process of curriculum review' (*ibid*, p. 6). Apart from a passing reference to 'poor guidance and counselling' (*ibid*, p. 35), the whole study has the usual Schools Council silence on pastoral care.

[. . .] the SSRC funded a little-known project from 1980 to 1983 on 'Curriculum Guidance and Differentation at 14 + ' (Smith 1984, which includes a good bibliography). His findings highlight 'cues which pupils have acquired about their own levels of ability', that 'through processes of guidance and counselling from teachers (formal or informal), pupils' choices are moved more in line with what teachers believe about their real level of ability', and, very significantly, that pupil ambitions are a 'relatively stronger' effect 'in schools where the options are less stratified' (*ibid*, p. 8). The research does not support Woods' 'social structure' model. Once again, the study does not focus on the process of guidance itself.

There have also been a number of small-scale studies considering the relationship between choice and specific subjects, especially in relation to the sciences and girls. For instance, Keys and Ormerod (1976) have shown that girls rating physics high in their preference scale are less likely to be able to study it than boys with the same level of preference. (See also Ormerod and Duckworth 1975, and Ormerod *et al* 1979). These all have implications for the educational guidance given by tutors and house or year heads, but this dimension is rarely if ever recognised. As I have stated elsewhere 'the corollary of choice is counselling' (Marland 1980 a, XV.1), and for the huge majority of pupils that means pastoral care via the tutor.

Thus those of us in schools have a very limited range of research (though much of it of good quality and interesting) to help us with the educational guidance aspect of pastoral care and options for the fourth year – and still less for post-sixteen! The research that has been done has usually been based on a very few schools, often pre-comprehensive reorganisation (e.g. Wood 1976) and almost all the time has been severely limited in terms of pastoral care application by having one of two focusses:

1 A sociological correlation model, in which the prime aim has been to correlate pupil choices with social class, ability, or earlier schooling.
2 A curriculum-planning model, in which the prime aim has been to map what subject range pupils have ended up with.

Almost nowhere in the literature of the research into choosing options is the pastoral process focussed upon. Unless we are to abandon choice, and that is both undesirable and unlikely, this research gap needs filling.

I have dealt with aspects of study skills in the previous section on the student as 'information-user', but it would be possible to take each aspect of the pastoral curriculum and demonstrate the lack both of a specific research focus into the topic, and how to weave it into the whole-school curriculum and pastoral programme. Indeed the absence of curriculum theorists and researchers from key focuses such as this is lamentable (e.g. Zeldin 1983, and Lee and Zeldin 1982, to name two Open University texts otherwise characterised by breadth and thoughtfulness). This is yet another aspect in which the curriculum demands of the aims of pastoral care have not been adequately researched or developed for those of us in schools to respond adequately to the exhortations. No wonder do HMI declare: 'Greater care in planning the time given to tutor periods and help and advice to tutors on how best to use this time would allow better use to be made of tutor periods.' (HMI 1979, p. 222). The [. . .] School Curriculum Development Committee's first six 'key themes' significantly included 'personal and social development' (TES 10.2.84) [. . .].

There is also a depressing separatism when the profession addresses itself to new issues: the enthusiasts overlook pastoral care. I find that two of the major [recent] thrusts, each of which has generated valuable research, have almost entirely overlooked the pastoral aspects of schooling: equal opportunities and multi-cultural education.

Equal opportunities

The mass of valuable research and discussion on aspects of equal opportunities and education has focussed heavily on the academic curriculum. Indeed there is hardly a word about pastoral care in the entire UK literature of equal opportunities and schooling. Conversely, there is little or nothing on the literature of pastoral care that addresses itself to equal opportunities. (In my own symposium, *Sex Differentiation and Schooling* (Marland 1983), I managed only five pages!) Of course some of the work of NISEC and some of the work on counselling relates to gender.

However, some researchers have focussed powerfully on aspects of sex differentiation and motivation and anxiety. The research of Carol Dweck (both in her contribution to Marland 1983, and her other papers) and Margaret B.

Sutherland (in 'Anxiety, Aspirations, and the Curriculum' in Marland 1983) show the need for a different approach to girls' anxiety. Carol Dweck can even demonstrate the different ways in which girls and boys react to 'peer' as opposed to 'adult' criticism. All these points have crucial implications for tutoring, but we have not yet begun to work them out. If equal opportunities is to be a real educational issue, it must be located in the central guidance processes of the school: pastoral care. At the moment we know, for instance, that science curriculum and methods alienate many girls, but we have not a single study of what happens to them in tutor periods.

Multi-cultural education

If the literature of feminism is reticent on pastoral care, that on the intensely urgent issue of multi-cultural education is positively empty. I intend by 'multi-cultural education' the twin complementary considerations of the Swann Committee, that is the educational needs of the children of ethnic minority families to ensure that they obtain their full rights to a good education, and also the educational needs of all pupils to be prepared for a multi-cultural world.

[An . . .] admirable book *Teaching in the Multi-Cultural School* (Lynch 1981), covers many aspects of the curriculum and has chapters on most 'subjects'. However, the pastoral programme is *never* mentioned, and 'tutor', 'form teacher', or 'pastoral' do not appear once in the index! I may have missed some work, but as far as I know, the entire range of research studies and educational discussion texts on aspects of anti-racism in the UK has been blind to the pastoral perspective. The important research by David Milner (Milner 1983) has endeavoured to establish how young people develop their attitudes to race identity. The essential point is that these matters are 'taught', and therefore are amenable to school actions. Lawrence Stenhouse, before his sad death, did more than any other single person in this country to assist the research and intellectual consideration of *how* pupils develop attitudes, and how these could be influenced by teaching (e.g. Stenhouse *et al* 1982).

Despite the rapid growth of the number of bilingual pupils in certain parts of the country (18.6 per cent of the school population in the ILEA, for instance) and the fact that 'linguistic diversity . . . is so much a feature of everyday life in England today' (Linguistic Minorities Project, 1985, p. 1), there has been very little speculation, and still less research, about the pastoral needs of bilingual learners whose English is currently very limited. *How* is 'personal, educational, and vocational guidance' to be offered by a tutor or junior school class teacher who has no competence in the pupil's strongest language if the pupil does not sensitively and clearly understand the teacher's English? A recent report by a group of teachers and community workers in the ILEA, 'Educating Bilingual Learners' (Working Party 1985), recommends special 'complementary tutoring', but as yet we have no research on the results of pastoral care or into possible variations.

I have tried as a practitioner in a school to keep abreast of the research and writing on aspects of multi-cultural education. However, I have to stress that in the wide-ranging number of studies of aspects of ethnicity, immigration, and ethnic minorities in schools, I have rarely or never come across either an explicit or implicit understanding of the pastoral contribution. We know attitudes are amplified or created by schools; we know racial attitudes are an artefact of society. But we have not found a way of studying what actually happens and how it can be changed.

The report by the Committee of Enquiry, chaired by Lord Swann, might have been expected to have changed this, especially as throughout it emphasises the need for more research. However, the relationship between one of its major themes, underachievement and achievement, and pastoral care is not even touched upon (Committee of Enquiry into the Education of Children from Ethnic Minority Groups 1985, Chapter 3), and 'what can broadly be termed pastoral matters' appears to be seen (though no definition is attempted) as 'facilities for meals and dress . . . ''rules and regulations'' and . . . religious ''rights and duties'' ' (*ibid.*, p. 203). At one point one sees a glimmer coming into the Committee's mind of the centrality of the pastoral task when it requires 'the school to be able to cater for any ''pastoral'' needs which an ethnic minority pupil may experience, for example in relation to intergenerational conflicts or educational aspiration' (*ibid.*, p. 326). However, the limited view of 'pastoral' (almost always with those nervous quotations marks of disbelief in its meaning) is assumed to be 'rules' about 'such matters as school uniforms, showers and changing, physical education and swimming' (*ibid*, p. 513).

The relationship between pastoral care and the educational needs of ethnic minority children and of the whole population of pupils in regard to their perception of a multi-ethnic society is a major and urgent focus for educational research.

Conclusion

The common fallacies of pastoral care include an over-emphasis on individual work, an under-emphasis on content, and a belief that there is no theory but rather that it all depends on experience and getting to know the pupil. These fallacies combine with the unfortunate effects of promotion policies and the dearth of people with experience and interest in pastoral care in the advisory service and in colleges and departments of education to leave pastoral care without the research base it requires.

In this chapter, I have highlighted those aspects of pastoral care where properly focussed and effective research studies need to be carried out and their results disseminated to the teaching profession. For example, one of the central pastoral tasks is to help children to be pupils. But if tutorial work, tutorial team leadership, and middle-management casework are to develop as fully professional tasks, the presently available research bearing on aspects of the pupil role must be drawn together, and fresh research initiated into being a pupil and the help required.

We need to study the relationship between parenting style and pastoral approaches and the correlations between parenting style and school success. We have to find ways of inducting pupils into secondary school studies throughout their schooling, and of teaching them how to handle and make best use of information. We need pastoral procedures which enable tutors and classteachers to understand motivation and to know how to ensure pupils learn how to succeed.

There is little research on the structure and responsibilities for pastoral care within the school, including how teachers use their tutorial time. We simply do not know enough about pastoral care structures to adapt, service or rebuild them. We also know very little about how tutors work, with no research available on the quality of the tutoring that goes on and of the inter-relationships between tutor and tutee. Although the inadequacy of in-service provision for tutors is widely acknowledged, we have yet to find out the best ways of producing effective in-service work in pastoral care.

The development of tutorial programmes within a whole-school pastoral curriculum is hampered by a lack of adequate research into essential elements of that pastoral curriculum, including education for careers, education about sexuality and health, and option choice. In addition, research into contemporary social developments, such as equal opportunities and multi-cultural education, has ignored the pastoral care aspects and applications of such developments. [Recent] years have seen a major growth of work specifically directed to pastoral care, [which] . . . has provided the basis for a new professionalism. [. . .] However, the level of knowledge at all levels and in all sectors of the system of what we mean by 'personal, educational, and vocational guidance' and how to deliver effective pastoral care for all is depressingly low. We hope there will be an upsurge of research to help the next generation of pupils more than their predecessors. [. . .]

References

AVENT, C. (forthcoming): *Careers Across the Curriculum*, Heinemann Educational Books.
BALDWIN, J. and WELLS, H. (1979, 1980, 1981). *Active Tutorial Work*, Books 1–5. Basil Blackwell.
BAZALGETTE, J. (1983). 'Taking up the pupil role', in *Pastoral Care in Education*, 1 (3).
BECHER, T. and MACLURE, S. (1978). *Accountability in Education*, NFER-Nelson.
BECK, J. (1972). 'Transition and continuity: a study of an educational status passage', M. A. thesis (unpublished), University of London Library.
BENNETT, N. 1976. *Teaching Styles and Pupil Progress*. Open Books.
BERGER, M. and TAYLOR, E. (1984). 'Editorial', in *Journal of Child Psychology and Psychiatry*, 25 (1).
BEST, R. (1980). 'Review of Johnson *et al* (1980), *Secondary Schools and the Welfare Network*', Unwin Educational, in *British Educational Research Journal*, 6 (2), pp. 215–8.

BEST, R., JARVIS C. and RIBBINS, P.M. (eds), (1980). *Perspectives on Pastoral Care*, Heinemann Educational Books.
BEST, R., RIBBINS, P. M. and JARVIS C., with ODDY, D. (1983). *Education and Care*, Heinemann Educational Books.
BLACKBURN, K. (1975). *The Tutor*, Heinemann Educational Books.
BLACKBURN, K. (1983a). *Head of House, Head of Year*, Heinemann Educational Books.
BOLAM, R. (ed.) (1982). *School Focussed In-service Training*, London, Heinemann.
BREIVIK, P. S. (1977). 'Resources: the fourth R', in *Community College Forum*, USA, Winter, 1977, 49.
BULMAN, L. (1984). 'The relationship between the pastoral curriculum, the academic curriculum, and the pastoral programme', in *Pastoral Care*, 2, (2), June 1984.
BULMAN, L. and JENKINS, D. (1988) *The Pastoral Curriculum*, Basil Blackwell.
BUTTON, L. (1981). *Group Tutoring for the Form Teacher*. Hodder and Stoughton.
CSV (1982). *Health*, a school and community kit, (updated version of 1978 kit).
COMMITTEE OF INQUIRY INTO THE EDUCATION OF CHILDREN FROM ETHNIC MINORITY GROUPS, (1985). *Education For All*, (the Swann Report), HMSO, Cmnd 9453.
COULTER, F. (1979). 'Homework: a neglected research area', in *British Educational Research Journal*, 5 (1), pp. 21–33.
CRAFT, M. *et al* (1981). *Linking Home and School*, Harper and Row.
DAVID, K. (1982). *Personal and Social Education in Secondary Schools*, Longman, for the Schools Council.
DEPARTMENT OF EDUCATION AND SCIENCE (1973). *Careers Education in Secondary Schools*, Education Survey 18, HMSO.
DWECK, C. S. (1977). 'Learned helplessness and negative education', in Keisler, F. R (ed.), *The Education*, 19 (2).
DWECK, C. S., and BUSH, E. (1976). 'Sex differences in learned helplessness with peer and adult evaluators', in *Development Psychology*, 12 (2), pp. 147–56.
DWECK, C. S. and GOETZ, T. E. (1978). 'Attributions and learned helplessness', in Harvey, J., Ickes, W. and Kidd, R. (eds), *New Directions in Attribution Research*, 2, pp. 159–79, Halsted, New York.
DWECK, C. S., DAVIDSON, W., NELSON, S. and ENNA, B. (1981). 'Sex differences in learned helplessness: II The contingencies of evaluative feedback in the classroom, and III An Experimental analysis', in *Developmental Psychology*, 14 (3), pp. 268–76.
DWECK, C. S. and ELLIOTT, E.S. (1981). 'Achievement motivation', in Mussem, P. (general ed.) and Hetherington, E. M. (volume ed.), *Carmichael's Manual of Child Psychology: Social and Personality Development*. J. Wiley, New York.
GALLOWAY, D. (1983). 'Disruptive pupils and effective care', in *School Organisation*, 3 (3), pp. 245–54.
HAMBLIN, D. H. (1978). *The Teacher and Pastoral Care*, Basil Blackwell.
HAMBLIN, D. H. (ed.) (1981a). *Problems and Practice of Pastoral Care*, Basil Blackwell.
HARGREAVES, D. H. (1972). *Interpersonal Relations and Education*, Routledge and Kegan Paul.
HEALY, M. and GOODHAND, L. (1983). *Effective Learning Skills: a Pupil Guide*. ILEA.
HMI (1979). *Aspects of Secondary Education in England*, HMSO.
HMI (1980). *A View of the Curriculum*, HMI Series: Matters for Discussion 11. HMSO.
HMI (1982). *Pastoral Care in the Comprehensive Schools of Wales*, HMSO.
HMI (1982). *The New Teacher in School*, HMSO.

HILSUM, S. and CANE, B. S. (1971). *The Teacher's Day*, NFER-Nelson.

HILSUM, S. and STRONG, C. (1978). *The Secondary Teacher's Day*, NFER-Nelson.

HULL, C. and RUDDOCK, J. (1981). 'The effects of systematic induction courses for pupils' perceptions of an innovation', final report of project HR 6848/1 to SSRC, (available from British Library).

HURMAN, A. (1978). *A Charter for Choice*, NFER-Nelson.

ILEA (1980). *Consultation Paper on Curriculum in Schools*, ILEA.

ILEA, Division 2 (1984). 'Transfer to secondary school', Internal DO2 circulation.

IRVING, A. (1983). *Educating Information-Users*, British Library Research and Development Department.

IRVING, A. (1985). *Study and Information Skills Across the Curriculum*, Heinemann Educational Books.

IRVING, A. and SNAPE, W. (1979). *Educating Library Users in British Secondary Schools*, British Library Research and Development Report no. 5467, British Library, R and D Dept.

JACKSON, S. (1978). 'How to make babies: sexism in sex education', in *Women's Studies International Quarterly*, 1 (4) pp. 342–52.

JACKSON, S. (1982). *Sexuality and Childhood*, Basil Blackwell.

KEYS, W. and ORMEROD, M. B. (1976). 'A comparison of the pattern of science subject choices for boys and girls in the light of the pupils' own expressed subject preferences', in *School Science Review*, 58 (203), pp. 348–50.

LANG, P. (1983). 'Pastoral care: some reflections on possible influences', in *Pastoral Care in Education*, 2 (2), see also Ribbins, P.M., Lang, P. and Healy, M. 1984, editorial to *Pastoral Care in Education*, 2 (1).

LANG, P. (1984a). 'Pupils, problems and pastoral care', NAPCE seminar paper.

LANG, P. (1984b). 'Pastoral care and educational research', *Research Intelligence*, 15 BERA.

LEE, V. and ZELDIN, D. (eds) (1982). *Challenge and Change in the Curriculum* and *Planning in the Curriculum*, Hodder and Stoughton, for the Open University.

LINGUISTIC MINORITIES PROJECT (1985). *The Other Languages of England*, Routledge and Kegan Paul.

LYNCH, J. (ed.) (1981). *Teaching in the Multi-Cultural School*, Ward Lock Educational.

MAHER, P. and BEST, R. (1984). *Training and Support for Pastoral Care*, NAPCE.

MARLAND, M. (1974). *Pastoral Care*, Heinemann Educational Books.

MARLAND, M. (1980a). The New Fourth-Year Curriculum, North Westminster Community School.

MARLAND, M. (1980b): 'The Pastoral Curriculum', in Best, R., Jarvis, C. and Ribbins, P. (eds), *Perspectives in Pastoral Care*, Heinemann Educational Books.

MARLAND, M. (ed.) (1981). *Information Skills in the Secondary Curriculum*, Schools Council Curriculum no. 9, Methuen Educational.

MARLAND, M. (1982). 'Preparing for promotion in pastoral care', in *Pastoral Care*, 1 (1). Basil Blackwell.

MARLAND, M. (ed.) (1983). *Sex Differentiation and Schooling*, Heinemann Educational Books.

MILNER, D. (1983). *Children and Race*, Ward Lock Educational.

MORTIMORE, P. and J. (1981). 'How to get the most out of the school night-shift', in *The Guardian*, 7 April 1981.

NIXON, J. (ed.) (1981). *A Teacher's Guide to Action Research*, Grant McIntyre.

NORDLING, J. A. (1978). 'The high school library and the classroom: closing the gap', in Lubans, J. jnr (ed.) (1978), *Progress in Educating the Library User*, Bowker.

ORMEROD, M. B. *et al* (1979). Girls and physics education', in *Physics Education*, 14, pp. 271-7.

ORMEROD, M. B. with DUCKWORTH, D. (1975). *Pupils' Attitudes to Science: a Review of the Research*, NFER-Nelson.

PRING, R. A. (1984). *Personal and Social Education in the Curriculum*, Hodder and Stoughton.

RAVEN, J. (1982). 'Educational home visiting and the growth of competence and confidence in adults and children', in *Curriculum Inquiry*, 12 (1), pp. 87-104.

REID, M. I., BARNETT, B. R. and ROSENBERG, H.A. (1974). *A Matter of Choice*, NFER-Nelson.

REYNOLDS, D. and MURGATROYD, S. (1977). 'The sociology of schooling and the absent pupil', in Carroll, H. (ed.), *Absenteeism in South Wales: studies of pupils, their homes and their secondary schools*, University College of Swansea.

RUDDOCK, J. and HULL, C. (1981). 'Pupils' grasp of classroom process', Paper to Educational Research Association.

RUTTER, M., MAUGHAN, B., MORTIMORE, P. and OUSTON, J. (1979). *Fifteen Thousand Hours – Secondary Schools and their Effects on Children*, London, Open Books.

SCHOOLS COUNCIL/HEALTH EDUCATION PROJECT (1983). *Health Education 13-18*, Forbes Publications/Holmes McDougall.

SHAYER, M. and ADEY, P. (1981). *Towards a Science of Science Teaching*, Heinemann Educational Books.

SMITH, I.R.H. (1984). 'Curriculum Guidance and Differentiation at 14 + ', end-of-grant report to SSRC on Grant c/00/23/0039/1.

STENHOUSE, L., VERMA, G. K., WILD, R. D. and NIXON, J. (1982). *Teaching about Race Relations*. Routledge and Kegan Paul.

SUTHERLAND, M.B. (1983). 'Anxiety, aspirations and the curriculum' in Marland, M. (ed), *Sex Differentiation and Schooling*, London, Heinemann.

TAYLOR, D. and HARRIS, P. L. (1981). 'Knowledge of strategies for the expression of emotion among normal and maladjusted boys', in *Journal of Child Psychology and Psychiatry*, 24, 1, pp. 141-5.

WEEKS, M. S. (1984). *A Brief Description of the Growth and Progress of the Clwyd Pastoral Care Professional Development Programme*, NAPCE.

WHITMORE, K., BAX, M., WATT, C. and HALL, K. (1984). *Health and Psychological Services in Inner City Primary Schools*, North Westminster Community School.

WILSON, H. (1980). 'Parental supervision: a neglected aspect of delinquency', in *The British Journal of Criminology*, 20 (3), pp. 203-35.

WILSON, H. and HERBERT, G. W. (1978). *Parents and Children in the Inner City*, Routledge and Kegan Paul.

WOODS, P. (1976). 'The myth of subject choice, in *British Journal of Sociology*, 27 (2), pp. 130-49.

WOODS, P. (1978). 'Negotiating demands of schoolwork', in *Curriculum Studies*, 10 (4), pp. 309-27.

WORKING PARTY INTO THE EDUCATION OF BILINGUAL LEARNERS IN DIVISION TWO OF THE ILEA, chaired by Marland, M. and Goodhand, L. (1985). *The Education of Bilingual Learners, Towards a Coherent Policy*, ILEA, Division Two.

ZELDIN, D. (1983). *Strategies in Curriculum Planning*, Open University.

Primary school resource management: a case study

Lynton Gray

The financial management of educational institutions is one of the great mysteries of education management. While the Audit Commission exhorts local authorities to devolve more financial responsibilities to their schools, we know next to nothing about the ways in which most institutions manage the financial resources already at their disposal. Headteachers and other education managers rarely have training in the basic financial management skills. This might be one of the reasons why so many headteachers treat the details of finance allocation within the school as a highly classified secret. In consequence, we know very little about the total sums of money actually spent by schools on the education of their pupils. And we know even less about the ways in which decisions are made in schools about fund-raising, the allocation and deployment of those funds and the resources provided by the LEA, and financial monitoring. This case study attempts to explore those management processes in one primary school. There is no claim that this school is in any way typical – we do not have enough knowledge to make that judgement as yet. It is hoped, however, that others can use the case as a basis for comparative studies.

Milton Primary School is the oldest of the three primary schools in a small town about 40 miles from London, in a large shire county. With over 300 pupils, there are 12 teachers and the head teacher. Teachers and classes are organized into three 'departments' according to pupil age, as lower (5–7 year olds), middle (7–9) and upper (9–11) school teams. There are 11 classes; the 12th teacher has responsibility for small groups of children with special needs for part of the time, and for a small and fluctuating number of gipsy children for the rest of the time. The school is a large, rambling two-storey building, about 70 years old.

The present system of financial management has evolved since the head was appointed seven years ago. She inherited a system whereby each member of staff had been allocated a proportion of the school allowance, decided how it should be spent, and then stored the purchased items in each classroom, so that the central stock cupboards lay empty. The incoming head felt that this was an inefficient system. There were no store cupboards in the classrooms, which in consequence were cluttered with consumable stock at the beginning of each year; and there was no continuity from year to year, nor any schoolwide resource policies.

At about this time schools were beginning to feel the first impact of national and local government policies of financial stringency. The new head looked for a resource management system which would cut costs, and deploy available resources as efficiently as possible. To this end a centralized ordering system was introduced, with a limited number of different types of consumable goods, in order to maximize the benefits of bulk purchasing. Since then the system has evolved with modification each year, but with the central objective of meeting a communal set of needs as efficiently as possible, while providing as wide a range of educational experiences as possible within the resources available.

The system of financial allocation used by the LEA is not dissimilar from that found in most English LEAs. A *per capita* allocation is agreed by the Education Committee according to the age of the pupil, and schools are notified of their provisional capitation allowance on the basis of the returns made on the termly staffing return in January each year. Schools are permitted to spend up to 90 percent of that allocation from the beginning of the financial year. The final capitation figure is calculated near the end of the financial year, when the following January's returns are received, to give the actual number of children on roll (see Figure 1). In 1983/84 the Authority was also able to make an additional 5 percent capitation allocation to schools, after reviewing overall expenditure.

In Milton Primary School the allocation for 1983/84 was based provisionally on the 336 pupils recorded in January 1983. The initial agreed *per capita* allocation for pupils of primary school age was £11.30 for 1983/84, (raised to £11.85 in December 1983). The school was told in March 1983 that it could spend up to 90 percent of £3,797 (336 × £11.30) – a total of £3,417. By January 1983 there were only 320 pupils on roll, as pupil numbers have continued to fall. The final 1983/84 allocation was, therefore, £3,792 (320 × £11.85), so the additional funds available towards the end of the financial year amounted to a further £375. The school also receives a small extra allowance of about £100 to cover the additional costs of educating an uncertain and fluctuating number of gipsy children, the costs of which are recouped by the LEA from a national 'no-area pool' to which all LEAs contribute to pay for the education of children without any fixed permanent residence, or whose parents, though UK residents, normally work abroad. An allowance of £77 is made for office stationery, and a separate allowance is made for cleaning materials.

Internal allocation procedures

Within the school, discussions about the spending of the next financial year's capitation allowance begin in February. A major part of the expenditure is committed in the form of consumable items – mainly paper, exercise books, writing and art materials. Other expenditure is committed annually to medical supplies and office needs, the annual television licence and the costs of pamphlets to accompany school broadcasts, as well as piano tuning and the servicing and repairing of office and audio-visual equipment. This regular committed expenditure amounts to something over two-thirds of the total allowance – about £2,500 in 1983/84, as is shown in Table 4.6.1.

Table 4.6.1 Estimated income and expenditure, Milton Primary School, 1983–4[1]

Expenditure	£		Income	£	
Capitation:			LEA:		
Exercise books, paper, et.	1400		Capitation allowance	3797	
Art and craft materials	1550		Administrative printing &		
Mathematics equipment &			stationery	77	
books	270		Replacement Fund	237	
Library books	165				
Physical education apparatus	140		LEA total		4111
BBC pamphlets, etc.	75				
Television licence	46				
Medical supplies	40				
Repairs	60		PTA:		1287
Total capitation		3746	Donations	1188	
			Waste paper collection	99	
LEA Replacement Fund:		237	School Fund:		2088
Physical education					
equipment	108		Photographer's commission	149	
Iron, ironing board, cooker	129		Tuck shop profits[2]	118	
			Voluntary contributions		
			for swimming	961	
PTA donations:		1287	Payments for field trip	860	
Seats for playground	411				
Micro-computer	327		Brought forward from		
			1982/83:		648
Computer trolley	50		LEA sources (inc. GRIDS)	324	
Reading books	499		PTA donations unspent	324	
Swimming pool maintenance & tuition	619				
Field trip to Norwich	849				
Minor consumable items (from					
School Fund)	550				
Total expenditure		7288	Total income		8134

Notes:
1. Income and expenditure for 'travellers' children in separate fund, not included here.
2. Tuck shop profits for part-year only.

The deputy head takes on the job of compiling the list of consumable items:

> The way I do this is to go around the school to all members of staff and talk to them
> about things they see that we may need, except for the usual supply of pencils, scissors
> and the other things that you can imagine would be needed in a primary school. I then
> go and discuss it with the head, and ask whether there is anything she feels we need.
> Then I go away and order it.

This is done on the LEA's pre-printed requisition forms, which are then signed
by the head and sent off to the LEA's area office for transmission to the suppliers.

The remaining part of the capitation allowance is earmarked for equipment,
apparatus and any special needs. In 1983/84 this amounted to about £1,000 (or
about £3 per pupil). The first stage in allocating these funds is a meeting of
head, deputy head and each of the scale post holders: each department is led by a
scale 3 post holder, and there are five holders of scale 2 posts, each for a designated curricular area. The broad priorities for the coming year are discussed,
and each of the scale post holders is asked to draw up a list of requirements. In
1983 priority was given to the purchase of books for pupils and teachers' guides
for the Nuffield Mathematics Scheme, which was being purchased in stages as it
became available.

The post holders are not given a budget ceiling within which to construct their
lists. Nor are they given guidelines as to the types of resources to be ordered or
the processes to be undertaken in identifying the school's needs. In consequence
this is done differently by different teachers. The scale 3 teachers tend to hold
departmental meetings to identify preferences and priorities. One scale 2 teacher
goes about the task thus:

> I haven't been given a specific sum, but I've been asked to write down what we
> need. . . . Basically I look at what we've got, talking to members of staff and finding
> out what they feel they need. I look through catalogues, have a word with the head,
> and see what we can afford. Whatever list I make out is trimmed down. Obviously you
> order more than you want, hoping that you'll get what you really do need in the end.
> One of the failings of the system is that things I really want can get cut out. Some of the
> things you categorize as really urgent are very expensive. . . . This list, once drawn
> up, goes to (the head) and that's the end of it as far as I'm concerned, until I get stock
> coming back. I find that things have been deleted when they don't arrive at school.
> There's no notification that things have been chopped off. If there's any committee
> which looks at the list I'm not aware of it.

Some teachers make a point of talking with all colleagues individually: others
generate a staffroom discussion on needs. Some put up a list in the staffroom, for
colleagues to write in their needs. Most undertake some form of consultation,
although a couple of teachers seem to have depended mainly on their knowledge
of previous years' usage, helped by visual inspection of the stock cupboards and
their perusal of the available catalogues from educational suppliers. One teacher
mentioned that she consulted her pupils before drawing up a list of reading
books.

As with the teacher quoted above, there is a general expectation that the list submitted to the head will be trimmed. Some mark on to their lists those items which are of highest priority. There is normally no need to make out a case for the items listed, although the head might question individual teachers, and occasionally will return a list for pruning. Usually, however, the head takes the lists, then makes her own judgements as to which items should be retained and which deleted, in order to contain the total costs within the resources available. The retained items are included on the official requisition forms along with the consumable items.

Most of the order goes to the local authority's centralized purchasing system, known as 'County Supplies', getting the benefit of a very large bulk purchasing and discounting system – with a warehouse conveniently close to the school. By arrangement, the consumable goods are divided into three equal amounts and delivered to the school near the beginning of each term, in April, September and January. Items not available from County Supplies are ordered directly from commercial educational equipment suppliers. No moneys change hands through the school. On receipt of an official school order, goods and delivery note go to the school, and the invoice goes to the Education Offices, where the cost is added to a running total of each school's annual expenditure. The LEA's financial management system is more flexible than many, in that schools are allowed to 'overdraw' their entitlement in any one year, with equivalent reductions in the following year's allocation. Conversely, unspent funds can be carried over to the next year.

Schools rarely receive specific and direct guidance as to the types of materials and equipment to be purchased. The LEA inspectors can and do influence choices indirectly through their advice to County Supplies as to items which should be carried in stock. There are also advisory teams of teachers who meet to advise on such items. The influence of LEA inspectors is more potent through their involvement in the LEA's extensive programme of in-service courses for teachers. There, teachers learn of the availability of new materials and equipment: for example a new type of graph paper and Latin American percussion instruments have been introduced to Milton Primary School after teachers had learned of them on in-service courses. Attendance on a science course brought with it a grant for the school from the science inspector, in order to purchase science apparatus. This came from the curriculum development fund allocated by the inspectors: some years earlier the school had received a £200 grant from this source, after a visiting LEA inspector had noted a shortage of equipment in the lower school. The teacher with responsibility for travellers (gipsy) children has been successful in obtaining a grant from the adviser for remedial education for the last couple of years, to purchase learning materials for use with these children.

The LEA inspectors also manage a fund for the replacement of major items of equipment. As an old school, Milton's needs here are greater than those of many schools, and the head has made regular requests, which have largely been successful because of her ability to keep the inspectors – and particularly the primary inspector with specific responsibility for the school – informed as to the school's needs, by letter, telephone and invitations to visit. Thus the school has received a new kiln, a new sewing machine (together with the services of an advisory teacher to instruct the staff in the uses of the new model), and in 1983/84 a replacement cooker, iron and ironing board. A bid is pending at the time of writing for a second sewing machine, necessitated by the introduction of courses in machine embroidery.

Each school is also invited to submit an annual bid for furniture and fittings. This goes to the LEA's area office, where, after consultation with LEA inspectors, approval was given in 1983 for the provision of wide work benches in three of Milton's infant classrooms.

The separate budgets for cleaning supplies and kitchen needs are dealt with by the school caretaker and kitchen supervisor, who assess needs and draw up the official orders, which are then signed by the head.

Table 4.6.2 The annual resource management cycle.

Identifying and meeting needs throughout the year

Jan.	LEA staffing return completed and returned to area office.
Feb.	Meeting of scale post holders to establish priorities: lists of needs compiled.
Mar.	Provisional capitation allowance figure received: annual order completed by head and sent off.
Apr.	First delivery of consumables from County Supplies.
May	
Jun.	Summer Fete – PTA fund-raising event.
Jul.	
Aug.	
Sept.	Second delivery of consumable items.
Oct.	
Nov.	
Dec.	Christmas Fair – PTA fund-raising event.
Jan.	Third delivery of consumable items. LEA staffing return. Final capitation figure received. Remaining orders placed for delivery before end March.

During the course of the year, as teachers identify the need for materials and equipment, they can meet them in a number of ways. At the beginning of each term every teacher submits a plan of the term's work to the head, who discusses it with teachers, commenting on resource implications and referring where appropriate to available materials or equipment within the school. Thereafter, as needs arise teachers draw on the paper, books, art, science, mathematics, writing and other materials and equipment from the relevant stock cupboards, which are open to all teachers to draw on freely.

If they are not to be found there (either because they have been used up, or have never been acquired by the school), teachers have four courses of action open to them. The first is to ask the head for permission to purchase the required item. If obtainable from County Supplies, the head might well call at the warehouse on her way to or from school, and collect it in exchange for an official order form. Otherwise, with permission, the teacher can buy the goods from a local shop, submitting the receipt to the head for reimbursement, either out of the LEA petty cash provision for very inexpensive items, or from the non LEA funds kept in the 'school fund' (see below). Teachers are unlikely to ask for items costing more than £10 or £15 from these sources.

More expensive items might be requested, again through the head, for inclusion in the annual order, or for submission to the PTA Committee as a request that the PTA might purchase the item for the school. This route would, of course, usually involve a long delay between request and receipt of the desired goods, even if successful. The third option is for the teacher to buy the items herself, or to borrow them from her own home or from friends. Teachers regularly spend their own money in purchasing teaching materials and equipment. Asked to estimate the amount they spend annually in such ways Milton teachers indicated sums ranging from £10 to £100, but averaging about £20 per year. One commented:

> If a thing only costs a couple of pounds you go out and buy it yourself. Most teachers do. They don't always bother to ask for the money back.

Only one of the 12 teachers indicated that she did not contribute out of her own pocket to the school in this way. Most mentioned that they would approach the head only occasionally for reimbursement, preferring to pay out themselves rather than submit a bill for every item purchased.

The final option open to teachers is to do without. They indicated that this was most common towards the end of each term, when certain kinds of consumable items had been used up, and replacements would not be received until the beginning of the next term. In some subject areas this can in part be countered by teacher enterprise in building up personal collections of 'junk materials' – margarine containers, cardboard boxes, plastic bottles and the like. But while these have their uses in science, mathematics and art, it was pointed out that you could not improvise apparatus for physical education in this way, and the musical range of a yoghurt cup was severely limited!

Non-LEA funds

To some degree resource shortages can be countered in primary schools by seeking funds from sources other than the LEA. As in many schools, Milton both has a 'school fund' for resources raised directly by the school and receives donations regularly from a lively PTA, whose president is the head teacher, with all teachers as committee members. Fund raising by the PTA is concentrated economically into two major annual events – a Summer Fete and a Christmas Fair. There has been an agreement with the PTA that parents and staff should not be asked to take on a larger regular involvement in fund raising than these. Otherwise the PTA activities are of a social nature, with only minority staff participation, such as the annual bonfire night party.

Control of PTA funds rests with the committee, which meets once a month. The key financial meetings are those immediately after the two major events. These are attended by the head and some senior staff. Informal soundings have usually been made by the head, among staff and parent members of the committee. Suggestions for ways of spending the money raised come from the head or from parent committee members: in theory teachers can put up their own suggestions to the committee, but in practice they would only do so through the head. It is recognized that the committee prefers to buy tangible, 'glamorous' items for the school – items which can readily be identified by visitors to the school. In recent years the school has received a colour television, stage lighting, PE equipment, display screens, carpets, sinks and workbenches. In 1983 the committee donated half the cost of a micro-computer, purchased under the national scheme whereby the Department of Industry met half the costs. A trolley for the computer was also bought, and the committee considered that the need for books in the school was so urgent that, on receiving a request for £200 for book purchase, they doubled that amount, and made a promise of future regular donations for book purchase. The committee has also agreed to provide new curtains for the school hall. Occasionally the committee has been reluctant to support a proposal from the school, as was the case a few years ago, when a request to fund a visiting theatre company was withdrawn. Some staff would like to see the school redecorated with PTA support, but anticipate reluctance there also:

> I'm not sure that the parents wouldn't necessarily see the value of a number of things the money could be spent on, like decorating, for example. I mean the school can be very depressing to work in: it hasn't been decorated for years. The PTA are not really going to want to spend money on decorating, and there's no reason why it should. But it would make an awful lot of difference to the people that work here, and the children who come here, if the school were decorated nicely . . .

There is no strong pressure to spend all the money raised by the PTA, however, and the money is sometimes left to earn interest in the Association's deposit account while alternatives are considered. Altogether the PTA raises between £1,000 and £1,500 from the two events, and another £250 from the collection of waste paper on a weekly basis, organized by a couple of parents. This latter is held as a separate book purchase fund for the school.

The staff role in relation to the PTA is normally a reactive one. They support PTA functions, but rarely initiate proposals for fund-raising activities, or for items on which funds might be spent. The major effort is concentrated into the summer and Christmas events, when the staff run stalls and organize activities. When asked to estimate their annual time commitment to fund-raising activities, half the staff indicated not more than two or three days per year. The other half's estimates ranged from four to 20 days. In spite of this commitment they did not feel that they should have any greater stake in the decision-making processes for the allocation of funds raised in this way. They felt it legitimate that

parents should have a major say, as they had made the major effort. In consequence, there was no general staff discussion to identify needs before a PTA
committee meeting.

The 'school fund'

The school raises money directly, in addition to PTA donations. Nearly
£10,000 per year is handled, mainly through one or other holding accounts for
regular school activities. Thus the school's swimming pool is managed on a
self-financing basis, with parents making voluntary contributions to cover the
costs of their children's swimming lessons. The money is then used for tuition,
pool heating and maintenance – costs which few LEAs are prepared to meet
these days. A separate fund handles weekly contributions from the parents of the
'fourth year' (10–11 year old) pupils who go away for a week in the summer term
to a residential study centre, to cover the costs of travel, subsistence and pocket
money.

The school organizes a 'tuck shop', where crisps are sold daily by pupils, and
whose profits amount to about £300 per year. As in most primary schools,
annual photographs of individual pupils reap a commission to the school – here
of about £150 – and a similar commission comes from an annual toy fair before
Christmas. A weekly bookshop is organized by one of the teachers, with an
annual turnover of about £1,200. This earns a commission of 15 percent from
the commercial firm providing the books for sale to pupils, taken in 'kind' as
extra library books. The children themselves also organize occasional 'shops' to
raise money for the school fund.

The monies so raised are used for a wide range of purchases which either the
head thinks that the LEA would not countenance, or for which LEA funds are
insufficient. The former category includes the school's hamsters and guinea
pigs, together with their cages and food; coffee for the mothers who meet in the
school on Fridays; ingredients for cookery lessons; and the contributions
towards the cost of educational visits for those children whose parents are unable
or unwilling to pay. Books dominate the second category, followed by various art
and craft materials.

The funds are controlled closely by the head – so closely that many staff are
not aware of them as being distinct from LEA funds or PTA donations. Careful
accounts of the minutiae of income and expenditure are kept by the head, and
are presented to the school's governing body after they have been audited each
year. The head sees none of the money, however, which is collected, banked and
recorded by the school's welfare assistant.

In general, the school is heavily dependent on non-LEA funds for its normal
educational operations. Even excluding the costs of swimming lessons, the total
sums received amount to some two-thirds of the LEA capitation allowance, and
when swimming is included, non-LEA funds equal capitation allowance. When
asked to estimate this figure only one member of staff estimated anywhere near

accurately, most of the rest underestimating by at least 50 percent. Teachers are not aware, then, of how dependent they have become on non-LEA funds, although several expressed some concern at this trend, partly because of a fear that growing PTA donations might encourage the LEA to reduce capitation allowances, and partly because of a realization that many schools do not enjoy the benefits of a supportive PTA – and that these tend to be in areas where levels of deprivation are already high.

Resource management and its relation to school policies and other aspects of school management

In this section the processes of resource management found at Milton Primary School are examined in relation to their impact on other aspects of the school, and particularly to the processes of policy making, evaluation and accountability in the school.

Resource management is a prime means by which policy is implemented, and a number of examples of this are seen at Milton. In general, school policies are not laid down formally by the head: however, it is well known by teachers that the head encourages some practices and wishes to discourage others, and that this is promoted through the ordering of school resources. For example, children are encouraged to write on plain (unlined) paper, and to write in ink, using a semi-italic handwriting style. These policies are supported through the purchase of inks, italic pens and plain paper, and by the restricted purchase of exercise books – although where teachers express a firm preference for exercise books, they are still made available. As explained by the deputy head:

> We are using stock ordering to influence school policies. For example printing inks. There weren't half as many when we started doing this. Now there are a lot of fabric printing materials, book-making and huge supplies of paper, but a dwindling stock of exercise books. Although children still do write in exercise books for certain lessons, most of their work goes in books they have made themselves. So they need the paper to do it on. So there we are making some changes, and discouraging some practices . . . we order the minimum number of (exercise) books, and that discourages people.

Other policies are less explicit, so that it is not clear as to the extent to which they are supported – or even recognized – by teachers appointed since the decisions were made. The head is committed to the development of pupil literacy through the provision of as wide a range of reading materials for pupils of all ages as possible, at the expense of class sets of textbooks or a single reading scheme, but some teachers perceived the lack of textbooks as a result of resource shortages rather than a school policy. Similarly, the head's belief in first-hand experiences has led to low priority being given to forms of teaching which emphasize second-hand experience, as, for example, through radio and television. The school's colour television was provided at the initiative of parent members of the PTA, and it is not yet backed up by a video recorder, rendering it a lot less usable than it would be otherwise, as the video recorder is accorded a lower priority than several other items of equipment. In some cases teachers perceived that the policies being followed were prescribed for the school by the LEA. Thus the introduction of the Nuffield Mathematics Scheme throughout the school, with the resource implications arising from the need to buy workbooks for all pupils, was thought, erroneously, by some teachers (appointed since the decision was made) to be an LEA decision – the LEA does not prescribe any specific mathematics scheme of work.

The school's resource management policies are recognized by teachers as being 'top down', with the head steering resources to achieve particular ends. Thus there is a policy of pump-priming in areas of identified need, and there are no expectations that resources should be spread evenly between age groups or curriculum areas in any one year. The thrice-yearly delivery of materials is in part the result of the school having limited storage space, but is also a deliberate resource management policy, in that demand is constrained towards the end of each term as stocks dwindle, and some items are used up.

In making resource management decisions, there is no formal consultative framework: consultation within the school, as in many primary schools, is informal – even casual. Staff meetings are held twice termly, but they would seem to discuss resource issues only rarely, dealing rather with administrative matters and operational curriculum issues. The annual requisition is not discussed at a staff meeting, and in 1983 the staff were not informed as to the total capitation allowance for the school.

Instead, most discussion about resources seems to take place informally in the staffroom over coffee, or as teachers meet in corridors and classrooms. The departmental meetings are also important arenas for resource discussions. The lower school team would seem to operate particularly cohesively in this respect – suggesting that the traditional autonomy of a primary school's infant department is not lost when that particular terminology is avoided!

Resource evaluation

As in most schools, the processes of evaluation in Milton are informal and piecemeal. The school was involved in the Schools Council's GRIDS School Self-Evaluation Project, in which the teachers collectively undertook an evaluation of their needs. They decided that they would spend the £500 grant received from Schools Council on calculators, manipulative apparatus and musical equipment, and that they would develop their individual competence as teachers of music so that the pupils would not suffer from the absence of a specialist music teacher. When asked as part of this case study how they would make use of an extra £1,000 for the school, half of the staff said that they would spend it on books, and a third of them referred to extra teaching hours, to assist pupils with special needs.

However, in spite of their experience in using self-evaluation strategies, there did not appear to be mechanisms for raising such issues collectively within the school, nor any consciousness among teachers either of themselves as 'resources', costing the taxpayer from £7,000 to £15,000 a year, or of the possibilities for evaluating the effectiveness of resource usage in the school.

Resource evaluation is more explicitly part of the work of the head teacher. In keeping with the management style at Milton, this is undertaken informally, as part of the head's daily rounds in the school:

> I'm in and out of the classrooms all the way through the day, and could tell you the kinds of equipment that every teacher needs: and I could tell you the equipment we've ordered and is never used. . . . When I see something happening that can be supported by a piece of apparatus that's not being used I go and get it (if they don't know about it) . . . but I don't make it deliberate policy, going off on my travels thinking 'what can I introduce today!' I do know the materials we have available, and because the teachers produce a plan of their work every term I know what's going on, and I know when that plan is drawn up roughly the kinds of materials that I can suggest can go in here, that they may not know about. I can also do it . . . when I'm actually visiting a class, either working with a group or going in and seeing what's happening . . . I don't make a policy of teaching every class every week or every so often, but I do go in on a supply basis (when one of the teachers is absent), and whenever I'm needed.

Commentary

The resource management system at Milton Primary School might be summed up as informal, centralized and efficient. The latter two characteristics are related in that the firm central control over the resource allocation procedures taken by the head reduces waste by avoiding the duplication of equipment and materials, and by restricting the accumulation of materials whose usage would be only occasional or limited to just one teacher. Resource investment is focused on items which are perceived to promote schoolwide policies, and to assure continuity and sequence in the educational experiences of the pupils. Conversely, covert forms of resource deprivation are employed to discourage approaches which are perceived as incompatible with those schoolwide policies. In consequence, teachers are encouraged, through the school's resource management policies as elsewhere, to see their responsibilities as extending beyond their own particular classroom and group of pupils, to encompass the school as a whole.

However, there are elements of the head's approach to resource management which might be seen to inhibit that broader, schoolwide perspective. In part these arise from the informality of the system; in part from the firm central control with its concomitant limited staff participation. The small size of most primary schools encourages informal rather than formal approaches to decision and policy making within the school. There are quite strong arguments, however, in favour of rather more formalization than is commonly found in this sector. The provision of clear resource information formally to all teachers is one simple way of doing this. Few schools provide a budget statement in which the expenditure of the capitation allowance is clearly itemized; still fewer schools compile a comprehensive budget, from which the resources acquired from LEA and non-LEA sources can be related to expenditure. If teachers are to take a professional responsibility for their schools and the resources with which they are expected to provide quality education, they need to know the resource constraints within which they are working. If they are to be asked to expend additional time and effort raising funds for the school, it is useful to be able to relate that effort to the particular resources thereby acquired. The [. . .] DES White Paper *Teaching Quality* (DES, 1983) underlined the relationship between self-assessment by schools and improved standards. Milton has been a pioneer school in the move to more effective forms of school self-assessment, but thorough and comprehensive evaluation is likely to require consideration of the effectiveness of the school's procedures for the mobilization, allocation and deployment of resources. This cannot be achieved without the relevant information available to all staff.

This in turn relates to issues of consultation and participation. In Milton these are more extensive than in many schools. All teachers are involved informally in the annual resource allocation procedures. There are again arguments in favour of some clarification and formalization of these procedures. Teachers drawing up lists of needs for their departments and curricular areas would benefit from the discipline of a budgetary target within which to work, individually and collectively. It might also be of benefit for them to be required to make out a case explicitly, either to the head or to a staff meeting, for the items requested and the priorities proposed. At the least this would be a useful form of staff development, promoting the acquisition and reinforcement of useful management skills. It is also likely to promote more effective resource management.

Some clear specification of the expected forms of consultation to be undertaken in drawing up lists of needs would also contribute to staff development and resource effectiveness. The inclusion of specified department and full staff meetings in a clear sequence of activities leading to the preparation of an annual order would not seem to be particularly burdensome. Such a sequence of consultative activities could form part of a relatively informal annual evaluation process, whereby the school looked back at the ways in which its policies and objectives had been achieved over the last year, and the resources required in the process, before looking forward to the next year's priorities with their related resourcing needs – and ways in which they might be met from both LEA and non-LEA allocations. In this way the extent of staff involvement in extra fund-raising activities could be adjusted to needs, rather than forming a semi-automatic annual cycle.

The approach outlined above would develop logically from the school's efforts already in self-evaluation. They might help to promote higher levels of satisfaction in the school's decision-making processes, as examined in the case study questionnaire which found substantial differences in the perception of half of the teachers between current practice and what they felt should be the practice (although it must be stressed that differences of perceptions between 'what is' and 'what ought to be' were smaller overall in Milton than in many other schools where this instrument has been used).

One final comment looks at the effect of a national climate of contraction and resource constraint on resource demand. Byrne (1974) and others have found at LEA level that financial stringency over a period of time has the effect of restricting demands for resources. There is some evidence for this process occurring within the school. It is not that resource shortages produce in teachers high levels of frustration because of their inability to undertake some types of teaching and learning activities. It is rather that the available resources and the class sizes lead to only those forms of teaching and learning which are compatible with the available resources being selected. The words of one teacher echo those of several others when he said:

> It's not often that I find myself unable to do something because the resources aren't there. Psychologically one knows that the money isn't there, and I tend to make use of what is available.

The effects of resource constraints on teaching and learning were spelled out lucidly by another teacher, who commented:

> (The head) will say once a year 'we've got the money: I have to warn you it's very little. Could you please write down what you think you'll need'. You go away and write out a list, bearing in mind what she's said about not having much money. . . . Ever since I've been teaching – five years it's been – we've been told so many times that they keep cutting back on spending that you don't bother to ask in the end, unless you're absolutely committed to believing that you desperately need this particular piece of apparatus or books.

References

BYRNE, E. (1974), *Planning and Educational Inequality*, Windsor, NFER Nelson.
DEPARTMENT OF EDUCATION AND SCIENCE (1983). *Teaching Quality* Cmnd 8836 London, HMSO.

Information technology in schools: responses and effects

David Lancaster

Introduction

One of the most remarkable changes in the technology of education, in both its broad and narrow senses, in British schools in the early 1980s has been the phenomenal growth in the use of microcomputers. In 1980 less than 5 per cent of secondary schools and virtually no primary schools had microcomputer facilities. Five years later almost every primary and secondary school had such provision. The adoption rate in education changed from nearly zero to 100 per cent within three or four years, which far exceeded the rate of growth in any other sector of the economy, and this at a time when the education system was contracting financially and in terms of numbers of clients. Why did that change take place and what are its effects within the education service?

This paper addresses these questions in relation both to the use of micro-computers for computer-assisted learning across the curriculum and in administration. The paper is not centrally concerned with the use of micro-computers in computer studies.

In this paper the development of the innovation in schools is related to promi-nent issues concerning technological innovation more generally. The first half of the paper addresses factors within schools and external to them which have affected schools' response to the availability of relatively low-cost micro-computers. In the second half the currently manifest and potential effects of the innovation in schools are considered in comparison with the impact of the microcomputer innovation in a range of other organizations.

Technological innovation can be categorized as 'needs pull' innovation, where a new product or process is developed to meet an identified need, or 'technological push' innovation, where the impetus is based on the technical capability to do something which was previously difficult or impossible. Some educators have advocated the use of computer-based instruction to provide learning experiences which are not available using a conventional teaching technology. However, although research has been and is being conducted on the effectiveness and efficiency of computer-assisted learning in various areas of the curriculum, the injection of resources into such developments has been carried out largely on the basis of an expectation of benefits rather than as a solution to a need identified in terms of the technology of learning.

A need which has been identified is for pupils to gain familiarity, confidence and skills with new technology in preparation for working life:

> Britain's greatest natural asset has always been the inventive genius of our people. This is the asset which we must tap if we are to profit from advances in technology. In microelectronics and information technology, we must do everything to encourage and train people with the ability and skills needed to design systems, write software and develop new businesses and products. We must start in our schools. The micro computer is the basic tool of information technology. The sooner children become familiar with its enormous potential the better.
>
> (Thatcher 1982, p. 1)

The innovation has been funded from many sources. The two major government initiatives have been the Department of Trade and Industry scheme, giving financial assistance in the purchase of (British-made) hardware, and the Microelectronics Education Programme (in Scotland the Scottish Microelectronics Development Programme), which are concerned with the production and dissemination of software and the provision of training. Local education authorities have to varying extents supported educational computing via funding of the purchase of hardware and software and the provision of training courses and advisory support. Schools have used some of their capitation and school funds for purchasing hardware and programs, and the purchase of computers has replaced minibuses as the target of many PTA fund raising efforts. The extent of resource commitment is very large. If each of 25,000 primary schools has an average of two microcomputers and each of 5,000 secondary schools has an average of ten microcomputers this represents a total of 100,000 computers, which at an average price of £500 (including those systems to which disk drives and/or printers are attached) represents a market value of £50,000,000 for equipment in the schools sector. The direct costs of training and the purchase of software probably push the total expenditure to date beyond £100,000,000, which at a time of financial contraction in the education sector represents a major input of resources. Indeed, it can be argued that it is possible to view educational computing as a resource-driven innovation in which schools have been given incentives to acquire microcomputers and then devise ways in which they can be utilized. Microcomputers may be viewed to some extent as a solution in search of a problem.

That may apply particularly to the administrative uses of microcomputers. There are few areas of school administration in which the need for computer processing has long been recognized and for which the barrier has been the availability at the right price of the appropriate hardware and software, though computer-assisted timetabling has been and still is a notable exception. The arrival of microcomputers in schools has certainly given rise to a vast proliferation of administrative applications and provides some support for the technological-push interpretation of the innovation.

A study of the innovation

To investigate the factors affecting the response to the innovation and its effects at the level of the school as an organization a research study undertaken by the author used both survey and case-study methods. A postal census of the approximately two hundred secondary schools in four LEAs, referred to here as Northlea, Southlea, Eastlea and Westlea, was carried out in 1984 and again in 1986. The response rates were 84 percent and 85 percent respectively. The surveys were carried out in parallel with longitudinal case studies in one school in each of the four LEAs, supplemented by interviews with relevant LEA officers and advisers, to enable the mechanism of the innovation to be studied. Although different sources of funding – capitation, fund raising events, funding from the DTI and LEAs – have been used to different extents, one source of funding which has had a major effect on the extent of information technology facilities in schools is the LEA. The extent of financial support from LEAs is directly related to the number of microcomputers per school in the different local education authorities. Westlea which provided the greatest financial support has the largest number of microcomputers per school, and Northlea which provided directly the least financial support has the fewest microcomputers per school. Differences in the average number of microcomputers per school in the different LEAs are statistically significant at the 0.1 level.

	Average number of microcomputers per school, 1984
Westlea	16.4
Eastlea	10.0
Southlea	8.6
Northlea	7.6

The number of microcomputers per school is, in turn, consistently related to various measures of the extent of use of computers for teaching purposes – for example, the number of subjects in which computers are used, the number of teachers who use computers in their teaching and headteachers' evaluation of the success of the innovation in terms of the extent of use in teaching.

The surveys found that the pattern of use of microcomputers is very different in different schools, both in the classroom and in administration. An obvious difference relates to priorities given to learning about computers (via examinable computer studies courses or computer appreciation courses) and learning with computers in different areas of the curriculum.

The relative priority attached to examinable computer studies is of considerable importance. According to one adviser:

If it didn't exist I think very few schools would want to invent it as this stage. It only exists for historical reasons. But given that it does exist it has all sorts of effects on whatever else goes on.

Those effects were explicated by an adviser in another authority:

> Some of the schools face a serious problem in that their computer studies work is very considerable and in some cases very successful and tends to dominate the use of equipment and so it is difficult to encourage the whole-school view because people feel that they are not going to get the resources to do it. So I can go into many departments and find a great interest, a great willingness to be involved, but a reluctance to do anything about it at the moment until they feel they are definitely going to have the resources to do it. And many of them find that the way that the resources are manipulated at the moment is so administratively frustrating that they are very reluctant to become involved. And so the development of that sort of policy depends on the school freeing the resources that are presently dominated by computer studies.

In the initial survey, in about half of the schools the main priority was attributed to computer studies, while in the other half computer assisted learning was stated to be of higher priority. In computer studies, approximately equal numbers of schools attached greater importance to examinable computer studies courses as to computer appreciation to all pupils in a particular year group or throughout the school. Within computer-assisted learning, the pattern of use is again highly variable between schools with examples of computer-assisted learning found in different schools in each of more than twenty areas of the curriculum. Similarly, within administration – although use in pupil records, option choice processing and word processing are the most common applications in those schools which used computer-based administration – a total of more than twenty different administrative applications were identified, though the average was only three applications per school.

The external pressures on schools to respond to information technology and the level of funding potentially available results in some schools in the attitude that 'computers are important; we should be doing something; who can do it?'

That may be indicative of a garbage can model of decision making (Cohen, March and Olsen 1976) in which the four streams of problems, solutions, participants and choice opportunities, merge. This innovation has been described earlier as partly a resource-driven innovation. When resources are provided by external organizations (Department of Trade and Industry, LEAs, Parent Teacher Associations) at a time of diminishing resources otherwise, and equipment enters a school in a highly visible way, a choice opportunity – 'an occasion when an organization is expected to produce behaviour that can be called a decision' (Cohen, March and Olsen 1976, p. 27) – arises. That can create a problem if there is a feeling that 'we ought to be doing something', but the rational decision-making approach (determining goals, evaluating alternatives relative to those goals, and choosing the optimal alternative) is felt to be impossible or inappropriate. In many such decision arenas goals remain obscure, perhaps by default, but also perhaps by intention – in situations of clashes of values and ideologies it may be possible to arrive at resolutions which are not

challenged when goals could not have been agreed. Different individuals may
have very different objectives but be able to agree that 'we ought to be doing
something'.

In those situations innovative ideas may be successful in a 'search' for problems, and it is possible for solutions ('A-level computer studies', 'computer-
assisted learning in geography', 'a computer awareness course for first-year
pupils', 'computerized timetabling') to emerge which both solve problems and
enable goals (perhaps different goals for different actors) to be discovered and
rationalized retrospectively. The range of solutions available depends, of course,
on the actors who are interested in participating in the choice opportunity.

Key organizational roles in schools

Given an expectation that schools will respond to information technology, and
funding to ensure that can happen at least to some extent, the innovation can be
of great symbolic importance. It is important that it is seen to be successful and
the uncertainty about how computer facilities will be used and with what effects
needs to be controlled and minimized. That scenario provides a classic opportunity for a 'project champion' to emerge – to build, to enhance or to risk a
reputation by backing and promoting the innovation. That opportunity has
been taken in many schools by a computer studies teacher. It has not occurred in
all schools, of course, and in some a person other than a computer teacher has
emerged as project champion. The computer teacher may choose not to get
involved in the innovation to a large extent, particularly as that involvement
may require a significant amount of the person's own time at weekends, vaca-
tions and so on. But in many schools the computer teacher has chosen to devote
considerable energy to the innovation.

There is certainly variability between schools, but a clear picture emerges that
computer studies teachers were perceived by headteachers to have more influence in determining the pattern of use than were headteachers, deputy headteachers, subject, general or information technology advisers, or, in respect of
administration work, clerical staff. As one headteacher said:

> In all honesty I haven't got much personal involvement with the computer. I do my
> best to encourage the various developments but I've not a great personal
> involvement. . . . It was a very good appointment when we appointed Alan. Not
> many schools placed the importance on computer education that we did at the time.
> We knew that we wanted someone who was a real expert in this field and we were
> lucky – we got Alan. We couldn't have found a better person. We've tried to get the
> best possible mileage out of him whilst he has been with us.

The extent of involvement of computer studies teachers has been closely associated with the extent of computer use and headteachers' assessment of its
success, both in the curriculum and in administration. For example, in the initial
survey there was an association, statistically significant at the 1 per cent level,

between the extent of involvement of computer teachers in the innovation and the number of teachers in a school using microcomputers in their teaching:

| | *Involvement of computer studies teachers* | | | |
	No involvement	Little involvement	Some involvement	Large involvement
Number of teachers using microcomputers	5.1	5.7	7.8	10.0

The influence of technical experts relative to headteachers and deputy head-teachers is particularly interesting in relation to administrative applications such as timetabling and option choice processing. These have traditionally been the responsibility of a deputy headteacher partly on the grounds that the main requirement was experienced educational judgement rather than technical pro-cessing of data. The relatively low influence which headteachers perceive them-selves and their deputies to have relative to technical experts is significant in respect of the consistent conclusion from research in business organizations in the 1960s at the time when computer systems were first being installed, on the relationship between managerial and technical influence in determining com-puter applications and the success of those applications. One of the major firms of management consultants (McKinsey and Co 1968) concluded that the key to computer success was strong leadership from senior management in directing the applications of the computers, and that where computers were ineffective it was generally because senior management had abdicated responsibility. Lamb, in relation to local government computing, similarly suggests that:

> Policy for computer development should be determined at senior levels, and priority in operation, development and equipment selection should not necessarily be control-led by a major user.
>
> (Lamb 1972, p. 230)

Stewart agrees:

> It is most important that management should not abdicate in the belief that it cannot understand or that it can safely leave computer development to the specialists.
>
> (Stewart 1971, p. 203)

Although there are differences between schools, the relative lack of senior man-agement involvement in many schools is a cause for concern in view of the conclusions of research in non-educational organizations.

There are substantial differences between schools within the same LEA in terms of the support received from advisers relative to that which the head-teacher would wish to receive, which tends to support the finding of Bolam *et al* (1975) of the 'adoption' of certain schools by advisers. In relation to administrative use, the lack of consideration of views of clerical staff, who might be expected to operate microcomputer equipment for some administrative tasks and to have some reservations about its use, is remarkable. Secretarial and clerical staff were perceived to have had very little influence in the decision about which, if any, administrative tasks were to be computerized, and the extent to which computer processing might result in an improvement or deterioration in the quality of jobs of clerical staff was taken into account in very few schools' decision making. The use of microcomputers by clerical staff is covered by new technology agreements in many local authorities, and although most head-teachers were aware of the existence or otherwise of a new technology agreement in their authority, there were significant numbers who admitted to not knowing the position (even in schools in which clerical staff were operating micro-computers), or where headteachers were wrong.

Effects of technological innovation

Innovations are introduced with the aim of changing organizations, but their introduction can have unintended effects in addition to those which were antici-pated. In evaluating the effects of the innovation of microcomputers in schools the model proposed by Leavitt *et al* (1973) provides a useful framework. If a school is viewed in terms of the Leavitt model as a system consisting of four main subsystems – people, tasks, technology and structure, then a socio-technical systems perspective would lead to the expectation that a change in one subsystem, such as technology, would result in changes in others. This model is consistent with the findings of much of the research work investigating the effects of the introduction of computers in non-educational organizations. Tomeski and Lazarus (1973 p. 21), for example, claim that:

> It is virtually impossible to introduce a computer into an organization without creating changes in work flows, structure and organizational relationships.

Two main types of effect of technological innovations, of considerable signifi-cance for schools, will be addressed here: firstly, effects at the level of the organization, and secondly, at the level of individuals working within the organization.

Effects on organizations

There are two different ways by which the introduction of computers may affect organizations. Firstly the computer may, intentionally or unintentionally affect job roles and the reasons and ways in which individuals and groups interact with each other, with changes in the formal structure following such changes in the operation of the organization. Secondly, the opportunities offered by the com-puter to bring about radical changes in organizational structure may be exploited. Lamb (1972) and Rowan (1982) suggest that the latter mechanism of change in structure is much less frequent than the former.

The impact on organizational structure depends, of course, very much on the uses of the technology. Mumford and Ward (1968) distinguish between the automation of existing tasks which may be associated with very little structural change and the use of integrated data-processing systems, where the structural consequences may be more extensive. That is clearly relevant, given that the trend in computer-based school administration systems is away from isolated applications and towards integrated systems.

The most extensive analysis of the structural consequences of the introduction of computers has concerned the centralization–decentralization dimension. When this was discussed in the 1960s in connection with the widespread introduction of mainframe computers, a major issue was whether the centralization of data inevitably or normally led to a centralization of decision making. Certainly one of the reasons for decentralized decision making – an overload on senior managers of information and its associated processing – was to some extent removed by the use of computers which thus enabled a recentralization of decision making. Whilst such centralization was more frequently reported than further decentralization, a common conclusion was that the use of computers could facilitate either centralization or decentralization. Gilman, for example, concluded that:

> The computer can serve equally well to support a move toward greater decentralisation as toward greater centralisation. If change in either direction develops, it will be the result of managerial choice, as it always has been. The computer's role in this respect is neutral – except as it offers the possibility to do what ought to be done in any case.
>
> (Gilman 1966, p. 89)

In education, it is useful to view centralization–decentralization at two levels, firstly within the institution and secondly in relation to the interaction between the institution and local and national government educational organizations.

Within the institution considerations similar to those addressed in relation to commercial organizations may apply to administrative work. In relation to the use of microcomputers for instructional purposes it is possible organizationally for the responsibility for and the physical location of equipment to be either centralized in, for example, a computer services department, or distributed, for example, with separate provision and responsibility being located in various teaching departments.

At the interface between the institution and the LEA the possibilities afforded by microcomputer technology to transfer information (particularly administrative information in the direction from the institution to the centre) for monitoring purposes clearly implies the possibility of increased central control. On the other hand, a number of LEAs are devolving some decisions, particularly financial decisions to institutions (Hinds 1982). In such cases the availability within institutions of appropriate microcomputer-based accounting systems may give the LEA increased confidence in the administrative systems within the institution and thus be a catalyst towards decentralization.

Effects on individuals

At the level of the individual, two areas of concern are relevant: effects on the number of jobs and effects on the content of jobs. The impact of new technology on job numbers is a major concern in non-educational organizations. It has also been identified as an issue by some teacher unions (e.g. NAS/UWT 1980) and this aspect of the concern of clerical staff unions, particularly NALGO, has been instrumental in the introduction of new technology agreements.

In terms of the effects on job content, the main emphasis in a substantial part of the literature on technological innovation, following Braverman (1974), is on the tendency for the introduction of new technology to be associated with job fragmentation, de-skilling and/or the polarization of skills. Although the focus of such analysis is mainly on manual jobs, Cooley cites evidence of the introduction of new technology resulting in the de-skilling of intellectual and professional jobs and views computers as 'the Trojan horse with which Taylorism is going to be introduced into intellectual work' (Cooley 1980, p. 1).

The educational technology literature, on the other hand, (for example, Hawkridge 1982) emphasizes the re-skilling effects on the role of the teacher – particularly a move from a traditional didactic role to that of a manager of learning.

Such concerns, of impacts on numbers of jobs, de-skilling or re-skilling, were reflected hardly at all in the responses of headteachers to questions about the effects of the introduction of computers on their own jobs and those of the staff within their schools. The majority of headteachers suggested that the use of microcomputers would have very little effect on their own jobs, other than by providing them with information more quickly. The effects were seen to be somewhat greater on the teacher's job and as a professional challenge to teachers to develop their own knowledge and expertise about microcomputers and hence to use them appropriately for the benefit of pupils. There were notable exceptions. One head suggested the effects on teachers were likely to be 'more than they realize!', but the overall response was that the effects were likely to be relatively small, and characteristic of the view of technology which Kanter (1974) attributes to 'traditionalists' rather than that which he associates with 'futurists'.

Schools, like other organizations, can be considered as being segmented both horizontally and vertically; the effects of technological change on job content are likely to be different in different horizontal and vertical segments. Areas where there is evidence in some schools of changes in job content are for computer studies teachers, deputy headteachers and clerical staff.

There are obvious advantages to computer studies teachers' career progression in involvement with other subject departments and with the administrative work of the institution. A number of them are taking an increasing advisory role in some other subjects in the curriculum, by searching in the educational computing press for information on available software, writing or modifying software, and providing technical advice and support to other teachers. In the administrative work of schools, some computer studies teachers are again becoming increasingly involved in the production, acquisition or evaluation of software for particular tasks but, more significantly and particularly for home-produced software, are often also taking the role of computer operator. There are many schools in which the tasks which were previously undertaken by clerical staff, for example, the production of pupil lists, are now being carried out by computer studies teachers. In some schools this has resulted from the provisions within new technology agreements, in others because clerical staff individually do not wish or have not been encouraged to become familiar with the equipment, and in others because home-produced software has been developed only to the stage where it can be made to work by the author but is not sufficiently robust to be used by others. Although in economic terms it could make sense for a computer studies teacher to process an administrative task in half an hour rather than that task being done manually by clerical staff in three or four hours, the transfer of some clerical work to the computer studies teacher is often a change which was not planned in advance. There is evidence in some schools, too, of some of the professional work commonly carried out by a deputy headteacher, for example in connection with timetabling, option group processing and the analysis of examination results, having been transferred to computer studies teachers. Whether these are permanent effects, or merely transitional, remains to be seen.

Conclusions

How can the concerns in the literature on technological innovation and the research findings in non-educational organizations on the effect of new technology on the jobs of both managers and others be reconciled with the perception of headteachers about those effects and with the evidence which has emerged so far within schools?

A concept which may usefully relate response to impacts, and the results of previous research in non-educational organizations with the author's findings in schools, is that of control. Studies in the health services, banking and retailing (Child *et al* 1984) have shown the effects of microcomputers on jobs to be related to the control over job content possessed by different occupational groups. Loveridge (1971) suggests that at an early stage of technological change or development, the attainment of expertise or control over the use of technology can enable the successful individual or group rapidly to grow in power and prestige.

In schools where the introduction of computers into administrative work and into the curriculum has been treated as a technical matter, the person who is in a position to control the 'critical uncertainties' (Hickson *et al* 1971), often the computer studies teacher, can be in a position of considerable influence. Pettigrew (1973) discusses a similar situation in which computer experts used their technical knowledge in 'managing dependency', in maintaining the centrality of their position in the decision-making process surrounding the introduction and use of a new computer system. This is associated with one of the most intriguing aspects of the effect of this innovation in schools – that relating to clerical staff, who have frequently been ignored in decisions about whether and how to use microcomputers and have often been by-passed when uses directly related to the tasks which they have commonly carried out have been introduced. We are concerned here, of course, with the control of job content, and specifically whether new technology can be used as a vehicle for the de-skilling of jobs, which is an issue of central importance in many sectors of the economy.

The potential for using microcomputer technology to de-skill and make more routine some aspects of the teacher's job is clearly antithetical to the professional norms of teachers and a process which, if perceived, will be resisted. As Etzioni (1969 p. 39) states:

> Most teachers apparently see the exchange of technical assistance as one which is theirs to control; ideas and suggestions may be solicited from various sources, but it is the teacher who tests them in the crucible of classroom experience. The norms maximize teacher freedom to seek assistance without granting authority to those who give it.

There is clearly a potential for microcomputers to be used as a means of introducing a more standardized curriculum, with individual teachers having less discretion concerning the content and delivery of curriculum topics. But the model of innovation underlying the production and dissemination of software by the Microelectronics Education Programme and the Scottish Microelectronics Development Programme takes into account recent thinking about educational innovation (e.g. House 1981; Fullan 1982) concerning the need for users to be able to adapt an innovation to the specific requirements of their teaching situation and preferred style. As one MEP officer stated:

> What is most acceptable in the classroom has been developed close to the classroom. . . . Past history must show that to treat teachers as just the passive receivers of materials developed from on high is courting disaster.
>
> (Avis 1985, p. 396)

This is in contrast with the research, development and diffusion strategy underlying the introduction of a number of computer-based administrative systems such as the Schools Computer Administration and Management Project (SCAMP) in Scotland, the Further Education Management Information System (FEMIS) and systems developed by a number of LEAs. The use of centrally designed administrative systems is clearly significant in terms of the control of what tasks are carried out and how they are carried out, and has obvious implications in terms of appropriateness and acceptability to users. Similar considerations apply, of course, to centrally produced teaching materials.

The conclusion at this stage must be that the technological determinism thesis in its crudest form is not supported – the introduction of microcomputers into schools does not have inevitable effects. The technology does, however, impose constraints on choice and makes some alternatives more attractive and others less attractive than they would otherwise be. Although some patterns of change are emerging, there are a range of possible consequences of the introduction of microcomputers into the curriculum and administrations, which are systematically related to the relative influence of key actors and explainable only in the context of processes of decision making in individual institutions. Although resourcing organizations, particularly central government and local education authorities, can significantly affect the *extent* of use of the technology, the *way* in which it is used and the effects which that has on job roles and organizational structures is primarily determined within individual schools.

References

AVIS, P. (1985). 'An LEA approach to software', *Education* 165(18):396.

BOLAM, R., G. SMITH and H. CANTER (1978). *LEA Advisers and the Mechanism of Innovation*, NFER.

BRAVERMAN, H. (1974). *Labour and Monopoly Capital*, Monthly Review Press.

CHILD, J., R. J. LOVERIDGE, J. HARVEY and A. SPENCER (1984). 'Micro-electronics and the quality of employment in services', in P. Marstrand (ed.) *New Technology and the Future of Work and Skills*, Frances Pinter.

COHEN, M.D., J. G. MARCH and J.P. OLSEN (1976). 'People, problems, solutions and the ambiguity of relevance', in J.G. March and J. P. Olsen (eds), *Ambiguity and Choice in Organisations*, Universitetsforlaget.

COOLEY, M. J. E. (1980). *Architect or Bee?*, Langley Technical Services.

ETZIONI, A. (1969). *The Semi-professions and their Organisation*, Free Press.

FULLAN, M. (1982). *The Meaning of Educational Change*, Teachers College Press, Columbia University.

GILMAN, G. (1966). cited in D. H. SANDERS (1974), *Computers and Management*, McGraw Hill.

HAWKRIDGE, D. (1982).*New Information Technology in Education*, Croom Helm.

HICKSON, D. J., C. R. HININGS, C. A. LEE, R. E. SCHNECK and J. M. PENNINGS (1971). 'A strategic contingencies theory of intraorganisational power', *Administrative Science Quarterly*, 16(2):216–229.

HINDS, T. M. (1982). 'Giving heads and governors the control of the purse strings', *Education*, 160(22):417.

HOUSE, E. R. (1981). 'Three perspectives on innovation: technological, political and cultural', in R. Lehming and M. Kane (eds), *Improving Schools*, Sage.

KANTER, J. (1974). 'Impact of computers on business organisations', in D. H. Sanders, *Computers and Management*, McGraw Hill.

LAMB, G. M. (1972). *Computers in the Public Service*, Allen and Unwin.

LEAVITT, H. J., W. R. DILL and H. B. EYRING (1973). *The Organisational World*, Harcourt Brace Jovanovich.

LOVERIDGE, R. J. (1971). 'Occupational change and the development of interest groups among white collar workers in the UK: a long-term model', *British Journal of Industrial Relations*, 10(3):340–365.

MCKINSEY and CO. (1968). *Unlocking the Computer's Profit Potential*, McKinsey and Co.

MUMFORD, E. and T. B. WARD (1968). *Computers: Planning for People*, Batsford.
NATIONAL ASSOCIATION OF SCHOOLMASTERS/UNION OF WOMEN TEACHERS (1980). *Microelectronics: Is there a Future for Teachers?*, NAS/UWT.
PETTIGREW, A. M. (1973). *The Politics of Organisational Decision Making*, Tavistock.
ROWAN, T. G. (1982). *Managing with Computers*, Pan.
STEWART, R. (1971). *How Computers Affect Management*, Macmillan.
THATCHER, M. (1982). 'Introduction' in Department of Industry, *Micros in Schools Scheme*, HMSO.
TOMESKI, E. A. and H. LAZARUS (1973). 'A humanised approach to computers', *Computers, Automation and People*, 22(6):21–25.

Section 5

Issues in staff management

Reference groups in primary teaching: talking, listening and identity

Jennifer Nias

> It's the teacher's disease. You have to talk about it all the time, get someone to listen, tell you you were right . . . It's a wonder we still have any friends, isn't it? But I couldn't manage without them . . .

In the tradition of symbolic interactionism, the individual knows of herself both as 'I' and as 'me'. The self is a social yet reflexive product, shaped by the responses of others but capable of initiating behaviour and reflecting upon it. Mature actors are self-conscious even though, paradoxically, they know themselves through their social identities. In the formation and maintenance of this reflexive relationship a crucial part is played by 'significant others', that is by those who have the most intimate socializing capability for the individual. It is through the responses of, for example, parents, siblings, and teachers to the actions of the developing 'I' that we come to see ourselves as others appear to see us and begin to incorporate this 'me' into our growing concept of 'I'. Cooley's 'looking glass self' is both the 'ego' formed through perceiving how others view the 'alter' and the 'alter' shaped by the initiated actions of the 'ego'. A distinction is also sometimes made between the self as 'ideal' and as 'real', although in this chapter I have not explored the potential of this difference.

As we grow older and our range of interaction increases the 'significant other' is supplemented by the 'generalized other', a term which Mead coined to describe an individual's understanding of the organized roles of participants within any defined situation. It does not refer to an actual group of people but to the supposed attitudes and opinions of others which are then invoked by the self for the regulation of behaviour. These views are often mediated through the beliefs and behaviours of 'reference groups', that is, groups which individuals use for self-evaluation and as a source of personal goals and values. Significant others are distinguished from the generalized other and from reference groups by their crucial role in early socialization and by the fact that normally they are or have been in direct contact with the person to whom they are 'significant'. By contrast, reference groups need not be friendship or membership groups and may indeed exist only in the individual's imagination. Their importance lies not in their physical but in their symbolic presence and their influence is transmitted by communication rather than by face-to-face contact. Membership of such a group is thus a question of identification, not of affiliation or allegiance. Indeed, it is possible for an individual's actions, taken in response to the norms of her reference group, to run counter to the interests of her membership group.

In addition, we all encounter many different social settings or are called upon to play varied roles. Symbolic interactionists therefore posit the existence of 'multiple selves' which reflect the individual's perception of herself (as both 'ego' and 'alter') in relation to the different groups in which she participates or with which she identifies. As these multiple selves are formed and negotiated, reference groups change, over time and with alterations in circumstances. They may even conflict, inducing the need for the resolution within the individual of dissonance between the warring 'selves'. [. . .]

In this chapter, I explore the normative and perceptual reference groups of ninety nine primary teachers as these relate to the defence of self. Elsewhere (Nias 1981) I described the varying self-perceptions and types of commitment which characterized these teachers' substantial selves. I argued that many of them chose teaching because they believed that as primary teachers they would be able to propagate or at the least live consistently with the values which formed the core of their professional activities. Here I show that values and personal identities were anchored in and sustained by in- and extra-school reference groups. For each individual, discussion with members of these groups served the interrelated functions of defending the substantial self and defining the reality to which that self had to react. As a result teachers who failed to find referential support within their schools – that is, who had no-one to whom they felt they could talk – came progressively to deny the social reality of adult life within them and, in many cases, left the profession. Those who found confirming responses within school from at least one other person gained the confidence to continue behaving consistently with their sense of self-image, even when this was divisive for the school as a whole. A few felt able to take the membership group of the school as a reference group, a development which strengthened their commitment and increased their job-satisfaction. For all except the last group, extra-school groups were of critical importance in defining and sustaining the individual's sense not just of personal but also of professional identity. Although primary schools are relatively simple in organizational terms, members of them evidently experience the conflict between frames of reference which for Shibutani (1955) characterizes complex societies. That they do so is a reflection both of their social isolation within school and of their access to others outside school who share their values and beliefs.

Data collection

[. . .] My enquiry relied heavily upon the personal accounts of ninety nine graduates who trained in one year Post graduate Certificate in Education courses for work in infant and junior schools and who had, at the time of interview, taught for between two and nine years. Two-thirds of them had attended, over five years, a course of which I was tutor. The remainder were a random sample who had between them attended similar courses at seven universities, polytechnics or colleges of education. Altogether there were thirty men, and sixty nine women the balance of sexes in each group being roughly the same.

I knew all the members of the first group very well, and three-quarters of them had been in touch with me between the time that their course ended and my enquiry began. Few of the second group knew me previously. To my surprise I found that members of both groups were not only equally keen to talk to a neutral but interested outsider about their professional experience, but that all of them were free (sometimes to the point of indiscretion) in their comments. Twenty two members drawn from both groups also kept a diary for one day a week for one term and the perspectives revealed in these accounts were very similar across the groups.

I contacted all the members of each group by telephone or letter. Six of the first group did not wish to be included in the project. With their prior consent, I visited in their schools (in many different parts of England) fifty three of the remainder and all the second group. I spent roughly half a day with each of them in their classes, making unstructured observations which I subsequently noted down before each interview. I also visited in their own homes twenty of the first group who had left teaching and were bringing up families. I had long telephone conversations with a further eight from the first group (six were at home, two teaching outside England). [. . .]

Pupils as reference groups

The most frequently invoked reference group of these teachers was pupils. Teaching is (notionally at least) a client centred occupation, so children naturally become a potent influence in shaping and reinforcing teachers' values and the actions which stem from them. In addition, teachers spend more time with their pupils than with their colleagues. It was common therefore to hear them say, 'I didn't much mind about anyone else, I had to make it work for them'; 'It doesn't matter that I don't agree with the rest of the staff, I can cut myself off from them by working with kids'; 'Blow the other (teachers) – I keep going because the kids enjoy what I'm doing and that tells me I'm right'. Since however many teachers work in physical isolation from each other and are protected even in open-plan schools by the 'norm of disregard' (Hitchcock, 1982), it was difficult for anyone to challenge their claims about client-satisfaction. In short, as long as classroom processes remain largely hidden from all except participants, pupils may be invoked as a reference group to justify many different decisions and types of behaviour.

Referential support for 'commitment'

Pupils then were the joker in the hand of every teacher, capable of being used to confirm any number of beliefs and practices. However, other reference groups specifically supported teachers in particular views of themselves. Earlier (Nias, 1981) I distinguished five senses in which these teachers were 'commited' to their occupation. Many were motivated by the desire to 'care and give' and about half of the total number expressed their debt to referential support for their political or religious views. This they received either through their own involvement in extra-school activities (e.g. 'I am a Christian first and everything else is shaped by that'; 'I couldn't keep going in teaching if I wasn't politically involved') or through their families. Many spoke of a Christian or Hebrew upbringing or of parents who were socially or politically active. Sustained by these forces they believed, for example, 'Most of what I do is because I think it's *right* to do that. It doesn't matter what the others do'; 'My own upbringing, my family especially – that's stronger than any influence in school'.

The lasting influence of such groups is encapsulated in the career of one particular talented and hard-working young woman, a convent-educated Catholic who had been actively involved in student protests at her university. She entered teaching believing strongly in the importance of cultivating creativity and individuality in her pupils, and her first teaching post, by her own choice, was in a self-styled 'progressive' school in a large city. There she was inescapably confronted by the dissonance between her frames of reference. All of the rest of the staff were committed to encouraging autonomy and creativity in their multi-ethnic, inner-city pupils. When she decided, at the end of her first year to give up teaching, she explained: 'The real problem for me was not being able to decide how much was up to the teacher. I'd spend the weekend making reading materials for (a seven-year old) because he needed to learn his phonics, and give them to him on Monday morning. When he turned round and said, ''Piss off, Miss, I want to make a monster'', I honestly didn't know whether he'd learn more about reading if I insisted he do the cards, or if I let him make a monster and then write about it. The rest of the staff were quite happy – they believed in the monster – but I could never completely see it that way. I felt I had a responsibility to teach him what he needed to know . . . It happened to me'.

Most were also committed to the pursuit of 'occupational competence'. In interviews they expressed their need for one or more reference groups which would help them to work out and maintain their own professional goals and standards. Ashton *et al.* (1975) have suggested that the factor most likely to distinguish among primary teachers in terms of orientations to teaching is their views on teachers' control over children's behaviour and learning. There is an alternative view, that teachers themselves see 'commitment' (and, in particular, acceptance of teaching as a professionally demanding occupation), as the most distinguishing characteristic. Certainly, it was the latter and not the former for which these teachers looked to the headteacher to 'set a standard' or 'to help shape my ideas' and were disappointed if he/she did not live up to this expectation

(Nias, 1980). In default of the head they turned to senior teachers. As one said, of an older colleague in her first school. 'He wasn't a model for the way I behaved, but it was tremendously supportive to find someone else on the staff who thought the way I did and was prepared to say so. That helped a lot'.

In addition, they frequently confirmed their own professional views and attitudes by using others as negative reference groups (Newcomb, 1943), that is, as groups of which they would not want to become members. Sometimes this took a general form (eg. 'It's easier to find teachers you wouldn't want to be like than ones you would . . . You don't meet many teachers who make you feel "That's the sort of person I'd like to be", do you? Usually it's the other way round'.) More often they located 'the opposition' or 'the enemy' (two phrases in frequent use) within their own school. However, as with negative role-models (Nias, 1984a), such polarization was normally made without intimate knowledge of the values of the teachers of whom they spoke. Moreover, teachers employing negative reference groups spread out along a wide political and ideological continuum. To assume, as sometimes happens, that graduate teachers see themselves as more 'progressive' than their fellows is to oversimplify their individual complexities and the rich variety of motivation which they bring to the job.

A minority were also committed to teaching because they saw 'being a teacher' as part of their self-image. The contact which they maintained with their own ex-teachers and tutors and sometimes with teachers in their families served to support them in this view. One said, 'All my family teach, and I didn't want to be the only failure – I *had* to keep on trying'. Another claimed, 'My family used to say, "You'll be a marvellous teacher one day", so I can't go back to them and say I've failed, can I?' This type of reinforcement was summed up by the man who said, 'Whenever I have doubts about whether it's for me, I go and see my old primary school head, he's retired now and he says "I've always seen you as a teacher – how's it going?", and I sit down and tell him'.

By contrast, three teachers bound by financial commitments and similar 'side bets' (Becker, 1960) but disillusioned by teaching, had rejected the teacher self-image. Instead, they had become privatized workers (Goldthorpe *et al.*, 1968). In the process they had adopted reference groups within their own and other schools which supported their psychological separation from their work. One man put it his way: 'It's a job – nothing more. I need the money, but I don't put more into it than I have to. My real life is with the band. That means I often come in exhausted in the morning – my main aim is to keep the kids quiet – off my back . . . I'm not the only one who sees it this way, you know . . . we talk about it . . . If society doesn't put itself out for us, why should we bother for them?'

In addition, a few teachers were, as Woods (1979) argues, 'committed' in the sense of being entrenched in an occupational structure. These alluded to reference groups which supported their aspirations in this or other concerns. Four teachers had begun seriously to aspire to senior posts and and were invoking the real or imagined standards of their local Deputy Heads Association or of headteachers generally. By contrast, others were using alternative groups to plan

futures in educational psychology, community and social work or in par-
enthood. Such normative groups helped individuals move from one career stage
to another, but they do not seem to have been especially influential in
determining subsequent educational policy or practice. Teachers who shaped
their behaviour by reference to a specific occupational group (eg. deputy heads)
still needed, once they had attained their new status, to seek or maintain a 'frame
of reference' which would help them translate their beliefs into action.

My interviewees did not see themselves simply as teachers. They also
regarded themselves as people with intellectual interests and capacities. Unfortunately, although they looked for appropriate referential support within their
schools, they tended to find it outside them. The cumulative effect of this was to
alienate many of them from teaching. One of my interviewees put it this way, 'I
didn't identify with (my colleagues) as people like me. I'm more aware of other
things outside school than someone who has been trained as a teacher and to do
the things teachers do'. Similar comments were: 'They're not like me, and I'm
not like them'; 'My educational reference group is certainly not in school – it's a
few intimate friends from university and scientists generally'; 'I'm intellectually
lonely at school. I'm the only one who reads *The Guardian*, the only one interested
in politics or literature and there is only one other who's ready to talk about art
and music'; (from a man teaching in an infant school) 'I love the children and the
work, but I have no contact with any adults with whom I have any ideas in
common. I feel intellectually starved'; 'For me, it was the three years at university that counted'; 'All our friends are doing postgraduate work, I've begun to
feel left out.'

It was this felt-need to maintain contact with the world of ideas and of passion-
ate debate that led several teachers towards advanced courses, kept them actively
involved in politics or para-political organizations (such as the Child Poverty
Action Group), reinforced their ties with non-teacher, graduate friends, caused
them to remember their university teachers or PGCE courses with enthusiasm
(eg. 'It was there that eduction became ideals, not just ideas in the file'; 'My
course made me interested in ideas – even more than in practicalities'). Two
had begun to write for educational journals, three were actively seeking posts as
college lecturers or advisers. Three left junior school work for posts in further
education and two took jobs as specialists in secondary schools 'because I miss
the stimulation of my subject'. [. . .]

In-school reference groups

Reference groups within the school varied considerably in size. Many teachers
appeared to need the referential support, 'to confirm my values', of only one
other, be it colleague, headteacher or sometimes adviser. The mutual support
afforded by such a person was out of all proportion to either the size of the group
or the time spent in communication. The existence of 'just one other' confirmed
their goals and aspirations, kept them from leaving the school, supported them

in innovation or retrenchment, deepened their satisfaction and fuelled their discontents. As one teacher said of such a reference person, 'We fed each other'. Such pairing may be a launching pad for new ideas or a powerful obstacle to change within the pair and amongst their colleagues. It can also have a destructive effect upon social relationships within the school as a whole.

Indeed, the influence of school-based reference groups upon their members was not always seen as working in the direction of greater professional commitment. A few teachers candidly said, for example, 'We make each other lazy'; 'It's difficult to work hard if no-one else does. The norm here is about putting teachers' interests first'; 'It was better when she left . . . I'd begun to share her lack of commitment to the job', and 'I know I'm a worse teacher than I was three years ago. It's difficult to do what you think you should do when you know you're an island. If only there was just one other person in the school who shared my ideas'. They described themselves as 'feeling less worried by my own conscience', 'learning to grow a skin when things aren't perfect,' 'learning to compromise'. Siegel and Siegel (1973) argue that individuals are particularly strongly influenced by membership groups which become reference groups. These comments may reflect, for some teachers, attitude changes resulting from a realignment of this kind.

In a few instances, individuals were able to point to a group of like-minded colleagues. When such a group existed, it tended also to be seen as a membership group. As such, it had a social dimension which strengthened its referential impact (see also Sherif and Sherif, 1964). Members could identify one another and indicate where they usually interacted (eg. 'We have a pub lunch once a week'; 'We stay behind after school'; 'We don't talk in the staffroom but we often meet in (the year leader's) classroom'; We're the mob in the corner – you'll see us there at lunchtime most days').

Moreover, when a reference pair or group developed an affective (as distinct from social) dimension it could become a potent force within a school. Three examples make this point very clearly. In one case, a value difference brought to the surface by a new headteacher led to the formation of a forceful staffroom group ('There's four of us – all women. We share the same political views, we do a lot socially together and two of us live together. He'll find it hard to break us up . . .'). In another, a married couple who taught together in a double unit, each independently said to me, 'I don't listen to what anyone else on the staff says. They all think differently to me, and now I'm working with (my spouse) I can just talk to him/her and we support each other'. Thirdly, two teachers working as a team – each married to teachers in other schools – began to live together. They explained: 'To make the team work we had to talk a lot, and that meant we spent a lot of time together and we began to realize how many ideas we had in common and how much we liked each other . . . well, team-teaching, especially in a shared unit, has to be a bit like a marriage if it's going to work, you have to want the same things, have the same values, and if one of you is male and the other's female and you obviously get on well together, the kids begin to treat you like mum and dad . . .'.

On the rare occasions that a whole staff was perceived as being concurrently a membership and reference group, it had a powerful effect upon its members. Five teachers spoke of being at schools where 'we accept that we all have common beliefs and that gives us a common basis for discussion,' or 'there's a basic level of understanding and therefore we can disagree and there's lots of lively talk in the staffroom'. By contrast, I was given three examples of staffs which were so tightly knit, philosophically and socially, that other teachers felt 'driven out – they had to leave if they wanted to survive'. In all of these cases, shared goals and standards were reinforced by joint social activities (eg. staff parties, theatre visits) and by a good deal of open discussion.

Extra-school reference groups

Unfortunately, at some point in their careers, the majority of my interviewees found themselves in a school in which there was no group other than pupils by reference to whom they could affirm their values. So great was their felt-need for referential support that, lacking it in one school, they actively sought for it outside. They went on courses (see also Schools Council, 1981). Some claimed: 'I don't care whether or not the rest of the staff approves of what I'm doing, but I do wish I had someone to discuss my ideas with. I'm so desperate I've signed up for a course at the Polytechnic' and 'I go to courses for reassurance/to listen to people agreeing with me/to find someone like-minded to talk to'. Others became involved in politics or union activities (eg. 'Branch meetings give you a chance to meet people who think like you do'), returned to their training institution or the friends they made there (eg. 'I don't see all that much of them, but I'd hate to lose touch with them because they're there to talk to if I need them'; 'I draw a lot on the PGCE course. It's there in my mind and bits come back . . . I suppose that's why I keep in touch with (my tutor). It keeps me from losing all my ideals which I would if I just listened to the teachers (in my school)'. This piece of research really started when an ex-student from my PGCE course came back three years later from 300 miles away to talk about her work and said, 'I do wish you could come and see what I'm doing now. No-one at my school seems to care and I'm losing heart'. Many others telephoned, wrote, dropped in at half-terms or in the holidays. 'No,' said one, 'I didn't really want your advice. I just wanted someone to tell me I was right'. It appears to have been for that reason too that several turned to educational books and, especially later in their careers, sought confirmation for their ideas in the writing of educationalists as widely disparate as A.S. Neill, Chris Searle and Rhodes Boyson. As one said. 'You need to know that someone else shares your views – someone with a wider view than teachers can have'.

Individuals also looked to teachers in other places – different schools, family and university friends, their own families. Ten teachers had kept in touch with a particular teacher or headteacher from a previous school at which they had taught, either before or after training, and regarded him/her as a 'very influential person in my development'. Most had teacher friends whom they perceived as very important (eg. 'If you're isolated you begin to question whether you're right'; 'I've got one friend from another school and we meet in a pub once a week . . . it helps reinforce your belief that you are right'). Four referred to people who had taught them at school (eg. 'I still keep in touch with her, I'm always interested in what she has to say about education'). Eleven of the men were married to primary school teachers and eleven of the women to secondary school teachers (none to primary school teachers). Despite the relatively small number of spouses in like employment most (but not all) of the sample cited their spouse as someone with whom they discussed their educational problems and ideas 'all the time'. One said, 'He's never been inside the school and I don't think he'd want to, but he really helps me sort my ideas out. He's a sort of touchstone, I suppose. If he thinks it's OK then it usually works'.

Parents were important too (eg. 'My father (a retired HMI) – I ring him a lot'; 'My mother still teaches and I talk to her a good deal') and even more frequently cited were parents-in-law (eg. 'Richard's mother kept me going. We used to go to see her in the holidays and she used to support me in what I was trying to do'; 'Frank's father is a headmaster of a junior school (in another part of the country) and I rely a lot on his reassurance.') Siblings (especially sisters) were occasionally mentioned. Five referred to their own children (eg. 'I think – would I want that to happen to them?'). [. . .]

Conclusion

Members of this group of primary teachers were characterized by a strong sense of personal identity which was by definition unique to each individual, but which contained many common elements. In particular, they saw themselves as 'committed' to teaching, especially as an occupation which would enable them to pursue humanitarian ideals and as a job which they wanted to do well. Some also saw themselves as 'being teachers' and a few as entrenched in a career structure. Most also perceived themselves as people with intellectual interests and concerns. These attitudes to themselves appear to have been deeply embedded; certainly individuals used a number of strategies to defend them from influence or assault by their colleagues and headteachers. Chief among these was the use of reference groups, especially as a perspective-confirming device. In Shibutani's (1955) terms, they defined reality through, communicated with and directed their actions towards selected audiences, many of whom had existed long before they made the decision to teach. The traditional isolation of the classroom teacher and the reluctance of many primary school teachers to engage in a potentially conflictual debate about ends served to confirm them in membership of these groups. Lack of appetite and/or opportunities within school for the discussion of values impeded the negotiation of new attitudes so, needing the confirming responses of others, they sought contact (often by telephone, if meeting was difficult) with those who they knew would provide such support. The more ego-gratifying this reinforcement, the less incentive there was to talk to their colleagues, and the more isolated they became within school, fortified in their personal convictions by contact with those outside it.

To be sure, these teachers were not impervious to the pressures of the membership group. In particular, they found it hard to sustain social isolation. As a consequence, they sometimes aligned their frames of reference more closely with those of their colleagues; more often they changed schools or left the profession. In addition, pupils became very important to them as a reference group. However, the presence on the staff, or among those very closely associated with the school, of only one other person with similar aims and values, frequently enabled individuals to sustain their sense of personal identity, to preserve their substantial selves. A reference group need not, it appears, be numerous, as long as the reality it stands for can be symbolically confirmed within the adult world of the school by a single representative.

Reference groups, it seems, may simultaneously promote and impede the development of the profession and of the individual within it. On the one hand, they are crucial in establishing and maintaining shared values among groups of teachers, a state which, if achieved, facilitates mutual understanding and provides encouragement and support in a lonely occupation. On the other, they may frustrate the negotiation of shared collegial norms. Reference groups used for the defence of one set of values can obstruct the open discussion of and agreement on others.

Viewed this way the notion of reference group membership is an important key to our understanding of schools' often-reported imperviousness to change. When these teachers reported having modified their practice they usually claimed it was out of a felt-need to survive socially within the staff group, or because they found identification with a particular sub-group in school to be in other respects reinforcing of their sense of identity. In most cases they did not change but continued to act in ways which were consistent with their view of their substantial selves. In this they were supported by referential contact, within the school or outside it. In other words, opposing views of reality, confirmed by communication with distinctive groups, led to actions which were directed to different audiences (whether real, imaginary or potential).

In short, teachers may hear what is said to them but not respond to it because they are listening to other voices. There are times, of course, when such deafness may be beneficial to the development of the profession as a whole. Equally however the formation within one school, or across many, of well-defined sub-groups with divergent aims may impede collective progress or distract attention from the need to tackle common problems. The problem then becomes one of helping teachers to overcome this kind of selective inattention to their colleagues' voices. One answer may be to provide opportunities and encouragement within primary schools for teachers to talk to one another about those aspects of their jobs which really matter to them. If the person makes the agenda, the practitioner may join in the debate.

References

ASHTON, P. *et al.* (1975). *The Aims of Education*, London, Macmillan.

BECKER, H. (1960). 'Notes on the concept of commitment', *American Journal of Sociology*, **66**, pp. 32–40.

COOLEY, C. H. (1964). *Human Nature in the Social Order*, New York, Schocken Books.

GOLDTHORPE, J. *et al.* (1968). *The Affluent Worker: Industrial Attitudes and Behaviour*, vol 1., Cambridge, Cambridge University Press.

HITCHCOCK, G. (1982). 'The social organization of space and place in an urban open-plan primary school', in Payne, G. and Cuff, E. (eds), *Doing Teaching*, London, Batsford.

MEAD, G. H. (1967). *Mind, Self and Society*, Chicago, University of Chicago Press.

NEWCOMB, T. (1943). 'Attitude development as a function of reference groups: the Bennington Study', in Maccoby, E., Newcomb, T. and Hartley, E. (eds), *Readings in Social Psychology*, London, Methuen.

NIAS, J. (1980). 'Leadership styles and job-satisfaction in primary schools', in Bush T. *et al.* (eds), *Approaches to School Management*, London, Harper and Row.

NIAS, J. (1981). 'Commitment and motivation in primary school teachers', *Educational Review*, **33**, pp. 181–90.

NIAS, J. (1984a). 'Learning and acting the role: in-school support for primary teachers'. *Educational Review*, **36**, 1–16.

NIAS, J. (1984b). 'Definition and maintenance of self in primary teaching', *British Journal of Sociology of Education*, **5**, 267–280.

SCHOOLS COUNCIL (1981). *Making the Most of the Short In-Service Course*, Working Paper 71, London, Methuen.

SHERIF, C. and SHERIF, M. (1964). *Reference Groups: Exploration into Conformity and Deviation of Adolescents*, New York, Harper & Row.

SHIBUTANI, T. (1972). 'Reference groups as perspectives', in Manis, J. & Meltzer, B. (eds.) *Symbolic Interaction: A Reader in Social Psychology*, 2nd edition, Boston, Allyn and Bacon. Originally published in *American Journal of Sociology*, **60**, pp. 562–69, May, 1955.

SIEGEL, A. and SIEGEL, S. (1973). 'Reference groups, membership groups and attitude change', in Warren, M. and Jahoda, M. (eds), *Attitudes*, Harmondsworth, Penguin.

WOODS, P. (1979). *The Divided School*, London, Routledge and Kegan Paul.

5.2

Some legal aspects of employment in schools

Geoffrey Lyons and Ron Stenning

[This is an edited version of a chapter of a book which reports on research, funded by the DES, and carried out by the authors between 1981 and 1985, on how managers in maintained secondary schools – especially headteachers – conduct employment relations in their schools. Its major purpose was to help heads to become more effective managers by giving guidance and providing training materials on the processes of staff management (see also Lyons and Stenning (1986) *Managing Staff in Schools: Training Materials*. The chapter below deals with some ways in which employment law influences the day-to-day management of staff and the problems which may arise if legal requirements are not understood fully.]

Introduction

As the manager of the school the headteacher is involved in:

- writing job advertisements
- staff appointments
- allocation of duties
- staff promotions
- maintenance of staff discipline
- staff dismissal
- health and safety

This list is not exhaustive but it includes the key processes of staff management, and all of these functions have legal implications.

Consider these incidents taken from real life:

1 Shortly after she was appointed, a teacher told the pupils that they needed extra coaching in French and that she was willing to do this for a fee outside school hours.

Q *What advice would you give this teacher with respect to her contractual obligations?*

2   Two teachers refused to comply with the deputy headteacher's instruction that they go to their respective classrooms and take their classes.

Q   *What is the contractual significance of this incident?*

3   A teacher could not account properly for the money given by the pupils towards a holiday trip.

Q   *Is the contract of employment relevant in this case?*

4   A headteacher placed a note on the staff noticeboard which stated that he had promoted an existing member of staff. This was the first the staff had heard about the potential promotion opportunity and the LEA had not been informed. *

Q   *What are the contractual implications arising from the headteacher's action?*

Headteachers who can confidently answer the questions posed in relation to these incidents may not wish to read any further. However, it may be prudent for them to check their answers against those provided at the end of this [chapter]. For less confident readers, the primary purpose of this [chapter] is to provide a *layman's* guide to matters which are of common concern to those with responsibility for the conduct of staff management in schools. To this end, emphasis is given to what is usually termed employment law.

The following text proceeds from a brief discussion about recent developments in employment law. This provides the broad context for an examination of some relevant provisions of selected statutes. These have been identified with reference to the list of staff management functions indicated above, and are thereby what the effective headteacher needs to know. ** [. . .]

Trends in employment law

There was relatively little statute law concerned with individual rights in employment until the early 1960s. This was because employers, unions and successive governments were agreed that workplace relationships were largely a matter for the parties directly involved and that the settlement of differences was best achieved by voluntary rather than legal means. There was, of course, the common law and disputes about breaches of contract were based on common law rights, though in the main employers and employees chose not to exercise these rights.

Over the past twenty years employment statutes have become the most significant feature of public policy concerned with employment relations. This reflects an important departure from the voluntary tradition since all sectors of employment, including education, are governed by a comprehensive legal framework.

The main themes of this legislation have been as follows:

• extension of individual rights
• anti-discrimination

*A commentary on the incidents presented in the text is provided at the end of this chapter
**For further legal guidance see Lyons, G & Stenning R (1986) pp. 37–50

- strengthening of trade union rights
- reduction in trade union power

These strands of public policy may be identified to a greater or lesser extent with the following legislation:

Contract of Employment Acts 1963 and 1972*
Redundancy Payment Acts 1965 and 1969*
Equal Pay Act 1970
Trade Union and Labour Relations Act 1974 and 1976*
Health and Safety at Work Act 1974
Employment Protection Act 1975*
Sex Discrimination Act 1975
Race Relations Act 1976
Employment Protection (Consolidation) Act 1978
Employment Act 1980
Employment Act 1982

This legislation is extremely significant for the conduct of staff management in the school. The prudent headteacher will, therefore, keep abreast of the main points of the law and especially cases that occur in the education service.

Unions representing both teaching and non-teaching staff have long recognised the importance of briefing their lay representatives about the relevant provisions of the law, especially those relating to employment protection and the contract of employment.

The main concern here is to examine some major aspects of the legislation applying to individual employees, rather than the legal provisions relating to collective employment matters. To this end, the contract of employment is the first major point of reference.

Contract of employment

5   An assistant caretaker sold plants grown in the school greenhouse to the pupils.
Q   *Does the law of Contract offer any guidance in this case?*

The contract of employment is the fulcrum of the employment relationship between individual members of school staff and the employer. In essence, a 'contract' means a bargain between two people which is legally enforceable. Thus the contract of employment is effectively a bargain whereby the parties to the contract agree to do something in exchange for an act or promise from the other side.

It should be noted that a contract of employment exists between the employer (either the LEA or governing body of the school) and an employee from the time the offer of employment is made and the employee's acceptance of the offer.

---

*The Employment Protection (Consolidation) Act 1978 brought together in one Act the provisions on individual employment rights previously contained in these earlier Acts. It was itself amended by the employment Acts of 1980 and 1982.

Further, while the headteacher is not normally empowered initially to formulate the substance of the employment contract, as the person responsible for the conduct of staff management within the school, the headteacher inevitably influences the way(s) in which contractual relationships develop, such as the introduction of rules applying to staff.

Sources and elements of the contract of employment

- job advertisement
- selection interview
- letter of offer and acceptance of appointment
- job description
- custom and practice
- LEA rules
- school staff rules
- collective agreements between employers and unions
- statutory minimum individual rights
- common law terms

These are the main sources of the employment contract and these are elaborated below. First consider these questions:

Can you give an example of an 'express term' in your contract of employment?

Can you give an example of what might be 'implied' in your contract of employment?

The two main elements of the contract are the terms which are *express* and those which may be *implied*. These can be a major source of difficulty where there is a difference over the interpretation of an employment contract.

The contract of employment reflects changes of procedure and substance over time. The terms of the contract include not only those expressly agreed between the individual teacher and the employer, but also those implied from other sources. Express terms can either be in writing or they may be verbally agreed between the parties to the contract. The letter of appointment, and a verbal explanation of the system of staff 'free' periods in the school, are two examples of what might constitute express terms of the contract.

Where a contract of employment is reasonably detailed the express terms usually pose few problems, at least in statute law, because the interpretations of the contract by the parties concerned are necessarily constrained by the governing legal provisions. However, it is not uncommon for differing opinions subsequently to emerge of what was said or promised at a selection interview, and great care should be taken by the participants to ensure that the contractual position is clarified before offering and accepting an appointment.

Consider this case:

6　A teacher was appointed as a full-time permanent teacher (with a standard contract of employment) in charge of the Resources Centre at the school. She was told at the time of her appointment that she would be required to apply herself almost full-time to the Centre's work. To begin with she had no regular teaching commitments, but after two years she was instructed by the headteacher to teach eighteen lessons a week. The teacher refused to comply with this instruction.

Q *What advice would you give the headteacher in this case?*

[. . .] Headteachers should make every effort to familiarise themselves with both national and local collective agreements on conditions of employment in education and the associated provisions which are part of the individual teacher's contract of employment. [. . .]

[If] national collective agreements concerning such matters as the 'teachers' day' and duties do not exist the implied terms of the contract, which may be drawn from common law, custom and practice, are a very important feature of employment relations in the school. In circumstances of mutual recognition of obligations and duties the implied terms of the contract of employment are rarely an issue.

[. . .] Reference to what the individual contract states is an obvious starting point, followed by an investigation into the local and national agreements operating at the time.

Changes in the contract

Consider these cases:

7   A typist in the school office was informed by the headteacher that her working hours were to be reduced from 18 hours to 12 hours a week.

Q   *Is this unilateral change in the terms of employment contract permissible in law?*

8   The headteacher instructed the school caretaker to clean the windows on the second floor of the school. Previously they had been cleaned by 'contract' window cleaners 'employed' by the LEA. The caretaker refused to comply with the instruction.

Q   *What are the contractual implications here?*

It was indicated above that the contract of employment is subject to change over time. For the contract to remain in being, however, there has to be agreement between employee and employer about any changes in its terms. Of course, if an existing term allows for a change by reference to a collective agreement, then this is permissible under the contract. It is not unusual for a headteacher (knowingly or otherwise) to attempt to change the terms of the contract.

If the member of staff concerned concurs and continues to carry out the assignment, then the courts usually find that the employee has agreed to the different arrangements or changes in the terms of the contract. There is the reservation that if the employer unilaterally changes the terms of employment and the employee works under the new terms, that is not sufficient evidence of agreement with the new terms. The employee can, during a 'reasonable period', try out the new terms before losing the right to resign and claim unfair dismissal or redundancy. A difficulty here is that a 'reasonable period' is not (except in the case of redundancy) defined in law. Thus it will be determined by the courts with reference to the particular circumstances.

An employee who is dismissed for not agreeing to a change in the terms of contract may, in certain circumstances, successfully claim that the dismissal was unfair. Thus the local Authority that dismissed seventeen school dinner ladies who refused to accept new contracts (which reduced their holiday entitlement and discontinued half-pay holiday retainers) were judged by an industrial tribunal to have been dismissed unfairly. The chairman of the tribunal declared that 'the county effectively tore up the national agreement which covered the employment of the ladies'. The decision of the tribunal was subsequently upheld by the Court of Appeal.

In accordance with the legal doctrine of 'freedom of contract', no court will normally order an employee to accept a contract, nor will an employer be ordered to employ a particular person. The courts' jurisdiction is with the award of compensation (damages) where one party to the contract breaches the rules mutually agreed.

Part-time employees

There is no legal definition of a 'part-time' worker, and under *common law*, whatever hours are worked, part-time workers have the same rights and obligations as full-time employees. However, under *statute law* employees whose contract of employment normally involves them working less than sixteen hours a week are excluded from certain rights; though those who are contracted to work at least eight hours a week gain similar protection to full-time workers if they have at least five years' continuous service with the same employer.

Temporary contracts may be fixed term or open-ended, but may terminate upon the occurrence of an anticipated event. Such contracts are extensively used in the following circumstances: to cover a member of staff who is ill over a long period; to stand in for a teacher on maternity leave; where there is a delay in filling a vacant post on a permanent basis; and to cover staff undertaking in-service training.

Thus, such contracts can, to some extent at least, relieve the headteacher of the burden of arranging for the permanent members of staff to cover for colleagues absent through illness or as a consequence of maternity leave. They facilitate the professional development of permanent staff because of the opportunity to engage in training activities outside the school or indeed within the school. Temporary contracts also provide a means of introducing 'new blood' into the school if only for a given period of time. These contracts may also relieve the pressure for making a permanent appointment from among an unsuitable list of candidates, for example, so that more time may be spent to ensure the school gets the person that it is seeking.

Temporary appointments are also made, however, in circumstances of school reorganisation, usually as a consequence of falling rolls and/or budgetary reasons. This can lead to staff tensions for a host of reasons including insecurity of teachers on temporary appointment and frustration by their permanent colleagues who believe their opportunities for career advancement may be reduced as a result of vacancies being filled by temporary appointments. The headteacher may thus be confronted with problems of staff motivation and poor morale with all that implies for innovative activities.

Consider this question:

9 Is it necessary to give notice to a teacher who is on a fixed term contract of employment?

Given the complexities of the contract of employment, effective staff management requires the headteacher to:

- take great care when writing job advertisements
- be alert to the dangers of making injudicious statements when appointing staff
- make sure they understand the contractual obligations of their staff
- keep abreast with national and local collective agreements for both teaching and non-teaching staff
- take heed of the LEA rules and notes of guidance relating to employment contracts of school staff
- beware of the advice offered by other headteachers (they may have been lucky!)
- seek proper legal advice from the LEA where there is any doubt about the most appropriate form of action to take in respect of the contracts of staff

Individual statutory minimum rights

The extension of the legislation concerned with the individual 'rights' of employees was identified earlier. These flow from a number of statutes but it is the contract of employment which, to a large extent, determines whether the 'rights' legislation applies.

The headteacher is involved in decisions about the following matters:

- staff dismissal
- time off for staff union representatives
- staff redundancy
- staff maternity leave

What 'rights' does the law confer here, and in what circumstances?

Common law 'rights' apply irrespective of whether the contract of employment relates to full or part-time employees. However, the Employment Protection (Consolidation) Act 1978 and the Employment Act 1980 provide a wide range of individual statutory rights, most of which are allied to the length of continuous service of an employee. A selection of these 'rights' are summarised in the table below, together with the related continuous service requirements.

While there are a number of other 'rights', they have been excluded because they are outside the headteacher's sphere of concern.

It will be noted that 'part-timers' as defined below do not enjoy some of the statutory rights which only apply to full-time employees. Further, statute law is concerned only with providing minimum employment rights to individuals. Employers may therefore provide better terms than those prescribed by law; here the headteacher needs to check on:

- the local agreements between the LEA and unions(s)
- the national agreements between the employers and union
- the individual staff contracts of service
- the related conditions of service documents

Having indicated the link between the individual rights legislation and the contract of employment, attention needs to be addressed to those aspects which have got many headteachers into 'hot water', beginning with employee dismissal (see Table 5.2.1).

Table 5.2.1 Statutory rights and minimum length of service required

Statutory rights	*Minimum length of continuous service required*
1 Protection from unfair dismissal	1 year
2 Written reasons of statement for dismissal	6 months
3 Protection against dismissal on the grounds of pregnancy	1 year
4 Protection against dismissal on the grounds of union membership activities	None
5 Time off for trade union duties or activities	None
6 Maternity pay entitlement	2 years
7 Pregnancy – pre-natal visits	None
8 Right to return to work after confinement	2 years
9 Entitlement to redundancy payment	2 years
10 Time off to look for work if under notice of dismissal for redundancy	2 years
11 Protection against sex or race discrimination	None

Dismissal of staff

Dismissal can take any of the following forms:

- termination of employment by the employer with or without notice
- termination of employment owing to redundancy
- constructive dismissal
- refusal by the employer to allow a woman to return to work following pregnancy

- refusal by the employer to renew a fixed term contract that has expired

While the legislation details what constitutes unfair dismissal, it is for the tribunals to decided whether a particular case of dismissal was fair or unfair.

There have been many instances where the intention to dismiss a member of school staff has not resulted in the lawful termination of the employment contract, usually because of one or more of the following reasons:

- a failure of the headteacher to provide the evidence that would justify dismissal
- the headteacher did not observe the appropriate procedure
- the LEA did not observe the appropriate procedure
- the inadequacy of the procedure was recognised by the LEA or industrial tribunal
- the decision to dismiss was based on inadmissible reasons

In circumstances of a dismissal of a member of school staff the headteacher is involved in:

- the appropriate application of the disciplinary procedure
- the collating and submission of evidence to the governing body and LEA
- the recommendation that the individual concerned be dismissed

Here, the overriding aim is to part company with an individual who, in the view of the headteacher, has demonstrated a lack of suitability for employment in the school, though it must be stressed that the headteacher is not empowered to dismiss a member of the school adult community. But this should not impair the judgement and actions of the headteacher. There is plenty of scope for dismissing an employee fairly through the procedures laid down by the LEA.

However, potentially fair reasons for dismissal must relate to the following:

- conduct;
- capability, i.e. skill, aptitude, health, physical or mental abilities;
- qualifications relevant to the position held where continuing employment would contravene the law (either on the part of the employee or employer);
- redundancy;
- some other substantial reasons which could justify the dismissal in the light of the position held

Potentially unfair reasons for dismissal include the following:

- trade union membership or activities
- pregnancy
- discrimination by race or sex

The legislative criteria in respect of the grounds for fair dismissal reflect the difficulties inherent in the notion that employment relations matters of this sort can be rigidly prescribed for all situations and circumstances. The key question which the tribunals invariably address is whether in the light of the known circumstances the employer acted *reasonably* in dismissing the employee with appropriate reference to the legal provisions.

Thus, conduct, capability and qualifications are an attempt to delineate specific matters that are an integral part of the contractual relationship. As the person responsible for the effective conduct of staff management within the school, the alert headteacher will monitor staff behaviour and be aware of their capability and qualifications. Nevertheless, problems may arise as a consequence of inappropriate action or reluctance to make an early decision where a member of staff is in breach of the staff code or has problems in the classroom.

Consider these incidents:

10 A newly appointed headteacher discovered that over the past year a teacher had persisted in disrupting staff meetings and was frequently abusive to colleagues, many of whom were so distressed that their teaching was adversely affected.

Q   *What action should the previous headteacher have taken?*
    What advice would you give the present headteacher?

11 On the advice of the headteacher, the LEA dismissed a teacher for incompetent teaching. The teacher subsequently pursued a claim for unfair dismissal which was upheld by the industrial tribunal.

Q   *What questions need to be addressed here?*

The remaining potentially fair reasons for dismissal range from the specific to a wide range of possibilities including:

- Contravention of a statute. This refers to a situation where retention of the employee in his job would involve a breach of statutory obligation by the employer or employee, for example employing a disqualified bus driver to drive the school bus.
- Dismissing an employee on the grounds of redundancy, because the need for the employee to carry out work of a particular kind has ceased or diminished thereby making the employee surplus to requirements.

Finally, other substantial reasons will be judged by the particular circumstances, but note:

- Long-term illness and a criminal act committed in the course of employment are examples which may fall within the scope of fair dismissal.

It was noted earlier that a crucial factor in the consideration of dismissal cases is whether the employer acted reasonably in the circumstances. Here, the notions of equity and natural justice are important especially in relation to the way in which the dismissal was conducted. The headteacher's actions and the provision of evidence to the LEA can, therefore, exert a powerful influence on the outcome of an industrial tribunal hearing. Whether a dismissal was unfair is for the tribunal to decide. Certain legal provisions, however, give specific guidelines where a dismissal could be deemed to be unfair.

- Dismissing an employee for engaging in trade union activities may be considered *unfair*, if the activities took place outside normal working hours, or indeed during working hours where the employer had given consent.
- Selecting an employee from others to whom the circumstances of

redundancy apply because of trade union activities, or where he/she was selected in contravention of an agreed procedure or a customary arrangement without good reason, may also be considered unfair.

- Dismissal for pregnancy is potentially unfair unless either the employee cannot or will not be able to undertake her work properly, or to continue to employ her would violate the law. For example, the employee may not be able to do work involving exposure to chemical substances that are known to be harmful to pregnant women and therefore constitute a breach of the Health and Safety at Work Act.
- Dismissal on the grounds of colour, race, ethnic origin or sex is inadmissable under the law and therefore unfair.

From the brief examination of the guidelines referring to potentially fair and unfair dismissal respectively, it would seem that the task of dismissing an employee fairly is not particularly difficult in the legal context. This observation is based on a number of assumptions:

- existence of carefully formulated policies and procedures
- observance of relevant procedures
- systematic collection of 'hard' evidence
- imposition of sanctions that are clearly articulated and understood
- standardisation of forms and letters dealing with such things as breaches of staff discipline and leave of absence
- a keen sense of judgement as to the appropriate action that should be taken in any given situation
- clear channels of communication between the school, governors and the LEA [. . .]

Staff appointments

A significant feature of the headteacher's role is the appointment of academic and non-teaching staff. The extent of involvement is determined by a whole range of factors including the procedures followed by the LEA; the part played by the school governors; and the headteacher's commitment to recruit staff of the calibre necessary to meet the current and future identified needs of the school.

While these aspects vary according to local circumstances and personal aspirations, a common aspect is the legal context, since employment law does not discriminate between schools and local authority boundaries. Here, there are four main areas that require early attention when the opportunity arises to appoint staff to the school, or when internal promotions are being considered. These are:

- job advertisements
- candidate long and short lists
- selection interview
- appointment

The law intrudes on all of these processes, in particular the:

Sex Discrimination Act 1975 (SDA)
Race Relations Act 1976 (RRA)
Defamation Act 1952

Job advertisements

With specific exceptions it is normally unlawful for anyone to publish, or cause to be published, any advertisement or notice which indicates an intention to discriminate on the grounds of:

- race
- sex
- marital status

This includes internal circulars on staff vacancies, promotion and training opportunities and any other benefits. Further, qualifications or requirements applied to a job which would effectively restrict it to applicants from only one sex or racial group have to be justifiable under the law, otherwise they constitute indirect discrimination.

Discrimination is lawful where sex is a 'genuine occupational qualification' or where there is a need to 'preserve decency' in situations where close physical contact between the sexes is likely to occur, such as in physical education.

Checklist for guidance

When staff vacancies or promotion opportunities occur in the school, the head-teacher should consider the checklist below before writing a job advertisement and/or internal circular:

- Avoid using titles such as 'master' or 'mistress' unless the post falls within the specified legal provisions, i.e. 'genuine occupational qualification' or the need to 'preserve decency.'
- Make sure the advertisement for the job (e.g. school typist) could not be understood to indicate a preference for one sex.
- If you wish to use words like 'he, or 'she', make sure that they are used as alternatives, e.g. 'he or she', and are consistent throughout the advertisement.

Selection for interview

The process of selecting applicants for interview usually entails the identification of those candidates who appear to be the most suitable. Whether a long list or short list is compiled will depend largely on the number and quality of the candidates applying for the vacancies or promotion.

This can be a daunting task, but the law requires (with specific exceptions) that

applicants are not excluded on the grounds of their race, sex or marital status.
Consider this case:

> 12 A headteacher, together with the LEA, advertised for a craft teacher. A short list was
> subsequently drawn up and the chosen candidates were invited to attend an inter-
> view. Before the interview took place a redeployed teacher from within the Author-
> ity was appointed to the post. The headteacher advised the shortlisted candidates
> that the post had been filled and therefore the planned interview was cancelled. One
> of the applicants subsequently claimed that he had been discriminated against on
> the grounds of his race since he was more experienced and had better qualifications
> than the person who had been appointed.

Selection interview

The interview is the forum which is perhaps most prone to the pitfalls posed by the
legal provisions applying to discrimination on the grounds of sex, marriage or
racial/ethnic origin.

Experienced interviewers will be aware of this danger and forestall it by
planning carefully their line of questioning and indeed the phrasing of questions
in sensitive areas. This is not always easy where an interviewing panel is con-
vened comprising school governors, LEA advisers and senior school staff. In
these circumstances, it is not uncommon for some members of the panel to ask
the candidate questions which may give the interviewee the impression that
his/her sex or racial origins are being taken into account in assessing their
suitability for the post in question.

It is good practice, therefore, for the headteacher, together with the chair of the
interviewing panel, to remind members before interviewing commences that the
questions they ask of candidates should relate to the qualifications, experience,
and personal qualities previously identified as relevant to the post.

Below are some examples of the kinds of questions that are best avoided.

Of a woman:
When do you intend to start a family?
Who will look after your children if they are sick?

Of a man:
Most of the other staff here are women. How do you think you will fit in?
Do you plan to get married?

Of a candidate who belongs to an ethnic minority:
Have you ever suffered any prejudice in your previous posts because of your colour?
There are very few Asian families in this area. Do you think you could settle down here?

Such questions reflect simple prejudice.

Interviewers should ask themselves: 'Would I also ask that question of a
male/female, English candidate who was white?' Frequently, a question which
appears to be discriminatory simply reflects a clumsy attempt to ascertain the
relevant information.

Internal promotion

There are additional legal implications here which require careful consideration by the headteacher. Unless one of the exceptions applies, it is unlawful to discriminate on sex or racial grounds when opportunities for promotion or training arise.

The headteacher has a responsibility, therefore, to ensure the selection criteria for promotion and training remains within the law.

Consider this incident:

13 A member of staff successfully applied for promotion to a Scale 3 post, and a colleague who had also applied claimed she had been discriminated against because she had better qualifications and was more experienced than the successful candidate.

Staff references

The Defamation Act 1952 provides a legal remedy for a candidate who suffers as a consequence of a false characterisation. Under the terms of this Act a plaintiff may seek compensation through the civil courts. It is normal practice for the headteacher or a senior member of staff to give a reference to a member of staff seeking promotion or employment elsewhere, but as the employer, the LEA (governing body in the case of voluntary aided schools) may be vicariously liable for defamatory comments expressed in the reference. The statement need not be explicit to constitute a defamation. A legal action may be successfully pursued by a plaintiff if an innuendo could be drawn from the reference.

Guidelines for staff references

An employer is not under any *legal* obligation to provide a reference. The provider of a reference is not obliged to reveal its contents to the member of staff concerned. If the reference is substantially true and accurate then it may be justified on those grounds. No legal liability can result unless the plaintiff can establish malice.

Where an unintentional falsehood is included in the reference an apology should be conveyed to the wronged person and all other recipients of the libel should be informed it was untrue. Slander is also covered by the Act, but for obvious reasons it is very difficult for a plaintiff to substantiate that a false characterisation was made on the phone and/or during a private conversation.

The headteacher should take all reasonable steps to ensure a reference is accurate.

Health and safety

The modern school is an extremely complex institution and it is not the intention here to offer technical guidance covering the plethora of school activities and building environment. [. . .]

The health, safety and general well-being of all those who participate in the life of the school is of obvious concern to the headteacher. While there has long since been a general duty under common law for reasonable care to be taken in the conduct of the school, the Health and Safety at Work Act 1974 places additional responsibilities on the LEA as the employer and on school staff.

The primary concern here, therefore, is with the Health and Safety at Work Act 1974, and the implications for staff management in the school.

Under the Act, the LEA as the employer is charged with the following general duties:

- provide and maintain plant and systems of work without risk to health, including a safe and healthy working environment
- ensure that handling, storage and transport of articles and substances are carried out safely
- provide information, instruction, training and supervision necessary to ensure the health and safety of employees at work
- ensure that entry to and exit from the workplace is safe and without risk
- ensure that the conduct of the school does not expose the public, or persons on the site who are not employees, to health or safety risks in so far as it is reasonably practicable

For school staff the following general duties apply:

- take reasonable care for the health and safety of himself/herself and other persons who may be affected by his/her acts or omissions at school
- co-operate with the employer so far as is necessary to perform any duty under the Act
- not intentionally or recklessly interfere with or misuse any equipment, safety device etc. provided to keep up with the Act's requirements

In keeping with the common law tradition, the Act places the responsibility for the 'management' of health and safety on the employing Authority. However, under the Act, an individual is liable to prosecution under criminal law as well as liable to be sued under civil law for errors and omissions having a detrimental effect on health and safety. Here the headteacher may be particularly exposed as the person responsible for the supervision of health and safety matters in the school.

A breach of the Act could lead to any of the following penalties:

- improvement notice
- prohibition notice
- up to £1000 fine for most offences in summary proceedings

- up to two years imprisonment coupled with an unlimited fine if there is a prosecution on indictment

Improvement notice

If the inspector considers a law has been broken, or will be broken, he/she can issue a notice to the responsible person requiring that the contravention be remedied within a certain time.

Prohibition notice

If there is a risk of serious personal injury, the activity giving rise to the risk, e.g. a lathe in the woodwork room, can be closed down until the specific remedial action has been taken.

The other penalties may be imposed in the event that the two notices above were not observed, for example, or where some other breach of the law has been proven.

A defence may be offered against civil or criminal action where:

- the offence was committed by, or due to the neglect of, or negligence of another person
- it was not known and could not have been reasonably ascertained that an offence was committed

Role of school staff

The Act places emphasis on a system and procedures approach rather than prescribing minimum health and safety standards which must be complied with. The aim, therefore, is to get employers to introduce a method of organisation and system and procedures, that will become self-regulatory. The main burden of responsibility for developing the appropriate organisation structures and procedures is with the employing Authority.

Consider this incident:

14 The headteacher reported to the LEA that a piece of masonry had fallen from the lower school building. On this occasion nobody was injured. Three months later a piece of debris fell from the same building and a pupil was slightly injured and received first aid in the school.

Most members of staff will recognise the importance of supervising pupils, especially where dangerous substances are involved in craft rooms generally. They will also acknowledge the need to follow the manufacturer's instructions attached to bottles and items of equipment and any additional regulations supplied by the LEA. However, accidents do occur which sometimes might have been avoided, usually for any one of the following reasons:

- The member of staff responsible did not follow the manufacturer's instructions.
- The manufacturer's instructions were unclear.
- The injured person was grossly negligent.
- The building where dangerous chemicals were stored was unsuitable for the purpose.
- The activity was inadequately supervised.
- The people involved were genuinely unaware of the health and safety hazards associated with the particular activity.
- The external contractors were negligent.

From this list it is apparent that the responsibility for accidents is very wide-ranging and that it has to be acknowledged that it is impossible to legislate for all eventualities. Nor can codes and guidelines be sufficiently embracing to relieve the headteacher from having to make judgements and decisions about health and safety matters.

Consider this action:

> The LEA safety regulations stated that the door leading from a classroom corridor to the back stairway should remain unlocked during school hours. The headteacher was concerned about the pupils' safety on the stairway and consequently kept the door locked.

To perhaps a lesser extent, all staff within the school are from time to time presented with such dilemmas. The Act implicitly, if not explicitly, recognises that a collective approach to the development and maintenance of effective procedures can ease the individual burden in making difficult decisions, while retaining responsibility for personal behaviour. Thus the regulations provide for the appointment of safety representatives from among the organisation's employees by recognised trade unions.

The Health and Safety Commission provides guidelines on the functions of safety representatives as follows:

- *Representation*: represent the employees in consultation with the employer over arrangements for developing health and safety at the workplace.
- *Investigation*: investigate complaints and make representations about health, safety or welfare to the employer on particular or general matters.
- *Inspection*: carry out inspections of the workplace (normally quarterly) during which the employer may be present. Carry out inspections after a notifiable accident, dangerous occurrence or in the event of a notifiable disease. Inspect relevant statutory documents held by the employer, except personal medical records.
- *Safety committees*: attend safety committee meetings.
- *Time off*: time off with pay will be given to safety repesentatives in order to carry out their function and to receive training.
- *Legal liability*: no additional legal liability is attached to the functions of a safety representative beyond the general duties of employees.

It is common practice for schools to have safety representatives and safety committees which are in keeping with the notion of self-regulation and the participation of staff in the decision-making processes concerned with health and safety. Their presence can be of great assistance to the headteacher, especially in drawing early attention to potential health and safety hazards.

Nevertheless, while in matters of detail the practice varies between LEAs, it is normal procedure for the headteacher to be assigned the responsibility for general oversight of health and safety in the school. To this end the headteacher should:

- keep informed about relevant legal requirements
- be familiar with the employing Authority's health and safety policy and its implementation
- be alert to hazards associated with the life of the school
- keep abreast with the documentation provided by the LEA
- encourage the co-operation of staff in promoting measures to improve health and safety
- identify the reporting channels to the LEA

Finally, a note of comfort for the hard-pressed headteacher. In the absence of specific legal requirements or other sources of guidance, subsequent judgements about particular decisions made by the headteacher in relation to health and safety will normally be based on whether, on balance, the headteacher's action, or indeed non-action, was reasonable in the prevailing circumstances. The same would apply to any other individual member of staff.

This brief survey of [some] aspects of employment law which are of [major] concern to the headteacher represents the legal dimension of the day-to-day practice of staff management in the school.

Commentary on the incidents cited in the text

1 This matter was quickly resolved when the teacher gave an assurance to the headteacher that she would cease forthwith to offer pupils of the school private tuition for personal financial gain.

   In the absence of an express term in the teacher's contract with the employing authority which excluded such activity, there remains the common law obligation which may be implied. Thus, by implication, no person in the employ of another should use their position for personal financial gain unless the contract of employment specifically allows for this. It is possible, therefore, that the teacher in this case was in breach of contract.

2 In this case the teachers concerned were refusing to carry out a *reasonable* instruction, which was to do the job they were paid for. They were, therefore, in breach of their contract. If the deputy headteacher had instructed the teachers to (say) empty the school litter bins, then the question to be

addressed is whether the instruction was *reasonable* in the light of their contract of employment.

3 Here the teacher was expressly obliged under the terms of his contract to take proper care of any monies for which he was responsible in the school. Moreover, the teacher is obliged, under common law, to account for money entrusted to his care in the course of his employment. The teacher was therefore in breach of contract.

4 This offer of promotion was subsequently withdrawn with the teacher's agreement. However, the LEA view was that the headteacher had offered a new contract to a member of staff and had published this decision. The LEA, therefore, felt that they were bound to honour the new contract if the teacher concerned had insisted.

5 The assistant caretaker was dismissed for breach of contract. He had in fact used the school facilities for purposes of private financial gain.

6 The headteacher acted in good faith when he informed the teacher, on her appointment, that she would be required to spend most of her time in the Resources Centre. The central issue is whether, in the light of the changed circumstances, the headteacher's instruction that the teacher teach eighteen lessons a week was reasonable. Matters to be considered here are: the competence of the teacher; the subject(s) she was instructed to teach; the level(s) of classes she was assigned to; and her future role with regard to the Resources Centre.

7 Providing the contract does not state to the contrary, there is nothing illegal in either party seeking to change its terms. However, if the typist refused to accept the reduction in her hours and was dismissed as a consequence, the Authority may have been liable to a claim for unfair dismissal. In this case, the question would focus on whether the Authority had acted reasonably in the light of all the circumstances.

8 No action was taken against the caretaker for refusing to obey the headteacher's instruction, but the incident raises a number of contractual implications that might be considered.

Since the windows had previously been cleaned by outside contractors it might be argued that as it was not the caretaker's customary task it was no part of his existing contract. If this is established, it is then chiefly a question of whether the headteacher's attempt to introduce a new term into the caretaker's contract, i.e. change it, was reasonable in the circumstances. Here such matters as: the medical condition of the caretaker; his age; and the degree of risk to the caretaker and others would almost certainly have a bearing on the outcome. Indeed, the headteacher's instruction may have been unlawful if the safety of the caretaker and/or others was clearly at risk.

9 This is a particularly murky area of law. Where people are on fixed term contracts, the law considers that they have been given notice at the outset of

the contract, and this equals the length of the fixed term. However, in the celebrated case *Ford* v. *Warwickshire County Council*, the House of Lords ruled that a teacher employed for eight years under a succession of fixed term contracts was 'continuously employed' throughout that period for the purposes of the Employment Protection (Consolidation) Act 1978, since during the annual summer vacation between the expiry of one contract and the commencement of the next she was 'absent from work on account of a temporary cessation of work'. Ford could therefore claim to an industrial tribunal that she had been unfairly dismissed and that she had a similar right in relation to redundancy payments. It should be stressed that this case was decided on its own particular merits, and the legal position may be clarified in the light of future cases.

10 The previous headteacher should have acted immediately to ascertain that the possible causes for this teacher's behaviour were not attributable to his medical condition, domestic circumstances or unwarranted provocation by his colleagues. If these factors were inapplicable, the headteacher should have disciplined the teacher and if necessary recommended his dismissal. In this case the problem was exacerbated because of the lack of a staff disciplinary procedure within the school and a breakdown in communication between the headteacher and the LEA.

The present headteacher must, therefore, monitor the behaviour of the teacher concerned, investigate the possible causes, compile a dossier, develop an appropriate staff disciplinary procedure and apply it, if necessary, to resolve this matter.

11 In this case, the industrial tribunal sought to establish the criteria used to assess the teacher's competence; the evidence of incompetence and the period of time the evaluation took place; whether the teacher had received the necessary training to teach the subject(s) he had been instructed to take, and any other appropriate support; the way in which the disciplinary procedures were applied.

The tribunal ruled in favour of the teacher because he was 'judged' in relation to the competence of his colleagues rather than against objective criteria.

12 In this case the headteacher followed the LEA procedures relating to redeployment of teachers and appointments. While the headteacher was not aware that one of the candidates who had been shortlisted for interview was coloured, his position, and indeed that of the Authority, was extremely vulnerable, because they could not produce the criteria on which the selection and appointment was based.

13 The school and LEA were unable to provide an acceptable defence in this case because they could not produce the selection criteria used to promote the successful candidate and the unsuccessful teacher clearly had better qualifications and experience.

14 The maintenance of the fabric of school buildings falls within the general
   duties placed on the Authority by the Health and Safety at Work Act 1974. In
   this case, there was a clear breakdown in communication between the headteacher and the LEA. This explained the lack of action of the Authority in the
   intervening period between the first incident and the second occurrence.
   While the main responsibility for developing appropriate communication
   systems resides with the Authority, a question mark remains over the headteacher's position in not passing the matter to the LEA when no action
   followed from his report.

References

LYONS, G. and STENNING, R. (1986). *Managing Staff in Schools: Training Materials*,
   London, Hutchinson.

The selection and appointment of heads

Colin Morgan

Introduction

In 1985 the procedures for selecting and appointing head teachers in England and Wales were substantially unchanged from those established at the beginning of the century.

The main features of traditional British practice are that candidates are selected by a lay interview panel of local authority members and school governors which is advised 'professionally' by an education officer; successful candidates are given a tenured position in a specific school (rather than a school district as in some countries). Once appointed, head teachers can remain in post for the rest of their working life, unless they voluntarily move to another school or, in very rare cases, are dismissed.

However, this situation seems likely to change. In 1984 the Government, via the Secretary of State for Education, publicly called into question the viability of the selection procedures in current use and challenged the tenure appointment principle by suggesting a period of probation for newly appointed heads. This major concern with headship selection and appointment followed publication of the Open University research – the POST project – on the selection of secondary head teachers (Morgan et al, 1983). This three-year project had itself originated in the debate about the overall importance of headship for school success initiated by the 'great debate' speech of Prime Minister James Callaghan at Ruskin College Oxford in 1977, which found formal statement in the Department of Education and Science (DES) publication *Ten Good Schools* (DES, 1977). 'Without exception, [these] heads have qualities of imagination and vision, tempered by realism, which have enabled them to sum up not only their present situation, but also attainable future goals.'

The POST project had been commissioned in 1979 to 'find out what currently happens in head teacher selection; to compare it with the methods used outside education; and to propose modifications and alternatives'. Head teacher selection and appointment, as well as curriculum appropriateness, the quality of classroom teaching and appraisal of teacher performance generally, emerged from the 'great debate' as major policy concerns of central government. This chapter will summarize some of the findings of the POST project, refer to relevant selection procedures elsewhere in the world, and indicate the emerging issues as they affect innovation.

The POST project

The POST project's brief was to evaluate the selection of *secondary school heads*, within England and Wales. However, from what is well known about procedures for selecting primary school heads, as well as the empirical findings of several unpublished dissertations, POST's findings are generalizable across all maintained schools. Also, informed commentators in Scotland, having read the research report, are clear that the ways the procedures operate in England and Wales are equally applicable there. As the methodology of this research is fully described elsewhere (Morgan *et al*, 1983), it is only pertinent to make clear the main basis which the research team adopted for evaluating the evidence. This was a *job analysis to procedures match*; that is, did selectors have a clear view of the job for which they were appointing, and did the procedures in use appear to measure those competencies which a job analysis of the secondary head's duties would indicate as necessary? Four of the main findings were:

1 selectors had a meagre knowledge of the job and used undeclared criteria;
2 the roles of the different groups of selectors were ambiguous;
3 the selectors used a restricted selection technology;
4 (of most significance) non job-related factors dominated the selection decision!

Absence of job analysis and declared criteria

Selectors were not helped in their task by the absence of a written description of headship duties. In fact, among the 59 local education authorities (LEAs) visited, only one was found where a written analysis of the secondary head's job had been made, and nowhere among the 26 LEAs where appointment stages were observed did selectors have a formal job description from which to work. This did not prevent selectors individually having their own ideas on what a head does, as will be seen below. Even these individual perceptions, though, were not shared; nor were selectors observed to brief or consult each other on criteria for selection or the appointment process. All selectors were observed to bring to bear their own variable and unstated criteria on their choice of candidate. It was not therefore surprising that candidates, unsuccessful at one final interview or failing to get through the first paper stage of eliminations in some places, continued until they successfully met the combination of individuals' undeclared criteria in another place.

Selector role ambiguity

Even within the distinctive 'province' of local government selection practice in England and Wales, the selection of head teachers presents a unique context because there are two lay groups – the LEA members and school governors – who participate as the ultimate decision makers. The members and governors are advised by a third selection group: the officers; though what the status or nature of their advice is to be is nowhere formally prescribed. Therefore it was little surprise for POST to find that current practice was characterized by considerable ambiguity of roles. There was even conflict between the participating groups on the fundamental issue of accommodating the necessary technical assessment and equity for candidates, with the local needs viewpoint expressed via school governors, and the LEA members' accountability for the final appointment decision. Often there was contention as to when in the procedure, with whom, and by what methods, 'tests' of *technical competence* as distinct from *social acceptability* were to be made. In fact, the whole notion of technical assessment in the job-related areas of educational leadership and management skills, as distinct from the more social concerns of the lay members, was sometimes lacking and generally undeveloped. Indeed, not everyone accepted that it was necessary. A need for an explicit definition of role duties was invariably apparent.

A restricted selection technology

The unsure status of technical assessment was reflected in the primitive selection methods used. For example it was found that, in one-third of LEAs, heads of even the largest secondary schools can be appointed on the basis of a two-stage procedure: just one formal meeting (averaging an hour) to consider the application form and references, and a final interview in which a candidate may be seen for as little as 20 minutes. Also, half of all LEAs did not have a preliminary interview stage. This not only ensures that candidates are seen twice on a formal basis, but also provides the opportunity for officers to examine in detail professional concerns of less interest to lay members. Even in those LEAs with a preliminary stage, selection methods were, however, restricted to interviewing, and this usually on a very ill planned and unstructured basis rather than in combination with the type of written and oral exercises which have been found to have such good predictive value in other occupational contexts (Anstey, 1971). Also, there was little tradition of using other types of selectors. External assessors, for example, officers from another authority – are unknown, though external assessors are, in fact, used in the health service in Britain. Only three LEAs involved experienced head teachers in the selection process. Technically, both preliminary interviews and the selection procedures as a whole were found to be entirely dependent on the interview, a tool repeatedly shown to have low or nil predictive value (Morgan, 1973; Tenopyr, 1981).

Decisive role of non job-related factors

The most striking finding of POST's research was what did and did not count among selection criteria. Fifty-two observations were made of LEA appointment stages by the researchers 'playing the fly on the wall' and writing down the criteria statements made by the selectors. Afterwards these statements were categorized according to the ideas which all panel members, whether officers, governors, or LEA members, used as eliminating criteria, whether positively to commend that a candidate go forward or be appointed, or negatively to assert that a candidate should not be considered further. The categories constructed, and examples within each category, were as follows.

1 *The right career track record*: selectors made positive or negative statements which encapsulated their idea of what was a correct or incorrect path, independent of the quality of performance on that path. They covered notions such as: the previous pattern of posts held, right age, right type of schools to have been in, the right pace of mobility etc. For example: '35 – the right age' (positive); 'A shade on the young side at 34' (negative). For this category, and the others which follow, many more examples are given in the book reporting the research (Morgan *et al*, 1983).

2 *Education and training*: selectors used their own judgements about the value of a particular pattern of education and training, type of qualification, or about the place where the candidate received them, to make positive or negative recommendations. For example: 'I have a naive belief in the quality of a first class honours degree' (positive); 'Don't want anyone with a first as they are too clever to employ' (negative).

3 *Quality of experience and performance to date*: for example: 'Worked hard in a difficult school' (positive); 'Very narrow experience' (negative).

4 *Fitness for the particular type of school*: selectors used a variety of comments to convey that a candidate was fitted or unfitted for the distinct circumstances, as they saw them, of the appointing school. For example: 'Comes from this part of the world and therefore has sympathy with the kind of children we have to educate' (positive). 'Comes from a progressive school and we are appointing to a traditional one' (negative).

5 *Seal of approval*: this term was used to include a range of statements, usually based on available documents, which indicated in the mind of the selectors that they conveyed a seal of approval or disapproval. For example: 'Excellent letter of application' (positive); 'Duplicated letter of application' (negative).

6 *Motivation*: selectors inferred judgements about candidates' motivation from their autobiographies or statements. For example: 'Candidate wants to move – he's tired of commuting' (positive); 'Is it preparation for retirement?' (negative).

7 *Previous interview performance*: selectors sometimes knew about candidates' previous interview performance. For example: 'Did well at last interview with us' (positive); 'Doesn't make a good impression at interview' (negative).

8 *Job related skills and knowledge*: for example: 'Very good ideas about the 14 +

curriculum' (positive); 'Not demonstrated enough sensitivity or leadership in his current deputy's job' (negative).

9 *Personality/personal qualities*: selectors made judgements about candidates' personalities, personal appearance and personal qualities and used them as evaluative criteria. These may have been perceptions either from information contained in the documents or generated by seeing the person. For example: 'Tall and physically distinguished' (positive); 'Hail-fellow-well-met type' (negative).

It is important to realize that the possession of a quality encapsulated in a statement by one selector can be a positive recommendation for a candidate, whereas the same quality when expressed by a different selector can damn another candidate. Given the absence of explicitly agreed criteria by all selectors before the process of elimination begins, it is inevitable that the criteria constructed individually are as varied and idiosyncratic as the selectors' views of headship and its requirements. Among the nine categories described above, what counted most reveals why current procedures fail any *job analysis to procedures match*. Table 5.3.1 shows which of these nine categories of criteria occupy the first three places in a ranking for each of the main elimination stages.

Table 5.3.1 Secondary head teacher selection: main criteria used

Rank of criterion category	Long and shortlistings		Preliminary interviews		Final interviews	
1	Personality/ personal qualities	30%	Personality/ personal qualities	42%	Personality/ personal qualities	39%
2	Right career track record	17%	Interview performance	19%	Interview performance	17%
3	Experience and performance to date	14%	Fitness for this school	10%	Fitness for this school	13%
			Specific job knowledge or skills	10%		

The percentage figures indicate the weight of usage of that category of criteria among the nine categories used at these elimination stages.

The picture presented by Table 5.3.1 speaks for itself; only three points need to be made. First, there is a low weighting given to job-related skills and knowledge, that is, the abilities that a job analysis would indicate were necessary. In the absence of any job analysis by the employers, or a statement of job-related criteria for selectors, this finding is hardly surprising. Second, the low weighting given to the category 'the quality of experience and performance to date', seems surprising at the level of common sense expectation, until one recalls that the LEAs had no formal systematic performance appraisal policies to reveal such information. This absence was well illustrated by POST's analysis of the head teacher references, where mention of a candidate's experience and performance was made in only very general terms: 'sound organizing ability', 'respected by staff', etc. Third, the decisive weighting given to personality/personal qualities stages is both surprising and to be expected: surprising, because this category is predominant at the paper stages, the long and short listings, when no candidates were present in person. This is to be explained by the fact that selectors had to hand the references which POST found to contain 'personality' mentions as their major constituent. Also, selectors were observed to construe personal qualities by projecting from information in the documents on the basis of 'feel' and 'impression' generally. It does seem that, in the absence of the controls dictated by explicit job criteria and training, the human selector has a marked penchant for the personal traits he believes are job related. This weighting given in head teacher selection to 'hunt the right personality', rather than to measure the required competencies, is wholly consistent with all major research on interviewing. This has shown that panel selectors work from their own stereotypes. These are not shared; each individual selector works from his or her own notions of the image and values appropriate for the job. At final interviews for secondary comprehensive school headships, the POST researchers found the panel members' statements frequently revealed their preferred stereotypes: 'We need a character, someone like the heads of the other two schools, someone who can compete. They are over large characters who can speak' (LEA member); '[We need] someone like my headmaster when I was at school – I went to a boys' grammar school, we all knew he was the headmaster and respected him. I look for someone like him' (LEA member); 'He [the candidate who was appointed] will look like Mr X [a local head] in 15 years' time and be just as good' (LEA member). [. . .]

If head teacher selection can be seen to involve [. . .] two different, and sometimes competing, requirements the assessment of technical or professional abilities (however difficult these are to define) and the assessment of social acceptability or fit by the lay controllers it is the latter category that universally engages selectors' major concern. [. . .] it seems, [. . .] assessment of *acceptability* in a range of social criteria is emphasized at the expense of a rigorous attempt to assess technical competence in the job-related skills of headship.

It is important to realize that in Britain, at least, this emphasis does not distinguish education from the major part of industry or commerce, though there is a widespread belief that it does. A 1980 survey of the selection of managers for British industry makes this clear: 'Companies had not changed their approach to the selection process in any significant way in the last 10 years . . . (and) executives, particularly senior executives, are largely judged on a set of personal non-ability related criteria, and by a method which is ill-suited to the task of assessing such criteria' (Institute of Personnel Management/British Institute of Management, 1980). What, then, is the 'state of the art' in the occupational selection of top leaders, and to where does one look for exemplary practice that can guide innovation within education? The POST project studied a range of what it deemed exemplary practices, each of which was characterized by the following features: rigorous job analysis and stated selection criteria, a multiple-assessment approach, ie using more 'tools' than just the interview; and a policy of evaluating the validity of the procedures, ie measuring the extent to which a particular selection tool or set of procedures were good predictors of subsequent good performance in the job. In fact, it is this latter condition that is the essential feature of 'state of the art' status, because, unless alternative features can be demonstrated to give a significantly better prediction of on-the-job success than the miserable predictive record of the interview as a selection tool, the groups who at present hold the ultimate power in head teacher selection are unlikely to be impressed by exhortations to innovate. The exemplary procedures studied by POST were: the selection of two senior managers for industry by different private management consultancy firms, selection of administrative class and executive officer entrants in the British Civil Service, the selection of senior staff in the health service, police senior command selection, and the National Association of Secondary School Principals (NASSP) assessment centre policy in the USA. The findings of these studies of selection external to education are discussed elsewhere (Morgan *et al*, 1983), and here it is relevant only to consider the NASSP assessment centre policy which is remarkable for two reasons.

First, it is an assessment process which has been pioneered by the secondary heads themselves through their union. Second, it is an assessment process which concentrates heavily on specific skill dimensions of headship and places considerably less emphasis on experience or career track criteria *per se*. It aims to assess these skills by a battery of analogous tests, which are exercises designed to simulate real work demands, and structured interviews (Hersey, 1980).

The National Association of Secondary School Principals' exercises have been the subject of a validation study (Schmitt *et al*, 1982). Schmitt found that the exercises designed to provide information on the skill dimensions of headship met this purpose, and confirmed that the skills tested were relevant to headship. NASSP assessment centres are attended by 12 participants at a time, who have been identified according to specified criteria as eligible in each school district. Each centre has a team of six assessors, including principals and other administrators from school districts and the county office. All assessors have successfully completed 30 hours of residential training before undertaking assessor duties. They work to a detailed Manual for Assessors prepared by NASSP, in which every exercise, together with the criteria and behaviour to be observed and recorded, is set out. Marking schemes are provided, with 5-point rating scales of the behaviour to be sought and descriptions of what constitutes that behaviour.

The NASSP package came about because of the widespread belief that candidates in conventional selection procedures are rarely observed or evaluated with regard to their performance of skills needed on the job. Typically, appointments were made with little more than an educated guess of potential administrative abilities. In other words, the NASSP approach was tackling a selection process resembling the one that POST found operating in England and Wales. The purpose of the assessment centre approach was to ensure that elimination decisions would in future be based on the skills vital to good headship performance. Twelve skill dimensions to be assessed were derived by a job study that covered the tasks and responsibilities set out in the job descriptions and performance appraisal instruments used by school districts, and as described in interviews with people with a thorough knowledge of the job.

In order to test these skills, NASSP has devised a variety of situational or analogous tests which allow an assessment to be made on the basis of each candidate's observed performance. In addition, personal interviews lasting two hours are held with each candidate. The final assessment report prepared on each participant is based on collation and discussion of individual assessors' scores and comments on each of the activities. Once the assessment programme is completed, each candidate receives a four-page assessment report. Although the NASSP assessment centres do not make decisions about selection for headship, the information generated about the participants' state of readiness for headship is available to school districts if they wish to use it when an appointment is to be made.

The significance of the NASSP methods is that, like the British Civil Service, police senior command selection, and (in part) the health service, they apply rigorous definitions of the job competences required, analogous tests, and in-depth structured interviews, all of which have been absent in educational circles and most of industry in the UK. In addition to observing and describing the existing practices the POST project carried out action research in 10 LEAs to test the feasibility of applying these three features in actual headship appointments. In devising their tests, POST drew extensively on NASSP and British Civil Service experience. POST found that many selectors expressed a greater sense of security about making decisions based on a wider variety of more systematically collected evidence using analogous tests and a better range of prepared interviews.

Conclusions

The POST research and its 50-plus recommendations have received unusual support from central government in the form of additional funding to prepare a handbook on selecting senior staff for schools (Morgan *et al*, 1984). In 1984, the Government called for a national conference representing LEAs, governors and teachers to discuss the issues. [Also], the White Paper, *Better Schools* (HMSO, 1985), drew the attention of LEAs and governors 'to the more detailed recommendations in the report of the Open University research'. The White Paper made it clear that there would be legislation to establish the main features of the procedure for appointing a head teacher in maintained schools, but whether these will specify the nature of the technical assessments that should be carried

out is not known. It does, however, indicate that the Government had dropped
the idea of a probationary period for newly appointed heads: 'assessment of the
suitability of newly appointed head teachers is best pursued as part of a general
appraisal system embracing all teachers' (HMSO, 1985: 56). In the meantime,
some LEAs have changed their selection procedures and are using some of the
exemplary practices discussed above. For example, Table 5.3.2 shows the preliminary 'interview' programme devised by a metropolitan borough authority to
assess candidates for two secondary headships.

Table 5.3.2 The secondary headships preliminary programme of one LEA

Wednesday 4th May	
9.15 am	Arrival
9.30 am – 10 am	Introduction to programme (Committee Room 4, Council Suite)
10 am – 12 noon approx.	Visit to school A
12.15 pm – 1.30 pm	Lunch at teachers' centre
1.45 pm – 3 pm	Visit to school B
Friday 6th May	
9.15 am	Arrival reception office, education department
9.30 am – 9.45 am	Introductory session (Committee Room 4 Council Suite)
9.45 am – 10.30 am	Crisis management exercise Part I (Committee Rooms 1 and 4, Council Suite)
10.30 am – 11.30 am	In-basket exercise
11.30 am – 1.00 pm	Crisis management exercise part 2
2 pm onwards	Individual interviews in the education depart- ment (Deputy Director and Chief Inspector)

However, despite the public impact of the research report, in mid-1985 LEAs
appeared to be changing their headship selection procedures only very slowly. In
fact, the author has evidence that innovative head teachers in the selection of
their teaching staff are more prepared than the LEAs to move into exemplary
practices, especially with the application of oral and written analogous tests. The
present slow pace of change within education authorities may be explained by
the fact that the rigorous systematization of the selection process which innovation would bring at the same time would eliminate or considerably reduce officer
patronage. This was a topic discussed in the research report, where a tradition of
patronage was seen to be one of the greater blocks to reforming head teacher
selection practices.

Whether the necessary changes are eventually achieved by legislation or,
more likely, by a gradual dispersion of best practice, they will need to ensure the
accommodation of two requirements which can be seen as conflicting: the need
for impartial technical assessment methods to gather the evidence of candidate
fitness for headship; and the need to satisfy demands for a visible democratic
accountability and social legitimation by the local community.

References

ANSTEY, E., (1971). 'The Civil Service administrative class: a follow up of post-war entrants, *Occupational Psychology* 45 1: 27–43.

DEPARTMENT OF EDUCATION AND SCIENCE (1977). *Ten Good Schools. A Secondary School Enquiry*, Her Majesty's Stationery Office, London.

DEPARTMENT OF EDUCATION AND SCIENCE (1985). *Better Schools* (Cmnd 9469), Her Majesty's Stationery Office, London.

HERSEY, P. (1980). 'NASSP's Assessment Center: practitioners speak out', *National Association of Secondary School Principals Bulletin*, 64 439: 87–117.

INSTITUTE OF PERSONNEL MANAGEMENT/BRITISH INSTITUTE OF MANAGEMENT (1980). *Selecting Managers – How British Industry Recruits*, IPM information report 34, BIM Management Survey Report, London.

MORGAN, C., HALL, V. and MACKAY, H. (1983). *A Handbook on Selecting Senior Staff for Schools*, the Open University Press, Milton Keynes.

MORGAN, T. (1973). 'Recent insights into the selection interview', *Personnel Review*, 4–13.

SCHMITT, N. *et al.* (1982). *Criterion Related and content Validity of the NASSP Assessment Centre, Research Report*, Department of Psychology, Michigan State University, East Lansing.

TENOPYR, M. I. (1981). 'The realities of employment testing', *American Psychologist*, 36 10: 1120–27.

INSET and professional development for teachers

Advisory Committee on the Supply and Education of Teachers

[. . .] The case for INSET

4 The case for INSET rests on the needs of the education service, of individual schools and of teachers themselves. First, it is, we hope, common ground that the education service needs an up-to-date, well-trained teacher force contributing to effective curricular change. Secondly, individual schools need a vital and committed staff, working to agreed goals in a climate which encourages effective developments in curricular change and teaching quality. Thirdly, teachers themselves need opportunities for INSET as part of their personal and professional development. The needs of the education service, of individual schools, and of individual teachers are, of course, closely interrelated. They call for a wide range of INSET activities and flexibility of response.

5 For many years the education service has been operating in a climate of rapid change. This climate seems likely to continue for the foreseeable future. It requires a continual process of adjustment on the part of all those involved. We give examples below of the ways in which curricular and organisational change have had or will have profound implications for the management of the teacher force and for INSET. Such changes may be initiated within schools, perhaps stimulated by major national reports on education, or may be in response to social change and other external pressures – for example, the raising of the school leaving age, falling rolls, or a desire for alternative forms of school organisation for other reasons.

6 Developments in the content and balance of the curriculum and in the examination structure are likely to continue apace. The requirements of the 1981 Act dealing with children with special needs, the implementation of the Cockcroft Report on Mathematics Teaching, the increased emphasis on the technical and vocational aspects of school learning, the growth of inter-cultural education and recognition of the need for differentiation to meet variation in the background, ability and aptitude of pupils have given and will continue to give rise to demands for appropriate in-service education and training. Such developments reinforce the need for INSET opportunities to be made widely available for curriculum development and to enable all teachers to contribute to and keep abreast of developments both in teaching methods and in their subjects. Many subjects, such as science, have changed so rapidly in recent years that teachers need to keep constantly in touch with new developments. Other subjects and cross-curricular emphases, like computer studies, are so new that INSET is required to help teachers to change or expand the range of their teaching if demand is to be met.

7 Curricular and other developments in education require new skills on the part of teachers. The advent of microcomputers in schools, for example, requires the development of skills in their application to the classroom. The development of records of achievement will add to the growing need for appropriate assessment skills on the part of teachers. The new criteria against which initial teacher training courses will be assessed, by requiring the involvement of practising schoolteachers in initial teacher training, have created a need for suitable skills on the part of some teachers, particularly in the supervision and support of students' school experience and assessment of their classroom performance. In-service education and training has an essential part to play in enabling teachers to acquire or sharpen such skills and, above all, to improve their practical teaching skills.

8 In addition, current expectations of teachers include an understanding of, and ability to relate to, the views of parents, governors, representatives of the working world and the wider community. They include also an awareness of the diversity of ability, behaviour, social background and ethnic and cultural origins of their pupils. As the new criteria for the assessment of initial teacher training courses indicate, teachers need to know how to respond flexibly to such diversity and to guard against preconceptions based on the race or sex of pupils. Again, INSET has an essential role to play in enabling teachers to develop or improve their understanding in these fields.

9 In recent years, too, there has been recognition of the importance of managerial skills on the part of head teachers and senior staff to enable them to carry out their increasingly difficult and complicated roles. INSET is an essential means by which those likely to become head teachers or to hold senior positions in schools can be helped to acquire the necessary skills. It plays an important part, too, in equipping teachers for new or extended roles including a change of school or type of school, for example, from large to small, or urban to rural.

10 In those cases where the management of falling school rolls has required the redeployment of teachers from one phase or subject to another, INSET has played a crucial role in enabling teachers to change or expand the range of their teaching. More generally, falling school rolls have led to a shift in the age structure of the teacher force towards the older age groups and to a reduction in promotion prospects. In these circumstances INSET has an important role to play in helping teachers to strengthen their sense of purpose and morale.

11 INSET thus serves many purposes and is essential to the maintenance of a well-trained, up-to-date teacher force. It also contributes to the effectiveness of the individual school. Increasingly it has been found that the basis for change and for effective identification of the need for training and its implementation is the quality and climate of the school. Whole-school self-evaluation against agreed goals and involving teachers as functional or whole-school groups in the identification of training needs can clarify the purposes of in-service provision, both school-based and externally provided, and so promote effective curricular change and improvements in teaching quality throughout the school.

12 Finally, INSET has a crucial part to play in assisting the teacher's own personal and professional development. It is inevitable that teachers, in common with other professionals, will become less efficient at their jobs if they do not obtain the stimulus of widened experience and continued education. Teachers need to be able to respond positively to the curricular needs of the individual pupil, of the class and of the school as a whole. INSET is likely to be the most effective way of strengthening their confidence and enabling them to re-invigorate their thinking and their approach.

13 Opportunities to undertake curriculum development and to up-date subject knowledge are needed by all teachers as a normal part of their professional development. We have already referred to the implications for in-service education and training of the rapid changes that have taken place in some subjects and the development of new subjects. In addition major [national] projects in different areas of the curriculum, major changes of emphasis in subject content as in the case of CDT, and developments such as the strengthening of the science element in the primary curriculum have reinforced the need for INSET for teachers in the fields concerned.

14 Some teachers will wish also to have opportunity to acquire or develop particular skills in order to enhance their professional development. We believe that where necessary women teachers should be encouraged and helped to take up these opportunities equally with their male colleagues. INSET serves too as a preparation for teachers wishing to move into new areas of work such as careers advice or counselling, or take on new responsibilities, for example increased pastoral responsibility, senior posts requiring management skills, or particular responsibility for children with special educational needs. In our report on teacher training and special educational needs we expressed the view that high priority should be given to the in-service training of teachers to meet special educational needs.

15 Further study through courses or research programmes leading to an advanced professional qualification or an appropriate higher degree is an important means of developing professional knowledge for teachers and will increasingly be sought as the profession becomes a graduate one. Second degrees may become as desirable a means of enhancing promotion prospects as first degrees have been hitherto. In addition secondment between schools, between schools and colleges of further education or training institutions, or between schools and industry or commerce can be a particularly effective way of gaining new insights and widening teachers' experience.

16 We believe that, against the background of major restructuring of the system to meet the needs of pupils at 16 + and of other current and prospective developments in the curriculum and in examinations, the need for opportunities for in-service education, training and professional development and the much wider involvement of teachers in INSET has never been greater, nor has the case been stronger. We consider that the education service owes teachers improved opportunities to enhance their professional development. In turn the education service will be best served by a vigorous, up-to-date force of teachers who have a personal and professional commitment to INSET, who have the benefit of access to adequate and appropriate INSET opportunities and who are fully involved in the process of identifying their learning needs and how to meet them. [. . .]

Conditions for the effectiveness of INSET

36 The ultimate goal of in-service training is the improvement of pupils' learning, through improvements in school and teacher performance. Judgement of the effectiveness of INSET is therefore made on the basis of the extent to which these improvements are achieved. But since appropriate resources and arrangements are necessary pre-requisites for effective INSET, it is important that suitable arrangements should be developed which will help to ensure that INSET is relevant to the needs of teachers and schools, and that optimum use is made of the resources available. Equally, appropriate and adequate resources at school, LEA and provider level are essential for the effective conditions to develop. Our recommendations for new arrangements for planning and for funding are dealt with later: this section deals with other conditions which must be satisfied for INSET to be effective.

37 As the White Paper 'Teaching Quality' points out, the task of managing the teacher force falls mainly to LEAs and needs to be carried out in a way which fosters professionalism and commitment among teachers. The provision of opportunities for in-service training is an important aspect of this management task. As we have indicated, there is a wide spectrum of INSET need and an equally wide spectrum of INSET provision. The task of matching need with provision is complex but central to the improvement of teaching quality, for which primary responsibility rests with the LEA. We do not believe that it is useful to prescribe any single model of INSET; rather we believe that it is important at all levels to match particular models of INSET to particular identified needs. As a first step, we have attempted to identify conditions for the effectiveness of INSET.

38 Three main conditions relate to the role of the LEA, of individual teachers and of the school. These and other conditions which the models, the resources and the arrangements should satisfy are set out below.

(a) Identification by teachers of their training needs in relation to the objectives of the school and the LEA, and their own professional development.
(b) Support of governors, the head teacher and senior staff and local authority advisers and involvement of the whole staff.
(c) A coherent LEA policy (which should include helping schools and colleges also to develop coherent INSET policies).
(d) Precise 'targeting' of provision.
(e) Choice of the appropriate form of INSET, whether individual to the teacher, school-based or externally-based.
(f) Choice of appropriate length of course and mode of activity.
(g) Relevance to the teachers' need and focused on practice.
(h) Appropriate expertise on the part of higher education institutions and other providers of INSET.
(i) Appropriate preparatory and follow-up work in schools.

We discuss each of these in turn below.

Identification by teachers of their training needs

39 Whole school self-evaluation schemes and practices, as well as success in creating a climate where professional self-assessment is possible, greatly assist in helping teachers to become professionally articulate about their own in-service needs. Teachers' practice in the classroom is most likely to be affected when they themselves have identified a need for training, and when it has been possible for them to relate their training to the needs of their own pupils. In this way, it is possible for the in-service training provided to take as its starting point the pedagogic and subject expertise which teachers have already acquired.

Support of the governors, the head teacher and senior staff and local authority advisers

40 The support of the governors, the head and senior staff and local authority advisers is crucial in helping the staff of a school to identify their overall goals and their training needs in relation to them as individuals, groups or as a whole staff. It is also the task of the head and senior staff to ensure that the INSET received is translated into effective action or changes in policy or practice. Some form of process for sharing what has been acquired through INSET is also necessary, for new developments to be accepted and implemented by all members of staff. These processes may be greatly helped by the designation of a suitable member of staff as teacher tutor or professional tutor with responsibility for co-ordinating INSET policies and provision.

A coherent LEA policy

41 It is important that the LEA should have well defined strategies for the training of teachers and for the identification of needs at LEA, school and individual teacher level. The success of LEA policies will depend in large measure on a strong advisory service, in touch with national developments and well informed of local needs and performance, which will be able through its knowledge of schools to identify strengths and weaknesses across the authority as a whole and to relate this to INSET, working with teachers in schools. Advisers can also play an important part in the selection of teachers for courses and in ensuring that the school undertakes adequate preparatory and follow-up work. Close co-operation between LEA advisers, teachers and providing institutions in the design of courses as well as in the choice of course members can help to ensure that the courses provided are directly relevant to classroom needs and the professional needs of teachers.

Precise 'targeting' of provision

42 INSET activity cannot be effective, no matter how good the design, if the participants do not have broadly similar aims and expectations, appropriately matched to the overall goals of the activity. Schools and local authorities alike should identify teachers who will benefit from school-based and LEA provision, and should join in careful discussions with higher education providers before teachers are released to attend courses.

Choice of appropriate form of INSET, whether individual to the teacher, school-based or externally-based.

43 Some forms of training take place most appropriately at classroom level, where teachers can be assisted in identifying their training needs in relation to their teaching and given immediate feedback and help in improving their response to pupils and their ability to stimulate pupils' thinking and imagination. Such work is greatly enhanced when teachers have time to reflect on their practice and plan for improvement, preferably in partnership with colleagues. This form of school-based work frequently leads to the identification of a need for other more formal modes of INSET, externally provided, or can itself become part of an external course. Every school needs the input which external providers, whether in the LEA or in higher education institutions, can offer from their own wider knowledge of the system. HE institutions can provide for schools their special expertise and the resources of large departments and can assist in identifying needs and developing appropriate forms of provision; local authority advisers can also provide their knowledge of LEA policies and of the performance of the whole of the LEA's schools.

Choice of appropriate length of course and mode of activity

44 Some training needs are best met by short courses, while others demand a long process involving school-related activity with formal training. Short courses can identify a need for changes in practice which should be followed up at the school level, while long courses can best provide a re-training or extension of professional skill. Subject up-dating may best be provided by a combination of full-time study and personal reading and written assignments. Part-time activities offer the opportunity for teachers to try out their newly acquired ideas and strategies in the classroom, and then to report back and analyse the effectiveness of these strategies in further meetings of the learning group. Full-time courses are now particularly valuable where intensive learning of a new academic subject or extension of a subject is undertaken. They can also be valuable where the new skills being learnt are very different from those in the teacher's present post. Distance learning is particularly useful to many teachers wishing to enhance their own knowledge and skill through guided private study.

Relevance to teachers' needs and focused on practice

45 The main aim of school- and classroom-related in-service education is to improve the conceptual framework, subject expertise and pedagogic technique of teachers and ensure that both theory and practice are closely related to classroom teaching and more effective learning strategies. This form of INSET, often described as school-focused, is planned from the beginning to improve the effectiveness of teaching and is normally aimed at individual teachers or at a functional group of teachers within a school or schools. It is particularly important that INSET of this type should take account of teachers' current expertise and experience and that those involved in providing the training should themselves be models of good practice in designing INSET and in pedagogy. Most forms of INSET are likely to be more successful and result in tangible outcomes when teachers have the opportunity to contribute from their knowledge and expertise to the particular in-service activity being undertaken. Moreover, it is important for teachers to be involved in monitoring the outcomes of various in-service activities as this can help to promote further commitment by teachers, schools and LEAs and can also assist with follow up activities (see paragraph 47) and the identification of further training needs.

Appropriate expertise on the part of higher education institutions and other providers of INSET

46 Teachers are rightly critical if they encounter poor teaching or low expectations on any INSET course. They do however respond with enthusiasm if high academic standards are demanded and if the quality of teaching and guidance offered is good and is geared to the needs of adult learners who are experienced in their field. It is important that providers of INSET should offer only those aspects of subjects in which they have adequate expertise, that they should collaborate with others if that is necessary to ensure adequate expertise, and that they should themselves be models of good practice in their academic and professional knowledge as well as in the example of pedagogy they offer in their own teaching.

Appropriate preparatory and follow-up work in the schools

47 While school-based training has the advantage of providing immediate classroom feedback it is all too often the case that the benefits of externally provided INSET are not fully realised because of a lack of preparation on the part of the school, or providing institution, or LEA, or the teacher concerned, and because of a lack of support work, follow-up and evaulation when the teacher returns. Steps should be taken to ensure that the conditions for implementing new ideas are met and to enable the benefits of INSET to be shared as widely as possible. A skilful head teacher or head of department can take the opportunity of one teacher's secondment to arrange a valuable programme of implementation and dissemination within the school. Similarly, an LEA can make the most of the secondment of teachers by arranging for them to contribute to in-service programmes on their return. The overriding importance of INSET being seen as an integral part of the strategies of all LEAs and all schools for improving the provision of education to all pupils is inherent in our recommendations for its effectiveness.

Planning and implementation of INSET

48 As we have already indicated, identification of need and match between need and provision – whether school or externally-based – are essential if INSET is to be effective. We have drawn attention to the need for a coherent LEA policy and to the importance of the role of the head teacher and senior staff in the identification of needs and the follow-up of training. The LEA, mainly through the advisory service, will clearly need to be closely involved at every stage. In the following section we describe the arrangements that we consider are necessary at school, LEA and area level for the planning and delivery of effective INSET. The arrangements have implications for the funding of INSET, which we deal with subsequently.

The school and INSET

49 Our thinking on INSET and the school owes much to the 1978 pamphlet 'Making INSET Work', produced by the INIST Sub-Committee of the former ACSTT* and distributed to each school with a view to raising levels of awareness

*The Induction and In-Service Training Sub-Committee of the Advisory Committee on the Supply and Training of Teachers

about the importance of INSET. This pamphlet stemmed from the development in many places of the concept of the "thinking school", which in turn related primarily to the responsibilities of the school for its curriculum and staff development and for the INSET necessary to support it, but which we suggest could usefully be extended.

50 We consider that every school should have an agreed procedure for ensuring that:

(a) The needs for in-service training and professional development of individual teachers, of groups of teachers within, the school and of the school as a whole are regularly reviewed.

(b) The priorities for in-service training, and the most appropriate means of meeting the different needs identified, are assessed in consultation with the governors and the LEA in the context of declared curricular aims and objectives.

(c) The LEA is informed at the end of each year of the level of school-based INSET carried out during that year, the staffing implications and the extent to which resources outside the school were drawn on for the purpose.

(d) On the basis of the review of INSET needs ((b) above) each year the school should assess its priorities for the following and succeeding years, including the release of staff to externally provided courses, to enable the LEA to take these priorities into account in establishing programmes of release. For short courses with a short planning lead time the school should review the case for the release of staff to attend such courses against its already declared annual assessment of priorities for release.

(e) INSET activities are prepared for, followed up and evaluated within the school.

The head teacher and senior staff will have a crucial part to play in this procedure, in consultation with the governors.

51 The needs of a school's staff for INSET will manifest themselves in different ways and at different levels. We consider that the head teacher or senior member(s) of staff with delegated responsibility for INSET matters (eg a teacher tutor/professional tutor) should take the initiative in reviewing needs for training and professional development. We recommend that this review should be carried out annually. Possible approaches might be as follows:

(a) By inviting individual teachers to consider their needs for training and professional development, with guidance as necessary (possibly based on a system of assessment) on priorities for INSET and the range of INSET opportunities available.

(b) By inviting groups of teachers, say heads of department, year group teachers, or pastoral teams, to consider their needs as a whole.

(c) By inviting senior staff to review their own needs – eg for management training – and the needs of the school as a whole, including the implications of the new criteria for the assessment of initial teacher training which require the involvement of practising school teachers in initial training.

(d) By inviting the school governors to offer views on training needs in relation to the curricular objectives of the school.

It is important that, whatever the approach adopted, teachers should have the opportunity to review their needs not only individually but through discussion with colleagues. Staff meetings especially at departmental level may be useful, provided they are arranged specifically for this purpose.

52 As we have already indicated (paragraph 39 above) school self-evaluation schemes and practices in relation to defined goals, as well as measures for professional assessment of teachers, can be of particular value in stimulating professional awareness of INSET needs. They provide the opportunity for the staff of the school to assess their strengths and weaknesses and to go on to identify the consequent training needs.

53 Identification of needs will be a valuable process of itself, but it is only a starting point. The next step is to consider how those needs may be most appropriately met and to plan, in so far as it is possible, a programme of implementation. Consideration will need to be given to the scope for meeting the needs so identified by: (1) training within the school from the school's own resources; (2) school-based activity drawing on outside expertise; and (3) externally-based activity. This process will require close collaboration between the head teacher and senior staff and the LEA advisory staff; and we consider the LEA's role in more detail in the next section.

54 We have already indicated that some forms of training can best take place within the school, where teachers can be directly helped in their own teaching performance and given immediate feedback. We consider that, increasingly, schools should seek to meet the everyday training needs of their staff, wherever possible, themselves, with help as appropriate from the LEA advisory service, from other schools in the area, from the staff of training institutions in the area and from other agencies, including diocesan advisory services where appropriate.

55 We recognise that school-based INSET, while avoiding the need for staff to be released from the school, is demanding of staff time: for example a teacher may be required to discuss his or her classroom work with a colleague, a visiting adviser or college tutor. We recommend therefore that every LEA should satisfy itself that there are adequate staffing resources for each school to enable such activity to take place and that, in turn, the school should satisfy the Authority at the end of each academic year that the level and nature of its INSET activity in relation to agreed objectives continue to justify those resources. In making this recommendation we are aware that it implies the provision of additional resources for INSET and that it may also entail a critical examination within schools and within LEAs of other uses of teacher time.

56 In some cases the head teacher or senior member(s) of staff responsible for INSET will judge, in consultation with the LEA advisory staff, that the INSET needs of certain teachers can be effectively met only through their attendance on courses or other forms of activity based outside the school. It is essential that such judgments are based on careful consideration of the purpose and likely value of the particular course and that, on the teacher's return, the extent to which the course fulfilled its purpose is evaluated. In order that needs and provision can be matched as effectively as possible, we recommend that each school should make an annual submission to the LEA setting out the case for the release of any teachers for whom externally-based courses or other training opportunities are proposed. The school would, of course, be helped in making its submission by guidance on the LEA's own priorities, and there would need to be some flexibility to accommodate short courses mounted at short notice.

57 Finally, we consider that the head teacher in co-operation with the responsible senior member(s) of staff should ensure that school-based INSET activity is properly evaluated and that teachers embarking on externally-based courses or other activities are adequately prepared; and on return encouraged to share their new insights with colleagues as well as to put their new skills into practice. Schools should discuss with the LEA their need for outside help in order to evaluate their own INSET activities. Staff seminars or departmental meetings should be arranged as appropriate to enable teachers returning from courses to pass on the lessons they have learned to their colleagues.

The LEA and INSET

58 We believe that the main role of the LEA should be to decide on its priorities for and policies towards INSET in the light of regional and national priorities, to set a budget for INSET and to allocate funds between the different types of activity in the light of its own priorities and the needs identified by the schools in its area. At present there appears to be a wide disparity between LEAs in their approach to, and provision of, INSET. Some LEAs have developed well-considered policies and produced effective arrangements. Others have minimal provision. As a result, teachers' opportunities to undertake INSET vary depending on where they work. We see a need for much greater consistency across the country and we therefore recommend that each LEA should develop clear and coherent policies towards INSET and programmes for implementation.

59 We have recommended that each school should make an annual submission to its LEA setting out the needs of its staff for INSET based outside the school. We envisage that the proposals from individual schools would provide a major input to the LEA's consideration of priorities for INSET across all its schools. The next step would be for the individual LEA to identify the training needs to be met, in the light of its own priorities and the submissions from schools, and to secure as close a match as possible between those needs and its direct INSET provision (ie through advisory staff, teachers' centres etc), the use made of the release of teachers to courses and the levels of support for part-time study. We consider in the next section a possible mechanism for securing effective match between needs and provision in higher education institutions.

60   A number of LEAs have found that advisory committees, involving advisers/inspectors officers, teacher educators, teachers' centre leaders and school teachers, have a useful role to play in consideration of INSET matters. We suggest that others might well find it useful to establish such committees. We envisage that their functions would be to consider the staff development needs of the Authority's schools in the light of national and regional developments as well as submissions from individual schools, and the Authority's own identification of priorities for INSET, and to advise on how those needs should most appropriately be met and on the resource implications. Where there is a high proportion of denominational schools, it will be necessary to take account of the views of the appropriate diocesan body.

61   In addition to careful assessment of need, a coherent LEA INSET policy will require clear identification of the resources available for INSET. We consider that each LEA should set a budget for INSET and that information about the components of this budget should be readily available to those interested. We envisage that the budget should cover the cost of staffing resources for schools for school-based activity, course fees, travelling and subsistence expenses and materials, the cost of employing replacement teachers as necessary to enable teachers to be released for INSET activities, payments for consultancy work, an agreed allocation of advisers' salaries and expenses and the necessary administrative support, and the costs of teachers' centres.

62   The direct INSET provision made by LEAs varies both in scale and in quality. We note that some provision based in teachers' centres enables teachers to share experiences and pool new ideas between schools, and that these centres play very important roles in providing resources and workshop facilities as well as a network for dissemination of teaching materials and information. Some make a substantial contribution in the form of short courses. They do not normally however provide courses of substantial academic subject study, or the dissemination of relevant research, which is best provided by higher education institutions. We recommend that LEAs should review their locally based INSET provision, having regard to the relative advantages and disadvantages of such provision compared with using provision made by higher education institutions which itself may be based in teacher's centres or other LEA local accommodation.

63   We have considered whether to make recommendations on the scale of LEAs budgets for INSET by reference, for example, to the size of their teaching force and the proportion of each teacher's time that might reasonably be devoted to INSET. It would be possible, for example, to make recommendations based on assumptions about the rate of release. [One] survey of in-service training, suggested that in 1982–83 release for this purpose stood at 1.3 per cent of the teacher force. This is well below the target of 3 per cent adopted in the 1972 White Paper. Indeed, it could be argued that this target is now itself too low on the grounds that new training needs have since emerged. Thus the training needs arising from current and prospective developments, in particular new policies for the curriculum and for improved match between teachers' training and their teaching programme, developments in the examination structure and in pre-vocational education, the introduction of records of achievement and the need to make provision in ordinary schools for pupils with special educational needs are likely to require teachers to be released to externally-based courses. Further, we have [also] made recommendations, in another report, on in-service training needs for special education which have implications for release. The release of teachers, however, is only one element, albeit the largest one, of the cost of INSET and, as we have already indicated, much valuable provision is made without release. It would therefore be arbitrary to make recommendations on the size of LEAs' budgets for INSET by reference only to the rate of release.

64 We concluded that a target for local authority expenditure on INSET, covering all the items set out in paragraph 61 above, would most usefully be expressed as a percentage of LEAs' expenditure on teachers' salaries. A major difficulty in reaching a view on what that figure should be is the lack of reliable and consistent information about the current costs of INSET. To assist our consideration we attempted to seek comparable information on expenditure on post-initial training for other professional groups both in the public sector and in industry and commerce. Our enquiries have shown, however, that few employers establish separate budget headings for the continuing education of professionally qualified staff in such a way as to enable useful comparisons to be drawn: any figures which we might quote would be likely to be misleading. Nonetheless we believe that it would be helpful for a target to be set and we judge that, if adequate resources are to be available to meet the range of INSET needs described in the first part of our report, it would be reasonable for that target to be equivalent to about 5 per cent of LEAs' expenditure on teachers' salaries or about £120m at 1983–4 prices. This would cover not just the cost of teachers' centres and of inspectorate/advisory staff time, [. . .] but all the components set out in paragraph 61. In the case of some LEAs, their expenditure on INSET may already be close to our proposed target. For the majority of LEAs, however, such a target would seem likely to imply a substantial increase in the level of their current expenditure on INSET. In the absence of consistent information on the current costs of INSET it is difficult to quantify the scale of the increase required, but we judge that across the country as a whole something like a doubling of current LEA expenditure on INSET would need to take place. We do not suppose that such an increase would be possible without the provision of additional resources for INSET.

65 In making decisions on the most appropriate way of meeting INSET needs, it is important that LEAs should have regard to value for money considerations. This is not always possible at present because the fee in respect of attendance on a course at a higher education institution is heavily subsidised [. . .]. In a later section on new funding arrangements we make suggestions for changes which would leave LEAs better placed to make judgements on value for money in respect of some courses and activities.

Area Co-ordination and INSET

66 We have emphasised the central importance of LEAs in the determination of local INSET policies and in securing as effective a match as possible between the INSET needs identified by schools and the provision available. Where, however, INSET needs are identified which can most appropriately be met by courses or other activities based on higher education institutions, there is a case for some sort of mechanism to bring together LEAs and providing institutions in their areas. Regional planning structures do exist and, in some areas, work well. But the existing RACs are not trans-binary and existing INSET co-ordinating bodies are, in many areas, only ad hoc committees without any formal structures.

67 The main function of any new mechanism would be to act as a 'broker' in securing a match between the INSET needs of LEAs which could not be met adequately from within their own provision and the INSET provision made by higher education institutions including award-bearing courses. The task of the 'broker' would be to collect relevant information from LEAs and pass it to the providing institutions with a view to facilitating a satisfactory match between needs and provision and enabling the institutions to respond quickly and appropriately to new needs. As we explain in the next section of our report, a brokerage role would be particularly significant if, as we recommend, higher fees were introduced for some INSET activities since it would offer providing institutions some guidance on whether proposed INSET activities would be sufficiently well subscribed to cover the costs which fees were intended to cover.

68 We suggest that this brokerage role might appropriately be undertaken on an area basis and that groupings of LEAs and providing institutions in their areas might come together to form area committees for the purpose. It seems likely that twenty such committees would need to be established in England, with at least one further area committee in Wales. We envisage that these area committees would have a tripartite membership, drawn from the LEAs, the higher education institutions in the area and local teachers. The establishment of these committees would not necessarily impose a new burden on LEAs and training institutions, since they would in some cases replace existing arrangements. A new administrative structure would be needed, which might be based on a constituent LEA, a higher education institution in the area, whether in the public sector or a university, or on sub-regions of the existing HMI divisions. Each area committee would need to have a salaried officer. While recognising that our proposed model for area co-ordination would need to be developed in considerably more detail and would clearly require discussion among the interested parties, we recommend that the Secretaries of State should invite proposals for area INSET committees, including the necessary administrative support.

69 The proposed area INSET committees, if properly constituted, might well take on a number of roles besides that of brokerage. They would, most importantly, need to identify centres of expertise in their region to meet identified INSET needs, especially the need for award-bearing courses. They might also play a part in the approval of long courses [. . .], so long as the present system of individual course approval continues. They might be involved in offering advice on the funding of INSET in their areas, for example by contributing to the advice formulated by NAB/WAB and by offering views to the UGC.

70 In recommending the establishment of area committees, we do not pretend that all INSET needs will be capable of being met on a local or area basis. The area committees should recognise that, if needs are to be appropriately matched with provision, some teachers will need to travel to INSET activities outside the area or look to national providers, including the Open University.

National priorities for INSET

71 We see a continuing case for identification of national priorities for INSET and consider that the in-service teacher training grants scheme introduced in 1983 has played an important part in stimulating INSET in the priority areas designated under the scheme.

72 There might well be advantages in the establishment of machinery which would provide opportunity for collective consideration of national priorities for INSET and for identification of training opportunities which needed to be organised on a national basis. We envisage that representatives of our proposed area INSET committees would wish to meet together regularly and we would expect them to keep in close touch with ACSET.

Towards a staff development review

Geoffrey Samuel

In December 1980 the Policy Committee of The Heathland School, which comprises the twelve senior members of staff, met to review various aspects of our in-service training. [. . .] A Senior Teacher (soon to be promoted to Deputy Head) had been given the responsibility of leading a team of staff concerned with initial training, induction and in-service training.

The initial training role was taken seriously. Close links were forged with a number of colleges and the Senior Teacher herself was appointed as a teacher–tutor at the London University Institute of Education. Resources in Hounslow were devoted to the induction programme: every probationer counted as 0.9 against the school's establishment and, under a comprehensive and well-planned programme, two-thirds of the induction activities were held in the school and the remaining one-third organized by the Authority. We had already developed this programme further than the Borough required: for example, we prepared a full report at the end of each probationer's induction year in addition to the December review laid down by Hounslow. In-service training meant not just the dissemination of information about other people's courses but the mounting of an ambitious school-focused programme. [. . .] These responsibilities were extended further: a programme of support was established for all teachers in their second year with a personal tutor assigned to the staff concerned, a series of professional meetings and a final end-of-year appraisal and report; the Deputy Head (Staff) became involved in all staff appointments – and promotions; she also had the only (and final) say on the release of staff for courses, study leave etc. There were also several lesser developments such as a Staff Professional Library.

It was against this background that the committee met in December 1980. [. . .] But the discussion on the extension of the probationer scheme to second-year teachers and its future development into the third year took an unexpected turn. If teachers in their first, second – and soon their third year – were to be assessed, why should not the same principle apply to every member of staff?

The conditions seemed ripe for such a move. The Heathland School had opened as a purpose-built comprehensive in 1973 and many of the staff had come to the school as probationers. All probationers were inspected in their classrooms. A very small number of open-plan areas existed, which encouraged a degree of openness in classroom 'visits'. Since 1975 the Headmaster had inspected every Department on a biennial basis and the presence of senior staff in the classroom was not seen as an unusual or particularly threatening occurrence. Indeed, many staff seemed positively to welcome the regular inspections. Since 1979 the school has voluntarily undertaken an annual evaluation which was presented to the Governors. The climate for the development of a programme of staff evaluation, therefore, seemed highly favourable.

Nevertheless, the proposal to include all staff in an appraisal scheme produced a divide between the hawks and doves on the committee. It passed by one vote. The informal response of staff to the proposed new policy was sufficiently critical to suggest a more measured approach. The Headmaster and the [Senior Management Team] sat down to work out a scheme that would satisfy both the majority on the Policy Committee and be broadly acceptable to staff. A senior officer of the Authority and the Adviser assigned to the school then took part in the final stage of discussions. The Staff Development Review was born.

In essence, it differed from the ideas of its original sponsors in a number of respects. It was to be voluntary and offered to all staff except those in their first two years, for whom a scheme already existed. A large amount of self-appraisal was to be incorporated. And the review would give staff the opportunity to discuss their own career development. The review Panel would comprise the Headmaster, Deputy Head (Staff) and Professional Tutor, of whom any two would appraise a particular member of staff. For the Deputy Heads the Panel would consist of the Headmaster and the assigned Adviser: the Headmaster would be assessed by the Adviser and a senior officer.

The new scheme was then revealed to staff the following summer and received a warm and constructive response. In September 1981 staff were, for the first time, invited to 'opt' for a Staff Development Review. Volunteers were issued with a copy of the Oxfordshire booklet 'First Steps in Self Evaluation' (Oxfordshire County Council, 1979) and invited to make use of it, if they wished. They were told that the discussion would be divided into three parts: first, they would discuss their work with the panel: then they would be asked to mention any factors which limited their job satisfaction (particularly if they were capable of remedy); finally, they could turn to their own career development!

In preparation for the review, panel members sought informal advice from the teacher's immediate superiors. It was agreed that any criticism of the teacher would be introduced at an appropriate time in the interview. Panel members decided who would raise the various points: issues likely to be raised by the teacher were identified and considered in advance so that a constructive response could be given. We were clear in our own minds that, if there appeared to be no solution to a constraint mentioned by the teacher, we would make this clear: we did not intend to raise unrealistic expectations.

Most of the reviews seemed to be successful. The exceptions were those staff who were looking for a detailed, objective appraisal of their performance – one or two seemed to expect grades! – and those few who saw the review as an opportunity to stake a naked claim for promotion. We were delighted with the manner in which personality clashes were handled: teachers rarely evaded the issue, they spoke with honesty, delicacy and professionalism. Most simply relished the chance to talk in an open and relaxed way about their job. We had some successes in the two latter areas of discussion: there were some constraints which we were able to remove, there were some teachers' careers which we were able to advance. The most common constraint was 'lack of time' and to this there was rarely a solution: equally common, was the complaint that the teacher was given no real and worthwhile responsibility. To this we responded by mounting an appropriate in-service course. Inevitably, the reviews of the most senior staff were somewhat different: the Headmaster's was a gruelling eighty-minute interview which was constructive and helpful.

The panel met at intervals to reflect on the reviews and to consider how best to honour any promises given. Inevitably, we were already concerned at the amount of time involved: it was rarely less than three hours in total for a review. The second year of the scheme operated on the same basis: the only difference was that the discussion with the teacher's superiors became more structured. But, in general, the relaxed and flexible approach continued: although a 'formal' review with a long written statement was offered, nearly all staff preferred the informal approach with no notes or documentation at the end.

As the scheme approached the end of its second year it was clearly time to assess its successes and failures. An analysis of the volunteers showed that the 1983/1984 academic year would begin with only seven eligible staff (from a total of over 80) not appraised in a review. Although this was encouraging, it did nothing to answer those critics who insisted that it should be compulsory: virtually every visitor to the school who came to talk about our programme focused on this aspect. In a justifiably critical letter to *Education* in November 1982 Peter Dawson of PAT made the same point. Reluctantly, we had to agree that our critics were right.

We also had to admit that we were rather too soft in our approach: in this we were influenced by *Teaching Quality* (HMSO Cmnd. 8836, para. 92) and in particular the references to the need for 'accurate knowledge of each teacher's performance . . . formal assessment of teacher performance is necessary and should be based on classroom visiting . . . and an appraisal of both pupils' work and of the teacher's contribution to the work of the school'.

The offer of two alternative forms of review was untidy and unsatisfactory: we felt that in future there should be one approach only: the time involved was a great concern: when schools were facing all the exigencies of falling rolls and contracting curricula, could we really justify the massive investment of time which the scheme required? A Panel of three seemed threateningly like an elite corps: but if we increased the panel and included, for example, the other two Deputies, the time spent on communication (already considerable) would increase even further. And, finally, was there a place for the Advisers? The administrative task of setting up 50 or 60 panels with 10 or more different Advisers was daunting: instead, we undertook to talk informally to Advisers whenever the opportunity occurred so that we could appreciate their view of the performance of our staff.

Before we presented our report to the Policy Committee, one thing was needed: the view of an outsider. At present our self-assessment was far too inward-looking. We were fortunate in obtaining the advice of an expert from public sector industry – an industry which has a national reputation for its performance appraisal. She proved to be an ideal assessor: as the wife of a Head of Department in a London comprehensive, she was sensitively aware of the differences between industry and schools. She spent a morning with us and 'observed' two reviews in action.

She was trenchant and critical in her appraisal. We were too cosy: the human relationships were excellent but was there really enough genuine assessment? We were confusing performance appraisal with career development. The two were incompatible. (This proved to be the only piece of her advice which we rejected). By attempting to cover too much ground we did everything superficially. She recommended a two-stage approach with an immediate superior as the first assessor who concentrated on performance, e.g. in the classroom, and a second assessor, further removed from the teacher, who could take a wider and a longer view. The interview would benefit if both assessor and assessed agreed in advance to limit the discussion to two or three particular topics. And, at the end, there should emerge agreed targets.

We presented our report to Policy Committee together with the outside assessor's comments. In general they accepted the recommendations. Targets had to be defined: they were not to be targets of the payment-by-results genre but professional objectives. For instance, an agreed target might be that the teacher should rewrite the second-year syllabus, or prepare himself for 'A' level teaching – or just go on a course. But there was one unwelcome surprise: Policy Committee insisted that the review should be annual. The sheer demands in time required to review our entire staff each year were awe-inspiring. Was the time really justified? 'Yes,' our assessor had said, 'your staff are the most valuable resource at your disposal'.

The new scheme introduced in September 1983 has provided a formidable challenge for all those Heads of Department and Heads of Year who are required to act as the first assessor. Most of them have found it exceedingly difficult. If we had given them precise guidelines and instructions about their modus operandi we would have produced a tidy but rather faceless scheme: by laying down nothing but the principles we have an approach that is individual, personal – but somewhat chaotic!

How has it worked in practice? First it had to be sold to the staff. Of course there were misgivings. But a meeting with an agenda item designed to enable staff to articulate their complaints (or opposition) produced not a single speech from the floor. That is not to imply that the new compulsory appraisal has the full-hearted consent of every single member of staff. We have permitted two members of staff to postpone their reviews until next year because their personal and domestic circumstances warranted such a course of action. The Deputy Head (Staff) then had to draw up a programme whereby both stages of every review could be completed within the academic year. Unfortunately, this has necessarily meant in this first year the imposition of arbitrary deadlines for both stages of each review.

'Immediate superiors' receive their programme. They consult their staff, arrange a date and an 'agenda' for discussion and then proceed: the actual reviews appear to have lasted anything from a few minutes to two hours. (A two-hour review is surely an indication of past omissions). A note of the agreed targets is then sent in writing to the Deputy Head. The second stage is then conducted by members of the same panel as in previous years except that the Deputy Professional Tutor becomes an assessor for teachers in their third year.

We began with those staff who had not opted in to the previous scheme. We were also under instruction to place considerable emphasis on performance appraisal. Inevitably, the cosy, expansive atmosphere of previous reviews was lost. Inevitably, also, some of the criticism was not easily accepted: perhaps again that points to management failures in previous years. In this first term we concentrated on middle management; it was encouraging to observe how many Heads of Department and Heads of Year looked forward to a genuine appraisal of their performance and welcomed the setting of targets. In particular, several asked for an assessment of their success as managers.

Although the second assessor has naturally read the targets agreed with the first assessor, there is no suggestion that progress towards the attainment of those targets should be discussed: that will be the job of the first assessor next year. However, some of the same ground may be covered again if that seems appropriate. In appraising performance and setting targets for Heads of Department, we have covered areas such as: syllabus review, management of teaching and non-teaching staff, contribution to the general life of the school, etc. The second review also provides an opportunity to discuss aspirations and development.

After one term is it too early to judge our new scheme? Insofar as this is a completely new experience for our Heads of Department and Heads of Year, it is inevitable that the first year will produce some untidy and inconsistent reviews. But we have decided to wait until July and then identify 'good practice' worthy of imitation rather than impose excessively rigid rules. However, our professional tutors have already noted a marked improvement in the work of Heads of Department in relation to probationers: the spin-off from the main scheme has made them far more professional in their support and appraisal of their new young staff. The time involved is excessive: it now makes major demands on three senior members of staff and it is unlikely that we shall be able to operate a scheme of such depth and detail every year for every teacher. Fortunately, the abandonment of the cosy approach in favour of colder appraisal of performance has not resulted in any deterioration in human relationships among the staff: on the contrary, the staff seems more professional and more realistic in facing the problems of contraction.

But the scheme must be judged by two criteria. In Professor Wild's [. . .] book, *How to Manage* (Wild 1982: 14), the Chairman of Unilever, Sir David Orr, lists five aspects of good management. The first is 'Making the right key appointments'. The second is stated as follows: 'Having the right people available for the key appointments means continuous attention to the whole area of training. It also involves the interchange and cross-posting of those who are going to hold key positions in order to ensure mutual understanding'. Already we can see the benefits of our scheme in this respect. We have a keener understanding of our staff – their strengths, their weaknesses and their training needs. As a result we should make better appointments and promotions in the future and relate our in-service training to our real needs.

In the last resort an outsider would ask us: What is the *effect* of your scheme? Are the targets being achieved? Were they the right targets in the first place? Is teaching in the classroom actually better? Are the syllabi more appropriate? Is the school better able to achieve what ratepayers regard as success? But most important – and this must be the ultimate and only real test of any programme in any school – are the *children* benefiting? To this question it is too early to give an answer. But in the final analysis it is the only answer which counts.

References

OXFORDSHIRE COUNTY COUNCIL (1979). *Starting Points in Self-Evaluation*, Oxford, OCC.

WILD, R. (ed.) (1982). *How to Manage*, London, Pan Books, p. 14.

The management of school-based staff development: an example

David Oldroyd

Priory School is an 11–16 Comprehensive in an expanding suburb of Weston-super-Mare. Since its opening in 1975 its senior staff have given a high priority to staff development activities, partly in response to the relative inexperience of the newly appointed staff. Many of these activities, and materials used, have been described elsewhere (Oldroyd, Smith and Lee, 1984) but this article will first describe the pattern of school-based staff development activities, then illustrate the programme content and finally, analyse the process of managing staff development in the school.

Pattern of activities

The aims of staff development at Priory are listed in the staff handbook as:

1 To provide continuing development of the professional knowledge, skills, and commitment of staff and student teachers.
2 To encourage individual teachers to plan their careers and to identify and exploit career opportunities.
3 To clarify the staff's awareness of the school's philosophy, aims and objectives and assist them to implement these effectively.
4 Through the above, to improve the education of the pupils.

These aims encompass personal, professional and organisational goals which appear to be essential ingredients of a balanced programme of staff development (Bolam, 1982). Personal development would include, for example, career counselling for staff; professional development, INSET activities designed to improve classroom or managerial performance; and organisational development would be the improved functioning of the school, for example, when policies were modified or better implemented.

Table 5.6.1 Pattern of staff development at Priory School, 1981–2

Forum	Responsibility (P) = Pastrol (C & SD) = Curriculum & Staff Development	Meetings per year	Time of meeting[1]	Usual length (hours)	Number attending
A WHOLE STAFF					
Staff Meeting	Senior Staff Working Party Chairperson	3	1545	1	65
Staff Conference	Senior Staff	2	0900[2]	6	65
B EXISTING GROUPS					
Senior Staff	Collective	6	time-tabled	1	5
Management Team	Collective	10	1545	1½	17
Heads of Faculty	Deputy Head (C & D)	8	1230	½	9
Heads of Year	Deputy Head (P)	6	1545	1½	6
Faculty Teams (7)	Heads of Faculty	0 to 12	time-tabled	1	7–11
Year Teams (5)	Heads of Year	0 to 6	1545	1	12
C INTEREST GROUPS					
Probationers	Deputy Head (C & SD)	20	1545	1	4
Staff Development Workshop	Deputy Head (C & SD)	11	1545	1	12–20
Multi-cultural Ed Workshop	Head of Geography	8	1545	1	8–10
Developmental Group Workshop	Deputy Head (P)	4[3]	1545	1	20
Self-Regulating Groups (3)	Collective	5 to 10	1230 or 1545	½–1	6–10
Student Teachers	Deputy Head (C & SD)	15	1230	½	3–5
D INDIVIDUALS					
Professional Counselling	Deputy Head (C & SD)	on demand	Various	Various	c30

External courses	By application to Senior Staff and LEA. (Supply cover and 75% funding provided).

1 The school's published annual calendar allocates after school activities as follows:
  Monday – Staff Department
  Tuesday and Thursday – Pupil Extra Curricular Activities
  Wednesday – Team Meetings
2 The LEA provides two inservice days within each school year.
3 Excluding observations in tutorial time and a residential weekend.

Table 5.6.1 identifies fifteen forums used in 1981-82 for staff development. Whole staff and existing group forums are in effect, if not contractually, 'compulsory'. The prime function of most of these forums is administrative and their use for in-service training has arisen gradually, though in some faculty and year teams this has not yet happened. The management team, which includes five senior staff, seven faculty heads and five year heads, decided, in 1980 when it was set up, to adopt a pattern of alternate administrative and INSET meetings to avoid the erosion of INSET time by 'administrivia'. Priory has a blocked timetable which releases the staff of each faculty for the same period each week for a faculty meeting. The three deputies and the senior teacher also meet with the head within the timetable, though their INSET meetings tend to be held at other times. Avon LEA's tangible support for in-service education in the form of time and resources is evident in the chart.

The interest group activities are entirely voluntary and the individual sessions are based on self-referral. While the 'compulsory' forums are the responsibility of a range of staff, the staff development function is being written into all managerial job specifications, and the role of the deputies is larger in organising the voluntary forums, particularly the deputy head (curriculum and staff development). He also plans the annual calendar which has resulted in reducing former conflicts between the various after school activities. For example, in 1981-82 there were no clashes between the interest group meetings, allowing the highly motivated to attend all of them if they so wished. The three organised workshops gave way in the summer term to three self-regulating groups each of which planned its programme. This experiment was an extension of the principle of adjusting the organised workshops to the wishes of the participants. The multicultural education workshop was based on a BBC TV In-Service transmission. [. . .]

The school day runs from 08.55 to 15.30 which allows most after-school sessions to be finished by 16.45. Lunchtime sessions are avoided where possible as there are too many other demands on people's time and sessions of half an hour are too short for most activities. A tradition has grown of adhering to the guillotine time at which meetings are supposed to finish. One hour seems to be an optimal session length unless workshop activities are involved.

Table 5.6.1 illustrates the high level of involvement of the staff both in taking responsibility for and participating in a wide range of in-service forums. An impressive number of hours per year are devoted to implementing the aims listed above.

Programme content

A useful way of analysing what participants get from in-service provision is suggested by Joyce and Showers (1980) who, from their survey of over 200 research studies of the effectiveness of in-service training, identify four 'levels of impact' depending on the objectives of INSET sessions:

Table 5.6.2 A taxonomy of INSET objectives (After Joyce and Showers)

Level of impact	*Purpose of the activity*	*Outcome*
1	DESCRIPTION Knowing 'what'	Knowledge for Understanding
2	EXPLANATION Knowing 'why'	
3	PRESCRIPTION Knowing 'what ought'	Knowledge for Action
4	DEMONSTRATION Knowing 'how'	
5	PRACTICE (off-the-job) with feedback	Skills for Action
6	PERFORMANCE (on-the-job) with feedback	

1 Awareness
2 Concepts and organised knowledge
3 Principles and skills
4 Application and problem solving – 'on-the-job'.

They argue that very little in-service training is ever actually applied 'on-the-job', the main reason being that INSET rarely provides opportunities for the demonstration or practice of skills with feedback about performance, particularly in the classroom.

From the literature they identify five components of training necessary for in-service learners whether they are learning new approaches or simply 'fine-tuning' skills they already use. These are:

1 Presentation of theory or description of skill or strategy.
2 Modelling or demonstration of skills or model of teaching.
3 Practice in simulated and classroom settings.
4 Structured and open-ended feedback (provision of information about performance).
5 Coaching for application (in-classroom assistance with the transfer of skills and strategies).

Joyce and Showers conclude that for maximum effectiveness, all five training components need to be used in sequence. Only a tiny minority of teachers who are presented with theory or description of skills will be able to translate these into action.

Table 5.6.2 is adapted from the ideas of Joyce and Showers. It has proved useful in planning and evaluating in-service activities. If, for example, a head-teacher wished to improve staff performance in making their classroom environments attractive and tidy, he or she could:

1 Describe what was desirable (level 1).
2 Explain why (level 2).
3 Arrange the staff into discussion groups to review their performance (level 3).
4 Show a videotape of an effective lesson ending in which pupils leave the room tidy; or arrange for the head of art to demonstrate how to make attractive wall displays of pupils' work (level 4).
5 Get the head of art to run a workshop in which teachers practice the skills of wall display and receive helpful hints (level 5).
6 Release teachers for the last 10 minutes of lessons so that they can observe and analyse the lesson endings of other teachers on a reciprocal basis (level 6).

Each level is enhanced by and to some degree dependent upon the previous level. A headteacher could demonstrate 'how' something should be done but if 'what', 'why' and 'what ought' were not understood, the 'how' would appear mechanistic. Even if the demonstration was based on carefully presented knowledge for understanding (Levels 1 and 2) and a sense of their value (Level 3), there would be no guarantee that once the teacher returned to the classroom arena change in performance would result.

Tables 5.6.3 and 5.6.4 sample a wide range of INSET activities and suggest the level of impact they might have attained. There is an obvious and positive relationship between the level of impact and the degree of difficulty in attaining it. It is not too difficult to persuade a college lecturer to come in and give a talk. To enable colleagues to observe one anothers' lessons and provide them with the knowledge and practice required to do this effectively is not quite so easy, particularly as it probably requires a lengthy process of 'climate creation' before such a venture becomes possible.

Considerable progress has been made at Priory in the use of mutual lesson observation activities which are the only example of 'on-the-job' feedback about performance. The management of the observation initiative has been described elsewhere (Oldroyd, 1982) but it involves reciprocal observation of lessons by consenting teachers using a number of schedules developed in the school (Oldroyd, Smith and Lee, op.cit.). Such observations were linked with the probationers' meetings, staff development and developmental group workshops and used by one of the self-regulating groups. Two meetings of the heads of faculty team also examined the relevance of the techniques to faculty team INSET. A Staff Conference by Prof. Ted Wragg on 'Improving Class Teaching' also helped to promote the activity. Subsequently videotapes of participants' lessons were used for demonstration and analysis and a training video was made to illustrate how to make non-judgemental lesson observation notes and how a post-lesson discussion might be handled. These 'experiential' activities seem to have greater potential for professional growth than the more passive activities which make knowledge their objective, but they are very demanding on the time and skills of the providers of in-service training.

School-based INSET activities for staff differ from the learning activities which staff design for their pupils in one important way – the learners can opt out from most of them if they do not find them valuable. Teachers tend to measure the value of INSET by how much they can apply their learning to the job they have to do. This being so, the sessions which enhance 'skills' as opposed to 'awareness' are more highly regarded. The preference of teachers for job-related skill training, which can be applied to 'real situations' probably resembles the preference of pupils for 'action knowledge' as opposed to 'school knowledge' (Barnes, 1976).

In an effort to guarantee 'relevance' much of the Priory INSET programme has attempted to give the participants 'ownership' of their activities by involving them in planning and delivering the workshops, using materials and examples from their daily experience or analysing tasks and problems commonly-shared within the school.

Despite the demands of Figure 5.6.2, there is value in most of these activities, passive or active. They contribute to a climate of openness about, and a sharing of, professional tasks and they help staff acquire the characteristics which have been described as 'extended professionality' (Hoyle, 1974). Such teachers relate theory to practice, see their work in relation to school policies and goals, value professional collaboration and involve themselves in non-teaching professional activities such as external in-service and professional reading. The concept of 'extended professionality' was the topic of the first 'advanced seminar', a 1983 addition to the forums in Figure 5.6.1. Alongside the metaphor of 'extended professionality' goes that of 'the thinking school' favoured by Her Majesty's Inspectors. It is towards this metaphor for the organisation that Priory's management process has been directed. [   ]

At the 1980 'Improving Schools' staff conference, Dr Ray Bolam outlined the following conditions favourable to the effective management of change:

1 The setting

(a) The 'change agents' must be viewed favourably – have status, leadership qualities and a good 'track record'.
(b) The organisation must be receptive – good staff morale, active support from the head/head of team, etc., general support of the LEA, readiness to expend extra effort.
(c) The organisation must be adaptive – ready to change behaviour, timetable and structure.

Table 5.6.3 Examples of 'compulsory' INSET activities

Forum	Topic	Leader(s)	Lecture/Paper	OHP/Slides	Discussion	TV/Video	Demonstration	Skills Practice	Observation	Level of Impact
Staff Meeting	Principles of pastoral care	Visitor	•		•					2
	Implementing discipline policy	WPC	•	•	•	•	•			4
	Improving the school environment	DH(SD)/HF/AT	•	•						4
Staff Conference	Improving class management	Visitor	•	•						2
	Small group active tutorial work	DH(P)/AT/AT			•		•	•		5
	Practical methods of review	V/HF/HY					•	•		5
Senior Staff Meeting	Computers in education	HF	•		•					1
	Management review	Visitor	•		•					3
	Pupil profiles	Visitor	•		•					1
Management Team	Providing for gifted children	Visitor	•							1
	Staff Selection techniques	HF	•	•		•		•		5
	Curriculum notation	Headmaster	•	•						3
Faculty Heads' Meeting	Role of HF in improving teaching	Visitor	•		•	•				2
	Use of video to analyse teaching	HF	•		•		•			4
	Technique for clarifying aims and objectives	DH(SD)	•	•			•	•		5

Group	Topic	Person								No.
Year Heads' Meeting	Links with community agencies	Visitors			•		•			1
	Role of HY in Staff development	DH(P)			•					3
	Use of tutorial time	HY			•			•		1
Faculty Team (Humanities)	The RLDU experimental classroom	Visitor			•	•		•		4
	Annual retrospective-introspective – prospective faculty review	HF			•					3
	Designing resources for slow learners	AT	•	•		•				4
Year Team (Year Two)	The teacher and the law	HY			•			•		1
	Counselling skills	Visitor	•		•	•		•		5
	Improving links with community agencies	Visitors			•	•		•		5

WPC = Working Party Chairperson
AT = Assistant Teacher
HF = Head of Faculty
HY = Head of Year

Table 5.6.4 Examples of voluntary INSET activities

Forum	Topic (Brackets indicate number of sessions in the course)	Leader(s)	Lecture/Paper	OHP/Slides	Discussion	TV/Video	Demonstration	Skills Practice	Observation	Level of Impact
Probationers' Meeting	The local community	Visitor	•		•					1
	Parent-teacher interviews	Asst Teacher	•		•			•		5
	Lesson observation	Collective	•		•	•		•	•	6
Staff Development Workshops	Improving pupil motivation (6)	Collective	•	•	•	•	•		•	6
	Improving teacher-pupil relationships (5)	Dep Head (C & SD)	•		•	•	•	•	•	6
Developmental Group Workshops	Developmental group work	Dep Head (P) + 2 Asst Teachers	•		•	•	•	•	•	6
School-based Courses	Multicultural education (8)	Asst Teacher	•		•	•				3
Self-regulating Groups	Counselling skills	Visitor			•		•	•		5
	Problem sharing	Collective			•					4
	Lesson observation	Collective			•					6
Individual	Career planning	Dep Head (C & SD)	•		•					3
	Writing letters of application	Dep Head	•		•			•		6
	Dry-run job interviews	Dep Head	•		•			•		5

Methods used

2 *The strategy for implementation*

(a) Planning should be adaptive and continuing
(b) Staff training relevant and continuing
(c) Opportunities for developing local materials
(d) A 'critical mass' of participants should be developed to sustain the change.

(For a more detailed account see Oldroyd, Smith and Lee, op.cit.).

Most of these conditions seem to apply to the setting and strategy employed to manage staff development at Priory. The leaders were credible, hard-working practitioners, the deputies teaching over 50% timetables, enjoying status and support from the headmaster who was himself involved as a provider and planner. The LEA support for their work was clear. It was possible to adjust the blocked timetable to free staff for INSET activities, and the modification of roles, for example that of the deputy head (staff development), demonstrates the organisation's adaptability. Continuity of planning was ensured by the emergence of a staff development team within the senior staff and by the spreading of leadership responsibilities. The 'socialisation' of a considerable number of staff by means of the induction programme contributed to the formation of a 'critical mass' of teachers expecting and willing to take part in staff development.

Support for INSET was also encouraged by the provision of a substantial amount of 'personal' staff development by the deputy head (staff development) in the form of professional counselling. Above all, the strongly, participative 'job-related' approach adopted in many of the activities led staff to see them as relevant, particularly as more [. . .] of them 'took ownership' of the activities. Staff development must be seen not as something that is done to you, rather it is something that you do.

[. . .]

References

BARNES, D. (1976). *From communication to curriculum*, Penguin Books Ltd., Harmonsworth.

BOLAM, R. (ed.) (1982). *School focussed in-service training*, Heinemann Educational Books, London.

HOYLE, E. (1974). 'Professionality, professionalism and control in teaching'. *London Educational Review*, Vol. 3, No. 2, p. 13–19.

JOYCE, B. R. and SHOWERS, B. (1980). 'Improving in-service training: the messages of research', *Educational Leadership*, February, p. 379–384.

OLDROYD, D. (1982). 'The illegitimate progeny of TEP: an account of one school's adaptation of a TEP handbook', in Wragg, E. C. and Kerry, T. *Teacher Education Project: Final Report*.

OLDROYD, D., SMITH, K. and LEE, J. (1984). *School-based staff development activities: a handbook for secondary schools*, Longman for Schools Council, York.

Name index

Subject index